Approaches to Teaching
Gothic Fiction

Approaches to Teaching
World Literature

For a complete listing of titles,
see the last pages of this book.

Approaches to Teaching
Gothic Fiction

The British and American Traditions

Edited by

Diane Long Hoeveler

and

Tamar Heller

The Modern Language Association of America
New York   2003

© 2003 by The Modern Language Association of America
All rights reserved
Printed in the United States of America

MLA and the MODERN LANGUAGE ASSOCIATION are trademarks owned
by the Modern Language Association of America. For information about obtaining
permission to reprint material from MLA book publications, send your request
by mail (see address below), e-mail (permissions@mla.org), or fax (646 458-0030).

Library of Congress Cataloging-in-Publication Data

Approaches to teaching Gothic fiction : the British and American
traditions / edited by Diane Long Hoeveler and Tamar Heller.
p. cm. — (Approaches to teaching world literature ; 79)
Includes bibliographical references and index.
ISBN-13: 978-0-87352-906-8 (alk. paper)
ISBN-10: 0-87352-906-5
ISBN: 978-0-87352-907-5 (pbk. : alk. paper)
1. Horror tales, English—Study and teaching. 2. Gothic revival
(Literature) — Great Britain—Study and teaching. 3. Gothic revival
(Literature)—United States—Study and teaching. 4. Horror tales,
American—Study and teaching. I. Hoeveler, Diane Long.
II. Heller, Tamar, 1959– III. Series.
PR830.T3 A67 2003
823'.08725'071—dc21   2003010663

Approaches to Teaching World Literature 79
ISSN 1059-1133

Cover illustration for the paperback edition: *The Artist in Despair
over the Magnitude of Antique Fragments* (1778–80),
by Johann Heinrich Füssli [Henry Fuseli].
Red chalk and brown wash on paper, 42 x 35.2 cm.
© 2002 Kunsthaus Zürich. All rights reserved

Third printing 2013. Printed on recycled paper

Published by The Modern Language Association of America
26 Broadway, New York, New York 10004-1789
www.mla.org

CONTENTS

PREFACE TO THE SERIES

In *The Art of Teaching* Gilbert Highet wrote, "Bad teaching wastes a great deal of effort, and spoils many lives which might have been full of energy and happiness." All too many teachers have failed in their work, Highet argued, simply "because they have not thought about it." We hope that the Approaches to Teaching World Literature series, sponsored by the Modern Language Association's Publications Committee, will not only improve the craft—as well as the art—of teaching but also encourage serious and continuing discussion of the aims and methods of teaching literature.

The principal objective of the series is to collect within each volume different points of view on teaching a specific literary work, a literary tradition, or a writer widely taught at the undergraduate level. The preparation of each volume begins with a wide-ranging survey of instructors, thus enabling us to include in the volume the philosophies and approaches, thoughts and methods of scores of experienced teachers. The result is a sourcebook of material, information, and ideas on teaching the subject of the volume to undergraduates.

The series is intended to serve nonspecialists as well as specialists, inexperienced as well as experienced teachers, graduate students who wish to learn effective ways of teaching as well as senior professors who wish to compare their own approaches with the approaches of colleagues in other schools. Of course, no volume in the series can ever substitute for erudition, intelligence, creativity, and sensitivity in teaching. We hope merely that each book will point readers in useful directions; at most each will offer only a first step in the long journey to successful teaching.

Joseph Gibaldi
Series Editor

INTRODUCTION TO THE VOLUME

Ever since "horrid" novels (as Jane Austen called them in *Northanger Abbey* [40]) were the best-sellers of the late eighteenth century, the Gothic has been an important and influential literary genre. In its two hundred plus years of enduring popularity, the appeal of the Gothic has been both transhistorical—inspiring writers as separated in time and place as Ann Radcliffe, Edgar Allan Poe, and Isak Dinesen—and historically specific and contingent, since Gothic fiction responds to such events and trends as the French Revolution, the rise of the bourgeois family, developments in science and technology, racism and sexism, and postmodern alienation.

The Gothic has made us familiar with such paraphernalia as claustrophobic castles, beleaguered heroines, and animated corpses. But, more important, the narratives that employ these conventions have been a storehouse of themes consistently compelling to post-Enlightenment writers: the dialectic between reason and irrationality, science and religion; the nature and limits of human knowledge; and, in such texts as Mary Wollstonecraft's *Maria*, William Godwin's *Caleb Williams*, and Mary Shelley's *Frankenstein*, the conflict between the individual and the social order. The recurrent theme in Gothic fiction of the tension between the individual and society—a theme that reflects a variety of ideological perspectives—can be cast as the tension between subaltern and dominant classes, between children and parental authorities, and between women and men.

Moreover, in its representation of the family and the workings of the conscious and unconscious mind, Gothic fiction raises questions of identity and sexuality that have been major cultural concerns both before and after Freud. Thus the Gothic lends itself to a richness of theoretical approaches that examine the genre in the light of history, politics, and psychology—interdisciplinary perspectives that trace the complex relation between literary form and its cultural matrices. Because of the questions that Gothic raises about the interplay between genre and culture, during the last several decades there has been a strong revival of interest in, and reevaluation of, the genre. One aesthetic and cultural issue is the disjunction between the wide popularity of the genre and its descendants (such as mass-market romances, fantasy, horror, and detective fiction) and the relative marginality of the Gothic to literary canons. Interestingly, criticism is seeking to understand what this disjunction tells us about the development of a split between high and low cultures. As interest in the study of popular fiction and processes of canon formation has grown, the Gothic has become increasingly visible on college syllabi as students examine how it and the popular genres descended from it continue to fascinate readers.

In addition to courses on Romanticism and Gothicism, the history of the novel, and the eighteenth- and nineteenth-century novel, women's literature courses are one place in the literary curriculum where the continuing vitality of the Gothic is most evident. The study of the Gothic has been of particular importance to the development both of feminist literary scholarship and of the pedagogy influenced by it. The tradition of feminist scholarship of the Gothic—embodied by such studies as Anne Williams's *Art of Darkness* (1995), Michelle Massé's *In the Name of Love* (1992), Diane Long Hoeveler's *Gothic Feminism* (1998), and an entire 1994 issue of *Women's Writing* (*Female Gothic Writing*) devoted to articles exploring the nature and meaning of the female Gothic—reaches back to early classics of feminist criticism such as Sandra Gilbert and Susan Gubar's highly influential *The Madwoman in the Attic* (1979), whose guiding metaphor for the situation of the nineteenth-century woman writer is the Gothic image of the imprisoned wife in *Jane Eyre*. Like Gilbert and Gubar, in their studies of a female literary tradition Ellen Moers (*Literary Women*) and Elaine Showalter (*Literature*) identified the Gothic as an important genre for telling stories, as Moers puts it, of "female heroinism" (91).

Moers's term "female Gothic" has been used to describe the tradition of women writers of Gothic that includes Ann Radcliffe, Jane Austen, Charlotte Dacre, Mary Wollstonecraft, Mary Shelley, and the Brontës and continues in the work of such twentieth-century women writers as Margaret Atwood, Angela Carter, Iris Murdoch, Muriel Spark, Joyce Carol Oates, Anne Rice, Toni Morrison, Gloria Naylor, and Poppy Z. Brite. Themes central to the female Gothic are also central to women's literature courses. They include women's claustrophobic experience in the bourgeois family; father-daughter relations; the mother-daughter bond; and women's often ambivalent attitudes toward sexuality, the body, and artistic creativity. As courses on women's literature continue to grow in number, the study of the female Gothic tradition, already important, will become increasingly more so. The diversity and complexity of the Gothic tradition are reflected by the range of critical approaches that have been applied to it. Much feminist criticism of the Gothic (such as Claire Kahane's work on mother figures) draws on psychoanalytic models, which have been important to the reevaluation of the genre because they raise questions about how Gothic conventions like doubling relate to identity formation and the representation of familial tensions. Marxian, and more recently, new-historicist critics have also looked at how narratives about identity, sexuality, gender, and class in the Gothic reveal the construction of the bourgeois subject. And, as Kari Winter's book on women and power in Gothic novels and slave narratives suggests (*Subjects*), race and imperialism are also important themes in the Gothic, from *Frankenstein* and *Jane Eyre* to Naylor's *Linden Hills* and Morrison's *Beloved*. African American literature is inspiring vital and exciting new work in Gothic studies, a trend with great pedagogical relevance, given the courses in multicultural studies that are currently multiplying in, and significantly changing, the college curriculum.

The Gothic is, then, taught in a number of contexts and from a variety of perspectives in the contemporary English department curriculum. In addition to theme and genre courses—like women's literature, minority literature, or the history-of-the-novel course—in which Gothic conventions can be addressed, works of Gothic fiction are taught in period and survey courses (for example, Radcliffe's *The Mysteries of Udolpho* in a course on eighteenth-century literature, Poe's and Faulkner's Gothic works in a survey of American literature). And, while we have pointed to the importance of the Gothic in courses that widen the canon, a knowledge of Gothic conventions is useful also in courses on already canonical literary figures, such as the Brontës, Dickens, and Poe. Given the current critical visibility of the Gothic, many more courses will be developed that focus on the history and permutations of the genre itself.

It is appropriate that a volume on teaching the Gothic should appear at this time. The volume coincides not only with renewed critical attention to the genre but also with the greater number and variety of reprints and improved editions of Gothic texts now available for classroom use (two competing editions of Dacre's *Zofloya; or, The Moor* were published in 1997 alone). Note too the recent appearance of ánthologies such as Chris Baldick's two editions of *The Oxford Book of Gothic Tales*, Patrick McGrath and Bradford Morrow's *The New Gothic*, and Oates's *American Gothic Tales*. While there have been many new critical studies of Gothic literature published during the past decade, there is as yet no volume that distills this knowledge in a form specifically designed for the use of teachers who wish to apply these insights in the university and college classroom.

This volume begins with the section "Materials," prepared by Tamar Heller, who reviews and summarizes the nearly one hundred responses to the survey sent to MLA members and others who teach the Gothic. Heller also discusses the wide variety of bibliographic and teaching materials available in the field.

Perhaps the first pedagogical concern and one of the most important raised by the Gothic, given its vast influence but canonical obscurity, is simply one of definition: therefore, the first essay in the collection—contributed by Judith Wilt—addresses that issue. We hope to provide teachers with a clear sense of the issues involved in a study of the Gothic in fiction and help them recognize and make meaning out of Gothic conventions. We also hope to give a sense of the richness of interpretations suggested by these conventions and of the variety of theoretical models—psychoanalytic, feminist, Marxian, new-historicist, ideological, poststructuralist among them—that can be used to structure these interpretations. Marshall Brown supplies the philosophical background necessary to teach the Gothic; Robert Miles relates teaching the Gothic to ideologies of the period; Stephen Behrendt discusses teaching the Gothic through the visual arts; Anne Williams uses the Gothic to introduce students to feminist theory; and Carol Senf examines the Gothic in its extended scientific context. The next essays survey the major British and American Gothic texts commonly taught in the college curriculum: Horace Walpole and Ann Radcliffe; the early female Gothicists like Sophia Lee, Clara Reeve, Mary Wollstonecraft, Charlotte Dacre, Jane Austen, and Mary Shelley; the male Gothicists Matthew Gregory

Lewis, William Beckford, and Robert Louis Stevenson; the homosocial Gothics of William Godwin, James Hogg, and Oscar Wilde; the dramatic adaptations of popular Gothic novels in relation to their sources; the Irish Gothicists Charles Robert Maturin and Sheridan Le Fanu; the Victorian Gothicists in relation to commodity culture, gender, racial theories, and imperialism; the vampire motif in the British Gothic tradition; and the contemporary female Gothicists Iris Murdoch, Margaret Atwood, and Angela Carter.

The American section of the volume also surveys the major figures and texts in that tradition: Charles Brockden Brown's *Wieland*, Edgar Allan Poe, Henry James, Nathaniel Hawthorne, and Herman Melville; Sarah Orne Jewett, Mary Wilkins Freeman, Charlotte Perkins Gilman, and Edith Wharton; the African American Gothic; and finally Anne Rice and Stephen King. The final section of the volume contains essays that position the Gothic in relation to pedagogical practices: the Gothic as taught to honors students; the Gothic and techniques of role-playing and identity writing; the Gothic as taught through a number of filmic adaptations.

The coeditors wish to thank Sonia Kane for her patience and assistance throughout the editorial process. In addition, the series editor, Joseph Gibaldi, is owed a debt of thanks for his belief in this project and Michael Kandel for his copyediting.

DLH and TH

Part One

MATERIALS

Some Results of the Survey

Like one of the doppelgängers in its narratives, the Gothic has had a two-faced career—wildly popular, yet lurking ghostlike on the margins of canonical and academic discourse. Lately, however, the genre has been losing its outsider status, because of a growing critical and—as this volume attests—pedagogical interest. The history of this shift, which has accelerated during the last few decades, coincides with significant trends in the academy: a questioning of pre-established canons and the ideologies that create them; the rise of feminist criticism, in this case a tool for reevaluating a genre frequently associated with women writers and a female audience; an interest in psychology and fictional forms that, like the Gothic, are especially suited to portraying fantasies and hidden desires; and the growing interest in situating literary forms—both high and low—in their historical and social contexts. The recent explosion of criticism about the Gothic has responded to the popularity of a genre whose appeal, from its inception in the late eighteenth century, has not lessened but, if anything, accelerated, given such phenomena as the best-selling fiction of Stephen King and Anne Rice; the success of mystery, horror, and science fiction in general; and the rise of Goth music and culture among teenagers.

As our survey established, the ongoing vitality of the Gothic extends to its pedagogical permutations. Survey participants have taught Gothic fiction in an impressive array of contexts: literature surveys and period courses, introductions to literature and composition courses, and a creative range of courses devoted to the genre—for example, Documents of Darkness: The Gothic Imagination; The Gothic Tradition in Literature and Film; Melodramatic Narratives: Ways of Telling a Gothic Story; Romanticism and Gothicism; Terror in Nineteenth-Century British Fiction; American Gothic; Gender, Law, and the Gothic; Women and Their Monsters; and Cybergothic.

One challenge of teaching such a popular genre is that, as one respondent put it, "some students discover they don't like to analyze their pleasure in such texts—'thinking too much about it' destroys the toe-curling delight of reading a Gothic novel late at night all alone by the light of a single lamp." But, as instructors also found, the familiarity of Gothic makes a wonderful resource for teaching students critical thinking and analytic skills, enabling them to sound the depths of cultural knowledge about literature that they already have in their possession in order to explore its implications. One strategy used by several instructors was to have students define Gothic as a semester-long project. In general, both instructors and students find the ambiguous boundaries of the genre one of its most fascinating features. To our survey question asking instructors to define the Gothic, respondents, although the genre is "notoriously difficult to define," tended to agree on certain features. One instructor offered the following list of typical elements of Gothic:

- conventions of Gothic: haunted or decayed structures (castles, mansions, abbeys, etc.), obsession with the past, the supernatural, entrapment and confinement (especially of the Gothic heroine), terror, horror, family lineage, curses

- additional Gothic elements and concerns: unreliable or compulsive narrators, displaced cultural or social anxiety, concerns with "bad parenting" and "bad education" practices, nightmare or inverted domesticity, embedded texts and embedded narratives (including frame narratives), fascination with liminal states (often signaled by a literal threshold), boundary transgression

At the same time, instructors stressed that the genre was not just a collection of "paraphernalia" but an evolving and vital form. As one who teaches a course on Romantic-era Gothic said:

I am of two minds about the definition of *Gothic*. As a teacher—and a teacher specifically of undergraduates—I find a limited definition of the genre useful. . . . As a scholar, on the other hand, I am convinced that the presence of certain formal and thematic elements in texts published well after 1820 makes the term *Gothic* meaningfully applicable to a much wider range of texts.

Whatever the paraphernalia of a particular narrative, instructors agree that the Gothic focuses on a "confrontation with an uncanny other," and many see it as a genre shaped by history because it "seems to appear at times of great social stress and economic uncertainty."

The following discussion of materials useful to the teacher of the Gothic surveys a wide field, from the early inception of the genre in the late eighteenth century to its contemporary versions. This list is not meant to be exhaustive. Rather, we have concentrated on those materials singled out by survey participants. Also, although a section on selected criticism of writers in the Gothic pantheon (Beckford, Lewis, Maturin, Radcliffe, and Walpole) is included, articles and books on other authors are listed because of their relevance to understanding the genre as a whole. They are not meant to be a complete catalog of works available on a single author; for this, instructors will want to consult other sources such as the bibliographies cited below and the *MLA Bibliography*.

Editions

One of the most telling signs of a text's tenuous canonicity is the amount of photocopied pages that an instructor must generate in teaching it. For those instructors who have had to deal with cumbersome photocopies of out-of-print Gothic texts—and the resultant sense of deauthorization that accompanies the lack of a real book—there has been good news. Teachers of the Gothic will discover one great benefit of its reevaluation: that it is much easier to find the materials one needs in the classroom, including accessible and reasonably priced editions and anthologies. During the 1990s, in fact, there have been a number of reprints of hitherto unavailable Gothic texts, such as Charlotte Dacre's *Zofloya; or, The Moor*, and, as Angela Wright notes in her essay in this volume, another important early female Gothic, Sophia Lee's *The Recess*, until now long out of print. Instructors wishing to check new arrivals in reprints and anthologies of Gothic are urged to log on to Frederick Frank's *The Sickly Taper* Web site (www.toolcity.net/~ffrank/index.html) and click on the link "Recent Reprintings and New Anthologies." Despite this greater availability of texts, there are persistent problems; editions go out of print, and there are some significant gaps in the texts available. For instance, despite the growing number of courses devoted to the Gothic, there is as yet no single anthology available for classroom use that surveys Gothic works and authors in Britain and America from the eighteenth century through the present. (Nicola Trott's recent anthology of late-eighteenth-century English and Irish Gothic novels is the closest thing.) Among existing anthologies, those mentioned most frequently by survey respondents were the two volumes of Christopher Baldick's *Oxford Book of Gothic Tales*, Joyce Carol Oates's *American Gothic Tales*, and Patrick McGrath and Bradford Morrow's *The New Gothic*. For those teaching drama, the anthology cited most frequently was *Seven Gothic Dramas* (ed. Jeffrey Cox). A noteworthy collection for those teaching Romantic Gothic is G. R. Thompson's *Romantic Gothic Tales, 1790–1840*.

Collections of novels used by respondents included Penguin's *Three Gothic Novels* (Fairclough); Oxford University Press's *Four Gothic Novels*, which contains *The Castle of Otranto, Vathek, The Monk*, and *Frankenstein*; and E. F. Bleiler's Dover edition *Three Gothic Novels* (*Otranto, Vathek*, and *The Vampyre*). Another edition of collected novels that includes *The Vampyre* is the University of Chicago Press one, which pairs it with *Frankenstein*; and Chris Baldick and Robert Morrison's The Vampyre *and Other Tales of the Macabre* combines Polidori's text with other nineteenth-century Gothics. An inexpensive Signet omnibus introduced by Stephen King contains *Frankenstein; Dracula*, and *Dr. Jekyll and Mr. Hyde*. Another recent addition to anthologies of Gothic novels, and a particularly promising one, is Nicola Trott's *Gothic Novels: An Anthology*, which combines six major Gothic texts—Walpole's *Castle of Otranto*, Reeve's *The Old English Baron*, Beckford's *Vathek*, Radcliffe's *Romance of the Forest*, and Maturin's "Tale of the Spaniard" from *Melmoth the Wanderer*—with contemporary reviews as well as headnotes and bibliography (although the absence of *The Monk* may prove a disappointment). For those interested in teaching early female Gothic, a useful collection is Deborah Rogers's *Two Gothic Classics by Women*, which contains Radcliffe's *The Italian* and Austen's

Northanger Abbey with a good preface. A set of volumes that offers reprints of several less well known female Gothics is *Varieties of Female Gothic*, edited by Gary Kelly; it contains works by Lee, Reeve, Butt, Dacre, Porter, and Owenson. These excellent scholarly editions are, however, priced for consumption by libraries rather than by individuals.

Among collections of ghost stories and tales of the supernatural are Anita Miller's *Four Classic Ghostly Tales* and Lincoln Child's *Dark Company: The World's Greatest Ghost Stories*; on the Victorian front are the indefatigable E. F. Bleiler's *A Treasury of Victorian Ghost Stories*; Baldick and Morrison's *Tales of Terror from* Blackwood's Magazine; and Michael Cox's *Twelve Tales of the Supernatural, Twelve Victorian Ghost Stories*, and (with R. A. Gilbert) *Victorian Ghost Stories*. Victorian ghost stories featuring women writers include Richard Dalby's collection *Victorian Ghost Stories by Eminent Women Writers* and Peter Haining's *Gentlewomen of Evil: An Anthology of Rare Supernatural Stories from the Pens of Victorian Ladies*, although the last two have unfortunately gone out of print. For American women's ghost stories, see Catherine A. Lundie, *Restless Spirits: Ghost Stories by American Women*, as well as the collection *Haunted Women*, edited by Alfred Bendixen. A collection of fantasy by women is *What Did Miss Darrington See? An Anthology of Feminist Supernatural Fiction*, edited by Jessica Amanda Salmonson. Vampire stories are represented in Alan Ryan's *The Penguin Book of Vampire Stories*, Christopher Frayling's *Vampyres: Lord Byron to Count Dracula*, and Leonard Wolf's *Blood Thirst: One Hundred Years of Vampire Fiction*. (Also see the essay on American women's supernatural fiction by Kathy Justice Gentile in this volume.)

Because of the variety of texts taught by respondents and the lack of a major anthology of Gothic fiction, many teachers use individual editions of Gothic novels. Editions recommended most frequently were Oxford's World's Classics paperbacks (coming first in popularity) and Penguin books. Norton Critical Editions were also popular, especially of *Wuthering Heights, Jane Eyre*, and *Dracula*, the last singled out by one correspondent because of its "impressive array of contextual and theoretical frames for the text." The Bedford–St. Martin's series (general editor Ross Murfin) that combines the text with examples of different types of criticism won particularly enthusiastic praise; of these, editions of *Jane Eyre, Wuthering Heights, Secret Sharer*, and *Turn of the Screw* were mentioned, and *Frankenstein* was a favorite with several instructors because of the especially high quality of its critical offerings. The new Riverside edition of *Wuthering Heights*, edited by Diane Long Hoeveler, places the novel most fully in its Gothic tradition by reprinting for the first time the Gothic short story believed to have most influenced Emily Brontë, Bartholomew Simmons's "The Bridegroom of Barna" (1840). At the time of this writing, a new edition of *Dracula*, edited by John-Paul Riquelme, is also notable for its excellence. (See the section "Readings for Students" for more details.) As one instructor says of the Bedford series, they are "no more expensive than a Penguin or an Oxford UP edition" but give students "some sense of the critical possibilities for reading the text." (One drawback of the series, however, is that it contains only a limited range of the more "canonical" Gothic fictions.) Wolf's *The Essential Frankenstein* and *The Essential* Dracula combine useful notes, bibliography, and filmography with the text of the novels. Respondents also noted that Dover Thrift Editions (costing only a dollar or two) make inexpensive alternatives when a work one is teaching is available in that series.

In addition to Joyce Carol Oates's collection of American Gothic fiction, another anthology, edited by Charles Crow, *American Gothic*, overlaps with many of Oates's prose offerings but, unlike hers, contains selections of poetry.

Another recent collection of source materials should be immensely helpful in the classroom, E. J. Clery and Robert Miles's *Gothic Documents: A Sourcebook, 1700–1820*, a gathering of primary texts (historical, aesthetic, cultural) that contextualize the rise of Gothic fiction and that are organized under the headings "Supernaturalism, Religion, Folklore, Shakespeare," "Gothic Origins," "The Gothic Aesthetic: Imagination, Originality, Terror," "Anti-Gothic" (including sources such as Coleridge's attack on Gothic), "Gothic and Revolution," and "Gothic Renovations."

The Instructor's Library

Reference and Background Sources

Helpful bibliographic references mentioned by respondents were Robert David Spector, *The English Gothic: A Bibliographical Guide to Writers from Horace Walpole to Mary Shelley*; Dan McNutt, *The Eighteenth-Century Gothic Novel: An Annotated Bibliography of Criticism and Selected Texts*; Benjamin F. Fisher's *The Gothic's Gothic: Study Aids to the Tradition of the Tale of Terror*; as well as indispensable guides by Frederick Frank, *Gothic Fiction: A Master List of Twentieth-Century Criticism and Research*, *The Guide to the Gothic II: An Annotated Bibliography of Criticism, 1983–1993*, *The First Gothics: A Critical Guide to the English Gothic Novel*, *Through the Pale Door: A Guide to and through the American Gothic*, and his recent *Gothic Writers: A Critical and Bibliographic Guide* (Thomson, Voller, and Frank). Frank's extremely helpful Web site *The Sickly Taper* contains a link to *Guide to the Gothic III*, a bibliography of sources published after 1993 or overlooked in his other guides, as well as links to a number of other Gothic sites. (See "Web Resources" below for more details.) Also mentioned were Marshall Tymn, *Horror Literature: A Core Collection and Reference Guide*; Neil Barron, *Horror Literature: A Reader's Guide*, first published in 1990, which has been updated under the title *Fantasy and Horror: A Critical and Historical Guide to Literature, Illustration, Film, TV, Radio, and the Internet* (1999). Montague Summers's *A Gothic Bibliography* (1941; rpt. 1964) is one of the significant early reference works. Teachers of female Gothic will want to consult Kay Mussell's *Women's Gothic and Romantic Fiction: A Reference Guide*.

Other recommended background works for instructors are Ann Blaisdell Tracy's *The Gothic Novel, 1790–1830: Plot Summaries and Index to Motifs* and Clery and Miles's *Gothic Documents*, which contains a number of sources that help situate the rise of Gothic in a discursive context. Instructors will also want to be aware of the resources offered by the International Gothic Association and its journal *Gothic Studies* (for more on the IGA Web site, see under "Web Resources" below).

Historical Background

Sources used by respondents that contextualize the historical background of eighteenth- and nineteenth-century Gothic include Roy Porter, *English Society in the Eighteenth Century*; J. H. Plumb, *England in the Eighteenth Century*; Basil Wiley, *The Eighteenth-Century Background: Studies in the Idea of Nature in the Thought of the Period*; Arthur O. Lovejoy, *The Great Chain of Being: A Study of the History of an Idea*; John Brewer, *Sinews of Power: War, Money, and the English State, 1688–1783*; Harold Perkin, *Origins of Modern English Society*; Boyd Hilton, *The Age of Atonement: The Influence of Evangelicalism on Social and Economic Thought, 1785–1865*; Neil McKendrick, John Brewer, and J. H. Plumb, *The Birth of a Consumer Society*; Leonore Davidoff and Catherine Hall, *Family Fortunes: Men and Women of the English Middle Class, 1780–1850*; and Nancy Armstrong, "Emily Brontë in and out of Her Time." (For more specifically on gender and social history, see the section on gendered criticism of the Gothic.)

Critical Background: Overviews of the Tradition and Its History

Instructors mentioned a number of general studies of the Gothic as useful introductions to the field. The most frequently cited overview of the Gothic tradition—and, indeed, the most popular secondary source of any kind among survey respondents—was a volume that one called "indispensable," David Punter's *The Literature of Terror: A History of Gothic Fictions from 1765 to the Present Day* (in the second edition, *The Gothic Tradition* is vol. 1, *The Modern Gothic* vol. 2), which links the rise of the Gothic to the rise of bourgeois culture. Three other top choices among respondents offer a good introduction to the Gothic tradition, its conventions, and its history: Fred Botting's *Gothic*, an accessible and concise survey; Maggie Kilgour's *The Rise of the Gothic Novel*, which explores the relation of early Gothic fictions to the revolutionary and reactionary ideologies of the late eighteenth century; and Markman Ellis's *History of Gothic Fiction*, an informed and extremely useful survey of the genre. Ellis's survey is intended for undergraduates, with chapters "History and the Gothic Novel," "The Female Gothic," "Revolution and Libertinism in the Gothic," "Science, Conspiracy, and the Gothic Enlightenment," "Vampires, Credulity, and Reason," and—most originally—"Zombies and the Occultation of Slavery." Several older (pre-1960) works were cited as still of value: Edith Birkhead, *The Tale of Terror: A Study of the Gothic Romance*; Eino Railo, *The Haunted Castle: A Study of the Elements of English Romanticism*; Montague Summers, *The Gothic Quest: A History of the Gothic Novel*; Michael Sadleir's pamphlet *The Northanger Novels*; and Devendra Varma, *The Gothic Flame*, the last one of the first modern reevaluations of the Gothic novel from the late 1950s. Other works mentioned by respondents were Elizabeth MacAndrew, *The Gothic Tradition in Fiction*; Maurice Lévy, *Le roman "gothique" anglais, 1764–1824* (called by one respondent "still unmatched"); Ann Blaisdell Tracy, *Patterns of Fear in the Gothic Novel, 1790–1830*; Brendan Hennessy, *The Gothic Novel*; and Coral Ann Howells, *Love, Mystery, and Misery: Feeling in Gothic Fiction*. In addition to Punter's, several works surveying the rise of the Gothic associate it with history and ideology: Robert Miles, *Gothic Writing, 1750–1820: A Genealogy*, a particularly lucid historicization of the "Gothic aesthetic and the Gothic as discourse"; David Richter, *The Progress of Romance: Literary Historiography and the Gothic Novel*; David Jarrett's brief monograph *The Gothic Form in Fiction and Its Relation to History*, which contains a useful discussion of Gothic motifs; E. J. Clery, *The Rise of Supernatural Fiction*; and James Watt's *Contesting the Gothic: Fiction, Genre, and Cultural Conflict*. (See the section on historicist criticism for more on this approach.)

Feminist overviews of the tradition were extremely popular: Anne Williams's *Art of Darkness: A Poetics of Gothic*, which employs a Kristevan approach; Kate Ellis's Marxian-inflected *The Contested Castle: Gothic Novels and the Subversion of Domestic Ideology*, which surveys early Gothics through Emily Brontë; and Eugenia DeLamotte's *Perils of the Night: A Feminist Study of Nineteenth-Century Gothic*. An important psychoanalytic study is William Patrick Day, *In the Circles of Fear and Desire: A Study of Gothic Fantasy*. Diane Long Hoeveler's *Gothic Feminism: The Professionalization of Gender from Charlotte Smith to the Brontës* has a feminist psychoanalytic slant, influenced by French feminism, on the rise of the female Gothic. (See the section on feminist criticism of Gothic for more on these and other feminist works.) Judith Wilt's *Ghosts of the Gothic: Austen, Eliot, and Lawrence*, which contains a section on eighteenth- and nineteenth-century Gothic, addresses the genre's influence on canonical British writers. See also Joseph Wiesenfarth, *Gothic Manners and the Classic English Novel* for more on this subject.

Useful collections of essays mentioned by respondents were Kenneth W. Graham's *Gothic Fictions: Prohibition/Transgression* and G. R. Thompson's *The Gothic Imagination: Essays in Dark Romanticism*. Other collections are *Gothick Origins and Innovations*, edited by Allan Lloyd Smith and Victor Sage, and *Exhibited by Candlelight: Sources and Development in the Gothic Tradition*, edited by Valeria Tinkler-Villani, Peter Davidson, and Jane Stevenson. A book published after the survey was administered, David Punter's *A Companion to the Gothic* contains a number of essays by important Gothicists and surveys areas of interest from the origins of the genre through its contemporary transmutations. Another recent addition to the essay collection is Glennis Byron and Punter's *Spectral Readings: Towards a Gothic Geography*. Fred Botting's new volume of essays, *The Gothic*, contains articles on authors ranging from Horace Walpole to Angela Carter. Marie Mulvey-Roberts's *The Handbook to Gothic Literature* contains a number of concise and helpful entries. Victor Sage's *The Gothick Novel: A Casebook* is a selected overview of the critical heritage of the genre through 1980, including selections from late-eighteenth- and nineteenth-century reviews.

Those interested in linking the Gothic with the history of the Goths should consult Samuel Kliger's classic study *The Goths in England*, as well as a recent Foucauldian reading of the "dispersal of Gothic discourse," Edward Jacobs's *Accidental Migrations: An Archaeology of Gothic Discourse*. More sources on the Gothic revival are Arthur Lovejoy's "The First Gothic Revival and the Return to Nature" and Michael McCarthy's *The Origins of the Gothic Revival*.

Sources on Gothic drama include the introduction to Jeffrey Cox's *Seven Gothic Dramas, 1789–1825*; John Franceschina's *Sisters of Gore: Seven Gothic Melodramas by British Women, 1790–1843*; Paul Ranger's *"Terror and Pity Reign in Every Breast": Gothic Drama in the London Patent Theatre, 1750–1820*; Bertrand Evans's *Gothic Drama from Walpole to Shelley*; Steven Earl Forry's *Hidden Progenies: Dramatizations of* Frankenstein *from Mary Shelley to the Present*; Diane Long Hoeveler's "Gothic Drama as Nationalistic Catharsis"; Michael Gamer's "Authors in Effect: Lewis, Scott, and the Gothic Drama" and "National Supernaturalism: Joanna Baillie, Germany, and the Gothic Drama"; David Worrall's "The Political Culture of Gothic Drama"; and Paula R. Backscheider's "Reflections on the Importance of Romantic Drama."

For those seeking to situate Gothic in the literary culture of the Romantic period, recommended works that contain discussions of the genre are Robert Kiely, *The Romantic Novel in England*; Marilyn Butler, *Romantics, Rebels, and Reactionaries: English Literature and Its Background, 1760–1830*; Gary Kelly, *English Fiction of the Romantic Period*; J. M. S. Tompkins, *The Popular Novel in England*; Marilyn Gaull, *English Romanticism: The Human Context*; Aidan Day, *Romanticism*; Steven Bruhm, *Gothic Bodies: The Politics of Pain in Romantic Fiction*; John V. Murphy, *The Dark Angel: Gothic Elements in Shelley's Works*; Fiona Robertson, *Legitimate Histories: Scott, Gothic, and the Authorities of Fiction*; and Gamer's *Romanticism and the Gothic: Genre, Reception, and Canon Formation*.

Criticism by Period

Eighteenth-Century and Romantic Gothic

One of the first essays marking the modern reevaluation of the Gothic was Robert Hume's "Gothic versus Romantic: A Revaluation of the Gothic Novel" (1969), which claimed that the Gothic was not just a collection of paraphernalia but a psychological genre sharing, though differing in response to, the Enlightenment philosophies of Romanticism. Robert Platzner has a heated dissent to aspects of Hume's argument in "Gothic versus Romantic: A Rejoinder" (Hume and Platzner).

Additional selected sources on the eighteenth-century Gothic are Lowry Nelson, Jr., "Night Thoughts on the Gothic Novel"; Harriet Guest, "The Wanton Muse: Politics and Gender in Gothic Theory after 1790"; Anne McWhir, "The Gothic Transgression of Disbelief: Walpole, Radcliffe and Lewis"; Gamer, "Genres for the Prosecution: Pornography and the Gothic"; Kari Winter, "Sexual/Textual Politics of Terror: Rewriting the Gothic Genre in the 1790s"; Anthony Johnson, "Gaps and Gothic Sensibility: Walpole, Lewis, Mary Shelley, and Maturin"; Edward Jacobs, "Anonymous Signatures: Circulating Libraries, Conventionality, and the Production of Gothic Romances"; George Haggerty, "Literature and Homosexuality in the Late Eighteenth Century: Walpole, Beckford, Lewis"; Jerrold Hogle, "The Gothic Ghost of the Counterfeit and the Progress of Abjection"; Ruth Perry, "Incest as the Meaning of the Gothic Novel"; David Richter, "The Reception of the Gothic Novel in the 1790s."

Victorian Gothic

Sources on nineteenth-century Gothic singled out by respondents include Robert Heilman, "Charlotte Brontë's 'New' Gothic" (1958), a ground-breaking essay on Brontë's appropriation of the Gothic tradition, as well as George Levine and U. C. Knoepflmacher's collection of essays *The Endurance of Frankenstein* and Chris Baldick's *In Frankenstein's Shadow: Myth, Monstrosity, and Nineteenth-Century Writing*. (For more on *Jane Eyre* and *Frankenstein*, see the MLA volumes on approaches to teaching these novels—the editors, respectively, are Hoeveler and Lau; Behrendt.) Other sources mentioned by respondents were Alice Hall Petry, "Jamesian Parody, *Jane Eyre*, and 'The Turn of the Screw'"; D. A. Miller, "*Cage aux Folles*: Sensation and Gender in Wilkie Collins's *The Woman in White*"; Tamar Heller, *Dead Secrets: Wilkie Collins and the Female Gothic*, which examines the influence of the female Gothic on a Victorian male writer; and Alison Milbank, *Daughters of the House: Modes of the Gothic in Victorian Fiction*, which looks at Collins, Dickens, Brontë, and Le Fanu. Robert Mighall's *A Geography of Victorian Gothic Fiction* provides important new historicizing readings of a number of Victorian Gothics, drawing on medical, racial, and sexological discourses. A recent volume of essays is *Victorian Gothic: Literary and Cultural Manifestations in the Nineteenth Century*, edited by Ruth Robbins and Julian Wolfreys.

For more (in addition to Heller's and Milbank's work) on the Victorian sensation novel's version of Gothic, see Winifred Hughes's *The Maniac in the Cellar*, a particularly lucid introduction to the field; Ann Cvetcovich's Marxist-feminist study *Mixed Feelings: Feminism, Mass Culture, and Victorian Sensationalism*; Lyn Pykett's *The "Improper" Feminine: The Women's Sensation Novel and the New Woman Writing*; Nicholas Rance's *Wilkie Collins and Other Sensation Novelists: Walking the Moral Hospital*; Thomas Boyle, *Black Swine in the Sewers of Hampstead: Beneath the Surface of Victorian Sensationalism*; Pamela Gilbert's *Disease, Desire, and the Body in Victorian Women's Popular Novels*; Marlene Tromp's *The Private Rod: Marital Violence, Sensation, and the Law in Victorian Britain*; and the collection of essays *Beyond Sensation: Mary Elizabeth Braddon in Context*, edited by Tromp, Gilbert, and Aeron Haynie. Also recommended is Beth Kalikoff, *Murder and Moral Decay in Victorian Popular Literature*, which combines a discussion of sensation fiction with that of Victorian melodrama and detective fiction.

Sources on Victorian sensation fiction are particularly useful for tracing the rise of the literary canon and the distinction between high and low literature—the low a category in which the Gothic has historically been placed. Criticism of Victorian sensation fiction historicizes contemporary reactions to Gothic narratives and how their decanonized status reveals anxieties about types of otherness (gender, race, class). For more on the Gothic and the rise of literary canons, see Bradford Mudge's "The Man with Two Brains: Gothic Novels, Popular Culture, Literary History" and Patrick Brantlinger's chapters "Gothic Toxins: *The Castle of Otranto, The Monk*, and *Caleb Williams*" and "Novel Sensations of the 1860s" in his *The Reading Lesson: The Threat of Mass Literacy in Nineteenth-Century British Fiction*. In *Modern Romance and Transformations of the Novel: The Gothic, Scott, Dickens*, Ian Duncan situates Gothic in the context of discourses of nascent nationalism, as does Cannon Schmitt in *Alien Nation: Nineteenth-Century Gothic Fictions and English Nationality*.

Fin de Siècle and Later Gothic

Sources on fin de siècle Gothic are William Veeder and Gordon Hirsch's Dr. Jekyll and Mr. Hyde *after One Hundred Years*, Elaine Showalter's reading of *Dracula* in *Sexual Anarchy: Gender and Culture at the Fin de Siècle*, Kelly Hurley's *The Gothic Body: Sexuality, Materialism, and Degeneration at the Fin de Siècle*, Rhys Garnett's "*Dracula* and *The Beetle*: Imperial and Sexual Guilt and Fear in Late Victorian Fantasy," Kathleen L. Spencer's discussion of "urban Gothic" in "Purity and Danger: *Dracula*, the Urban Gothic, and the Late Victorian Degeneracy Crisis," and Stephen D. Arata's "The Occidental Tourist: *Dracula* and the Anxiety of Reverse Colonization" as well as his book *Fictions of Loss in the Victorian Fin-de-Siècle*. All these works associate the genre with nineteenth-century anxieties about types of otherness and illuminate the implication of Gothic in other cultural discourses that chart these anxieties—medical, scientific, imperialist.

For more on twentieth-century Gothic, see Victor Sage and Allan Lloyd Smith's *Modern Gothic: A Reader*; Punter's *The Modern Gothic*; Theo D'Haen's definition of postmodern Gothic; Steven Bruhm's "Stephen King's Phallus; or, The Postmodern Gothic"; and—a particularly valuable resource—the special issue of *Modern Fiction Studies* guest-edited by John Paul Riquelme entitled *Gothic and Modernism*. This collection, containing numerous useful articles divided into the sections "The 1890s," "Gothic Popular Forms," and "The Gothic and Language," is also noteworthy for the lucid introductory essay by Riquelme, "Toward a History of Gothic and Modernism: Dark Modernity from Bram Stoker to Samuel Beckett." For more sources on modernity and the Gothic, see under "Topics, Areas, Subgenres" below.

The Gothic Pantheon: Selected Criticism

It is impossible to provide a complete bibliography of criticism for all Gothic authors discussed in this volume; for more, see individual essays, the bibliographic resources mentioned above, the *MLA Bibliography*, and sources on individual authors cited elsewhere in "Materials." However, below is a list of selected criticism on "the Gothic Pantheon" (i.e., Walpole, Beckford, Radcliffe, Lewis, and Maturin).

Books on Beckford are James Lees-Milne, *William Beckford*; Brian Fothergill, *Beckford of Fonthill*; Andre Parreaux, *William Beckford, auteur de* Vathek *(1760–1844): Etude de la création littéraire*; Fatma Moussa Mahmoud, *William Beckford of Fonthill, 1760–1844: Bicentenary Essays*; Kenneth W. Graham, Vathek *and the Escape from Time: Bicentenary Revaluations*. Essays on Beckford are Parreaux, "Beckford: Bibliographie selective et critique"; James K. Folsom, "Beckford's *Vathek* and the Tradition of Oriental Satire"; Kenneth W. Graham, "Beckford's *Vathek*: A Study in Ironic Dissonance"; Adam Roberts and Eric Robertson, "The Giaour's Sabre: A Reading of Beckford's *Vathek*"; George Haggerty, "Literature and Homosexuality in the Late Eighteenth Century: Walpole, Beckford, Lewis."

Books on Lewis are Louis F. Peck, *A Life of Matthew G. Lewis*; Parreaux, *The Publication of* The Monk*: A Literary Event, 1796–1798*. Essays on Lewis are Peter Brooks, "Virtue and Terror: *The Monk*"; Wendy Jones, "Stories of Desire in *The Monk*"; Peter Grudin, "*The Monk*: Mathilda and the Rhetoric of Deceit"; the essays in *Matthew Lewis's* The Monk, a special issue of *Romanticism on the Net* guest-edited by Frederick Frank, including Frank's thorough "*The Monk*: A Bicentenary Bibliography." See also the essay by Haggerty under Beckford above.

Books on Maturin are Niilo Idman, *Charles Robert Maturin: His Life and Works*; Claude Fierobe, *Charles Robert Maturi: L'homme et l'œuvre*; Robert

E. Lougy, *Charles Robert Maturin*; Dale Kramer, *Charles Robert Maturin* in the Twayne Authors series. Essays on Maturin are Mark M. Hennelly, Jr., "*Melmoth the Wanderer* and Gothic Existentialism"; Kathleen Fowler, "Hieroglyphics in Fire: *Melmoth the Wanderer*"; Joseph W. Lew, "Unprepared for Sudden Transformations: Identity and Politics in *Melmoth the Wanderer*"; Jack Null, "Structure and Theme in *Melmoth the Wanderer*"; Regina Oost, "'Servility and Command': Authorship in *Melmoth the Wanderer*"; Amy Elizabeth Smith, "Experimentation and 'Horrid Curiosity' in Maturin's *Melmoth the Wanderer*"; David Punter, "Ceremonial Gothic." See also the chapters on Maturin in Robert Kiely's *The Romantic Novel in England*, Coral Ann Howells's *Love, Mystery, and Misery*, Punter's *Literature of Terror*, Terry Eagleton's *Heathcliff and the Great Hunger*, and Margot Backus's *The Gothic Family Romance*. See also the essays comparing Maturin with Le Fanu by Julian Moynahan ("Politics") and Victor Sage ("Irish Gothic"). See the essay by Hennelly in this volume.

Biographies of Radcliffe are Robert Miles, *Ann Radcliffe: The Great Enchantress*; Pierre Arnaud, *Ann Radcliffe et le fantastique*; and Rictor Norton, *Mistress of Udolpho: The Life of Ann Radcliffe*. Bibliographic resources are Deborah Rogers, *Ann Radcliffe: A Bio-bibliography* and *The Critical Response to Ann Radcliffe*. A useful study that situates Radcliffe in eighteenth-century literary history is Daniel Cottom, *The Civilized Imagination: A Study of Ann Radcliffe, Jane Austen, and Sir Walter Scott*. Essays found particularly useful by respondents are David Durant, "Ann Radcliffe and the Conservative Gothic"; Mary Poovey, "Ideology and *The Mysteries of Udolpho*"; Nelson C. Smith, "Sense, Sensibility, and Ann Radcliffe"; Alan D. McKillop, "Mrs. Radcliffe on the Supernatural in Poetry"; Cynthia Griffin Wolff, "The Radcliffean Gothic Model: A Form for Feminine Sexuality"; Barbara M. Benedict, "Pictures of Conformity: Sentiment and Structure in Ann Radcliffe's Style"; Terry Castle, "The Spectralization of the Other in *The Mysteries of Udolpho*"; Rhoda L. Flaxman, "Radcliffe's Dual Modes of Vision"; Kim Ian Michasiw, "Ann Radcliffe and the Terrors of Power"; April London, "Ann Radcliffe in Context: Marking the Boundaries of *The Mysteries of Udolpho*"; Mary Laughlin Fawcett, "*Udolpho*'s Primal Mystery." See also the essays by Schmitt and Hoeveler in this volume.

Full-length studies of Walpole are Timothy Mowl, *Horace Walpole: The Great Outsider*; R. W. Ketton-Cremer, *Horace Walpole: A Biography*; Brian Fothergill, *The Strawberry Hill Set: Horace Walpole and His Circle*; Kevala-Krishna Mehrotra, *Horace Walpole and the English Novel: A Study of the Influence of* The Castle of Otranto, *1764–1820*; Betsy Harfst, *Horace Walpole and the Unconscious: An Experiment in Freudian Analysis*. Peter Sabor's *Horace Walpole: The Critical Heritage* is useful for gauging the contemporary response. Essays on Walpole are Jill Campbell, "'I Am No Giant': Horace Walpole, Heterosexual Incest, and Love among Men"; Syndy Conger, "Faith and Doubt in *The Castle of Otranto*"; Lee Morrissey, "'To Invent in Art and

Folly': Postmodernism and Walpole's *The Castle of Otranto*"; Ian Watt, "Time and Family in the Gothic Novel: *The Castle of Otranto*"; Toni Wein, "Tangled Webs: Horace Walpole and the Practice of History in *The Castle of Otranto.*" See also the essays by Miles and by Norton in this volume.

Critical Approaches

Feminist and Gender Studies Approaches

We asked survey respondents to identify critical approaches of greatest interest to them in the classroom; the most frequently mentioned was feminist criticism. This response is corroborated by the richness of secondary sources about gender cited by them. The recovery of the Gothic tradition as a genre worthy of study has been in tandem with the feminist goal of rediscovering marginalized and deauthorized women writers, and feminist criticism of Gothic has sought to examine the attraction of Gothic conventions both to these authors and to their female readers. A number of recent works of feminist criticism on the Gothic juxtapose male and female writers, as do three of the critical works most frequently cited by survey respondents: Anne Williams's *Art of Darkness: A Poetics of the Gothic*, Kate Ferguson Ellis's *The Contested Castle: Gothic Novels and the Subversion of Domestic Ideology*, and Eugenia DeLamotte's *Perils of the Night: A Feminist Study of Nineteenth-Century Gothic*. Other frequently cited works of feminist criticism were Terry Castle's *The Female Thermometer*, especially her discussion of the "spectralization of the other" in *The Mysteries of Udolpho* and her introduction, and Michelle Massé's *In the Name of Love: Women, Masochism, and the Gothic*, a provocative psychoanalytic reading.

Among the originary work of feminist criticism of Gothic is Ellen Moers's *Literary Women*, especially the section "Female Gothic" (excerpted in Levine and Knoepflmacher's *The Endurance of* Frankenstein), which reads *Frankenstein* as a birth allegory rooted in female reproductive experience. Another important critical work that shifts the lens from maternal experience to the daughter's view of the mother is Claire Kahane's "The Gothic Mirror," cited by a number of respondents, which reads the female Gothic as matrophobic discourse—a genre about the daughter's fear of becoming like the mother in male-dominated culture. Other works of feminist criticism that help define the genre as a nightmarish refraction of female experience are Sandra Gilbert and Susan Gubar's *The Madwoman in the Attic*, Tania Modleski's chapter "The Female Uncanny: Gothic Novels for Women" in *Loving with a Vengeance: Mass-Produced Fantasies for Women*, and Margaret Anne Doody's important essay "Deserts, Ruins, and Troubled Waters: Female Dreams in Fiction and the Development of the Gothic Novel." A particularly popular work of feminist criticism among respondents was Juliann Fleenor's collection of essays *The Female Gothic*, which contains especially Wolff's "The Radcliffean Gothic Model: A Form for Feminine Sexuality" and Joanna Russ's "Somebody's Trying to Kill

Me and I Think It's My Husband: The Modern Gothic." Two overviews of female Gothic and feminist readings of the genre are valuable for those desiring an introduction to this field: E. J. Clery's *Women's Gothic from Clara Reeve to Mary Shelley* and Donna Heiland's *Gothic Novels: A Feminist Introduction.* Instructors might also want to look at the *Female Gothic Writing* issue of *Women's Writing.*

Other works of feminist criticism of eighteenth- and nineteenth-century Gothic singled out by respondents were Marilyn Butler, "The Woman at the Window: Ann Radcliffe in the Novels of Mary Wollstonecraft and Jane Austen"; Anne Mellor, *Mary Shelley: Her Life, Her Fiction, Her Monsters*; Mary Poovey, *The Proper Lady and the Woman Writer* (especially the sections on Wollstonecraft's *Maria* and *Frankenstein*); Margaret Homans, *Bearing the Word: Language and Female Experience in Nineteenth-Century Women's Writing* (which contains chapters on *Wuthering Heights, Jane Eyre*, and *Frankenstein*); and Diane Long Hoeveler, *Gothic Feminism: The Professionalization of Gender from Charlotte Smith to the Brontës* (which also contains chapters on Radcliffe, Dacre, Austen, and Shelley). Tamar Heller's *Dead Secrets: Wilkie Collins and the Female Gothic* (which contains a chapter on female Gothic from Radcliffe to Shelley) and Alison Milbank's *Daughters of the House* both employ a feminist approach to look at nineteenth-century male writers. Other works recommended by respondents are Frances Restuccia, "Female Gothic Writing: 'Under Cover to Alice'"; Kathy Fedorko, *Gender and the Gothic in the Fiction of Edith Wharton*; and two pieces on Daphne du Maurier's *Rebecca*—Alison Light, "'Returning to Manderley': Romance Fiction, Female Sexuality, and Class"; Modleski's chapter on Hitchcock's film version of the novel in *The Women Who Knew Too Much: Hitchcock and Feminist Theory.* (Another, more recent work on du Maurier and female Gothic is Avril Horner and Sue Zlosnik's *Daphne du Maurier: Writing, Identity, and the Gothic Imagination.*) Other noteworthy feminist full-length studies of Gothic are Bette Roberts, *The Gothic Romance: Its Appeal to Women Writers and Readers in Late-Eighteenth-Century England*; Susan Wolstenholme, *Gothic (Re)Visions: Writing Women as Readers*, a feminist-poststructuralist treatment; and Susanne Becker, *Gothic Forms of Feminine Fictions*, which focuses on postmodern neo-Gothic. Barbara Creed's *The Monstrous Feminine* and Elizabeth Bronfen's *Over Her Dead Body: Death, Femininity, and the Aesthetic* were recommended as useful for theorizations of the feminine in the Gothic.

Survey participants identified several works on women's literary and cultural history as particularly helpful for the teacher of female Gothic. Works on women's literary history are, in addition to Moers's *Literary Women* and Gilbert and Gubar's *The Madwoman in the Attic*, Eva Figes, *Sex and Subterfuge: Women Writers to 1850*; Jane Spencer, *The Rise of the Woman Novelist: From Aphra Behn to Jane Austen*; Janet Todd, *The Sign of Angellica: Women, Writing, and Fiction, 1660–1800*; Claudia Johnson, *Equivocal Beings: Politics, Gender, and Sentimentality in the 1790s: Wollstonecraft, Radcliffe,*

Burney, Austen; George Haggerty, *Unnatural Affections: Women and Fiction in the Later Eighteenth Century*; and Caroline Gonda, *Reading Daughters' Fictions, 1709–1834*. Works useful for situating the female Gothic in the context of women's history during the nineteenth century are the introduction to women in the Victorian period in *The Norton Anthology of Literature by Women* (Gilbert and Gubar); the three-volume *The Woman Question: Society and Literature in Britain and America, 1837–1883*, edited by Elizabeth K. Helsinger, Robin Lauterbach Sheets, and William Veeder; and Elaine Showalter's *The Female Malady: Women, Madness, and English Culture, 1830–1980*.

Several books on romances for women, while not explicitly on the Gothic, were cited as useful for understanding the appeal of narratives like the Gothic for a female audience; these works are Jan Cohn, *Romance and the Erotics of Property*; Janice Radway, *Reading the Romance*; Kay Mussell, *Fantasy and Reconciliation: Contemporary Formulas of Women's Romance Fiction*; and Carol Thurston, *The Romance Revolution* (see also Modleski's *Loving with a Vengeance*, which contains a chapter on Harlequin romances as well as one on female Gothic). Several essays that explicitly address Gothic romances are Kate Flint, "Romance, Post-modernism, and the Gothic: Fictional Challenges to Theories of Women and Reading, 1790–1830"; Radway, "The Utopian Impulse in Popular Literature: Gothic Romances and Feminist Protest." (See also Light ["Returning"] and Modleski [*Women* 43–55] on *Rebecca*.)

As Scott Simpkins says in this volume, the field of male Gothic has been undertheorized. Two works available on male Gothic are Joseph Andriano's Jungian reading of representations of the feminine in *Our Ladies of Darkness: Feminine Daemonology in Male Gothic Fiction* and Cyndy Hendershot's *The Animal Within: Masculinity and the Gothic*, which looks at images of masculinity in both male and female Gothic texts, focusing on discourses of the body, science, and imperialism.

Eve Kosofsky Sedgwick's chapter on "homosexual panic" in *Between Men: English Literature and Male Homosocial Desire* is an important example of criticism of what could be called "gay Gothic"—the genre's coded representation of homosexuality. D. A. Miller's "*Cage aux Folles*: Sensation and Gender in Wilkie Collins's *The Woman in White*" is a groundbreaking reading of homoeroticism in nineteenth-century sensation fiction. A number of works on vampire literature read the vampire as an embodiment of the gay male or lesbian—see Christopher Craft, "'Kiss Me with Those Red Lips': Gender and Inversion in Bram Stoker's *Dracula*"; Talia Schaffer, "A Wilde Desire Took Me: The Homoerotic History of *Dracula*," which reads Stoker's novel in the light of the Oscar Wilde trials; Sue-Ellen Case, "Tracking the Vampire"; Tamar Heller, "The Vampire in the House: Hysteria, Female Sexuality, and Female Knowledge in J. S. Le Fanu's 'Carmilla,'"; essays on lesbian vampires in Joan Gordon and Veronica Hollinger's *Blood Read: The Vampire as Metaphor in Contemporary Culture*; and the section "Lesbian Vampires" in Gina Wisker, "Love Bites: Contemporary Women's Vampire Fictions." For more on lesbian Gothic, see

Paulina Palmer, *Lesbian Gothic: Transgressive Narratives*. Other useful works on gay male Gothic are George Haggerty, "Literature and Homosexuality in the Late Eighteenth Century: Walpole, Beckford, Lewis"; Raymond Bentman, "Horace Walpole's Forbidden Passion"; Jill Campbell, "'I Am No Giant': Horace Walpole, Heterosexual Incest, and Love among Men"; and Steven Bruhm, "Picture This: Stephen King's Queer Gothic." See also the essay by Ranita Chatterjee and Patrick Horan in this volume.

Survey respondents interested in teaching gender issues recommended several texts discussing and theorizing the history of sexuality as useful background: Roger Shattuck, *Forbidden Knowledge from Prometheus to Pornography*; Thomas Laqueur, *Making Sex: Body and Gender from the Greeks to Freud*; and Michel Foucault, *An Introduction*, volume 1 of *History of Sexuality*.

Psychoanalytic Approaches

Given the Gothic obsession with dreams, fears, and desires, it is not surprising that psychoanalytic criticism was a popular approach among survey respondents, as it has traditionally been among literary critics. Psychoanalytic criticism can interwine with feminist or gendered criticism, as some of the important works of feminist criticism of Gothic mentioned above—by Williams, Massé, Kahane, Doody, and Hoeveler—employ a psychoanalytic approach. See also Norman Holland and Leona Sherman, "Gothic Possibilities," a work of reader-response criticism that explores the psychological appeal of Gothics to a female audience. To go to the source of psychoanalytic criticism in order to understand its revelance to the genre, see Freud's essays "The Uncanny" and *The Interpretation of Dreams*, as well as Ernest Jones's *On the Nightmare*. William Patrick Day's *In the Circles of Fear and Desire: A Study of Gothic Fantasy* is a psychoanalytic study mentioned frequently by survey respondents. See also David Punter's *The Romantic Unconscious* and *Gothic Pathologies*, the second a study that focuses, as its subtitle claims, on "the text, the body, the law"; Jerrold Hogle's "The Restless Labyrinth: Cryptonomy in the Gothic Novel"; Pamela Kaufman's "Burke, Freud, and the Gothic"; and Michelle Massé's discussion "Psychoanalysis and the Gothic." Catherine Belsey's "The Romantic Construction of the Unconscious" links the "textual fantasy" of the Gothic with the representation of subjectivity in Wordsworth. Valdine Clemens's *The Return of the Repressed: Gothic Horror from* The Castle of Otranto *to* Alien melds Jungian and historicist approaches to argue that the Gothic is a "type of psychosocial therapy" (1). A particularly provocative melding of psychoanalytic and historicist approaches is Ronald Thomas's discussion of Gothics and detective fiction in *Dreams of Authority: Freud and the Fictions of the Unconscious*, which situates Freud's interpretations of the self in the ideologies of Victorian culture. For psychoanalytic interpretations of the doppelgänger or double convention in Gothic, see "Topics, Areas, Subgenres" below. (See also the essay by Anne Williams on psychoanalytic criticism in this volume.)

Marxian-Historicist Approaches

Much of the recent criticism reevaluating the Gothic historicizes it by tracing the genre's implications in discourses of class, ideology, and politics. Several of the books mentioned as background works above—Punter (*Romantic Unconscious*), Miles (*Ann Radcliffe*), Clery (*Women's Gothic*), Richter (*Progress*), and James Watt—are examples of historicist criticism, which was also a popular approach among survey respondents. (Clery's work, which ties women's association with the genre to the rise of commodification, is an example of the fusion of feminist and historicist interpretation of the rise of the Gothic, as is Miles's.) On the Gothic's representation of class and politics in the era of the French Revolution, see Ronald Paulson's "Gothic Fiction and the French Revolution" as well as his chapter "The Gothic: Ambrosio to Frankenstein" in *Representations of Revolution, 1789–1820*; Lee Sterrenburg's essay "Mary Shelley's Monster: Politics and Psyche in *Frankenstein*," which reads the monster as an embodiment of fears of class unrest. Other works that examine the Gothic and ideology are Poovey's "Ideology and *The Mysteries of Udolpho*" and her chapters on Wollstonecraft and Mary Shelley in *The Proper Lady and the Woman Writer*; Terry Lovell's section "Gothic Fantasy: A Literature of Subversion?" in his *Consuming Fiction*; Franco Moretti's chapter on the "sociology of the modern monster," "Dialectic of Fear," in *Signs Taken for Wonders: Essays in the Sociology of Literary Forms*; Alok Bhalla's *The Cartographers of Hell: Essays on the Gothic Novel and the Social History of England*; Jacqueline Howard's *Reading Gothic Fiction: A Bakhtinian Approach*, also a helpful work for exploring gender issues; Stephen Bernstein's "Form and Ideology in the Gothic Novel"; Elsie B. Michie's "Production Replaces Creation: Market Forces and *Frankenstein* as a Critique of Romanticism"; Andrea Henderson's "'An Embarrassing Subject': Use Value and Exchange Value in Early Gothic Characterization"; Stefan Andriopoulos's "The Invisible Hand: Supernatural Agency in Political Economy and the Gothic Novel"; and David Richter's "The Unguarded Prison: Reception Theory, Structural Marxism, and the History of the Gothic Novel." Hogle's "The Gothic Ghost of the Counterfeit and the Progress of Abjection" is an important theoretical explanation of how the Gothic obsession with images of counterfeit and abjection are related to the transition from precapitalist to capitalist culture.

Formal and Aesthetic Approaches

Approaches that focus on the formal structure and aesthetics of the Gothic include Sedgwick's *The Coherence of Gothic Conventions*, cited by a number of respondents as a significant work of criticism, and Terry Heller's *The Delights of Terror: An Aesthetics of the Tale of Terror*. A provocative document for engaging the question of canonicity of the Gothic as literary form is Elizabeth R. Napier's *The Failure of Gothic*, which, as its title indicates, harks back to older devaluations of the genre by arguing that its fragmentation and instability, its inability to hold to neoclassical ideals of closure, signal aesthetic failure. Other critical works like Haggerty's *Gothic Fiction / Gothic Form*, which explicitly responds to Napier, argue for a more positive reading of these trends in Gothic, seeing them as a radical (and aesthetically valuable) innovation in affective form that gives literature a new vocabulary for feeling and private experience. Instructors interested in exploring the Gothic's link to melodrama will want to consult Peter Brooks's discussion of this genre, *The Melodramatic Imagination: Balzac, Henry James, Melodrama, and the Mode of Excess*.

Cultural Studies Approaches

Many recent critical works place the Gothic in the context of a wider culture, but particularly significant recent works employing a cultural studies approach are Mark Edmundson, *Nightmare on Main Street: Angels, Sadomasochism, and the Culture of Gothic*, a meditation on the American obsession with the Gothic; Judith Halberstam, *Skin Shows: Gothic Horror and the Technology of Monsters*, which focuses on messages about otherness in various cultural forms of Gothic, including variations of such texts as *Frankenstein* and *Dracula*; Nina Auerbach, *Our Vampires, Ourselves*, which examines both film and literary versions of vampirism and their embedded cultural messages.

While there has not yet been much critical discussion of other popular culture versions of Gothic, such as comic books, instructors interested in exploring them in the classroom might wish to consult a work mentioned earlier, Neil Barron's *Fantasy and Horror: A Critical and Historical Guide to Literature, Illustration, Film, TV, Radio, and the Internet* (see, for example, in this collection, Robert Morrish and Mike Ashley's discussion "Fantasy and Horror Magazines"). Students who are well versed in Gothic comic book culture will frequently bring such references into the classroom. It behooves the Gothic instructor, therefore, to be familiar with *Sandman*, *Watchmen*, and *Batman: The Dark Knight Returns* (all DC Comics). Known as graphic novels, these comic books for adults frequently develop traditionally Gothic themes and are part of a new, vital, and growing field (see Weiner).

Topics, Areas, Subgenres

Art and the Sublime   The relation between Gothic literature and Gothic architecture is addressed in several works. Linda Bayer-Berenbaum's *The Gothic Imagination*, which juxtaposes Gothic architecture, art, and literature, is an especially good secondary source to consult, as is Paul Frankl's *The Gothic: Literary Sources and Interpretations through Eight Centuries*, which traces the relation between Gothic architecture and philosophical and cultural trends.

Two analyses of Walpole's Gothic revival at Strawberry Hill that are particularly relevant to the teacher of the Gothic are Dianne Ames, "Strawberry Hill: Architecture of the 'As If,'" and D. D. McKinney, "The Castle of My Ancestors: Horace Walpole and Strawberry Hill." For the relation between landscape art and Radcliffe's novels, see Charles Kostelnick, "From Picturesque View to Picturesque Vision: William Gilpin and Ann Radcliffe"; Lynne Epstein, "Mrs. Radcliffe's Landscapes: The Influence of Three Landscape Painters on Her Nature Descriptions."

To introduce students to the idea of the sublime and its relevance to Gothic fiction, some instructors mentioned assigning Burke's *A Philosophical Enquiry into the Origin of Our Ideas of the Sublime and the Beautiful*. For secondary sources on the sublime, see Vijay Mishra's *The Gothic Sublime*, called by one respondent the best recent study of the Gothic; Jack Voller, *The Supernatural Sublime: The Metaphysics of Terror in Anglo-American Romanticism*; David Morris, "Gothic Sublimity"; and Hendrik van Gorp, "The Sublime and the Gothic." Background on the eighteenth-century sublime may be found in Samuel Monk's *The Sublime: A Study of Critical Theories in Eighteenth-Century England*, Walter J. Hipple's *The Beautiful, the Sublime, and the Picturesque in Eighteenth-Century British Aesthetic Theory*, and Frances Ferguson's *Solitude and the Sublime*. On gender and the sublime, see Barbara Claire Freeman, *The Feminine Sublime*.

Fantasy　For exploring the Gothic's relation to fantasy, see Rosemary Jackson, *Fantasy: The Literature of Subversion*; Tzvetan Todorov, *The Fantastic: A Structural Approach to a Literary Genre*; Neil Cornwell, *The Literary Fantastic: From Gothic to Postmodernism*; and Lucie Armitt, *Theorizing the Fantastic*.

The Double-Doppelgänger　Sources on the double or doppelgänger theme include Masao Miyoshi, *The Divided Self: A Perspective on the Literature of the Victorians*; Karl Miller, *Doubles: Studies in Literary History*; Carl Keppler, *The Literature of the Second Self*; Clifford Hallam, "The Double as Incomplete Self: Toward a Definition of Doppelgänger"; Otto Rank, *The Double: A Psychoanalytic Study*; Robert Rogers, *A Psychoanalytic Study of the Double in Literature*; David Ketterer, *Frankenstein's Creation: The Book, the Monster, and the Human Reality*; R. Jackson, "Narcissism and Beyond: A Psychoanalytic Reading of *Frankenstein* and Fantasies of the Double"; Mary K. Patterson Thornburg, *The Monster in the Mirror: Gender and the Sentimental/Gothic Myth in* Frankenstein.

Houses and Spaces　Many works of Gothic criticism address conventions such as the Gothic's use of space. Among several works that offer particularly provocative theories of the genre by looking at this topos is Jan B. Gordon's "Narrative Enclosure as Textual Ruin: An Archaeology of Gothic Consciousness," which interprets the "romantic attraction to the fragment" (214) in the Gothic by analyzing its images of ruins, buried secrets, and multilayered texts. Another look at houses in the Gothic is Maria Tatar's "The Houses of Fiction: Toward a Definition of the Uncanny," which concludes that the source of fantasy is, finally, a sense of "radical homelessness" (182). A Foucauldian reading of the carceral space of the Gothic is Paul Morrison, "Enclosed in Openness: *Northanger Abbey* and the Domestic Carceral." An important work that does not explicitly address the Gothic but is an essential analysis of spatial symbolism is Guy Bachelard's *The Poetics of Space*. Instructors might also want to consult Max Byrd's "The Madhouse, the Whorehouse, and the Convent," which examines the eighteenth-century preoccupation with sexuality and the carceral in works including Gothic novels. (For another approach to houses in Gothic fiction, see Hennelly's essay in this volume).

Religion and Philosophy   Works that examine the Gothic's relation to religion are Joel Porte's essay "In the Hands of an Angry God: Religious Terror in Gothic Fiction"; Victor Sage, *Horror Fiction in the Protestant Tradition*, which traces the Gothic's relation to anti-Catholic rhetoric; Edward Ingebretsen, *Maps of Heaven, Maps of Hell: Religious Terror as Memory from the Puritans to Stephen King*; Marie Mulvey-Roberts, *Gothic Immortals: The Fiction of the Brotherhood of the Rosy Cross*, which examines the Rosicrucian influence on the Gothic; and S. L. Varnado, *Haunted Presence: The Numinous in Gothic Fiction*. For philosophical approaches, see Marshall Brown's "A Philosophical View of the Gothic Novel" as well as his essay in this volume.

Race and Imperialism   For race and imperialism in the Gothic, see Patrick Brantlinger's "Imperial Gothic" in *Rule of Darkness: British Literature and Imperialism, 1830–1914*; H. L. Malchow's extremely useful and lucid *Gothic Images of Race in Nineteenth-Century Britain*; Stephen Arata's "The Occidental Tourist" and *Fictions of Loss in the Victorian Fin-de-Siècle*; Judith Wilt's "The Imperial Mouth: Imperialism, the Gothic, and Science Fiction"; and the first chapter of Jon Thompson's *Fiction, Crime, and Empire*, which looks at imperialism in Victorian detective fiction. For more on race in American literature, see the end of the section "American Gothic" below and works by Robert Martin ("Haunted"); Lesley Ginsberg; Kari Winter (*Subjects*); and Toni Morrison (*Playing*). Judie Newman's "Postcolonial Gothic: Ruth Prawer Jhabvala and the Sobhraj Case" offers a definition of an increasingly important but hitherto undertheorized area of Gothic studies. Lucie Armitt's "The Magical Realism of Contemporary Gothic" also discusses the relevance of Gothic fiction to the field of postcolonial literature, while Donna Heiland's *Gothic Novels: A Feminist Introduction* contains a chapter on postcolonial fictions.

Irish and Scottish Gothic   One historically important version of imperial or colonial Gothic is Irish Gothic. For more on this field, see William J. McCormack, *Sheridan Le Fanu and Victorian Ireland* and "Irish Gothic and After

(1820–1945)"; Julian Moynahan, "The Politics of Anglo-Irish Gothic: Maturin, Le Fanu, and *The Return of the Repressed*"; and, most recent, Margot Gayle Backus, *The Gothic Family Romance: Heterosexuality, Child Sacrifice, and the Anglo-Irish Colonial Order*. See also Sage's "Irish Gothic: C. R. Maturin and J. S. LeFanu" and Mark Hennelley in this volume.

For an introduction to the field of Scottish Gothic, see Ian Duncan, "Walter Scott, James Hogg, and Scottish Gothic"; Hoeveler, "Gendering the Scottish Ballad: The Case of Anne Bannerman's *Tales of Superstition and Chivalry*"; and Punter, "Heartlands: Contemporary Scottish Gothic."

European Gothic (outside the British Isles) Some sources on European Gothic are Neil Cornwell, "European Gothic," "Gothic and Its Origins in East and West: Vladimir Odoevsky and Fitz-James O'Brian," and *The Gothic-Fantastic in Nineteenth-Century Russian Literature*; Pierre-Georges Castex, *Le conte fantastique en France de Nodier à Maupassant*; David Glenn Kropf, *Authorship as Alchemy: Subversive Writing in Pushkin, Scott, Hoffmann*; Bernice Glatzer Rosenthal, *The Occult in Russian and Soviet Culture*; Eric A. Blackall, *The Novels of the German Romantics*; Roger Cardinal, *German Romantics in Context*; Glyn Tegai Hughes, *Romantic German Literature*; Virgil Nemoianu, *The Taming of Romanticism: European Literature and the Age of Biedermeier*. For the work of an important Scandinavian Gothicist, see Sibyl James, "Gothic Transformations: Isak Dinesen and the Gothic"; Susan Hardy Aiken, *Isak Dinesen and the Engendering of Narrative*; and Robert Langbaum, *The Gayety of Vision: A Study of Isak Dinesen's Art*.

American Gothic One respondent claimed that Leslie Fiedler's *Love and Death in the American Novel* "turned [her] on" to the field of American Gothic. Other works on American Gothic are Donald Ringe, *American Gothic: Imagination and Reason in Nineteenth-Century Fiction*; Lewis S. Gross, *Redefining the American Gothic: From* Wieland *to* Day of the Dead; Howard Kerr and John William Crowley, *The Haunted Dusk: American Supernatural Fiction, 1820–1920*; Dale Bailey, *American Nightmares: The Haunted House Formula in American Popular Culture*. Teresa Goddu's *Gothic America* is a historicizing approach to early Gothic fictions in America and their relation to developing nationalism (see her essay on Charles Brockden Brown's *Wieland* in this volume). Kathleen Brogan's "American Stories of Cultural Haunting" reads ghost narratives in American Gothic as a metaphor for "issues of acculturation in a polyethnic society" (150). Brogan has also published a book on this topic entitled *Cultural Haunting: Ghosts and Ethnicity in Recent American Literature*. Edmundson's *Nightmare on Main Street* is a provocative cultural studies interpretation of America's continuing obsession with Gothic. Showalter's "American Female Gothic" in *Sister's Choice: Tradition and Change in American Women's Fiction* (127–44) was singled out as a concise introduction to this topic. Hoeveler's "Postgothic Fiction: Joyce Carol Oates Turns the

Screw on Henry James" examines how one of Oates's many Gothic short stories rewrites James's classic. Karen Halttunen's *Murder Most Foul: The Killer and the American Gothic* traces the history of the mythology of the killer in American culture. David Mogen, Scott Patrick Sanders, and Joanne B. Karpinski's *Frontier Gothic* reads American Gothic as a manifestation of myths of the American frontier and their desire to tame the wilderness and the dark others who inhabit it. Martin and Savoy's *The American Gothic* contains important works on race and the American Gothic: Martin, "Haunted by Jim Crow: Gothic Fictions by Hawthorne and Faulkner"; Ginsberg, "Slavery and the Gothic Horror of Poe's 'The Black Cat.'" For more on the topic of race, see Kari Winter's book *Subjects of Slavery, Agents of Change: Women and Power in Gothic Novels and Slave Narratives, 1790–1865*, which reads slave narratives as a form of the Gothic, and Toni Morrison's sections on Gothic in *Playing in the Dark: Whiteness and the Literary Imagination*. (Also see Hogle's essay on African American Gothic in this volume.)

Horror Fiction   Sources on horror fiction mentioned by respondents are Noel Carroll, *The Philosophy of Horror; or, Paradoxes of the Heart*, a philosophical meditation on the attractions of the genre; James Twitchell, *Dreadful Pleasures: An Anatomy of Modern Horror*; Brian Docherty, *American Horror Fiction: From Brockden Brown to Stephen King*; Tony Magistrale and Michael Morrison, *A Dark Night's Dreaming: Contemporary American Horror Fiction*; Manuel Aguirre, *The Closed Space: Horror Literature and Western Symbolism*; Joseph Grixti, *Terrors of Uncertainty*; Martin Tropp, *Images of Fear: How Horror Stories Helped Shape Modern Culture*; Susan Stewart, "The Epistemology of the Horror Story"; Stephen King, *Danse Macabre* (also his "Why We Crave Horror Movies"); David J. Skal, *The Monster Show: A Cultural History of Horror*; and Judith Halberstam, *Skin Shows: Gothic Horror and the Technology of Monsters*. (For more on American horror fiction, see the essay on Stephen King and Anne Rice by Bette Rogers in this volume).

Vampires and Ghosts   Vampire literature is a popular subgenre of Gothic (see Daniel Scoggin's essay in this volume). A number of works on vampires can be considered codings of "gay Gothic" (see discussion of this above). Paul Barber's *Vampires, Burial, and Death: Folklore and Reality* gives some historical background on vampires. See also Twitchell, *The Living Dead: A Study of the Vampire in Romantic Literature*; Gregory Waller, *The Living and the Undead: From Stoker's* Dracula *to Romero's* Dawn of the Dead; Ken Gelder, *Reading the Vampire*; Carol Senf, *The Vampire in Nineteenth-Century English Literature*; and Jalal Toufic, *Vampires: An Uneasy Essay on the Undead in Film* (called "an incredibly important book" by one respondent). There are so many readings of the Transylvanian count that one might legitimately identify a subspecialty of Dracula studies, but among the works found most useful by respondents—not just for what they say about Stoker's novel but about vampire fiction in general—were Jennifer Wicke, "Vampiric Typewriting: *Dracula* and Its Media"; Arata ("Occidental Tourist") and Showalter (*Sexual Anarchy*) on *Dracula* (see "Fin de Siècle and Later Gothic" above); Margaret L. Carter, *Dracula: The Vampire and Its Critics*; and Leonard Wolf on *Dracula* (*Essential Dracula*). (See also the essays by Craft and by Schaffer in the discussion of gay Gothic above.) Nina Auerbach's *Our Vampires, Ourselves* is a particularly lucid survey of vampire tales in literature and film and their cultural meanings.

The presence of the supernatural in the Gothic is explored in Carter's *Specter or Delusion? The Supernatural in Gothic Fiction*. Criticism of the ghost story includes Julia Briggs, *Night Visitors: The Rise and Fall of the English Ghost Story*; Jack Sullivan, *Elegant Nightmares: The English Ghost Story from Le Fanu to Blackwood*. Since ghost stories have been a fruitful venue for women writers of Gothic, much recent criticism of the genre has been feminist: Vanessa R. Dickerson, *Victorian Ghosts in the Noontide: Women Writers and the Supernatural*; Lynette Carpenter and Wendy K. Kolmar, *Haunting the House of Fiction: Feminist Perspectives on Ghost Stories by American Women*; and Nickianne Moody, "Visible Margins: Women Writers and the English Ghost Story."

Detective Fiction　On detective fiction, one of the generic progeny of the Gothic, see Glenn W. Most and William W. Stowe, *The Poetics of Murder: Detective Fiction and Literary Theory*; Ian Ousby, *Bloodhounds of Heaven: The Detective in English Fiction from Godwin to Doyle*; Dennis Porter, *The Pursuit of Crime: Art and Ideology in Detective Fiction*; Martin A. Kayman, *From Bow Street to Baker Street: Mystery, Detection, and Narrative*. Criticism on the origins of detective fiction in the late nineteenth century examines its link to Victorian anxieties about gender, class, race, and selfhood. See D. A. Miller, *The Novel and the Police*; Gordon Hirsch, "*Frankenstein*, Detective Fiction, and *Jekyll and Hyde*"; Ronald Thomas, "Minding the Body Politic: The Romance of Science and the Revision of History in Victorian Detective Fiction" and his chapter on detective fiction in *Dreams of Authority: Freud and the Fictions of the Unconscious*. The first chapter of J. Thompson's *Fiction, Crime, and Empire* looks at imperialism and the emergence of the modern detective hero in Poe and Doyle.

Film Criticism　Criticism on film includes, in addition to the Toufic book on vampires mentioned above, Andrew Tudor, *Monsters and Mad Scientists: A Cultural History of the Horror Movie*; Skal, *Hollywood Gothic: The Tangled Web of Dracula from Novel to Stage to Screen*; Bruce Lanier Wright, *Nightwalkers: Gothic Horror Movies*; Jonathan Lake Crane, *Terror and Everyday Life: Singular Moments in the History of the Horror Film*; Will H. Rockett, *Devouring Whirlwind: Terror and Transcendence in the Cinema of Cruelty*; Vera Dika, *Games of Terror: Halloween, Friday the Thirteenth, and the Films of the Stalker Cycle*; James Ursini and Alain Silver, *More Things Than Are Dreamt*

Of: Masterpieces of Supernatural Horror, from Mary Shelley to Stephen King, in Literature and Film; William Everson, *Classics of the Horror Film*; Dennis Fischer, *Horror Film Directors, 1931–1990*; Ken Hanke, *A Critical Guide to Horror Film Series*; David Pirie, *A Heritage of Horror: The English Gothic Cinema, 1946–1972*; and John McCarty, *The Fearmakers: The Screen's Directorial Masters of Suspense and Terror*. Works that focus on gender issues in Gothic and horror films are Carol J. Clover, *Men, Women, and Chain Saws: Gender in the Modern Horror Film*; Barry Keith Grant, *The Dread of Difference: Gender and the Horror Film*; Isabel Cristina Pinedo, *Recreational Terror: Women and the Pleasures of Horror Film Viewing*; Rhona J. Berenstein, *Attack of the Leading Ladies: Gender, Sexuality, and Spectatorship in Classic Horror Cinema*; and Wheeler Winston Dixon, "Gender Approaches to Directing the Horror Film: Women Filmmakers and the Mechanisms of the Gothic." (Also see Dixon's essay in this volume.)

Readings for Students

The works mentioned above were often recommended, either as part of course reading or as library reserve, for both students and instructors, especially for instructors teaching graduate courses in which a range of criticism could be assigned. Those working with undergraduate students, however, were aware of the difficulties of teaching sophisticated criticism in the often rushed-for-time undergraduate curriculum; they suggested strategies for introducing secondary works that had worked particularly successfully.

Many instructors used Freud's two essays "The Uncanny" and *The Interpretation of Dreams* to introduce psychological readings of the genre. In addition to reading Freud in tandem with Gothic texts, some excerpted readings from intellectuals relevant to the period of the Gothic they were looking at: for example, Burke (on the sublime or the French Revolution) in conjunction with eighteenth-century Gothic or Darwin in conjunction with nineteenth-century Gothic. One instructor mentioned using Bishop Richard Hurd's *Letters on Chivalry and Romance* (1762), which analyzes feudal fantasies, because of its relevance to the rise of the Gothic's version of such fantasies. Another teacher used De Quincey's essay "On the Knocking at the Gate in *Macbeth*" because it is "a productive entry point for the defamiliarizing strategies of the Gothic." Coleridge's review of *The Monk* attacking Gothic romance is a good example for students of hostile contemporary responses to the genre.

Works by various philosophers and historians function as touchstone texts that help explain or illustrate a concept. For instance, excerpts from Bachelard's *The Poetics of Space* can be useful for introducing students to the symbolism of space in the Gothic (the excerpts work particularly well in conjunction with a psychoanalytic approach or a feminist introduction to the domestic, and frequently carceral, spaces of female Gothic). Michel Foucault appeared in a variety of classroom contexts—*Discipline and Punish* along with works that depict the carceral landscape of Gothic, or *Madness and Civilization* and *The History of Sexuality* to discuss sexuality and madness. Several instructors used Julia Kristeva's concept of abjection in *Powers of Horror* to explain the Gothic dual fear of taboos and fascination with transgressing them (for more on the pedagogical use of Kristeva, see the essay by Anne Williams in this volume). The introduction to Edward Said's *Orientalism* helps introduce students to an important strand of ideology in Gothic's descriptions of racial others.

Secondary works most frequently assigned to students were Punter's *Literature of Terror* (in the second edition, *The Gothic Tradition* is vol. 1, *The Modern Gothic* vol. 2), called "the most valuable introduction to the Gothic for students" by one instructor who has students buy it or copies chapters for them, and Fred Botting's *Gothic* (cited for useful overview and helpful bibliography). Other popular works assigned in whole or in part, or placed on reserve, were Maggie Kilgour's *Rise of the Gothic Novel*, Anne Williams's *Art of Darkness*, Kate Ferguson Ellis's *The Contested Castle*, Robert Miles's *Gothic Writing*, and Sage's *The Gothick Novel*. Essays assigned included Peter Brooks's "Virtue and Terror: *The Monk*," Anne McWhir's "The Gothic Transgression of Disbelief," Christopher Craft's "'Kiss Me with Those Red Lips': Gender and Inversion in Bram Stoker's *Dracula*," Susan Stewart's "The Epistemology of the Horror Story," Arata's "The Occidental Tourist," and Sedgwick's "The Character in the Veil: Imagery of the Surface in the Gothic Novel."

Among the many critical works on female Gothic the ones most frequently given to students (in addition to Williams [*Art*] and Ellis [*Castle*]) were Marilyn Butler's "The Woman at the Window," Terry Castle's "The Spectralization of the Other," Moers's "Female Gothic," Gilbert and Gubar's chapter on *Jane Eyre* in *Madwoman in the Attic*, Tania Modleski's "The Female Uncanny," and Claire Kahane's "The Gothic Mirror." Introductions to several collections of Gothic works were judged useful—for instance, David Mogen, Scott Patrick Sanders, and Joanne B. Karpinski's introduction to *Frontier Gothic* and Jeffrey Cox's to *Seven Gothic Dramas*. One instructor "swear[s] by" Chris Baldick's introduction to *The Oxford Book of Gothic Tales* as an accessible overview of the genre. Several instructors found Marilyn Gaull's discussion of Gothic in *English Romanticism: The Human Context* a "short but very helpful definition" of the genre for students.

To inspire debate on the definition of Gothic, one instructor recommended assigning Robert Hume's "Gothic versus Romantic: A Revaluation of the Gothic Novel" and Platzner's response to it (Hume and Platzner). Another definition cited frequently by survey participants is the attempt to define and delimit the meanings of *Gothic* by Maurice Lévy in his article "'Gothic' and the Critical Idiom." Works in the Bedford–St. Martin's series were considered especially useful for giving a sense of the range and varieties of critical approaches, with the *Frankenstein* volume (ed. Smith) particularly recommended, especially its essays by Lee Heller ("*Frankenstein* and the Cultural Uses of Gothic"), Mary Lowe-Evans ("Reading with a 'Nicer Eye': Responding to *Frankenstein*"), and Warren Montag ("The 'Workshop of Filthy Creation': A Marxist Reading of *Frankenstein*"). (Since the time of the survey, a new volume of the Bedford *Frankenstein* [Smith] has been released that retains the Montag essay but substitutes other essays for those by Heller and by Lowe-Evans; instructors will either want to use the new essays or work with photocopies.) Critical materials in Norton Critical Editions were judged useful, with the *Dracula* volume particularly recommended (ed. Auerbach and Skal). Alan Bewell's "An Issue of Monstrous Desire: *Frankenstein* and Obstetrics," which positions Shelley's depiction of reproduction in the context of nineteenth-century obstetrical discourses and their anxieties about the female body, was also recommended as a good introduction to cultural criticism.

Aids to Teaching

Art and Architecture

The Gothic is a genre ideally suited to teaching in an interdisciplinary manner, and a number of visual and audiovisual texts can be paired with written works in order to spark discussion and student interest. Several respondents reported particular success bringing in art contemporary to the inception of the Gothic as a way of setting the scene to introduce Gothic themes and conventions. (For more on using art in the classroom, see Stephen Behrendt's essay in this volume.) Showing the work of such artists as Salvator Rosa, Nicolas Poussin, Henry Fuseli, Joseph Wright, Giambattista Piranesi, William Blake, John Constable, and J. M. W. Turner helps students see how Gothic fiction participates in intellectual trends and ideological anxieties of its period and, like visual images, creates an iconography for representing them. Showing the work of Rosa and Poussin, for instance, introduces such concepts as the picturesque and the sublime while also demonstrating what one teacher calls the "eighteenth-century fascination with ruins, rugged landscapes, isolation of human figures, and visual strategies for producing impressions of isolation and vulnerability"—these impressions a significant feature of the Gothic. Several respondents also recommended showing slides or photographs of Gothic architecture. Recommended for preparing slides were Michael McCarthy's *The Origins of the Gothic Revival*, an "especially rich" source not only for pictures but also for images of locations in England that reflect the Gothic revival; Rose Macauley's *The Pleasure of Ruins*; Christopher Hussey's *The Picturesque*; Elisabeth Manwaring's *Italian Landscape in Eighteenth-Century England*; and John Dixon Hunt's works on landscape, gardens, and painting, such as *Gardens and the Picturesque: Studies in the History of Landscape Architecture.* Several instructors used slides of Walpole's antiquarian estate at Strawberry Hill with particular success. For a nice collection of illustrations from early Gothic novels that can be useful to introduce students to Gothic conventions, see Frederick Frank's "Illustrations from Early Gothic Novels."

Other instructors found slides or reproductions of Piranesi's carceral landscapes particularly helpful for introducing the emphasis on imprisonment and threatened autonomy in the Gothic (at least one instructor paired Piranesi's work with the theory of Foucault). One respondent, to underscore the surreal and grotesque elements of the Piranesi drawings, couples them with pictures by Bosch and Magritte; another pairs Piranesi with Goya and Friedrich; while yet another brings in slides of works by Dali, Duchamp, and Ernst to illustrate the surreal nature of Gothic narrative.

Music

Several teachers reported using music in the classroom, for example, the damnation scene in Mozart's *Don Giovanni.* To illustrate the shift from Enlightenment neoclassicism to Romantic angst, one instructor contrasted excerpts from baroque, classical, and Romantic composers (i.e., Telemann and Mozart followed by Tchaikovsky, Wagner, and Mahler). One extremely innovative interdisciplinary course on Gothic presents musical motifs (such as the melodic pitch repetition from Beethoven's Fifth Symphony and pedal point from Chopin's D-flat Prelude) as touchstones for correspondences in Gothic fiction, introducing the Gothic hero through the language of music (dissonance, chromaticism, arpeggiation). Other instructors used more modern music, including selections from 1980s Goth bands, such as Dead Can Dance, Sisters of Mercy, and Bauhaus, as well as Marilyn Manson, Transvision Vamp, Ministry, Christian Death, Shakespear's Sister, and Smashing Pumpkins.

Film and Audiovisual

A vast library of films can be used in the Gothic classroom—both adaptations of classic Gothic texts and original narratives. (For more on film adaptations of the Gothic, see Wheeler Dixon's essay in this volume.) The films most frequently mentioned as useful in the classroom are the various movie versions of *Frankenstein,* especially the original (1931) version, but also *The Bride of Frankenstein* (1935), which is actually closer to the novel; Kenneth Branagh's *Mary Shelley's Frankenstein* (several respondents thought this version "awful," but others seemed happy with it); and the 1993 TNT version with Randy Quaid. Ken Russell's *Gothic,* based on the events surrounding Mary Shelley's writing of the novel, was also mentioned, as was Mel Brooks's parody *Young Frankenstein.* The film versions of *Dracula* were the second most popular set of movies among respondents; these include the original (1931) version, with

Bela Lugosi and directed by Tod Browning; John Badham's *Dracula*; George Melford's Spanish-language version of the novel, filmed the same year and on the same set as the Lugosi film; Terence Fisher's *Horror of Dracula*; Coppola's *Dracula*; and, on the parody front, William Crain's *Blacula*. Given the number of filmic descendants of both Shelley and Stoker, recommended sources for teachers desiring to select a film version are the videos *Frankenstein: A Cinematic Scrapbook* and *Dracula: A Cinematic Scrapbook*.

Other films frequently used in the classroom are the early film version of *Jane Eyre*, with Orson Welles and Joan Fontaine (dir. Stevenson); *Wuthering Heights*, with Lawrence Olivier and Merle Oberon (there are other movie versions of these texts, but the black-and-white old movie versions, with their great Gothic atmosphere and renowned actors, were the ones singled out by respondents). Hitchcock's *Rebecca* was also popular, as were such other films of his as *Vertigo* (a powerful statement of the doppelgänger theme as well as a descendant of Wilkie Collins's *The Woman in White*), *Psycho*, and *Marnie*. In addition to the versions mentioned above of Stoker's *Dracula*, vampire filmography includes two versions of *Nosferatu*, the classic one by Murnau and one by Werner Herzog; Tony Scott's *The Hunger*; and the film version of Anne Rice's *Interview with the Vampire*. Other movies mentioned by respondents were Cronenberg's *The Fly* and *Dead Ringers*, Lynch's *Blue Velvet* (a retelling of E. T. A. Hoffmann's "The Sandman"), Kubrick's *The Shining*, Tourneau's *Night of the Demons*, as well as *Carnival of Souls*, *Cat People*, *Blade Runner*, *The Haunted Summer*, *Edward Scissorhands*, *Silence of the Lambs*, and *Hannibal*. All the films already mentioned have interesting gender politics, but two that are useful for introducing the conventions of female Gothic are Jean Cocteau's *La belle et la bête* and Roman Polanski's *Rosemary's Baby*, with its narrative of monstrous birth reminiscent of Ellen Moers's discussion of birth allegory in her essay on *Frankenstein* as "female Gothic." Several film versions exist of Le Fanu's "Carmilla," whose female homoeroticism is also a useful text for Gothic gender studies; see Roger Vadim's *Et mourir de plaisir* (the English release is *Blood and Roses*) and *Carmilla* (1989; dir. Gabrielle Beaumont).

Useful documentaries included A & E's *In Search of Frankenstein* and a 1994 special on *Frankenstein* (see Purinton's essay in this volume). A videocassette produced by BBC educational publishing, *Aspects of* Jane Eyre, narrated by Libby Fawcett, discusses a number of issues in Brontë's novel including its version of Gothic. Other resources are a CBC Learning Systems cassette *Terror and the Gothic*, which features Devendra Varma, author of *The Gothic Flame*, discussing the genre; a microfilm collection *Birth of a Gothic Novel* reproducing ninety-eight works by Beckford, Lewis, Radcliffe, Reeve, and Walpole photographed from original editions and letters in English libraries.

Web Resources

If there were one Web source essential for instructors, it is the site mentioned earlier, Frederick Frank's *The Sickly Taper*, which, in addition to a bibliography of awesome proportions, also contains links to a number of Gothic Web sites, including the following:

> Doug Thomson's *Gothic Literature: What the Romantic Writers Read* (www2.gasou.edu/facstaff/dougt/Gothic.htm)
> Jack Voller's *Literary Gothic Page*, an archive of online Gothic sources at Southern Illinois University (www.siue.edu:80/~jvoller/Gothic.html)
> the bibliography *The Gothic: Materials for Study*, assembled at the University of Virginia (www.engl.virginia.edu/~enec981/Group/title.html)
> *Women Romantic-Era Writers*, edited by Adriana Craciun (www. nottingham.ac.uk/~aezacweb/
> *The Gothic Literature Page*, maintained by Franz Potter (members.aol. com/iamudolpho/basic.html)
> connections to the International Gothic Association Web page (www. sul.stanford.edu/mirrors/romnet/iga/)
> *Romanticism on the Net* (users.ox.ac.uk/~scat0385/ron.html#ron); of particular note for this online journal is its special issue on Matthew Lewis, vol. 8, 1997)

Both Potter's *Gothic Literature Page* and the International Gothic Association Web site contain links to selected course syllabi on Gothic taught around the world.

Instructors will also want to be aware of the site for the exhibition *Sublime Anxiety: The Gothic Family and the Outsider* at the University of Virginia (www.lib.virginia.edu/exhibits/Gothic/) and *Gothic and Horror Literature: Online Resources*, a site that focuses on the categories of film, material culture, religion, and vampirism (www.centenary.edu/~balexand/goth20/resources. html).

Web sites on historical periods can contain useful materials on the Gothic: Jack Lynch's *Eighteenth-Century Resources* (andromeda.rutgers.edu/~jlynch/18th/), *Romantic Circles* (www.rc.umd.edu/indexjava.html), and *Victorian Web* (landow.stg.brown.edu/victorian/victov/html). Among the many nonscholarly sites on Gothic, several of higher quality are *Romantic Ghosts and Gothics* (www.autopen.com/ghost.Gothic.shtml), *Shadowvale: A Gothic Rendezvous* (www.geocities.com/Area51/Zone/6463), *Dark Minds* (www.darkminds.com/), *Gothic Romance Webring* (www.angelfire.com/ca/venuslove/RomGoth.html), and *Gothic Journal* (Gothicjournal.com/romance/).

Part Two

APPROACHES

Introduction

In Joanna Baillie's Gothic drama *Orra* (1812), the heroine exclaims at one point, "there is a joy in fear!" (29), and such a sentiment would seem to express the ambivalent attraction that readers have had toward the Gothic since its inception in the mid–eighteenth century. Critics have explored the vast variety of anxieties addressed by a genre that attempts to entertain and instruct its readers through fear, all the while producing in them a joy they are often embarrassed to confess. However, the mixture of emotions produced, both joy and fear, aptly describes not only the versatile symbolism of the Gothic genre but also the scholarship that explores it, which can employ a range of critical languages. The essays in this volume are testimony to the rich and exciting range of critical possibilities stimulated by the Gothic; they are also a tribute to how such criticism can be the product of the creative application of theory in the classroom. Indeed, these essays show how pedagogical experience can enrich critical and theoretical understandings of the Gothic while providing innovative strategies for introducing students to this culturally important genre.

The "Approaches" part of the book is divided into four sections. The first, "Teaching the Backgrounds," introduces instructors to important critical approaches to the Gothic as well as to larger disciplinary contexts (such as philosophy, ideology, the visual arts, psychoanalysis, and science) in which the Gothic can be situated. The second section focuses on the important tradition of British Gothic, primarily classic early Gothics of the late eighteenth century and Romantic period; it also contains several essays on the tradition's important nineteenth- and twentieth-century permutations. The third section surveys different aspects of teaching the tradition of American Gothic, from Brockden Brown through Stephen King and Anne Rice; it contains essays on such important figures as Hawthorne, Melville, Poe, and James. The final section, "Specific Classroom Contexts," looks at a number of pedagogical situations in which the Gothic can be taught, including honors classes; considers teaching Gothic through role-playing and identity writing; and discusses the use of audiovisual materials.

The section on backgrounds begins with Judith Wilt, who offers a definition of Gothic by comparing the issues raised by contemporary Gothic—both literary and film versions—with those raised by classic earlier Gothic fictions. Marshall Brown provides a counterargument to dismissive criticism of Gothic that has seen it as trivial and not cerebral; he points to the affinities between the genre and the larger aesthetic and philosophical movement of Romanticism. Brown makes a powerful case for the Gothic's engagement with questions of real philosophical depth, showing how the instructor can focus fruitfully on those parts of Gothic novels that explore the "mind and its reflections." His central claim, "Philosophy stands at the origin of the Romantic Gothic," allows the teacher to make interesting connections between canonical Romantic texts and Gothic texts that have been until recently dismissed. Similarly discussing the Gothic in the light of larger cultural trends, Robert Miles offers a sophisticated model for teaching early Gothic in the context of eighteenth-century values and beliefs—a particularly important endeavor, given the strong historicist emphasis in current criticism of the Gothic. Stephen Behrendt helps the instructor think of the Gothic in interdisciplinary terms, by discussing how to teach the early Gothic alongside contemporary works of art that depict similar themes. Anne Williams employs a feminist psychoanalytic approach, discussing how using the work of Julia Kristeva in the classroom enables the teacher of Gothic to address such issues as the Gothic's representation of abjection and the feminine. Finally, Carol Senf examines the interface of science and the Gothic in fictions from Shelley's *Frankenstein* to modern cyberpunk, analyzing how the Gothic responds to anxieties about technology in the aftermath of the Age of Reason. The essays in this section provide the sort of useful and specific intellectual background material that any effective instructor must introduce into the classroom, and at least one essay, Wilt's, raises the most problematic issue in the teaching of contemporary Gothic literature, namely, its dark other: slasher videos, snuff films, and violent pornography.

The next section, on the tradition of British Gothic, begins with James Norton's discussion of the important originating Gothic fiction of the 1700s, Walpole's *The Castle of Otranto*. Examining the work of two important early female Gothicists who have only recently begun to be rediscovered—Clara Reeve, author of *The Old English Baron*, and Sophia Lee, author of *The Recess*—Angela Wright discusses the gender politics of the Gothic canon and shows how these Gothic fictions reflect the political climate of their own day, particularly in regard to class issues, by being examples of what James Watt has called "loyalist Gothic" (7). Diane Long Hoeveler examines the early female Gothic, offering a teaching approach that emphasizes how the Gothic fictions of late-eighteenth-century women writers are part of a trend she calls "Gothic feminism," which helped normalize a model of femininity that would prove highly influential to the formation of the nineteenth century's ideology of domesticity. Taking a different perspective on the work of the premier female Gothicist, Ann Radcliffe, Cannon Schmitt explores the relation between suffering and spectacle in her work, placing it in the aesthetic and ideological context of Romanticism and showing the instructor how to teach Radcliffe by analyzing similar descriptions of sensibility in Wordsworth's poetry.

While the essays by Wright, Hoeveler, and Schmitt look at the female Gothic tradition, Scott Simpkins focuses on the important but hitherto underexplored genre of "male Gothic," analyzing the work of Lewis, Beckford, and Stevenson. Similarly focused on the male Gothic, Ranita Chatterjee and Patrick Horan analyze the representation of the homosexual and the homosocial in Godwin's *Caleb Williams*, Hogg's *Private Memoirs and Confessions of a Justified Sinner*, and Wilde's *Dorian Gray*, thus addressing the increasingly important topic of gay studies of the genre.

No overview of British Gothic would be complete without attention to the Gothic drama, a highly popular dissemination of Gothic conventions and narratives in the Romantic period. Despite the importance of Gothic drama, however, it is less frequently taught than Gothic novels and short fiction. Marjean Purinton gives the instructor of Romantic Gothic an erudite overview of the history of Gothic drama; she also offers creative classroom strategies showing teachers how to integrate Gothic fiction and drama by juxtaposing such important works as *Frankenstein* and their dramatic adaptations.

The remaining essays in this section address several other significant contexts for teaching Gothicism of the British Isles. Mark M. Hennelly's essay on Irish Gothicism, focusing on Le Fanu and Maturin, demonstrates how their work can be taught through reference to important architectural tropes of Gothic and also how Irish Gothic uncovers tensions in the colonial relation with England. Tricia Lootens surveys the Victorian Gothic, proposing a highly original theory of how it reflects the period's ambivalent relation to bourgeois values and commodities. Tamar Heller examines the Gothic's complicity in the ideological formations that circled around those anxiety-producing topics—race, gender, and imperialism—in mid- to late-nineteenth-century British literature. Heller demonstrates how the Gothic in Wilkie Collins's *The Moonstone* participated differently in racial and gender stereotyping, while anxiously examining the subject of British imperialism. Daniel Scoggin reads vampire fictions from Polidori to Stoker. Susan Allen Ford offers an interpretation of contemporary women's Gothic that not only considers the recurrent themes of matrophobia and anxiety about female sexuality and the body but also argues that these fictions use images of the feminine to address the loss of value and stable meaning in the modern world.

Critics from Leslie Fieldler to, more recently, David Mogen, Scott Patrick Sanders, and Joanne B. Karpinski; Eric Savoy; Robert K. Martin; and Mark Edmundson have argued for the affinity between Gothicism and American culture. American Gothic echoes the American preoccupation with violence as well as the anxiety that the other cannot be easily repressed and is in fact the ambiguous underside of the apparently tamed and civilized wilderness. The section on American Gothic in this volume begins with Teresa Goddu's analysis of one of the earliest Gothic fictions of the new republic, Charles Brockden Brown's *Wieland*; she shows instructors how to place it in the context of anxieties of the period.

Two essays on Poe and James address teaching important formal aspects of Gothic: Richard Fusco offers a theory for analyzing suspense in the Gothic, while A. A. Markley studies the doppelgänger figure in Poe's short fiction and James's *Turn of the Screw*. Focusing on two of the most canonical of American Renaissance writers, Hawthorne and Melville, Laura Dabundo examines the ambiguous boundaries between order and disorder in their Gothic fictions, arguing that the dialogue between these two writers is crucial to crafting a new version of American Gothic. Kathy Justice Gentile writes on the Gothic fictions of Mary Wilkins Freeman, Sarah Orne Jewett, Charlotte Perkins Gilman, and Edith Wharton, surveying the female tradition of American Gothic and discussing how it offers a critique of male-dominated culture. Jerrold Hogle provides a theorization of the important but critically underexplored area of African American Gothic fiction in his essay on teaching Toni Morrison's *Beloved* and Gloria Naylor's *Linden Hills*. Bette Roberts offers a model for connecting the wildly popular Stephen King and Anne Rice with the larger tradition of Gothic, focusing on their representation of vampirism.

The volume's final section addresses a few important types of pedagogical situations in which the Gothic can be taught. Sandy Feinstein offers an excitingly creative model for teaching Gothic in an interdisciplinary way. Mark James Morreale discusses teaching the Gothic through role-playing exercises in which students, using electronic discussion lists, both write and act out their own fictions, applying their knowledge of Gothic conventions and themes. Wheeler Winston Dixon considers films based on Gothic fictions and their usefulness in the classroom and suggests films that can be used to complement the vast number of Gothic texts currently being taught in the university and college classroom.

There are as many methods of teaching Gothic fiction as there are different types of Gothic texts. Instructors who introduce the Gothic into their curriculum will be rewarded, we think, with teaching works that excite, engage, and provoke students to ask two important if uncomfortable questions that a university and college education is supposed to pose: What is the meaning of life? And how can we understand and accept death?

"And Still Insists He Sees the Ghosts": Defining the Gothic

Judith Wilt

Luke: I'm not afraid.
Yoda: You will be.
—*The Empire Strikes Back*

In Stephen King's 1989 magnum opus *It*, the hero, a novelist who was once a stuttering twelve-year-old, recalls the speech therapist's sibilants-practicing sentence, "He thrusts his fists against the posts and still insists he sees the ghosts" (574). He recalls the sentence just in time to enable him to understand and contend against It—the monster who is eating his friends, his town, the universe. The idea is that for most adults the muscle of belief, strongest in late childhood, atrophies in one's mid-twenties as the social world directs belief toward such puny this-world powers as education, conventional marriage, insurance, and the claims of advertised products, leaving men and women blind to and helpless against the many things in heaven and earth that are not part of this philosophy. Stoker's *Dracula*, I'd argue, contains the same caution.

I like to teach the Gothic to show students how savvy these writers have always been about the this-world powers and the terrors of family, knowledge, desire, and the material goods (and evils) of the culture in which the story is set. The reason why I *love* to teach the Gothic, though, is to play devil's advocate, sometimes literally, about the paranormal and the supernatural. I insist that students see the ghosts. I want to give them a rationale, so to speak, to suspend disbelief, to make them afraid, very afraid, of simple immersion in this world and its comforts, or even in its rather homogenized terrors. It is necessary here, however, to say that it has been standard to begin many courses on the Gothic with a discussion of the difficulties of defining the term, and many instructors summarize the history of the term by presenting the variety of definitions proposed by Maurice Lévy in his article "'Gothic' and the Critical Idiom."

Although it is useful to introduce the historical and critical permutations of the term through an analysis of this article, I have developed another method that allows students to discover for themselves some of the meanings of the term *Gothic*. This essay describes that method as a contract between instructor and students formed with the intention of allowing the students to "see the ghosts" that inhabit the Gothic terrain.

Such a contract is all very well when agreed on by writer and reader, but as a teacher assigning required reading, I found it required a little thought. I have taught (and written about) classic Gothic from *Otranto* to *Dracula* before and relished the process of closing the distance between my contemporary students and the (only apparent) abstractions of Walpole or Shelley or Bram Stoker. When I decided more recently to design and teach a course that would follow the Gothic into contemporary territory, I found myself pausing for a qualm. How frightening would I be? How low would I go? How much killing and dying, how much violence and perversity, would I put us through? Syllabus by syllabus over two undergraduate versions and a graduate one of the course, I've been pushing the edge of the envelope. At first we used the metafictionally distanced film *Scream*: now we use the serial killer film that scares me most— *Seven*. I find that James's *The Turn of the Screw* works much better in my second version of the course, now that it's paired with Shirley Jackson's chillingly authoritative narrative of a deranged dwelling, *The Haunting of Hill House*. Next time I do the graduate version of the course I may even shift Poppy Z. Brite's grimly amoral and voluptuously engrossing *Exquisite Corpse* from the recommended to the required list.

Fully defining or covering the Gothic is an impossible task, of course; thank heaven for the sober urgencies of pedagogy in a thirteen-week semester. I need an outline of ideas to shape reading choices and keep some key questions on the horizon; I need a sample story or two to generate an opening-day discussion; I need a way of engaging both with the history of the genre and with its piquant present. I need to decide what to do about the centrality of film to young peoples' experience of *any* popular-culture genre (now, rather than choose two or three films to see and discuss, I assign eight or ten films to be viewed and reviewed by small groups of students, with one clip each to be shown and discussed with the class). And the writing component of the course? I'm getting good analytic papers and personal reflections, but the Gothic needs something more—will this be the year I assign students to write their own Gothic stories? And why have I been "afraid, very afraid" to do that?

The shaping ideas for the course, to which I return each time I teach a variant of it, no matter what text we read, have been mainly three:

1. The Gothic always blurs or even dissolves the boundary between life and death. Virtually all literature serves this purpose to some extent, of course: theoreticians from Freud and Bataille to Barthes and Kristeva have argued that some impulse in the human being to violate its own boundaries in order to test its dimensions makes this kind of playing with death a foundation of creative art. The special contribution of the Gothic to this enterprise, as a stable genre of its own, is the creation of a domain of the undead, the should-be-dead-but-isn't, the never-was-alive-but-is, the looks-alive-but-isn't. We look at the many kinds of undeath proliferated by the Gothic and what fears and desires we are expressing when we keep reading and writing about it. I want to provoke discussion about the killing and dying that are gateways to this domain, as part of a continuing debate about the limits of human will and agency and as part of the continuing dispute about the purposes of the Gothic genre. Is it moral outlawry or a social and psychic safety valve?

2. From the beginning of my interest in the Gothic I've been haunted by a phrase from *Frankenstein*: as the creature looks on the scientist-father whose death he has encompassed, he mourns, but also celebrates the fact, that "the miserable series of my being is wound to a close" ([Bedford] 186). Why does it seem so true, and yet so dangerous, to think of one's being as a series? And why do deaths in the Gothic always seem simultaneously, punlike, to be both a winding to a close and yet a wound to, a gap in, a refusal of closure? The domain of the Gothic is not just the philosophical problem of evil but the problematic of being itself, which refuses either to stay in place or to wind itself to a close.

3. The Gothic is a faithful record of human engagement with visible, political, cultural issues—race, class, gender, science, empire, authorities of all kinds. But it is also an insistent advocate for the importance of the invisible, the spiritual, even the religious. The Gothic keeps a steady critical pressure on organizations and institutions that want to package and sell the invisible, on all forms of religious dementia, but it is also the vehicle for a wild journey past the Garden of Belief to the countries of Defy Belief and Beyond Belief. From Charles Maturin's *Melmoth* through William Peter Blatty's *The Exorcist* to Thomas Harris's *Silence of the Lambs*, whose heroine quotes T. S. Eliot and whose dark hero "collects church collapses, recreationally" (22), we try to take that journey.

Shaping ideas are all very well, but for opening-day discussion there's nothing like a ghoulish sample of surprise readings to work on. In the spring 2001 version of the course I had the temporary benefit of a number of anonymous and sometimes scatological Gothic tales from the Internet centered on the presidential election (!), but a more reliable opening pair have proven to be two stories from Ray Bradbury and Harlan Ellison. Bradbury's 1951 "Marionettes, Inc." is an accomplished little future-history tale of husbands looking to live the double life of marriage and freedom, who rejoice to discover a company that will build substitute selves to keep the wife happy at home while they step out. The classic O'Henry twists of the story have a satisfyingly Gothic snap, and all the physical violence happens offstage. Ellison's 1975 "Bleeding

Stones," by contrast, piles gore upon gore, blasphemy upon blasphemy, as the carved gargoyles on Saint Patrick's Cathedral, breathing their hundredth year of mutation-producing polluted chemical air, come to life and imaginatively play out their demonic natures upon the godly and the ungodly below:

> A gargoyle crouches in a mound of bodies eating hearts and livers it has ripped from the not-quite-dead casualties. Another sucks the meat off fingers. Three gargoyles have found a nun. Two have lifted her above, and wrenching her legs apart like a wishbone they . . .   (184–85)

Well, you have the idea.

In all three versions of my course this opening set of readings prompted the same satisfying eruption of argument. The largest group insisted that the Bradbury story, with its faster pace, calibrated levels of surprise and suspense, and "subtlety," was not only "better" but also "more truly frightening" because it "left more to your imagination." A stout minority would defend the proliferation of bodily agonies and the enraged tone of the Ellison story as more genuinely Gothic, more unsettling and frightening. I would always join the minority, proposing that the Gothic was aimed squarely at whole being, challenging boundaries like inside/outside, mind/body, and imagination/reality. Above all, I would ask those who claimed to feel boredom at the repetitious goriness of the Ellison story to consider whether that boredom wasn't actually the beginning of deep horror at the Gothic element of repetition itself. The disgust that was spoiling their pleasure, I assured them, would give way to weird gusto if they could bear to read carefully. In this way, we can replay, right at the start and right on the pulses, the old Ann Radcliffe versus Monk Lewis terror versus horror argument.

Maturin's 1820 *Melmoth the Wanderer* is positioned as the first long work of the course; it is my way of serving up the history of Enlightenment and Romantic Gothic in one dish. *Melmoth* employs motifs of imprisonment in madhouse and convent that suggest the carceral tyranny of supposedly consoling institutions like family and church. It dissolves the boundaries between life and death by establishing a tension between the human hunger for knowledge and immortality and the equally human longing for the death that ends suspense, torture, and, above all, remorse. It offers in Melmoth himself a splendid example of the Gothic's dark tutor about the death wish, about the cannibal side of the parent-child relationship and the demonic side of romantic love. Melmoth is neither the wholly supernatural tempter of Monk Lewis's novels and plays nor the wholly human patriarch-tyrant of Ann Radcliffe's tales but something in between—a human being who wants immortality, an immortal who longs to die.

The students in the graduate version of this course, who had somewhere along the line already read Richardson's *Clarissa* and Byron's *Manfred* and even, some of them, the Marquis de Sade, were better able to use *Melmoth* as a glossary of Gothic past. They were better able too to see the theological arc of this long, twisting labyrinth of tales—the irrational clinging to hope against the rational argument of the tutor to accept despair and self-damnation, and the curious paradox of Melmoth himself as the sly argument *for* belief: if there were no God, there would be no damnation, and no human will to resist damnation, as every one of Melmoth's targets does.

What kept the undergraduates gamely traversing Maturin's novel was a series of vivid images from the stories pointing to later Gothic—the way that those routinized by religion became dead-alive automatons while others, exhausted by the roller coaster of hope and despair, deliberately sought that other kind of death in life, madness; the way every human relationship sinks toward the ero-tocannibal delights coming up in *Dracula* and *Silence of the Lambs*.

In my first undergraduate version of the course, anxious to cover the history of the genre, I spent a good deal of time on the great English and American short stories of the first half of the twentieth century, by M. R. James, H. P. Lovecraft, Fritz Leiber, and especially May Sinclair. But the short fiction seemed oddly to break up the rhythm of the novel reading, and students were anxious to reach the Gothic present. In my current version, moving on more quickly to Ira Levin's *Rosemary's Baby* and *The Exorcist* satisfies us both: for me these novels mark the beginning of my own reading engagement with pop-ular Gothic, while for students the film versions they vaguely recall having seen make a useful background for the novels, which in turn they recognize as a pre-lude to Gothic today.

Together the novels are the occasion for a very successful engagement with culture and the Gothic. Students picked up quickly the many similarities between Levin's 1967 New York apartment story and Blatty's 1972 Georgetown rental tale—a newly restless and rootless society at the mercy of the evil of place, the centrality of actors and acting, that curious love-hate for the medical and religious professions, the evil or absent fathers and the defensive mothers afraid of momism, the worship of baby-boomer children left over from the 1950s segueing into the 1960s paranoia that our children are possessed by the devil.

In addition, the equivocal surfacing of the Catholic into 1960s culture fasci-nated the students at my Jesuit university. Levin's post–Vatican II, post-Catholic Rosemary Reilly contends with dreams of demonized nuns and of such icono-graphic figures as Jackie Kennedy and Anna Maria Alberghetti in league with the devil, while the pope's triumphant visit to Yankee Stadium in 1965 coincides with her rape and impregnation, and the famous *Time* magazine cover story on death-of-God theology lies on the waiting room table of the big-time gynecolo-gist who smells of tannis root. Blatty's Columbo-like Jewish detective initially targets a spoiled priest as the likely source of the demonic violence centered around the possessed Regan MacNeil, and the doctors probe Chris and Regan's Catholic beliefs as the locus of what they assume is the mutual delusion of mother and daughter.

In both these novels the comforting modern assumption that the horrors are all in the imagination of crazed mothers gives way to a real-body Gothicism that profoundly materializes the disrupting, illuminating, destroying evil presence. William Friedkin's film version of *The Exorcist* memorably displays the versatility of the body under torture and manipulation, but it can't touch the novel's vivid evocation of the human body as a dynamic producer of grotesque and malignant smells, substances, and energies that ultimately penetrate and animate all material reality around. Nor does it ground this evocation, as the novel does, in the demons' hunger, beyond any element of good and evil, to be both at the controls and in the embrace of this marvelous producer—"sweet! it is sweet in the body! Ah, the blood, feel the blood, how it sings" (324). Roman Polanski's film version of *Rosemary's Baby* cleverly chooses the attenuated and shimmering body of Mia Farrow, then simultaneously playing Frank Sinatra's wife and the ultimate victimized waif-lure of the nighttime soap *Peyton Place*, for the baby's battered mother. Both novel and film vividly portray the alienation and Gothicism of pregnancy: "You look as if you're being drained by a vampire," comments Rosemary's friend (156).

After thinking about the sanctified killings by *Melmoth's* inquisitors and pondering *Dracula's* vampires, the students finally arrive at the present time and its new Gothic protagonist, the serial killer. While the Gothic has always been to some extent talking to other popular culture genres, especially the historical novel and science fiction, the present of the Gothic for my students is marked by its new entanglement with the powerful mass-market genre of crime fiction, which increasingly features this contemporary dark hero or, as Patricia Cornwell's *Point of Origin* (1998) would have it, white whale (191).

The students have seen this figure practically take over the screen in the last decade, and they can talk knowledgeably from the *Scream* series about the rules of the game between killer and victim as translated into the head game played between filmmaker and film watcher. My job, I think, is to connect this game with the metafictional game the Gothic has played since Walpole's *The Castle of Otranto* and Lewis's *The Monk*, but also to get students to think more deeply about the cultural why of the present moment's turn to this kind of monster.

The psychoserial killer is not a new figure in crime or even in Gothic fiction: the father figure of this genre, Jack the Ripper, was a contemporary of Stevenson's *Dr. Jekyll and Mr. Hyde*. But in recent decades, since Ted Bundy seized the American imagination and Jeffrey Dahmer whetted its appetite, the crime and detective novel as a best-seller genre has been dominated by this increasingly Gothic monster, whose humanity is always doubted at the start and confirmed at the end. The novel pays homage to an infinitely stranger, more mysterious and apocalyptic, actually a posthuman humanity. The serial killer is, to return to my three opening points, the ultimate artist of the beauty and boundarylessness of death, the next step in the series of our being, the newest of Gothicism's dark tutors about the dimensions and artifices of our belief.

Vampire killings are emphatically serial, of course. So, for instance, is the killing fury that hops from male to male owner of the car in Stephen King's *Christine*. But the center of the genre for the last twenty years in crime fiction and noir has been the artist-killer and his artist-pursuer, the psychoanalyst-detective, vividly embodied for our time in the FBI psychologist profiler and his-her evil twin, the psychologist serial killer and human gourmet Dr. Hannibal Lector.

Contemporary crime writers, working partly from Gothic myth and partly from real cases and from their imaginative expansion of the work of FBI profilers, view the serial killer either as a being-starved entity driven to reenforce his self through the collecting and symbolic ingesting of victims (shades of *Dracula's* Renfield) or as an artist creating a series of scenes or works that enhance and extend his being. In most such novels and films the psychoanalyst-detective seeks the source of this experience of insufficient or detachable-extendable being in some childhood or adolescent episode in the suspect's background: discovery, analysis, understanding, capture follow in consoling order.

What distinguished *The Silence of the Lambs* in this context is not only the protean reach of its monster, at once the psychoanalyst and the serial killer, the gourmand of lives and emotions, the artist of the beautiful and the father confessor of psycho killer and innocent detectives alike, but also the fact that he resists all analysis, even his own. "Nothing happened to me," says Lector, "I happened." No analysis can break him down. A posttheological philosopher, he thinks of himself as an act of God, challenging Clarice Starling to get out of the "moral dignity pants" of behaviorism and psychoanalysis (21). As pure act, he lives with equal facility in the body, when not straitjacketed, or in the mind; as a lector he produces and consumes text in uninterruptable cycles. In the hands of the novelist Thomas Harris he writes and reads—essays, case histories, letters—with the same instinct and for the same reasons as he sips the emotions of those in pain, and he frees his body eventually with a stolen portion of his captor's ballpoint pen ingested and smoothly regurgitated. In the film, as students saw immediately, Jonathan Demme reinvented Lector as an artist of the visual—he draws pictures of Clarice Starling.

In its two past versions my undergraduate course has closed with *Silence of the Lambs*: most recently we took a quick look at the film of *Silence* and ended with the novel *Hannibal* and most recently its filmic adaptation released in 2000. In the 1999 book sequel Harris plays head games with his audience, and with his previous texts in the series, in order to really churn the stomach. Students, like reviewers, were radically divided; some enthralled, others convinced that the head games were just headaches. Good. We were back in the territory of the opening-day argument: Bradbury's clever minimalism versus Ellison's rampaging gross-out. Well, even if we agree, I said, that in this latest novel and its filmic adaptation Harris has angered his readers, corrupted his characters, and trashed his elegantly constructed earlier series—might that be deliberate? the acme of Gothic? Might Maturin have meant *Melmoth the Wanderer* to do something similar, despite his footnoted apologies that he wasn't responsible for what his characters did or what history he had to report?

They could close the book, but they went home, I think, thinking.

Philosophy and the Gothic Novel

Marshall Brown

Though it sounds exciting and often is, Gothic fiction can also be frustrating. The early Gothic novels contain long passages of description, background, drifting, and waiting that lack the intensity supposedly characteristic of the genre. Critics are often apologetic or even positively critical, and students can be puzzled or worse. It is tempting to ignore the dry expanses and emphasize the juicy bits. Sex and violence carry the day. But why did the novelists write and their contemporaries consume the parts that subsequent readers have been inclined to skip over? Why do the body and the passions so often give way to the mind and its reflections? My contribution to this volume focuses on the portions of Romantic Gothic novels generally ignored or scorned and points to a variety of connections they have with Romantic thinking. Among the Romantic period writers likely to be familiar to students, it is only in the less familiar works of Poe that the Gothic mode becomes obviously thoughtful, and even in Poe it isn't obvious that the thoughtful parts are successful. But with the proper orientation much that seems vapid turns out to be rooted in its period, significant, and indeed powerfully interesting. Below, I juxtapose passages to illustrate various themes linking Romantic fiction to Romantic ideas.

"Habe nun, ach! Philosophie"

Goethe's *Faust* is not a Gothic novel. Still, it inspired several. Though it replaces Gothic sadism with humor, it presents most of the other characteristic features of theme, imagery, and construction found in Gothic dramas and, mutatis mutandis, novels. Faust may go off on a tangent, but he starts as a Gothic hero. And his launching pad, the first rhyme word in the play proper, spoken in his "high-arched, narrow Gothic chamber," is "philosophy":

> I've done, alas, philosophy
> Medicine and judgery
> And theological drudgery
> From the ground up, with ardency.
> . . . .
> So I've turned to magic art
> To learn what secrets it may impart,
> Declared through spirit's might and mouth.
> (my trans. of lines 354–57, 377–79)

It is tempting to look askance at Faust's philosophy. Doesn't he, after all, leave it behind? And his Gothic cousins, don't they turn thoughtlessly to realms beyond human ken? The most studious among them, Victor Frankenstein, like Faust, pursues mysteries beyond any legitimate human knowledge:

> It was the secrets of heaven and earth that I desired to learn; and whether it was the outward substance of things, or the inner spirit of nature and the mysterious soul of man that occupied me, still my inquiries were directed to the metaphysical, or, in its highest sense, the physical secrets of the world.   (Shelley, *Frankenstein* [Crook] 194)

Science here touches the unknown, seemingly bypassing wisdom. Yet it is a mistake to let the empiricist cast of British (and American) thought over-shadow the elements of reflection that lie in the Gothic impulse. Philosophy teaches Faust how to conjure the devil; "natural philosophy" is the mad sci-entist's most precious resource (*Frankenstein* [Crook] 34). *Naturphilosophie* was the Romantic designation for a particularly bizarre, quasi-mystical view of the universe as a living body. But it was philosophers and philosophically trained scientists who practiced the mode. Philosophy stands at the origin of the Romantic Gothic.

The following sampler of observations illustrates the variety of analogies and influences linking philosophical speculation with Gothic imagining:

1. Ask students or colleagues how Charlotte Dacre's sensational *Zofloya* begins, and they will probably answer, as one once answered me, "With the mother." That is true, so far as the plot goes. But the text opens with questions of precise knowledge and careful reasoning:

> The historian who would wish his lessons to sink deep into the heart, thereby essaying to render mankind virtuous and more happy, must not content himself with simply detailing a series of events—he must ascer-tain causes, and follow progressively their effects; he must draw deduc-tions from incidents as they arise, and ever revert to the actuating principle.   ([Craciun] 39)

Causality, the core of Kant's epistemology, is just as much a concern of narra-tives based on the unequal powers of natural and supernatural creatures. At one level, the obsession with the supernatural found in a number of Gothic novels can be understood as an exploration of the philosophical and scientific questions of how nature does and doesn't work.

2. Ann Radcliffe's famed landscapes are akin to devotional materials of the period. The following meditation, from a much reprinted tract of the 1780s, virtually identical to countless effusions in Radcliffe and her imitators, illus-trates affinities that have not been explored in the scholarship but that can eas-ily become a focus for classroom discussion, awaking sympathy for the less animated parts of Gothic novels.

> Solitude moves us in every one of its peaceful pictures. In sweet melan-
> choly the soul collects itself to all feelings that lead aside from world and
> men at the distant rustic tone of a monastery bell, at the quiet of nature
> in a beautiful night, on every high mountain, near each crumbling mon-
> ument of old times, in every terrifying forest. But he who knows not what
> it is to have a friend, a society in himself, who is never at home with his
> thought, never with himself, to him solitude and death is one and the
> same.   (Zimmermann 2: 105; my trans.)[1]

Defending itself against the terror or the temptations of the Gothic demon, the
soul composes itself toward higher thoughts. Thus, in Gothic portrayals of
nature we see the responsiveness of the individual toward the divine world.
They can be seen and analyzed as moments of spiritual power counteracting
the forces of evil.

3. More formal presentations of philosophical issues can be found in a number of Poe's stories. Though his sources were probably indirect, they are a treasure trove of German-style Romantic philosophy. The following excerpt is
typical (and chosen because its last two words are identical with a phrase made
notorious by Karl Marx and Gilles Deleuze); it is spoken in a trance by a character named Vankirk, a student of the French Kantian Victor Cousin and of the
"abstractions which have been so long the fashion of the moralists of England,
of France, and of Germany" (*Works* 2: 103; "Mesmeric Revelation"), but it
could well have come straight from the pen of one of the more lucid of the
German *Naturphilosophen*.

> There are two bodies—the rudimental and the complete. . . . The mat-
> ter of which our rudimental body is composed, is within the ken of the
> organs of that body; or, more distinctly, our rudimental organs are
> adapted to the matter of which is formed the rudimental body; but not
> to that of which the ultimate is composed. The ultimate body thus
> escapes our rudimental senses, and we perceive only the shell which falls,
> in decaying, from the inner form, not that inner form itself; but this inner
> form as well as the shell, is appreciable by those who have already
> acquired the ultimate life. . . . When I say that it resembles death, I mean
> that it resembles the ultimate life; for when I am entranced the senses of
> my rudimental life are in abeyance, and I perceive external things
> directly, without organs.   (2: 111–12)

4. Finally, Anglophone scholars often overlook the fact that the Gothic was
popular in Germany and France, not just in the English-speaking lands, and that
there it was frequently even more directly philosophical. E. T. A. Hoffmann, for
example, was immersed in the speculative writing of his time. His stories and
above all his early *Monk* imitation, *The Devil's Elixirs*, couch the assault on mental stability in the language of Kant and his successors, sounding like this:

It is one's own wonderful stepping forth out of oneself that permits an observation of one's own self from another standpoint, which then appears as a means that is subservient to a higher will, and that serves *that* purpose which has been set as the highest to be achieved in life.

(*Elixiere* 65; trans. mine)[2]

A related analysis of consciousness permeates the writing of the greatest of the Gothic novelists—though one not often classified under our rubric—Honoré de Balzac. The portrait of Raphaël's terminal madness in *The Wild Ass's Skin* is as abstractly conceptual as any in Poe.

This man of so powerfully active an imagination sank down to the level of those slothful animals crouching in the bosom of the forests, looking like decayed vegetation, without taking a step to seize an easy prey. He had even shut out the light of heaven, day no longer entered his room. Toward eight o'clock in the evening, he would leave his bed: without having a lucid consciousness of his existence, he would satisfy his hunger, then immediately go back to bed. His cold and frowning hours brought him only confused images, apparitions, chiaroscuros on a black ground. He had buried himself in deep silence, a negation of movement and of intelligence.   (279)

As my chrestomathy suggests, much of Romantic Gothic fiction depends so heavily on a philosophical analysis of psychological states as to be virtually impenetrable without some acquaintance with the underlying conceptions. There are of course other philosophical connections, such as the political philosophies of Rousseau and Godwin that resonate in Godwin's fiction and, a bit more remotely, in Mary Shelley's, and later in the century the evolutionary and racial issues from Darwin, Herbert Spencer, and Max Nordau that increasingly haunted the Victorians (see Arata, *Fictions*). It is not surprising that much in the novels remains alien unless philosophical issues are raised and, where necessary, formally introduced.

Transcendental and Supernatural

The "transcendental" is Kant's term for the foundation of experience. At the very start of the *Critique of Pure Reason*, Kant asks what makes it possible for us to have confidence in the validity and stability of the world we see around us. What guarantees the continuity of the self?[3] Romantic philosophy begins in such a questioning and questing tone; that is one of many elements it shares with the Gothic mood of wonderment and dissatisfaction. Consequently, we can productively discuss Gothic striving not just in psychological and moral terms but likewise as an epistemological or metaphysical issue. Kant undertook to answer these questions, with which Romantic speculation begins: he argued there must be something beyond experience that guarantees its truth. Indeed, there are two transcendental dimensions underlying experience—two things that must concur to provide the stability of our perceptions. First, if we can depend on the coherence and the universality of the objects around us— if we can trust that we will continue to see what we see and that others will see the same things—then something outside us must correspond to the objects we individually perceive. These are the famous "things in themselves" (*Dinge an sich*), the real entities we all share because they lie beyond the subjective contingencies of perception. Second, if we regard ourselves as enduring identities, it must be because our changing experiences inhere in an underlying self that Kant calls the transcendental unity of apperception or the transcendental consciousness. Notice that he does not absolutely say that either things in themselves or (to use yet a third designation) the transcendental ego necessarily exists. He only says that if we have a shared world and a meaningful experience, then they must derive from these two hidden realms. Otherwise, as he often says, the world would be like a dream, and indeed our dreams show us what life would be like without stable selves and meaningful experiences.

It's that straightforward. Our experiences are diverse, our persons shifting; what assures us of stability and consistency must therefore lie beyond experience, in the depths of the universe or of the self. For Kant this reasoning is pure logic and nothing more. He consciously cultivated a dry and forbidding style for discussing philosophy and repeatedly warns against trying to investigate the transcendental realms, for they would lose their transcendence and hence their stability if we ever experienced them (see Nancy, *Discours* and the more accessible "Logodaedalus"). But warnings can also be temptations. The link between the transcendental and the supernatural is forged even by Kant whenever he bars the gates to the higher or lower realm. Noteworthy is the Gothic-tinged language in section 33 of his attempt at a popular exposition, the *Prolegomena to Any Future Metaphysic*, which must be translated with deadpan literalness in order to capture the flavor:

> There is indeed with our pure concepts of the understanding something ensnaring with respect to the seduction to a transcendent use . . . , and so the understanding builds itself unobserved next to the house of experience a yet far roomier annex, which it [the understanding] fills up with mere creatures of thought, without once noting that with its otherwise correct thoughts it has transgressed the boundaries of its use.
>
> (A 106; my trans.)

Whether they resisted Kant or fell in with him, the lesser philosophers of Kant's day sanitized his ideas, but a few prescient philosophers and many medical writers pursued the imaginative directions he both opened up and strove to foreclose. Thus his student and erstwhile friend—but eventual antagonist—

Johann Gottfried Herder joked acidly about "the onanism of pure-impure reason" (388; letter to Jean Paul, Nov. 1798). A decade earlier, Goethe's friend Karl Philipp Moritz published the following remarkable assessment in an early number of the first journal devoted to experimental psychology, of which he was the founding editor:

> Apropos of Anton Reiser's observation, "Mysticism and metaphysics truly coincide insofar as the former often has chanced to produce by means of the imagination what in the latter is a work of speculative reason," I thought of Kant's "Dreams of a Ghost-Seer" in relation to his present writings. Kant now realizes his fantasies and dreams through serious, cold philosophy—which is all the more comprehensible since it was a philosopher who fantasized in that book, and philosophers are said frequently to reason better in dreams than awake.   (55–56; my trans.)[4]

Medical psychology in the Romantic decades, beginning in Germany and gradually spreading, preponderantly entailed an investigation of abnormal phenomena such as dreams and madness on an explicitly neo-Kantian basis (see M. Brown, "From the Transcendental"). Even against Kant's expressed intentions, many threads link the invisible worlds of transcendental idealism to the bizarre terrains of the Gothic novel.

Assigning Kant's epistemological writings to literature students is difficult, even at the graduate level. I have attempted the *Prolegomena*, the introductions to the *Critique of Pure Reason*, and the important but rather abstruse essay of 1786 "What Is Orientation in Thinking?," which allows problems of disorientation to surface. It takes patience and time to draw students into these works. However, transcendental epistemological issues can fruitfully be raised in connection with the Gothic supernatural, whether or not the novels are explicitly philosophical. "Obstinate questionings" that provoke Gothic thoughts in Kant or Wordsworth can be used to provoke transcendental ones in novels.[5] "And what was I?" asks Frankenstein's monster at one point; a few pages later he asks, "Who was I? What was I? Whence did I come? What was my destination?" and then, "Why did I live?" and "Why did I not die? . . . Of what materials was I made?" ([Crook] 90, 96, 101, 137). These questions can point in the direction of psychology, of race or gender, of science or ethics or even politics. But they can also be used to raise issues of ontology (What is a being?); of causality; of the constitution of consciousness; of cosmology, theodicy, teleology, and the existence of God. The philosophical problems presented by the transcendental worlds of the Gothic novel are multifarious.

Spirit and Spirits

The premise of transcendental idealism is that we participate in two worlds. One, the physical world, is known, determinate and determining. The other, the world of the transcendental ego and of things in themselves, is dark and unsearchable. Living on the edge, human beings are divided between matter and spirit, necessity and freedom. The imagery of boundaries and limits is all-pervasive and parallels the border regions haunted by spirits in so many Gothic narratives: Coleridge's Ancient Mariner crosses the line of the equator as he enters into his realm of moral and psychic disintegration, and he prevents the Wedding Guest from crossing the threshold back into the holy realm of the church (in Wordsworth and Coleridge).

Kant, still a figure of the Enlightenment, speaks of the drive we feel within to realize our participation in the dark world, bringing freedom to light. The drive to manifest freedom is the ground of morality, and without the moral drive we would not be truly human, only mechanical beings, no better than animals. Our appreciation of the sublime magnificence of nature directs us toward the heavens.

In other thinkers the impulses are less uplifting. Characteristic of Romantic thought is the fierce energy sparking conflict in the hero's soul. A nagging dissatisfaction with mere earthly existence provokes a spiritual restlessness that can lead to virtue but is also readily suborned to vice. The spectacular battles in Gothic novels test the intellectual and moral resources of the individual, whether in victory like Godwin's St. Leon or in defeat like Lewis's Ambrosio.

A good introduction to the moral philosophy of German idealism, and more teachable than anything by Kant, is Johann Gottlieb Fichte's *Die Bestimmung des Menschen* (1800; *The Vocation of Man*). Fichte, Kant's first great successor, began in the 1790s expounding a system that he termed the "doctrine of knowledge," the *Wissenschaftslehre* celebrated in the chapter of Carlyle's *Sartor Resartus* called "The Everlasting Yea." In his earliest and most formal complete exposition, Fichte focused on the self's need to test limits and find boundaries if it is going to have a concrete existence. Increasingly popularizing and nationalistic, Fichte then turned rather swiftly from abstract philosophy to stirring lecture courses on moral and political topics. *The Vocation of Man* is his most successful attempt at an accessible, emotionally gripping presentation of idealism as he understood it. Its first book, "Doubt," revisits Kant's two-world theory. If we possess any knowledge, Fichte argues, then we must abandon all hope of a freedom transcending the constraints imposed by that knowledge. Ending in despair, he pleads for rescue by a higher power. The plea is answered in the second book, "Knowledge," by a spirit who engages in dialogue with the self and turns Fichte's despair on its head. Knowledge comes from within our minds; not only is it certain, but it is more powerful than any external force. The Faustian impulse is evident here, and the spirit proves increasingly to be a ghostly and demonic figure. Total knowledge becomes solipsistic, and madness ensues. The philosophical rhetoric turns Gothic, in a passage that can serve as a commentary to many a Faustian moment in Gothic novels, as the recovery proves to rest solely in self-realization through dedication, striving, and duty.

If the whole of human life is not to turn into a spectacle for a malicious spirit, which has implanted this inextinguishable yearning for the imperishable in poor humanity merely to find amusement in their repeated grasping for what incessantly eludes them, their ever repeated snatching at what will again elude their grasp, their restless running around an ever repeated circle, and to laugh at how seriously they take this tasteless farce; if the wise man, who will soon see through this game and be irked at continuing to play his part in it, is not to throw away his life and [if] the moment of awakening to reason [is not to] become the moment of earthly death—then that purpose has got to be achieved. (Fichte 90–91)

The motifs accumulated in this passage from Fichte offer starting points for discussing almost any Romantic Gothic narrative, and many later ones, in a philosophical perspective. On the Gothic side lie: spectacle (think of the theatrics of Hoffmann's "Sandman," where taste and tastelessness are crucial themes, or the opening scene of Charles Robert Maturin's *Melmoth, the Wanderer* with the spectacle of a shipwreck seen from shore); repetition and circling (such as the Giaour's whirling motion in Beckford's *Vathek*); deep play (a motif in a vast number of Gothic fictions—central, for instance, in Pushkin's "Queen of Spades," initial in Honoré de Balzac's *Wild Ass's Skin*, nearly incidental in Valancourt's Paris gambling life reported in Ann Radcliffe's *The Mysteries of Udolpho* [3.13, 4.16]); death as the entry to a higher life, so often suggested in Poe. On the philosophical side, as if tested by the Gothic, lie the evaluation of the whole life, the critical meaning of yearning or striving, the quest for seriousness and vision. Needless to say, there are many lines to be drawn other than philosophical ones from the Gothic motifs I have itemized. Still, to comprehend the fascination the Gothic held for the most ambitious and intellectual writers of the Romantic period (including Schiller, Kleist, and Eichendorff in Germany and poets like Wordsworth and Percy Shelley in England), it is well to keep in mind the resonances of the Gothic as a theater for testing and proving the soul.

Madness

Though Kant warned against investigating transcendental realms, almost everyone who followed him except academic philosophers broke his injunction. In a period when psychology was not yet sharply divided from philosophy, many writers looked to states of mental alienation—dreams and madness—as manifestations of the spiritual essence amid empirical life. While the primary materials are rare even in German libraries and inaccessible to students, the leading physicians of the age were among the authors, and the general fascination with these mental states permeated Europe.[6] It is interesting to consider the profile of madness in Romantic Gothic novels. Madness is not ordinarily humorous or blustery as in *Don Quixote* and *King Lear*, nor is it aggressive and transgressive as in Robert Louis Stevenson's *Dr. Jekyll and Mr. Hyde*, several Sherlock

Holmes mysteries, or Lautréamont's *Songs of Maldoror*. Rather, it is most often passive, as the declining spirit is observed and analyzed. Here, in juxtaposition, are excerpts from Johann Christian Reil and from Poe, illustrating the notion that madness reveals the essence of the soul in both scientific and fictional texts.

> This pure consciousness, separate from all contingent determinants, is the foundation of our whole knowledge, . . . the I, entirely empty in itself, . . . on which the whole infinity of the manifold depends. What abstraction [i.e., Kant] presents to us as something merely thought appears to us in reality just before the outbreak of a collapse in which first the surrounding world of the senses, then our own objectivity, and finally subjectivity or the consciousness of the consciousness of self is extinguished. . . . The visible scene is wrapped in ever thicker fogs that finally remove it altogether from sight; sounds fade ever further away from us until they die off in the measureless distance. . . . Life has withdrawn from the boundary to the innermost focus of organization; absolute darkness and the stillness of death surround us. . . . Our whole prior existence seems but a dream to us. But at last our mental powers also vanish, even the memory of the past, the I hangs as but a single glimmering, but wholly empty spark in absolute night, of which naught but the consciousness remains, *that it still is and still thinks its empty being*, until even this passes into unconsciousness.   (Reil 551–52; my trans.)

> These shadows of memory tell . . . of a vague horror at my heart, on account of that heart's unnatural stillness. Then comes a sense of sudden motionlessness throughout all things. . . . After this I call to mind flatness and dampness; and then all is *madness*—the madness of a memory which busies itself among forbidden things. Very suddenly there came back to my soul motion and sound—the tumultuous motion of the heart, and, in my ears, the sound of its beating. Then a pause in which all is blank. . . . Then the mere consciousness of existence, without thought. . . . Then entire forgetfulness of all that followed.
> (Poe, *Works* 2: 237; "Pit and the Pendulum")

This Gothic madness is not frenzy but a disorientation or loss of anchorage that reveals the pure profile of the mind. Time stops as the victim struggles to re-collect himself. The characteristic vacancy of so many passages in Romantic Gothic fiction feels different from the sensational intensity of *Dracula* and its congeners, but it's possible to win sympathy even for Radcliffe's longueurs by analyzing how self-discovery emerges from solitude and confinement. Indeed, the landscapes of nature and those of the soul often coincide. Thoreau in prison—not a Gothic figure, to be sure, but experiencing a Gothic situation—sounds much like Radcliffe out of doors:

It was like traveling into a far country, such as I had never expected to behold, to lie there for one night. It seemed to me that I never had heard the town-clock strike before, nor the evening sounds of the village. . . . It was to see my native village in the light of the Middle Ages, and our Concord was turned into a Rhine stream, and visions of knights and castles passed before me.   (652; "Civil Disobedience")

Dream is a lesser madness, madness a greater dream, and both are potentially alike consoling and revelatory. Michel Foucault expressed the tonality perhaps most eloquently, in a commentary on Romantic dreams:

Thus, in the discourse common to delirium and to dream the possibility of a lyricism of desire unites with the possibility of a poetry of the world; since madness and dream are at once the moment of extreme subjectivity and that of ironic objectivity, there is no contradiction: the poetry of the heart, in the final, exasperated solitude of its lyricism, turns out to be an immediate reversal, to be the originating song of things.

                    (*Histoire* 536; my trans.)[7]

The thinker who systematized the twentieth-century understanding of dreams and madness as gateways to the soul was Freud, and he did it in part from meditations on a Gothic novelist, E. T. A Hoffmann. The unconscious in the modern sense was, if not a Romantic discovery, then in any event a Romantic coinage, revealed in moments of astonishment: "He recoiled from him, as if he had suddenly seen a serpent in his path, and stood gazing on his face, with an attention so wholly occupied as to be unconscious that he did so" (Radcliffe, *Italian* 51; ch. 4). Though Freud was a philosophobe, his understanding of the unconscious is also colored by his early familiarity with Kant, whose account of temporality he refers to in connection with the timelessness of the unconscious, in chapter 4 of *Beyond the Pleasure Principle*. From Freud the legacy of the Gothic passes to more recent speculative thinkers, including Foucault (who refers to *The Mysteries of Udolpho* in "What Is an Author?"), Derrida (in his books on Heidegger's "Geist" and Marx's specters), and Lyotard (in *The Inhuman*).

These dimensions of the Gothic novel, as it probes the human essence, by no means exclude or take precedence over the dimensions in which it simultaneously explores social formation and individual deviation. But philosophy accounts for much of the quieter and more expansive mysteries of the genre—above all in a Continental perspective—and it can help students understand why the books are so long and the events, in many cases, so sparse.

"Beatrice Takes the Veil"

In the Gothic-sounding chapter "Beatrice Takes the Veil" of her historical novel *Valperga*, Mary Shelley's murderously named heroine Euthanasia holds a remarkable philosophical discourse, sounding most of the themes sketched in this essay. Here is the gist:

> I will tell you what the human mind is; and you shall learn to regulate its various powers. The human soul, dear girl, is a vast cave, in which many powers sit and live. First, Consciousness is as a centinel at the entrance; and near him wait Joy and Sorrow, Love and Hate, and all the quick sensations that through his means gain entrance into our hearts. . . . But beyond all this there is an inner cave, difficult of access, rude, strange, and dangerous. Few visit this, and it is often barren and empty; but sometimes (like caverns that we read of, which are discovered in the bosoms of the mountains, and exist in beauty, unknown and neglected) this last recess is decorated with the strongest [strangest?] and most wondrous devices. . . . But here also find abode owls, and bats; and vipers, and scorpions, and other deadly reptiles. This recess receives no light from outward day; nor has Conscience any authority here. Sometimes it is lighted by an inborn light; and then the birds of night retreat; and the reptiles creep not from their holes. But, if this light do not exist, oh! then let those beware who would explore this cave. It is hence that bad men receive those excuses for their crimes; which take the whip from the hand of Conscience, and blunt his sharp crown; it is hence that the daring heretic learns strange secrets. This is the habitation of the madman, when all the powers desert the vestibule, and he, finding no light, makes darkling, fantastic combinations, and lives among them. From thence there is a short path to hell, and the evil spirits pass and repass, unreproved, devising their temptations.
> But it is here also that Poetry and Imagination live.   (355–57)

The caves of the Gothic novel, not least, are the recesses of the human mind, philosophically understood.

NOTES

[1]Zimmermann's bulky volumes appeared in English in dozens of editions beginning in 1779. Balzac is cited in French "in allusion to the well-known work of Zimmermann" in Poe's "Island of the Fay" (*Works* 2: 211).

[2]A more polished rendering of Hoffmann's typically clumsy early prose can be found in Taylor's translation, but it sacrifices the philosophical resonances I have struggled to preserve (such as "Anschauung des eigenen Ichs").

[3]Kant poses similar questions repeatedly at the opening of his major works. The most compact and familiar version is perhaps this: "How is pure natural science possible?" and "How is metaphysic possible, as a science?" (*Critique* 13, 15).

[4]*Anton Reiser* was Moritz's autobiographical novel. "Träume eines Geistersehers" (Dreams of a Ghost-Seer) is an early work by Kant satirizing the influential mystic Swe-

denborg. Despite its suggestive title (echoed in Schiller's unfinished Gothic novel) and a few relevant passages, "Dreams of a Ghost-Seer" offers little of direct importance to students of the Gothic, nor does the even earlier and pedestrian essay "On the Diseases of the Head."

[5]". . . those obstinate questionings / Of sense and outward things, / Fallings from us, vanishings; / Blank misgivings of a Creature / Moving about in worlds not realised, / High instincts before which our mortal Nature / Did tremble like a guilty Thing surprised" (lines 142–48). Wordsworth's most philosophical and most transcendental poem, "Ode: Intimations of Immortality from Recollections of Early Childhood" (as the title became in 1815), is practically a recipe for *Frankenstein*.

[6]Medical and scientific writers include C. W. Hufeland, court physician in Weimar and later in Berlin, and editor for over forty years of Germany's leading medical journal, the *Archiv für die practische Heilkunde*, who wrote extensively about the very Gothic topic of the premature burial of the dead; Johann Christian Reil, the leading German psychiatrist, who was a direct influence on Kleist and Hoffmann; and the school of *Naturphilosophen* ("philosophers of nature"), among them the philosopher (and scientist, and mythographer) Friedrich Wilhelm Joseph Schelling and the cosmologist and biologist Lorenz Oken. Author of numerous mystical speculations on the origin of life, editor for decades of *Isis* (then as now the name for the leading journal in the history of science), Oken is mentioned both by Carlyle (*Sartor Resartus*, bk. 1, ch. 3) and by Emerson, whose references to Oken date principally but not entirely after the publication of J. Stallo, *General Principles of the Philosophy of Nature*, as documented in Pochmann's invaluable source study (599n215, 610n463).

[7]This passage comes from one of the chapters omitted from Foucault's *Madness and Civilization*.

The Gothic and Ideology

Robert Miles

> The rude manners, the boisterous passions, the daring
> ambition, and the gross indulgences which formerly
> characterized the priest, the nobleman, and the
> sovereign, had now begun to yield to learning. . . . The
> dark clouds of prejudice break away before the sun of
> science, and gradually dissolving, leave the brightening
> atmosphere to the influence of his beams.
> —Ann Radcliffe, *A Sicilian Romance*

> For the rest it is not difficult to see that our epoch
> is a birth-time, and a period of transition. The spirit of
> man has broken with the old order of things hitherto
> prevailing, and with the old ways of thinking.
> —Hegel, *The Phenomenology of Mind*

Early Gothic writing's connection to ideology is at once obvious and elusive. Obvious, because the concept of ideology has its origin in modernity, in the Enlightenment's view of itself as a present that has broken with the past, and the Gothic, as David Punter some time ago pointed out, obsessively and ambivalently dwells on the meaning of this historical fracture (*Literature* 425). Elusive, because the Gothic appears to arise out of this nascent modernity without taking positions on it. For example, the Dissenters John Aikin and Anna Laetitia Aikin (later Mrs. Barbauld) were progressive radicals, and yet their influential fragment, *Sir Bertrand*, appears to deal with its subject (an aristocrat exploring the ruins of a castle) in purely aesthetic terms.

My aim in this essay is to suggest some strategies for enabling students to connect the Gothic with ideology. My approach has two parts. First, I suggest that Gothic writing and ideology share a common origin. To put it another way, I suggest that the history of Gothic writing and the history of how the ideological has been conceptualized are interlinked. Second, I approach the concept of ideology from the perspective of political philosophy rather than, say, from vantage points in the Marxist tradition. I do this because I am less interested in particular ideological explanations than in how one might think about the origins of ideological thought. In terms of teaching, my aim is not to show how the Gothic might be read ideologically, in the way that any given form is susceptible of being read, but to demonstrate how the Gothic's affinities with the rise of ideological thought influence the particular ways Gothic texts represent ideological material.

John Schwarzmantel's *The Age of Ideology* provides my political-philosophical starting point. Schwarzmantel argues that the concept of ideology is an epiphenomenon of modernity, and that for an analysis to qualify as ideological three conditions must be satisfied: "critique, goal and agency" (63). By "critique" he means the self-conscious analysis of the present as being no longer bound by previous structures of power. As Kant put it in his essay on the subject, Enlightenment "is man's emergence from his self-incurred immaturity" (qtd. in Schwarzmantel 26), where Kant means by "immaturity" instinctive or unthinking acceptance of traditionary authority. In different ways, both my epigraphs express this sense of awakening into freedom, or modernity, for "goal" signifies a notion of the good life, or happiness, and "agency" the means by which the transformation from the despotic old to the good new is to be effected. It is the contention of political philosophy that only with the Enlightenment does one encounter the coming together of critique, goal, and agency. As a consequence, while one finds the ideological prior to the eighteenth century, ideology as a concept satisfying the necessary and sufficient conditions outlined by Shwarzmantel awaits the birth of the modern.

My organizing suggestion is not that the Gothic fully articulates an ideology capable of satisfying a political philosopher but that the Gothic is fundamentally conditioned by the fact that its emergence—as that complex congeries of literary, architectural, and aesthetic phenomena we designate by shorthand the Gothic— is coeval with the rise of ideology. Thus, although the Gothic is only rarely clear about goals (the work of Ann Radcliffe, being, I think, an exception in having a strong sense of the good life) and while it is always vague or contradictory about agency, it is nevertheless grounded in critique. It deals in subjects no longer bound by traditional forms of authority. Beginning in a crisis of legitimacy, it is from the beginning ideologically self-aware. Looking back twenty years at Radcliffe's phenomenal popularity, William Hazlitt asserts that her "'enchantments drear' and mouldering castles derived part of their interest, no doubt, from the supposed tottering state of all old structures at the time" (161). As Hazlitt indicates, for the Gothic's first readership there was a direct connection between tottering castles and tottering constitutions, both regarded by radical innovators as feudal remnants. Contested authority and ideological self-consciousness may seem to be two sides of the same coin, but in fact the self-consciousness depends on a historical sense, on the belief in progress toward Enlightenment. The Gothic combines both things, contested authority and a historical sense, and as such embodies fictionally what Schwarzmantel labels "critique."

To demonstrate how the Gothic is from its inception grounded in critique and therefore ideologically self-conscious, I take my students through what I call the discursive hinterland of Horace Walpole's *Castle of Otranto*. Until recently, this would have meant digging out obscure sources, but a couple of developments have considerably altered matters. The proliferation of Gothic courses has led to a corresponding increase of curricular materials. For instance, my colleague E. J. Clery and I have produced the edited collection *Gothic Documents: A Sourcebook, 1700–1820*. Containing various materials, reviews, parodies, essays, works of political economy, aesthetic treatises, philosophical texts, and belles lettres, it provides a selective picture of the Gothic at its moment of origin. The other significant development has been the Internet. I refer not just to the growth of teaching materials on the Net but also to the availability of Web sites featuring, for example, virtual tours of the gardens at Stowe (panther.bsc. edu/~jtatter/stowe.html) or images of Strawberry Hill (oak.conncoll.edu/ccacad/eng309/picturesque/255.html). Students can be referred to this material, through the sites' URLs, or you can put it up on the screen during your lecture, given a link to the Internet and large-screen projection.

With the aid of these materials, then, we collectively explore *Otranto*'s discursive hinterland. It is one thing to tell students that readers equated tottering castles with fears of revolution; it is another for them to know this inwardly, with something like a contemporary's grasp of it. To gain some purchase on the Gothic's intellectual history, we examine some of the texts collected in *Gothic Documents*. Extracts from Tacitus, Montesquieu, and the novelist Henry Brooke (among others) familiarize the student with the Whig myth of the Ancient or Gothic constitution—the belief, as Montesquieu puts it, that Britain's "beautiful system" of government came from the "woods" of Germany (63), a system in which trial by jury, Magna Carta, parliamentary representation, the Glorious Revolution that forever secured the gains of the Reformation by excluding the Jacobite faction, and the Bill of Rights were all of a piece. The belief in an ancient, Saxon, or Gothic constitution has a complex history; but the fundamental point is that the term *Gothic* was already highly politicized at the time of Horace Walpole's first Gothic story, in 1764.

This is the point at which a virtual tour of Stowe gardens is particularly helpful. The gardens were largely designed and built in the eighteenth century by the Temples, a powerful family of Whig aristocrats, of whom the most significant was Sir Richard Temple, Viscount Cobham (1675–1749). A vast exercise in political iconography, the Stowe gardens formed an instructive spectacle open to suitable members of the public sphere. The numerous follies, or temples, encoded a series of subtle and not so subtle political messages, most turning on the fitness of the Temples to govern the country and the unfitness of their political enemies, especially Sir Robert Walpole, to do the same. Pedagogically, a virtual visit to Stowe dramatizes the political meanings of Gothic structures.

The Gothic Temple (panther.bsc.edu/~jtatter/Gothic.html), constructed during the years 1744–48 and designed by James Gibbs at the behest of Lord Cobham, was intended as an iconographic embodiment of the Patriot values of the Gothic constitution, in opposition to Sir Robert Walpole's ruling Whig government. Although Cobham and Walpole were both Whigs, they belonged to different factions and were bitter enemies. Thus, while the Temple of Ancient Virtue (which Cobham saw himself as embodying) was intact, the corresponding Temple of Modern Virtue was a ruin (panther.bsc.edu/~jtatter/ancient. html) and had in its middle a headless statue, said to represent Sir Robert (J. Robinson 90, 98). In effect, through these buildings Lord Cobham is asserting that he is a true Goth and Sir Robert a corrupt one. Horace Walpole was, by all accounts, highly put out by this lapidary satire on his father. We then virtually visit Horace Walpole's house at Strawberry Hill. I suggest to my students that "Choppd Straw Hall" began its transformation into a Gothic pastiche as a response to the attack on Sir Robert Walpole at Stowe. I suggest that if Lord Cobham sought the Whig high ground by building a temple proclaiming his allegiance to the core Gothic values, Horace trumps him by building a Gothic structure he actually lives in.

Armed with this context, we examine the prefaces to *Otranto*, asking the question, Why does Walpole masquerade as a Catholic gentleman, who in turn pretends to be a counterreformational priest, who in his turn forges a tale set several hundred years earlier, at the time of the Crusades? One can again use *Gothic Documents* here, making the point that the Gothic constitution was explicitly anti-Catholic; for Whigs and radical Whigs alike, the constitution was a bulwark of Protestant freedoms. Walpole frequently claimed to uphold his father's political legacy of true Whiggism. So why does he masquerade as a priest intent on pulling down the Reformation, a key pillar of the Gothic constitution? I suggest to my students that we're offered a clue when we notice the punning connection between Stowe's satiric accusation against Sir Robert and the plot of *Otranto*. The romance is about an usurper of a Gothic house, precisely the charge leveled at Sir Robert (Colton). In public life Walpole upholds his father's political image, but in fiction's private, dream spaces he dons the garb of the family's ancestral enemies and turns assassin.

The key point is not the oedipal reading but that Walpole's text begins as a pastiche, a "faked" imitation of a Gothic story (Walpole posing as an artful priest writing a bogus medieval tale) casting a pall of irony over the period's dominant political values. According to the Whig myth, the Gothic constitution was the incarnation of legitimacy and succession. A single organic line linked the Saxon witenagemot, Magna Carta, parliament, the two revolutions, and the present joyful status quo of constitutional monarchy, a line without any gaps or ruptures capable of throwing into doubt the appeal to Gothic precedent on which the whole ideological edifice rested (R. Smith; Kliger). But here was *Otranto*, obsessively dwelling on illegitimacy and usurpation, on gaps and ruptures. It's not just that Manfred's attitude toward divorce unhappily recalls Henry VIII and the Reformation or that the plot concerns usurpation; the theme of illegitimate possession pervades all aspects of the romance, from Theodore's suspect origins to incest to the prefaces with their references to textual fakery and generic miscegenation (the marrying of ancient romance and modern novel). In other words, in the tottering structure of the castle of Otranto we already find Hazlitt's revolutionary suppositions and Schwarzmantel's critique, where the artful priest's appeal to legitimacy (the restoration of the line of Alfonso) is self-consciously inserted into debates about history, progress, and reformation. Whig politicians such as Lord Cobham or, indeed, Sir Robert Walpole confidently pointed to the Gothic constitution as a cultural fact of undoubted authenticity, from which they derived their authority and legitimacy. By contrast, Horace Walpole slyly transforms the same material into a parable about the contested ambiguity of all such appeals to authenticating origins. His own text, like his own house, is a self-dramatizing Gothic fake. Thus, although *Otranto* does not constitute ideology per se, it does perform ideology's conceptual work.

This is all done with a light touch. For Walpole, the Gothic was meant to be light, stylish, and *Otranto* a clever jeu d'esprit. Nevertheless, he fixed two things at the center of the Gothic: a plot line turning on legitimacy and a ludic spirit based on the ironic self-consciousness that comes with skepticism toward origins. Walpole's light touch was much the same as what Susan Sontag meant when she called Gothic "camp" (109), and in my view this aspect of his sensibility has its origins in his homosexuality (Mowl 4–7). Walpole was a deep player who liked to write from cover. As a result his satires on the pieties of the Whig ideology never peep from behind their mask but like the ghost of Alfonso haunt the fabric of the text.

Through the narrative of questionable origins the Gothic creates a basis for ideological self-consciousness. I say "basis," because whether the Gothic became more than that depended on who took it up. That it was, in the immediate aftermath of *Otranto*, largely women writers who took it up has been much discussed. A less noticed but equally significant fact is that many were also from the middling classes, frequently with close links to rational Dissenters. Like Radcliffe (Norton 26–27, 55–56) they often came from that class Isaac Kramnick helpfully calls "bourgeois radicals." Walpole famously complained that starchy, conventional Clara Reeve did not get the point of his use of the supernatural when she endeavored to make her ghost behave in a more rational manner in *The Old English Baron* (1777) (Punter, *Literature* 54). In Reeve's story, the ghost acts to ensure that the proper line is restored and, with it, legitimacy. But the whole point of Walpole's ending and irrational ghost was that in the modern world, in the age of ideology, the fiction of unquestioned legitimacy is no longer possible, no longer imaginable. Two writers who understood this very well were the bourgeois radicals Sophia Lee and Charlotte Smith. *Otranto*-like, Lee's *The Recess* reverts to a moment of disputed legitimacy in English history, the usurpation of Mary Queen of Scots. In the panoramic narrative that follows, we go from Britain to Paris to a camp of rebellious slaves in the Caribbean and back again, as if on an Enlightenment tour of contemporary, contested power structures. Indeed, throughout this period the story of the dispossessed Scottish Queen served as a coded antinarrative to an emerging, conservative ideology that stressed the continuities of legitimacy stretching from the commercially prosperous reign of Elizabeth, with its uncontested hierarchy, to the supposed verities of the constitution of the present day (for an example of this antinarrative that is also self-consciously ideological, see Ireland 83–84).

But the event that really brought forth the ideological self-consciousness made possible by Walpole's experiment was Burke's *Reflections on the Revolution in France* (1790), which retrofitted the old Whig ideology with a new, Gothic identity. Burke did this by putting a novel spin on chivalry. The connection Montesquieu made between feudalism and chivalry was significant, because it linked the manners of the Goths (that is to say, chivalry) to their political institutions. As one expired, so did the other. When, in his *On Fable and Romance* (1783), James Beattie concluded that Cervantes's Don Quixote put an end to chivalry and the middle ages (or feudalism), he was rehearsing a convention (Clery and Miles 92). Burke defied this periodization: the spirit of chivalry lived on, just as the spirit of the British constitution survived in immemorial custom. He shifted the constitutional debate from one of statutes and what they did or did not permit to one of manners (meaning, as we would now say, culture). Wanting to insist that the Gothic constitution endured, Burke had to argue that so did the manners in which it inhered. Chivalry had not therefore perished with Cervantes's satire; it was rhetorically alive in the thousand swords that would have sprung to Marie Antoinette's defense had she been menaced by Billingsgate fishwives instead of Parisian ones.

Radicals lost no time in holding Burke to his rhetorical flourishes by linking the political status quo he chivalrously defended to feudalism, barbarism, backwardness, and effeminacy. Here is an example from John Thelwall, who is replying to Burke's *Thoughts on a Regicide Peace*:

> Are these the institutions which Mr. B. wishes to support? . . . Are these . . . the regular and orderly fabrics of the ancient legitimate "government of states" whose plans and materials were "drawn from the old Germanic or Gothic customary" and of which those famous architects, "the civilians, the jurists, and the publicists," have given us such flattering draughts, ground plots, and elevations? If they are, away with your idle jargon of venerable antiquity . . . they are Bastilles of intellect, which must be destroyed. They are insulting mausoleums of buried rights. (15)

As we can see, Gothic, the Bastille, and the immature surrendering to traditionary forms of authority are of a piece in Thelwall's answering rhetoric. Burke, through his reactionary defense of chivalry, had succeeded in invigorating, and polarizing, the meaning of *Gothic* in a way that created, for instance, a radical avatar in *Otranto*, for Manfred was nothing if not a Goth, in the new, pejorative, radical lexicon.

Ann Radcliffe (despite the long critical history of her being misconstrued as a political conservative) sided with the bourgeois radicals by keeping the transition between old and new, feudal and modern, at the heart of her fiction. Apart from her first romance, *The Castles of Athlin and Dunbayne* (1789), she set her stories on the cusp between past and present, thus ensuring that her fictions were structured around comparisons of systems of value that were to be historically understood. At the same time, the romance plot of usurpation restored works to the detriment of the ancien régime. The forces of modernism, embodied in the young lovers and marked as middle class by the lovers' sensibility, their devotion to domesticity and companionate marriage, always triumph; and they are seen to triumph on the grounds of a greater, ideological legitimacy. Radcliffe's heroes and heroines prevail, because unlike her antagonists who perish they appeal to spiritual (Protestant) merit rather than to class privilege. It is this spiritual appeal that invests them with legitimacy.

The Gothic's ideological matter is textual and implicit. In Radcliffe, the self-conscious comparison of systems of values is internalized as the conflict between generations, where, for instance, Ellena and Vivaldi in *The Italian* represent in the values they espouse the sort of rational, modern, companionate couple Wollstonecraft might approve of, whereas Vivaldi's mother embodies the outmoded values Burke perversely defends (for Wollstonecraft's attack on Burke's defense of the Gothic practice of primogeniture, see Clery and Miles 236). In Radcliffe, ideology is pursued through a revamping of *Otranto's* plot of dynastic failure and questionable legitimacy, where a heroine with a distinctly bourgeois complexion defends her rights against a patriarchal aristocrat. In *The Monk*, Lewis picks up a different aspect of Walpole's legacy: his devious role playing. Lewis's primary concern is the ideology of the unified subject, the belief that we are tidy, discrete entities with containable desires, a myth he principally explodes through the device of Ambrosio. Highlighting the performative and contingent in human identity is, as we can see from modern identity politics, itself highly ideological; it, too, is a form of awakening from traditionary forms of authority. If Radcliffe's generational conflicts conceal one kind of ideological charge, Lewis's treatment of the provisionality of identity hides another.

As one might expect, it is in the work of radicals such as Wollstonecraft and Godwin that ideological self-consciousness is most acute. Thus in *Maria; or, The Wrongs of Woman* Wollstonecraft highlights the ideological analysis she shares with Thelwall through the simple turn of phrase "Bastilled" in marriage (155), which recalls her polemic against Burke's defense of primogeniture and arranged marriages (Clery and Miles 237–38). One might as easily say that Godwin's Falkland is Bastilled in his own conservative ideology, immured in an outmoded form of chivalry.

Early Gothic writing, more interested in critique than goal, appears (to recur back to Punter) ambivalent. In this respect, ambivalence is a constituent aspect of the genre. According to Schwarzmantel, the "language of modern politics . . . saw the mass of the people as the source of sovereign power, as opposed to the king, or any power derived from a religious or supernatural body" (41). As a genre the Gothic features supernatural bodies that are no longer tied to a sovereign or at any rate to an uncontested power (Clery, *Rise* 17). Thus, as in Radcliffe, the supernatural body is merely meretricious (Schedoni's or the Inquisition's shabby tricks) or unreal (the waxen image). Alternatively, as in *The Monk*, the supernatural body is a sexualized, ambiguous object (i.e., the she-devil Matilda). In either case, the Gothic does not attempt to resurrect the old order by reinvesting it with an invincible supernatural aura, nor does it attempt to lay it bare as an imposture; but, like Walpole in his prefaces to *Otranto*, it appears to do both at the same time. As a result, what comes into focus as objects of possible supernaturalization are the bodies the new ideologies most keenly contest: of women (the genre tout court), of the third sex (followers of Lewis), of Catholic revenants (Radcliffe), of paragons of chivalry (Godwin), and of blacks (where Dacre's *Zofloya* is early and Melville's *Benito Cereno* late).

When I teach the Gothic and ideology, then, my question is not, What is ideological about this particular text? but, What kind of ideological analysis does this text make possible? The distinction may appear to be merely a matter of nuance, but I think it instructive for both teacher and students to ask how locating the Gothic in the historic rise of ideological understanding shapes our interpretation of the Gothic. The adjustment amounts to the difference between seeing Radcliffe's texts as benighted expressions of false consciousness (for too long the condescending approach to her work) and seeing them as actively engaged in the process of making the ideological visible, for which I strongly recommend Mary Poovey's seminal article "Ideology and *The Mysteries of Udolpho*" (1979). Poovey argues that Radcliffe's text works through without resolving a contradiction in the ideology of sensibility: while sensibility promised to empower women by placing them at the center of the civil project of improving society through the feminine powers inherent in domestic virtue, it simultaneously contributed to the mystification of women's condition by drawing a veil over the economic reality that truly determined their position in the world. Poovey shows how Radcliffe's romance manifests critique without having a clear idea about agency and goal and how the text remains, as a consequence, ambivalent and ambiguous.

While accepting Poovey's analysis as a model for understanding the conflicted attitude of the Gothic to the whole question of tottering structures, I would modify her approach by enlarging the circle beyond the ideology of sensibility. A historical concern for the decay of models of legitimacy pervades the Gothic, not accidentally or in a general manner, which might be said of almost any text, but as an integral aspect of the Gothic's generic origins. To put it at its simplest, a concern with authenticity, legitimacy, and power follows as a matter of course from pastiche, from the self-conscious bric-a-brac with which Walpole assembled both his house and his romance.

Teaching the Gothic
through the Visual Arts
Stephen C. Behrendt

The approach of this essay to teaching the Gothic is essentially historical, in that it draws heavily on the visual arts of the eighteenth and early nineteenth centuries, whose nature and reputation may be seen to relate in useful ways to works of Gothic literature, in whatever medium. The course format discussed here is that of the undergraduate classroom. The course may be full-semester, of the sort I have taught several times on the Gothic, in which we study the rise, flowering, and dissemination of the Gothic in British (especially) literature and culture in the eighteenth and nineteenth centuries in particular. Alternatively, the setting may be a segment of a course in British fiction, which I organize as a four-to-five-week block devoted to the Gothic. Student enrollment is frequently made up of no more than half English or English education majors; sometimes only a quarter is majors, the remaining students representing a broad cross-section of academic fields, intellectual abilities, and previous exposure to the arts and humanities.

Over many years of teaching I have discovered that students are willing to explore complex subjects when they can approach them through works in media other than the printed word. Perhaps when the lights are turned off, students gain some measure of safety from the relative anonymity the darkness provides; perhaps they simply feel safer when the subject matter is not literature and their responses to questions and comments by the instructor and by other students are presumably therefore not being graded. Whatever the cause, they tend to engage more eagerly and often more probingly in discussions about works of visual art. This fact is especially important if the enrollment covers a broad range of student interests, abilities, and experience.

That fact noted, I like to have students ground themselves a bit in the historical and cultural context for the Gothic by reading Burke's *A Philosophical Enquiry into the Origin of Our Ideas of the Sublime and the Beautiful* (1757). In predictable eighteenth-century fashion, in setting up the categories of the sublime and the beautiful, Burke's essay offers many terms for definition: *sympathy, terror, obscurity, power, vastness, infinity, delicacy, smoothness,* and the like. These terms themselves furnish material for discussion, and it is always productive to ask students to work out lists of the qualities they associate with such terms and to find examples of these qualities in works of visual art or in music, whether the examples are historical and academic or rooted in the popular culture (and media) of the moment. Invariably, students produce a mixture of associations, and this heterodox assortment itself occasions further expanding and refining of the definitions.

I begin by reminding students of Burke's suggestion that it is through the operations of the principle of sympathy that poetry, painting, and other affecting arts transfuse their passions from one breast to another (41). We can trace the term *sympathy* back through the writings of eighteenth-century philosophers like David Hume and Adam Smith, of course, but we can also move directly forward to Burke's subsequent comment that terror is a passion that always produces delight when it does not press too close and that pity is a passion accompanied with pleasure, because it arises from love and social affection (42). We consider a few examples suggested by the students to prove, disprove, or more likely complicate Burke's claim, then I ask them to consider one of the works most frequently introduced in eighteenth-century discussions of the sublime: Nicolas Poussin's painting *Winter; or, The Deluge* (1660–64; see essay appendix for available reproductions of artwork).

Poussin's harrowing image assembles a tableau of human and nonhuman figures all attempting to escape the rising waters. What makes the painting so terrible is our understanding of the futility of the efforts of these doomed souls. We know from our acquaintance with the biblical account of the Deluge that there is no escape, that all will drown. At the same time, what preserves this image as sublime rather than merely horrible is that we are also aware that *it is only an image*. While the painting appeals to the principle of sympathy that asks us to appreciate the desperation that grips humans and animals alike in Poussin's image, it likewise affords us the psychological distance that comes with our recognition that the image is not reality per se but a temporal and spatial portrayal of a story from the Bible. I ask students to examine some of the ways in which Poussin's painting draws us into the affecting scene at the same time as it provides the reassuring distance that comes from our being, finally, spectators rather than participants. Many of the devices Poussin uses in his painting, we discover when we turn to Gothic fiction, have clear analogues in literature.

Poussin's *Winter* opens the door to discussion of an important aspect of the Gothic: the prevalent sense of jeopardy. Over and over in classic Gothic literature, authors create physical and psychological environments of jeopardy, environments that threaten the characters (especially the most vulnerable, usually female) with harm and even death. The terror associated with their situations involves for the reader the sense that there is no escape. As in *Winter*, all rescue and all salvation appear cut off. Here it is helpful to have students study the fantastic drawings of Giovanni Battista Piranesi (1720–78) assembled under the title of *Carceri d'invenzione* (*Imaginary Prisons*), begun as early as 1745 and reworked, significantly, in 1761; these drawings are contemporary with both Burke's speculations and the rise of the Gothic. Piranesi's dramatic use of light and shade suggests the heightened verbal effects we associate with the Gothic. More important are the layers and layers of monumental staircases, walkways, and other architectural effects that dwarf the tiny human figures Piranesi includes in the drawings to underscore the prison's vast scale. Not only do these structures for the incarceration and torment of human beings exert oppressive psychological force on the viewer (as they surely would on anyone trapped in them), but many of the staircases and walkways appear to lead nowhere or to blind walls. As in much of Gothic fiction, the effect of being trapped, caged, permeates Piranesi's drawings.

The monumentality of Piranesi's *Carceri* allows students to consider other examples of physical and spatial vastness in later eighteenth-century art. One especially useful example of this visual vocabulary is the remarkable chalk drawing by Henry Fuseli (1741–1825), *The Artist in Despair over the Magnitude of Antique Fragments* (1778–80), which depicts the seated artist beside the enormous foot and hand of some dismembered colossal figure. The picture is doubly relevant, for its coincidental relation to the enormous body parts that appear in Walpole's *Castle of Otranto* and for its suggestion that the heroic (and therefore monumental) past has passed irretrievably beyond the lives, experiences, and aspirations of the modern world. This is the message conveyed as well by pictures of architectural ruins like those of Hubert Robert (1733–1808), who worked in Italy with Piranesi early in his career and was the first painter to make ruins the central subject of numerous pictures rather than merely a setting. Robert's *Ruins of the Grand Gallery of the Louvre* (c. 1796), for instance, or early sketches like the *Equestrian Statue of Hadrian* (c. 1757) typically depict the ruins of monumental classical structures, their columns truncated or fallen, their arches incomplete, their ground surfaces littered with rubble, while everywhere the stonework is being taken over by vegetation that sprouts from the cracks and fissures or springs from the broken upper surfaces. Nature everywhere and inevitably reclaims what humans have built, in other words, while tiny figures in modern dress go about mundane activities visibly out of context with the noble extravagance of the vanished ways of life to which the ruins point the viewer.

These recurrent images of ruins, which find their counterpart in the outsized and often crumbling castles, abbeys, prisons, and other man-made structures in Gothic literature, suggest the familiar Gothic theme of decline and decay; at the same time they reflect the later eighteenth-century interest in real and pseudo-antiquarianism brought about in part by the excavations at Pompeii and Herculaneum. Just as the buildings are deteriorating all around the human beings whose actions they dwarf, frame, and often inhibit or entirely prevent, so are the human participants in Gothic works frequently in a state of moral decline. Both active villains and passive, indifferent characters whose powerlessness facilitates the villains' designs embody the decline from nobility of character and deed characterizing the irretrievably past age of chivalry. Gothic fiction alludes again and again to this decline. Against the active or passive jeopardy posed by these figures, typically, stands the heroine: a woman who is repeatedly subjected to physical and psychological assaults that find their parallel in the dark passageways, winding staircases, and underground chambers of man-made structures and in the winding pathways, thorny thickets, and foul weather of Nature herself. Ironically, of course, it is this woman who, time after time, proves to be the most resilient figure in the fiction and who emerges (with or without the timely assistance of a male deliverer) victorious from her trials.

Anne Janowitz has written perceptively about how ruins function in English culture as both a topos of mortality and an ideological support for the masculinist paradigm of authority that propelled eighteenth-century commercial and imperialist designs in England. Students, given the chance to explore the complex relations that exist between visual and verbal depictions of ruins and the human activities that take place in them, especially when they are encouraged to think about how and why these themes relate to the particular historical moment that witnessed both the Industrial Revolution and the rise of the Gothic, often offer remarkably perceptive comments. They can be surprisingly sensitive to the ways in which cultural phenomena find representation in works of art in all media.

For the Industrial Revolution, I like to introduce the work of Philippe de Loutherbourg (1740–1812) and Joseph Wright of Derby (1734–97). De Loutherbourg, who was an accomplished designer of stage sets (a point of particular interest to students, who often remark on the theatricality of so much of Gothic literature), regarded the English landscape as especially rich in sources for the sublime. His later works interestingly link the physical sublime of nature with the technological accomplishments of humanity, and the results are often visibly related to characteristics of the Gothic. His famous *Coal Mine at Night* (1801) provides a remarkable vision of the hellish intrusion of industrial technology into the natural landscape: the buildings silhouetted against the great orange glow of the industrial hell's mouth is an apt image of what William Blake might have meant (had he been thinking only literally) by the "dark Satanic mills" he excoriates in the great anthem that precedes *Milton* (plate 1). Wright, whose *Eruption of Vesuvius* (1774–75) makes an interesting companion piece to de Loutherbourg's *Coal Mine at Night* in the classroom, offers another interesting approach to the subject. In pictures like *Experiment with the Air-Pump* (c. 1768), he provides an almost poetic commentary on the relation of technology to human and nonhuman subjects: the plight of the bird in the air pump, which is systematically suffocating it, is reflected on the face of the girl at the center, who is accompanied by a somewhat older woman covering her eyes. The age and appearance of the woman are not unlike those of the typical threatened Gothic heroine. Meanwhile, the male figures impassively sacrifice the bird's life to their scientific inquiry, intellectualizing its death in ways not unlike those methodical (if finally deranged) reasonings by which Gothic tormentors (like Zastrozzi in Percy Shelley's Gothic romance of the same name) rationalize the sufferings and deaths of their victims.

Returning to the subject of nature and the Gothic, I ask students to consider whether the images of decline and decay extend also to physical nature and whether we might think about the Gothic world as a postlapsarian one that presents us with a powerful echo of the lost Eden, a physical and psychological wilderness that threatens virtually everyone and in which no one can be trusted to be what she or he either appears or claims to be. Peter Thorslev, Jr., has suggested that the Gothic world is essentially tragic, with its central characters struggling against inscrutable and often insurmountable forces. In this environment the negative characters are often self-destructive victims of their own pride, passion, and ambition, all of which are often manifested as a consuming desire for revenge against real or imagined adversaries or as an insatiable thirst for absolute domination. Such characters are both unnatural and un-Natural, out of touch with nature and the laws of nature that formed a central core of discussion in later eighteenth-century writing on a broad spectrum of social, political, philosophical, and intellectual topics. The question of whether Nature is beneficent, benign, or antagonistic when it comes to human experience raises the question of whether Gothic literature tends primarily to bear out the positive Rousseauian view of human nature or the deeply pessimistic view of Rousseau's contemporary, the Marquis de Sade. If man-made structures, ancient and modern, dominate pictures and narratives, so too nature comes increasingly to dominate visual art at the dawn of Romanticism. Just as Robert made ruins the subject of many pictures, other artists did likewise with the natural environment, treating nature as subject rather than simply as a backdrop for human activity.

The disparity between nature's immensity and humanity's littleness was thus emphasized. In the paintings of the German visionary Caspar David Friedrich (1774–1840), this disparity becomes central, as in *Monk by the Sea* (1809), where the monk is visually submerged in the dark ocean that borders the desolate sandy coast, or in *Landscape with Oaks and Hunter* (1811), where students often require considerable time to find the small figure of the hunter among the lush foliage of oaks and brush that fills the painting. Looking at such depictions of the natural universe helps students appreciate that while Gothic characters frequently take refuge in nature (often in forests at night), these natural sanctuaries are not without their own dangers, nor is anyone in that postlapsarian world entirely released from the jeopardy that suffuses Gothic narratives.

I am not suggesting that works of visual art like those discussed here are either implicitly Gothic subjects or even illustrative of Gothicism. The instructor interested in pursuing that connection might trace contemporary copies of Gothic literature, which were frequently adorned with engraved illustrations. These illustrations typically fulfill the student's expectations about the melodramatic and formulaic trappings of the Gothic; imperiled maidens in diaphanous garb, armored knights, dark and ominous villains, moonlit forest prospects, dungeons, and flickering candles. One can usefully ask students whether such visual images help or hinder the reader-viewer, a question that always elicits good, productive discussion. Another strategy is to introduce a large selection of the works of Fuseli, which are more than usually steeped in visual effects we routinely associate with characteristics of the Gothic. Indeed, moving from Fuseli's painted subjects to his drawings (many of which were long suppressed) raises the matter of his misogynist portrayals of women as predators and tormentors, which bear a clear relation to the (mis)treatment of women in Gothic fiction and in misogynist visual art of the period in general, including pornography.

My point is that pictures of the sort I have discussed here reveal important intellectual and aesthetic analogies to the themes, subjects, and phenomena we typically associate with the literary Gothic. That these are not specifically Gothic pictures is important to the larger point I try to make about the literary Gothic: that while it is a body of writing that can be studied on its own, it is also part of a broad cultural dialogue about the nature and status of humanity at a historical moment of crisis and transition. An old world was, very literally, being swept away by the advent of a modernity replete with scientific and technological advances; with burgeoning nationalism and the imperialist designs that necessarily accompanied it; with major shifts in European political, economic, and social structures; and with complex redefinitions of people's relations to other people, to their God, and to their religious and humanitarian beliefs. I ask my students to list some of these changes and discuss how they might have had an impact on later eighteenth- and early-nineteenth-century life. Over and over, the answers involve anxiety: students rightly perceive that changes of the sort that were transpiring in this period deeply undermined long-standing, traditional values, belief systems, and protocols of human behavior. It is but a small step for them to consider, then, how the trials and tribulations we associate with the Gothic, and the physical and psychological environments in which they occur, can be read as fictional figurations of these anxieties, of their underlying causes, and of the various and frequently inadequate mechanisms employed by jeopardized individuals in their attempts to cope. For me and my students, taking this interdisciplinary route into the Gothic enables us to take a wider route out of the Gothic and into the arena of human activity in general.

APPENDIX
Print and Electronic Reproductions of the Artwork Discussed

Caspar David Friedrich, *Landscape with Oaks and Hunter* (1811), Reinhart Collection, Winterthur. See Joseph Leo Koerner, *Caspar David Friedrich and the Subject of Landscape* (New Haven: Yale UP, 1900) 21; *Art Brokers Intl.* (www.oil-paintings.com/cdf03.html).

Caspar David Friedrich, *Monk by the Sea* (1809), Natl. Gallery, Berlin. See Koerner 168; *Neoclassicism and Romanticism Images*, created by Patricia Vettel-Becker, Montana State U, Billings (www.msubillings.edu/art/Neoclassicism-Romanticism.htm).

Henry Fuseli, *The Artist in Despair over the Magnitude of Antique Fragments* (1778–80), Kunsthaus, Zürich. See Martin Myrone, *Henry Fuseli* (Princeton: Princeton UP, 2001) 7; *Art Online* (www.artonline.it/eng/opera.asp?IDOpera=368).

Philippe de Loutherbourg, *Coal Mine at Night* (also known as *Coalbrookdale by Night*; 1801), Natl. Science Museum, London. See reproduction in syllabus for course Aspects of the Industrial Revolution, taught by Gerard M.

Koot, History Dept., U of Massachusetts, Dartmouth (www.umassd.edu/ir/syllabus.html).

Giovanni Battista Piranesi, *Carceri d'invenzione* (1745–61), Ashmolean Museum, Oxford. Jonathan Scott, *Piranesi* (London: Academy, 1975) 74–103, reproduces a number of the *Carceri*; plate 7, first state, is on 84. An electronic reproduction is also available at *Sunsite CGFA* (sunsite.dk/cgfa/piranesi/p-piranes2.htm).

Nicolas Poussin, *Winter; or, The Deluge* (1660–64), Louvre, Paris. See Pierre Rosenberg and Véronique Damian, *Nicolas Poussin: Masterpieces*, trans. Sophie Henley-Price and Michael Worton (London: Cassell, 1995) 131; *Olga's Gallery* (www.abcgallery.com/P/poussin/poussin108.html).

Hubert Robert, *Equestrian Statue of Hadrian* (c. 1757), Metropolitan Museum of Art, New York. See Victor Carlson, *Hubert Robert: Drawings and Watercolors* (Washington: Natl. Gallery of Art, 1978) 31.

Hubert Robert, *Ruins of the Grand Gallery of the Louvre* (c. 1796), Louvre, Paris. See Paula Rea Radisich, *Hubert Robert: Painted Spaces of the Enlightenment* (Cambridge: Cambridge UP, 1998) 132; *Web Gallery of Art* (www.kfki.hu/~arthp/html/r/robert/louvre1.html).

Joseph Wright, *Eruption of Vesuvius* (1774–75), Tate, London. See Stephen Daniels, *Joseph Wright* (Princeton: Princeton UP, 1999) 65; *Arcadian Galleries* (www.mezzo-mondo.com/arts/mm/wright/WRJ016.html).

Joseph Wright, *Experiment with the Air-Pump* (c. 1768), Natl. Gallery, London. See Daniels 65; *Arcadian Galleries* (www.mezzo-mondo.com/arts/mm/wright/WRJ015.html).

The Horrors of Misogyny:
Feminist Psychoanalysis
in the Gothic Classroom

Anne Williams

Psychoanalysis offers obvious and yet provocative resources to the teacher of Gothic fiction. Professional criticism of the Gothic began about the time that Sigmund Freud's theories were becoming widely known. Gothic texts, fantastic and dreamlike as they are, have often been read through the lens of psychoanalysis. But orthodox Freudian readings of the Gothic usually tend to reduce these stories to allegories of Freud's theories, calling the reader's attention to the presence in the text of the hero's or villain's oedipal complex or incestuous desires. Such readings might be gratifying to Freudians who rejoice in confirmation of the master's "universal" truths, but they are less satisfying as literary criticism in which one hopes to elucidate form as well as content.

In *Art of Darkness: A Poetics of Gothic* (1995), I argue that Freud's writings may themselves be seen as belonging to the Gothic tradition. Freud posits a human psyche structured much like the Gothic mansion of literary convention. Shaped by its history, this haunted structure contains secrets that are hidden even from its master, the conscious mind, but that express themselves in bizarre effects such as hysterical symptoms. In the Freudian psyche as in the Gothic mansion, the past cannot lose its power until its secrets are disclosed. Furthermore, in this confining structure, the dangerous female other (the drives, the unconscious, sexuality) is usually incarcerated in the attic or the cellar, though she escapes from time to time to threaten the master of the house (239–52).

If this hypothesis is valid, it becomes clear why orthodox Freudian readings of Gothic works often seem so mechanical and so reductive: the theory and the text it is being used to analyze not only have conceptual affinities, they have the same blind spots. It is useful to remind ourselves that the Greek root of the word *theory* means "a view." Theory is most useful when it shows us things we otherwise wouldn't be able to see. In psychoanalytic theory, these things include most notoriously the "dark continent" of female sexuality and the supposed mysteries of female desire (see *The Question of Lay Analysis* in *Standard Edition* 20). ("What does a woman want?" Freud asked but did not stay for an answer [E. Jones, *Life* 421].) Thirty years of feminist Gothic criticism have revealed how the tradition's conventions of plot, setting, character, decor, and affect point to cultural manifestations of the female at many levels. But these became visible only after feminists recognized that the Gothic manifests the sexual politics of the culture(s) that produced it.

Since the 1970s or so, feminists have also been rereading Freud and his French disciple Jacques Lacan from the perspective of the female other.

Writers including Luce Irigaray, Sarah Kofman, Catherine Clément, Hélène Cixous, Madelon Sprengnether, and Jacqueline Rose have examined the psychoanalytic tradition's unconscious acceptance of cultural stereotypes in thinking about women and Freud's resistance to seeing psychic development as anything other than a drama of fathers and sons. I believe that this revisionist body of work offers readers of the Gothic what they have sought: a psychoanalytic context that enables us to talk about the form as well as the content of Gothic texts. In this essay I focus on the work of Julia Kristeva, which I have found most helpful in reading and teaching the Gothic. The titles of her books themselves range through an array of Gothic-sounding themes: *Powers of Horror, Tales of Love, Black Sun: Depression and Melancholia,* and *Revolution in Poetic Language.* Furthermore, her reading of language as fraught with tensions between the masculine, paternal, abstract symbolic order and the feminine, maternal, material, semiotic provides compelling insights into the formal properties of Gothic fiction.

My aim is to teach undergraduates about the basic concepts of psychoanalysis and to show them how to do a psychoanalytic reading of a literary text. This project is complicated by a number of problems. First, though students are unknowingly Freudians in many ways (they tacitly accept many of his major ideas as received opinion), they also tend to share our culture's skepticism about psychoanalysis and its methods. So this material often evokes some resistance in the psychoanalytic sense. Second, one cannot teach Kristeva without also first teaching Freud and Lacan. Third, Kristeva's writing is often difficult. Originally educated as a linguist and then as a psychoanalyst who did her training analysis with Lacan, Kristeva takes for granted a formidable knowledge of psychoanalysis, philosophy, and linguistics in propounding her theories. I have developed some strategies for confronting the second and third of these problems. As to the first, student resistance, I have found that as in analysis, some students work through their skepticism as they come to understand the concepts and learn to read from the psychoanalytic perspective. Indeed, those most talented as close readers often take to this method with enthusiasm, for good psychoanalysts read language as attentively as any New Critic ever did. Other students never overcome their resistance and unwittingly follow the example of Dora: they drop the course.

Though I have taught several versions of an undergraduate course on the Gothic that incorporate psychoanalysis and the work of Kristeva, I always include M. G. Lewis's *The Monk,* the tale of Bluebeard, Pope's "Eloisa to Abelard," Coleridge's *The Rime of the Ancient Mariner,* and Keats's "La Belle Dame sans Merci" among the primary texts, and Freud's *On Dreams,* Madelon Sprengnether's *The Spectral Mother: Freud, Feminism, Psychoanalysis,* and Toril Moi's *The Kristeva Reader* among the secondary ones.

I spend approximately the first four weeks of the semester introducing students to the basic information that they will need in order to read Kristeva. The first book I assign is Sprengnether's *The Spectral Mother,* because it provides a clear exposition of Freud's major concepts and of his evolving views through-out his career. At the same time it gives a feminist critique of these ideas and contains an equally clear description of his recent interpreters, including Lacan, Kristeva, and Irigaray. The book concludes with an essay in practical criticism, a reading of Marilynne Robinson's lyrical novel *Housekeeping* (1980). Though Sprengnether chose to discuss the novel because its narrative adumbrates an escape from the social and psychic structures of phallogocentrism, it also has surprising affinities with the Gothic tradition and can readily be seen as a kind of post-Gothic narrative. Having students read this last section of *The Spectral Mother* is particularly useful, because if they are to learn how to read texts from a psychoanalytic perspective in a relatively short time, they need, in addition to the theory, models of such readings.

After Sprengnether I assign Freud's own summary of *The Interpretation of Dreams*, called simply *On Dreams* (1901; *Standard Edition* 5: 629–86). In this brief book he gives an accessible overview of his ideas about the nature and mechanisms of the dream work. In discussing Sprengnether and *On Dreams*, I try to ensure that students acquire the fundamentals of a psychoanalytic vocabulary: the unconscious, repression, displacement, hysteria, narcissism, and the Oedipus complex, for instance. I also want them to understand Freud's description of the processes of dream work as a hermeneutic system. Dreams may be regarded as particularly ambiguous cinematic texts that emerge at the intersection of mind, which is inextricably linguistic, and body, which knows only sensations, urges, emotions. The resulting text is distorted, but distorted, according to Freud, in predictable ways. Indeed, one may find the equivalents of dream mechanisms in a context already familiar to students of literature, among the rhetorical tropes, another systematic catalog of linguistic distortions: Freudian displacement entails the same process as metonymy, for instance. Condensation is metaphor.

Throughout this class I encourage students who are puzzled by the concepts that we're learning to read several different explications of psychoanalytic theory. Useful summaries also appear in literary handbooks, such as M. H. Abrams's *Glossary of Literary Terms* and Françoise Melzer's essay "Unconscious." The exposition of psychoanalysis and the critical essays included in the Bedford series Case Studies in Contemporary Criticism are also helpful. If I teach *Frankenstein* among the primary texts, I use the Bedford edition (ed. Smith) so that my students will have ready access to this material. I also recommend that they consult Laplanche and Pontalis's *Language of Psychoanalysis*, particularly when we begin reading Kristeva, whose use of technical terms such as "primary narcissism" and "feminine paranoia" often cause confusion. Elizabeth Grosz's feminist critique of Lacan and John Lechte's book on Kristeva are also good resources for the confused.

When students have learned a basic psychoanalytic vocabulary, we pause for some practical criticism to help them begin to read texts from this perspective. I assign the tale of Bluebeard (Perrault) and lead them through a reading that explores the implications of that conventional Gothic structure, the house that hides a terrible secret. (Study questions are included in appendix 2 to this essay; I also require that every interpretive point be supported with specific textual evidence.) As I read the story, Bluebeard's castle is overdetermined in its realizing several fundamental aspects of patriarchy. The word *house* itself can mean "family line" as well as "structure." The structure of the house is also the structure of patriarchy and the Freudian image of the self. Thus Bluebeard's fourth wife is engaged in exploring the realities of her culture and her place in it, which is organized around binary pairs of opposite and unequal terms. (See Aristotle's line of good and line of evil, given in appendix 1, a handy list of some basic binary pairs; Hélène Cixous and Catherine Clément elaborate on that list of ten pairs in *The Newly Born Woman* [63].) Our heroine has no name, only a role as Bluebeard's wife. Because patriarchy aligns the female with materiality, it is inevitable that he murders his wives by separating their heads from their bodies.

The next stage of the course is an introduction to Lacan's ideas that Kristeva builds on, notably the mirror stage and the *nom du père* (translated as "law of the father" or symbolic order) (*Ecrits* 67–71). I spend a class meeting lecturing on a few of his major premises, particularly his emphasis on the linguistic aspects of his theories. I explain his use of Saussure's notion of the relation of the signifier and the signified, noting that for Lacan, more self-consciously than for Freud, language is the medium through which the self is both empowered and controlled: the Lacanian "speaking subject" has access to language and is also subject to its laws and to that of the culture the language both expresses and shapes. We then turn to Kristeva, and here I use *The Kristeva Reader*, edited by Toril Moi. This anthology contains a helpful introduction and headnotes for each of the essays that paraphrase and summarize Kristeva's arguments. (Moi's *Sexual/Textual Politics* [1985] also offers a useful summary of Kristeva's early theory.) In Moi's anthology, I assign the introduction, the excerpts from *Revolution in Poetic Language* "About Chinese Women," "Stabat Mater," and "Freud and Love: Treatment and Its Discontents." I then place *Powers of Horror* on reserve and ask students to read the translator's note and the first three chapters. As we work our way through these texts, I begin each class meeting by asking students to write down a question about the assigned reading. I find this exercise useful, because not only does it give me an opportunity to discuss and clarify the points they raise; it also provides me with information as to how well they are understanding the theories.

In class I emphasize Kristeva's narrative concerning the formation of the speaking subject and the accompanying concepts of abjection and melancholy. Kristeva assumes that an infant (a word whose Latin root means "incapable of speech") experiences its not-yet-self as neither unified nor differentiated from the mother. Lacan posits the mirror stage, in which the infant sees the reflection of a self that appears whole, unified in contrast to the earlier physical experiences of diffusion and diverse sensations. Accepting this fiction of unity, the infant takes a significant step toward the symbolic order. To see oneself from without as one, rather than as the disunified and dissimilar sensations hitherto experienced from within, effects the repression of those sensations and drives, their organization into a perceived unity. In order to enter the abstract realm of the symbolic, the infant must, Kristeva argues, "abject" or throw off the materiality encoded as female within the symbolic. She theorizes that this process occurs because from within the symbolic order certain phenomena maintain the power to evoke a visceral sensation of revulsion. Anything that subverts order, that threatens to violate the boundaries between the self and the other evokes horror: a bloody corpse, for instance, is disturbing, because blood, which should properly remain inside, is horrifying when outside the body. What should be animate is dead. The familiar monsters of horror movies all manifest such category violations: consider Dr. Frankenstein's creation, the vampire, the werewolf, the zombie.

Kristeva defines melancholia (depression) also in linguistic terms. This condition arises from a problematic relation with the maternal, both as representative of the death that eventually follows any birth and as failed or inadequate access to the symbolic. If one understands this narrative, one also understands the key concepts of the semiotic and the symbolic and her thesis that the speaking subject is not a stable, fixed entity but one always *en procès* (both "in process" and "on trial").

To review and reinforce this story of subject formation, the class reads and discusses Pope's "Eloisa to Abelard." The history of these two famous lovers offers a bizarre materialization of the Freudian oedipal crisis. The lovers' union, characterized by Eloisa in language evoking the infantile fusion with the mother, is interrupted by Abelard's literal castration, after which (as Pope remarks) they "retired each to a several convent." Eloisa's house, the Paraclete ("holy spirit") built for her by Abelard, is very much a house governed according to the law of the father, though whether that father is God or Abelard is unclear, since Eloisa tends to confuse the two. As the portrait of a woman who, by taking the veil, has renounced her will and her sexuality only in appearance, the poem may also be regarded as a fantasia on a patriarchal culture's notions of the feminine. Pope's imagining of the convent as Gothic is an anachronism; the real Paraclete would have been in the unmysterious Romanesque style. But Gothic architecture provides the claustrophobic complexity and mystery that Western culture associates with the line of evil. Eloisa herself is in many ways stereotypically feminine: hysterical and driven by only one thing, passion for her lost lover. I point out that indeed Eloisa is Pope's female impersonation. He is masquerading as a woman, just as anyone who has become a speaking subject by gaining access to the pronoun *I* is also engaged in a kind of masquerade, since " I" represents every subject speaking English. Why shouldn't she be a man's idea of what a woman wants? I tell the students that for centuries some scholars have argued that Eloisa didn't write the famous letters, that Abelard did. Speculation about this possibility always creates a lively discussion.

In the poem, as in the law of the father, language—Eloisa's letters—becomes the supplement, the substitution, that attempts to reestablish her relationship with her lost love. Eloisa is simultaneously conscious of the power of language and of its inadequacies. As Kristeva would predict of someone inadequately detached from the maternal, Eloisa suffers "black melancholy" (line 165). And as the rather lengthy heroic epistle shows, she is very much a speaking subject both in process and on trial. She circles around and around in her frustrated passion. There is no solution for her but a reunion with Abelard in the tomb, which she imagines future lovers reading and interpreting as if it were a text. Here as in Lacan's formulation of the symbolic order, access to language is inherently tragic, a Faustian bargain in which the speaking subject buys power by renouncing love.

In addition to Kristeva's narrative of the process of subject creation, I emphasize her notions of the relation between what she calls the semiotic to the symbolic order and her definition of poetic language. Kristeva names the infantile, presymbolic stage "the semiotic." This condition she describes as a nonrepresentable space called "the chora," "a non-expressive totality formed by the drives and their stases in a motility that is as full of movement as it is regulated" (*Revolution* 93). Though there can be no meaning here as such (because the infant has not yet been constituted as a speaking subject), there is the experience of rhythms, pulsions, energies, drives that "connect and orient the body to the mother" (95). When the infant becomes a speaking subject, the semiotic's transgressive, material, rhythmic energies are repressed but make their presence felt from within the symbolic: "The semiotic gives expression to a sort of lawlessness within the structures of language and society" (Sprengnether 213). In Kristeva's view, when the semiotic makes its transgressive presence felt within the symbolic, the result is poetic language.

Learning to speak a foreign language provides a useful analogy for understanding the movement from semiotic to symbolic. At first one hears the unknown tongue only as sounds and rhythms. Gradually as those sounds begin to coalesce into meanings, one tends to lose consciousness of the sounds as merely sounds. Kristeva argues that poetic language is potentially revolutionary, because poetry arranges words so as to foreground their material dimensions, through such techniques as rhyme, alliteration, assonance. Such arrangements recall the words' material dimensions, the repressed semiotic and its transgressive, subversive, nonsymbolic energies. Not only metaphor but also rhyme yokes heterogeneous ideas together with violence—or jouissance. Indeed, to unleash the materiality of language by arranging it into poetry is a bit like giving the madwoman the key to her attic.

I use Coleridge's *The Rime of the Ancient Mariner* (in Wordsworth and Coleridge) and Keats's "La Belle Dame sans Merci" to reinforce the concepts of the semiotic, the symbolic order, and poetic language. Each of these lyrical ballads can be read in this context as histories of the creation of a speaking subject. The Mariner uses the pronoun "I" for the first time when he says he killed the albatross. Keats's Knight at Arms "awoke and found *me* here / On the cold hill side" (my emphasis) after his nightmare of those repressive father figures whose damning name for the Lady apparently makes her disappear. Each experiences abjection: the Mariner's anguished exclamation, "The very deep did rot: O Christ!" (line 121); the knight's dream of "starved lips . . . with horrid warning gaped wide" (lines 41–42). And each gains access to language, the power to tell his tale.

This exercise concludes the theory portion of the course, but in our subsequent conversations about the conventions of Gothic fiction I emphasize how narrative devices, plots, and the genre's uncanny foregrounding of language embody the processes of Kristevan poetic language, eruptions of the maternal semiotic expressing its energies from within the paternal symbolic order. For instance, the Walpole tradition of Gothic fiction includes unexplained supernatural events. From a psychoanalytic perspective this admission of irrational and paranormal power adumbrates, in displaced form, experience of the pre-oedipal mother. I believe that this mode of Gothic originated with men and is more commonly produced by them because patriarchal social arrangements do tend to create the oedipal crisis that Freud described. The cultural demand to align oneself with the masculine and to repress the feminine leaves the male subject with an unconscious fantasy of the female as pre-oedipal mother: a terrifying figure that is all-powerful, arbitrary, and irrational. In male Gothic, this fantasy may appear in the guise of the terrible mother or femme fatale, or as Satan (as in *The Monk*), since in the symbolic order power is characteristically coded male. The Walpole tradition (which includes *The Monk*, Maturin's *Melmoth the Wanderer*, and Stoker's *Dracula*) employs an elaborate system of frame and embedded narratives. The device of the frame narrative is paradoxical. It both distances the reader from the framed material and at the same time anchors that material in reality. Nelly Dean, a down-to-earth person, has witnessed the implausible passion of Catherine and Heathcliff in Emily Brontë's *Wuthering Heights*. The Wedding-Guest has the same function in regard to the Mariner. The frame narrative is, in psychoanalytic terms, a compromise formation. The convention, originating with Walpole, that the present narrative is a translation of a document originally in a foreign language has a similar function.

Another characteristic narrative device, the compilation of documents, like the frame narrative provides purportedly concrete and reliable evidence. At the same time, the splitting of the narrative into multiple points of view both replicates the unconscious memory of a pre-oedipal lack of coherent subjectivity and simultaneously serves to displace unconscious anxieties while disrupting or discouraging "secondary revision," Freud's term for the mind's impulse to rationalize the dream, to fill in the gaps in the narrative (*Standard Edition* 5: 488–508). The Radcliffe tradition foregrounds secondary revision. Not only do we share the heroine's point of view, thus seeing the world from the unified perspective of a single self, but the supernatural is explained away.

Thus it is appropriate that in this mode of Gothic narrative from Charlotte Brontë's *Jane Eyre* onward, the novel usually purports to be the heroine's autobiography, the generic embodiment of Lacan's speaking subject, whose unity and wholeness is fundamentally fictional. Gothic plots dramatize the eruption of the semiotic from within the law of the father. In Gothic fictions, language frequently becomes uncanny, as in the prophecy of Walpole's *Otranto*, which is horribly materialized, embodied in the gigantic casque that crushes the hapless Conrad. These plots arise out of an anxious recognition of the gulf between meaning and intention, as when Raymond weds himself inadvertently to the Bleeding Nun by vowing himself to her in the belief that she is his beloved Agnes. These misdirected words conjure the Bleeding Nun, a highly overdetermined subverter of the law.

When a woman becomes a nun, she symbolically reenacts the movement from the semiotic to the patriarchal symbolic. By taking vows of poverty, chastity, and obedience, nuns renounce their materiality as women; their black-and-white habits transform their bodies into signs of that renounced materiality. A *vir*tuous woman, as the word's etymology declares, is a kind of honorary man. But the Bleeding Nun broke her vows to God the father, took a lover, and murdered him. At the manifest level, her habit now signifies that crime. She is not "bloody" or "blood-stained," however, she is "bleeding," which suggests not the blood of a single crime but an ongoing or recurrent shedding of blood. This poetic language betrays a deeper patriarchal horror of females, who bleed regularly. Raymond, incidentally, is saved from the marriage to his specter bride by symbolic intervention. Another supernatural being, the Wandering Jew, translates her desire for the burial of her bones: a final repression.

In Gothic, language that is lost or out of place is also conventional. Devices like the found manuscript, the lost will, the missing letters all materialize as literary conventions the inherent anxieties about language that inform Gothic fiction. Finally, Gothic plots are family plots. The patriarchal family is the cultural structure always already in place that generates Gothic plots. These plots tend to focus on certain pressure points that are situated at the intersections of nature and culture within patriarchy: wedding vows, wills, and the rules governing the family, such as legitimacy and legal inheritance. This is also the reason why in early Gothic at least (1764–1830), incest is so frequently the horror of horrors, for as the foundation of patriarchal culture incest is the Gothic mansion's heart of darkness.

APPENDIX 1
The Line of Good and the Line of Evil

In the *Metaphysics*, Aristotle writes that the Pythagoreans believed that reality may be divided into the following binary pairs (*Aristotle's* Metaphysics 64).

Well into the early modern period, these were familiar to philosophers as the line of good and the line of evil.

male	female
limited	unlimited
odd	even
one	many
right	left
square	oblong
at rest	moving
straight	curved
light	darkness
good	evil

APPENDIX 2
Study Questions

On Bluebeard

What are some relevant connotations of the color blue?

What assumptions about the female are taken for granted by Bluebeard and by the narrative?

Look closely at the language with which Bluebeard announces his prohibition: "Go into all and every one of them, except that little closet, which I forbid you, in such a manner that, if you happen to open it, there's nothing but what you may expect from my just anger and resentment." What are his unconscious expectations and desires in issuing this mandate? How do we know?

Why, according to the logic of patriarchy, is it inevitable that Bluebeard's wife will disobey her husband's prohibition? that the terrible secret is the bloody bodies of his murdered wives? that he murdered the wives by decapitating them?

On Pope's "Eloisa to Abelard"

Sort out the elements of oedipal conflict apparent or implied in Eloisa's story. In what ways does her plight realize the specifically Lacanian version of this crisis? Pay particular attention to the fact that she is writing a letter.

What evidence does the poem contain of Kristeva's semiotic?

How would Kristeva diagnose Eloisa's experience of "Black Melancholy"?

How does Kristeva's theory of abjection explain Eloisa's sense of horror?

Pope sees Eloisa's dilemma as a struggle between "Nature and Grace, Virtue and Passion"; how might Kristeva see her conflict?

List all the ways in which Eloisa might be seen as a speaking subject *en procès*?

On Keats's "La Belle Dame sans Merci"

Who asks the questions in the first two stanzas? What are the various possibilities?

This poem is famous for its ambiguity. Find the words and phrases that are subject to often opposing interpretations and look for details that seem odd. Tell as many alternative versions of what might have happened as may be supported by the text.

Trace the speaker's experience of language (and subjectivity) throughout the narrative that begins in stanza 4.

How might the poem be read as an oedipal crisis from the infant's point of view?

What constitutes the *nom du père*?

On Coleridge's *Rime of the Ancient Mariner*

Closely examine the figurative language. What elements in the poem manifest the culturally feminine? the culturally masculine? mothers and fathers?

Trace the appearance of first-person pronouns through the Mariner's narrative.

The Mariner tells a story and reaches a very firm conclusion about its meaning. Look for ways in which the story of his experiences do not justify that conclusion. Also consider the structure and the function of the narrative frames.

In the light of Kristeva's theory of abjection, analyze the Mariner's experience of the water snakes.

According to Kristeva, verse is more likely to manifest the semiotic than prose, because it foregrounds the material dimensions of language (sound, rhythm, etc). Analyze part 4, focusing on the relation between sound and sense.

Teaching the Gothic
and the Scientific Context
Carol A. Senf

Emphasizing the relation between the Gothic and science can prove useful in several very different types of classes, including classes in cultural studies or media studies, classes that study various literary periods, and classes on the Gothic in general. Because Georgia Tech is a technical institute, where most students graduate with degrees in engineering, computer science, chemistry, or biology and where the only undergraduate humanities degree is a Bachelor of Science in Science, Technology, and Culture, the classes in which I have taught Gothic literature have tended to emphasize the connection between the Gothic, a form of artistic expression that focuses on what is mysterious and beyond the realm of human control, and science, a discipline whose practitioners believe that the universe is ultimately knowable.

The connection between the Gothic and science is especially appropriate, because the Gothic arose at a time when scientific and human control over nature was beginning to replace belief in a deity who had created human beings in his image and who, while inscrutable, nonetheless retained a paternal interest in human endeavors. Certainly, the fear that science may open a veritable Pandora's box of uncontrollable horrors has existed almost since the beginnings of the Gothic and continues to exist in more recent works such as William Gibson's *Neuromancer*.

A useful approach to examining the relation between the Gothic and the science of its day initiates discussion by looking at twentieth-century popular culture. While this approach may be particularly suited to students in science studies or cultural studies, it can be adapted by teachers in more traditional humanities programs. Because concern over the potential power of science lies at the heart of many Gothic works, studying the Gothic is a way to examine such fears appearing in a number of works from different periods, including Hawthorne's "Rappaccini's Daughter," "The Birthmark," and "Ethan Brand"; Gilman's "The Yellow Wall-Paper"; Stevenson's *The Strange Case of Dr. Jekyll and Mr. Hyde*; Wilde's *The Picture of Dorian Gray*; Wells's *The Time Machine*, *War of the Worlds*, and *The Invisible Man*; Shelley's *Frankenstein*; and Stoker's *Dracula* and *The Jewel of Seven Stars*. This essay pays particular attention to *Frankenstein*, *Dracula*, and H. G. Wells's "scientific romances," because they appear in most discussions of Gothic and should therefore be in any teacher's repertoire. Moreover, because all these works have been interpreted in film, students are likely to be familiar with them. While addressing traditional Gothic works, I also examine cyberpunk, because it is something many students already know, either through its literary forms or through films such as *Blade Runner*, *RoboCop*, and *The Matrix*. Cyberpunk deals with many of the concerns that students voice about the power of science and technology over their lives. Examining the Gothic tradition helps them broaden their understanding of the Gothic and see the limitations in discussions that restrict it to a single historical period (the 1790s and the early nineteenth century) or to a limited set of conventions. In fact, exploring modern popular culture encourages students to recognize that the Gothic continues to flourish, because it satisfies the need of human beings to grapple with whatever frightens them.

I begin by asking students whether science and its ability to transform their lives frightens them. From there I lead to classic sci-fi films like *Alien*, then to that film's origins in *Frankenstein*. I introduce a handout of standard definitions of the Gothic in order to acquaint students with the genre and its characteristics. By going over these definitions, students quickly understand that even experts disagree, and instructors can also begin to illustrate the limitations in most of the standard definitions that students will encounter in their research. For example, teachers might explain that many definitions limit Gothic literature to the late eighteenth and early nineteenth centuries and therefore ignore much of what we intuitively recognize as Gothic. They might also note that the emphasis on certain conventions (supernatural events, medieval settings, persecuted maidens, and sexually depraved villains) eliminates certain arguably Gothic works. (It may, however, be interesting to see how these conventions are transformed in modern Gothic works.) Finally, examining definitions enables a class to trace quickly the development of the Gothic and note its emergence during different historical periods—the birth of Gothic in the late eighteenth century, the 1890s in England and the United States, and the late twentieth century.

While most definitions provide students with valuable insights about Gothic literature, two are especially useful because they explicitly link science and Gothic. *The Harper Handbook to Literature* (Frye, Baker, Perkins, and Perkins) examines the Gothic novel's origins as a response to contemporary rationality: Horace Walpole wanted "to blend the two kinds of romance, the ancient and the modern," having wearied of the

> strict adherence to common life in Richardson and Fielding. . . . He wanted to revive the mysterious and supernatural from seventeenth-century French romances while cutting them down to modern form. . . . Mary Shelley's *Frankenstein* (1818) transformed the Gothic into moral science fiction. Indeed, all mystery stories derive from the Gothic, and those that evoke terror . . . are frequently called Gothic.   (224–25)

In addition, this definition introduces Walpole, an important figure in the Gothic canon whose works do not fall within the perimeters of all classes that explore the relation between the Gothic and science.

Another definition, from Bette Roberts's *Victorian Britain*, extends the time of the Gothic and reinforces its connection with science:

> Fear of the present and future . . . distinguishes the most significant Gothics of the period: Robert Louis Stevenson's *Dr. Jekyll and Mr. Hyde* (1886), Oscar Wilde's *The Picture of Dorian Gray* (1891), H. G. Wells's *The Island of Dr. Moreau* (1896), and Bram Stoker's *Dracula* (1897). Analyzed in view of late Victorian cultural phenomena, sexual repression, loss of religious faith and moral absolutes, scientific and psychological research, and imperialism—these novels demonstrate the shifting anxieties of readers coping with the changes, uncertainties, and dangers of both Victorian and modern worlds. (334)

These definitions introduce three important ideas that I emphasize for students: that the interface between the Gothic and science has existed ever since Shelley created *Frankenstein* in 1818; that writers continue to express the fear that science, instead of helping human beings, will place them in peril; and that science reveals unpleasant truths about the human condition.

Most examples of late-nineteenth-century Gothic literature examine the ideological changes that took place as a result of the Darwinian revolution. No longer created in the image of God, both the decidedly apelike Mr. Hyde and the blood-drinking Dracula illuminate the fear of atavism, that primitive forces might reemerge to take over the civilized world. Wells's *War of the Worlds* suggests that human beings might not always be at the top of the food chain and hints at the horrors that might occur when advanced technology rests in the hands of an amoral force. More interested in politics, *The Time Machine* warns what might happen to human beings if the oppression of the working classes continues. As the novel reveals, our devolution to the cannibalistic Morlocks and the weak and effete Eloi would eventually lead to even more terrifying creatures at the end of time.

When asked whether science frightens them, many students, already familiar with *Frankenstein*, mention the threat of a scientific creation's rising up to overpower its creator—a concern that appears in the films *Blade Runner* (based on *Do Androids Dream of Electric Sheep?* by Philip K. Dick), Stanley Kubrick's *2001*, and other robot fantasies as well as in works like Stephen King's *Christine* (1983) and Tom Maddox's "Snake Eyes," which presents the computer as a kind of vampire that controls the central characters. Some students, mindful of the horrors wrought by thalidomide and DES, may mention works in which a medication or treatment originally intended for healing produces ill. This fear is evident in "The Yellow Wall-Paper," *Dr. Jekyll and Mr. Hyde*, and *The Invisible Man* as well as in "Solstice" by James Patrick Kelly. In Kelly's story, the ancient power associated with Stonehenge unites with modern drugs to produce overwhelming hallucinations. Finally, students often mention the fear that scientific exploration may bring human beings into contact with unspeakable monsters, such as those revealed in the popular *Alien* films. Worse yet, these originally external monsters may become indistinguishable from the human subject.

Another fear that occurs to students familiar with Darwin's theories is that human beings, instead of being created in the image of their creator, are simply another kind of animal and might evolve (or devolve) into something terrible.[1] Most of Wells's scientific romances (*War of the Worlds*, *The Time Machine*, and *The Island of Dr. Moreau*) include variations on the theme of what it means to be human in a world that has lost its notion of divinity—as do Stoker's *Dracula*, *The Jewel of Seven Stars*, and *The Lair of the White Worm*. In fact, all Stoker's Gothic works address the anxiety that primitive forces may take over the civilized world. (Instructors who teach any of these turn-of-the-century works have an excellent opportunity to introduce students to the Darwinian ideas of natural selection, sexual selection, and evolution in general as well as to the hostile reaction to those ideas.) Whether the primitive threat is a vampire, a mummy, a dinosaur or other specimen of the past, or a creature of another species—such as a Martian, a Morlock, or a giant crab—the practitioners of modern science are frequently powerless against it. Many of these novels also suggest that the scientific solutions are even more horrifying than the threats that they attempt to stop. Discussing what has frightened people about science in the past and examining the powerlessness of science provide an excellent transition to the Gothic elements of modern popular culture.

Moving to popular culture at this point offers four pedagogical advantages. First, because many students are already comfortable with the films that they see and the sci-fi that they read outside class, they quickly become comfortable with Gothic material as well. Second, beginning with popular forms takes advantage of students' existing knowledge of the Gothic. Because so many discussions of the Gothic emphasize magic, mystery, and medieval settings, Gothic literature may initially seem remote, inaccessible, and overly academic. Films and paperback novels, however, feel familiar to students. Indeed, most of my students have already seen several film versions of *Dracula*, *Dr. Jekyll and Mr. Hyde*, and *Frankenstein* as well as *2001*, *Blade Runner*, the *Terminator* films, *RoboCop*, and the *Alien* films, and some have already considered how these films present science.

Third, examining popular works makes the point that some of the films and novels that students know actually reinterpret earlier works. Thus, very openly, teachers can demonstrate that while films provide insight into older Gothic works, they do not substitute for reading the originals. Without threatening, scolding, or suggesting that film is decadent or inferior, teachers can indicate scenes that differ dramatically from the novels on which they are based. For example, several film interpretations of *Dracula* compress Mina and Lucy into one character, while others join Renfield and Jonathan Harker; and the 1960 version of *The Time Machine* is a dramatically cold war interpretation of Wells's classic. In this way teachers can subtly suggest the need to read original texts with care.

Finally, beginning with students' existing knowledge helps demonstrate that, because the Gothic is concerned with the social, economic, and political issues of its day, it has changed drastically since its beginning even as it continues to emphasize whatever is mysterious, frightening, and overwhelming for a particular culture. Gothic literature at the end of the eighteenth century can be shown to be quite different from Gothic literature of the 1890s, and both are quite different from the cyberpunk literature and film of our own day, but the very existence of this popular sci-fi demonstrates that the Gothic continues to evolve as a genre. Students quickly see that *Frankenstein* (Universal, 1931) and *The Bride of Frankenstein* (1935) reveal the machine-age fascination with technology, while *Mary Shelley's Frankenstein* (1994) is concerned with reproductive technologies, including surrogate motherhood and in vitro fertilization. Students worried about human cloning can make that connection as well. Indeed, the monsters that either erupt or threaten to erupt from their human hosts in *Alien* and *Alien: Resurrection* are expressions of concern about science's interference with natural reproduction. (All versions of *Frankenstein* along with the *Alien* films evoke the old-fashioned, pre-science fear of becoming the parent to something strange, dangerous, and uncontrollable.)

The theme of possession by the monstrous and alien continues to dominate cyberpunk, as is clear in Bruce Sterling's introduction to *Mirrorshades*. Sterling notes that, as technology at the end of the millennium has become more intimate, cyberpunk shifts the threat from external to internal: "Not for us the giant steam-snorting wonders of the past. . . . Eighties tech sticks to the skin, responds to the touch: the personal computer, the Sony Walkman, the portable telephone, the soft contact lens" (xiii).[2] Thus, cyberpunk transforms the ancient fear of demonic possession into the modern fear of scientific possession, of our being taken over by our technological developments. In the 1980s and 1990s, that fear became more and more wrapped up with the power that computers had over daily lives (though *Christine* demonstrates a comparable fear of the automobile that literally takes over the lives of its various owners)[3] and with our inability to distinguish what is human from what is manufactured.

In classes that are not devoted to a particular literary period, one may trace the evolution of various Gothic themes or ideas. For example, a class that begins with *Frankenstein*, an exploration of a scientific creation that ultimately comes to have life of its own, might continue that theme with Marge Piercy's *He, She, and It*, Dick's *Do Androids Dream of Electric Sheep?*, or *Blade Runner*. Another class, more interested in examining the horror of scientific hubris, might begin with *Frankenstein* and move to "Rappaccini's Daughter" and Wells's *The Island of Dr. Moreau* or his *The Invisible Man* before concluding with Gibson's *Neuromancer*. Pairing works that have similar themes is a relatively simple way to encourage students to examine how the fears of specific scientific developments have changed over the centuries, even though the fear of scientific endeavor per se remains a constant.

While all aficionados of film, science fiction, or Gothic literature probably have personal favorites, the following films are especially useful because they directly link science and Gothic literature: *Frankenstein, The Bride of*

Frankenstein, Dracula, Bram Stoker's Dracula: Love Never Dies, Blade Runner, Mary Shelley's Frankenstein, Alien, and *Alien 3.* All eight films are readily available on videotape and DVD. As popular culture continues to evolve, films, television series, and even advertisements will continue to provide ways to explore the interface between science and the Gothic.

The earlier films tend to demonstrate that science is powerless against an external evil (Frankenstein's monster or Count Dracula) or, in the Universal Studios interpretations of *Frankenstein,* an accomplice. Films and popular literature at the end of the millennium are more likely to reveal that the evil has become wed with the human and is, in fact, indistinguishable from it. Sterling, for example, notes several themes that he identifies with cyberpunk's invasion of the body: prosthetic limbs, implanted circuitry, cosmetic surgery, genetic alteration. He adds something even more terrifying and overwhelming, "mind invasion: brain-computer interfaces, artificial intelligence, neuro-chemistry techniques radically redefining the nature of humanity, the nature of the self" (xiii). Certainly, *Blade Runner* asks viewers to consider what makes human beings different from replicants (essentially androids who have been created to perform boring, dangerous, or tedious human functions). In the *Alien* films another species overcomes the human from within. This blurring of boundaries between scientific invention and the human seems to be a late-twentieth-century invention, a question that concerns writers and thinkers only at the end of the twentieth century. Istvan Csicsery-Ronay notes that cyberpunk explores the fascination of contemporary science with boundaries:

> The current scientific scene is entranced by the microstudy of boundaries no longer believed to be fundamental: between life and non-life, parasite and host, human and machine, great and small, body-brain and cosmos. Expansive SF [science fiction] was based on historical analogies of colonialism and social Darwinism, the power struggles of the old against the new, the ancient against the scientific. The topoi of implosive SF are based on analogies of the invasion and transformation of the body by alien entities of our own making. Implosive science fiction finds the scene of SF problematics not in imperial adventures among the stars, but in the body-physical / body-social and a drastic ambivalence about the body's traditional and terrifyingly uncertain integrity.   (272)

A return to traditional works shows the extent to which the Gothic has, almost since its beginnings, asked its readers to consider how science and technology have changed our idea of what it means to be human. Because students are frequently not aware of the importance of historical development, it is appropriate for teachers to introduce them to the long history of Gothic. "Rappaccini's Daughter" (1844), *Dr. Jekyll and Mr. Hyde* (1886), and *The Invisible Man* (1897) had already contemplated the extent to which science could alter the human being, while *The Time Machine* (1895) suggested that technology may determine the direction in which humans are evolving. Stoker's novels, however, suggest that modern science may bring human beings in contact with ancient evils against which it is powerless.

It is now almost a critical truism that certain Gothic works, notably *Franken-stein* and *Dracula*, address the scientific developments of their day. Science, if less prominent in other Gothic works, is nonetheless worth discussing if only because all Gothic literature features whatever is mysterious and overwhelming to the culture in which it was produced. Focusing on science has the added benefit of showing students that Gothic is not something medieval and remote but of vital importance in their lives today, because it confronts the forces that threaten to overwhelm them. If Gothic originated during a period in which writers and thinkers no longer believed that they were created in the image of God and that they were now in the control of science and its creations, the Gothic of today examines a world in which science and technology have become even more important. Looking in the mirror, these students see Frankenstein's creation looming behind them. Starting their cars in the morning, they may also be greeted by a voice that brings Kubrick's Hal into their lives. Perhaps more than any generation before, students today are prepared to examine the connection between science and the Gothic.

NOTES

[1]An excellent discussion of the Darwinian-Gothic connection can be found in Hurley.

[2]Sterling's introduction provides an excellent brief introduction to cyberpunk, as does *Mississippi Review* (16.2–3), which is devoted to a discussion of cyberpunk.

[3]Instructors interested in this theme can choose from several films, none of them particularly good, that feature possessed or terrifying automobiles: *The Car* (Universal, 1977), *The Wraith* (New Century Productions, 1986), and *Maximum Overdrive* (Warner Brothers, 1986), in addition to *Christine*. Showing one or two brief film clips, however, reveals a culture in which a familiar technological device wields enormous power over human beings. Some of these films respond to a particular cultural event, the gasoline crisis of the 1970s, not only to the generalized fear of the power of the automobile.

The First English Gothic Novel: Walpole's *The Castle of Otranto*

James Norton

Horace Walpole's *The Castle of Otranto, a Gothic Story* (1765) is considered the first English Gothic novel, because it pioneered Gothic fiction as a genre. Teaching the novel provides an excellent beginning for a Gothic literature course. Many early reviewers were morally shocked by the novel's "rotten materials" and "Gothic devilism" (Walpole, Castle [Mack] xi), but later critics praised it as a "master-piece of the horrible," honoring Walpole as "the actual founder of the literary horror-story" (Walpole, *Castle* [Scott] xxix; Lovecraft 24). Although the novel's Gothic imagery, such as a living skeleton, excited eighteenth- and nineteenth-century readers, modern students accustomed to the astonishing visual effects of shriek films usually find Walpole's descriptions of "the horrible" unarresting. The goal for teachers, then, is to engage students in a study of Walpole's Gothic imagery on its own historical terms. To achieve this goal, I recommend an approach that explores Walpole's Gothicism in an eighteenth-century historical context. History-based pedagogy has the advantage of preventing students from dismissing the story as cartoonish, and it provides a solid basis for comparative studies of later Gothic fiction and theory. My teaching approach focuses on seven areas: terminology, the Gothic revival, architecture, antirationalism, medievalism, supernaturalism, and church history.

Classroom instruction begins by considering Walpole's role in popularizing the term "Gothic" as a fiction label in 1765. I use W. S. Lewis's paperback edition (Oxford) of the novel because it reproduces the original title page and includes Walpole's first- and second-edition prefaces, necessary for understanding the novel's historical context. Attentive students often notice with some confusion that modern editions and online bibliographies of Walpole's novel use "A Story" or "A Gothic Story" or "A Gothic Tale" as alternative subtitles. For historical accuracy, they need to know that "Gothic" did not appear in the first edition, published anonymously 24 December 1764 (dated 1765) and titled *The Castle of Otranto, a Story*. The original title page and preface presented the novel as an eighteenth-century English translation of a newly discovered sixteenth-century Italian version of a twelfth-century story. In the second edition, which came out within months of the first, Walpole revealed his authorship by adding a new explanatory preface, and the title was changed to *The Castle of Otranto: A Gothic Story*. A best-seller, the novel was the first in England to use "Gothic" in its title to identify a new kind of fiction that combined the suggestion of ghastly, supernatural images of the dead with traditional themes of chivalry and romance. To see evidence of the literary fad Walpole created, students can find many late eighteenth- and early nineteenth-century Gothic fiction titles in Frederick Frank's bibliographic guides now available on his Web site, *The Sickly Taper*.

Knowledge of the novel's publication history and title prepares students to investigate what "Gothic" meant for English readers in 1765. They bring to class their own definitions of what they think the word denotes and connotes in modern popular culture. I also assign them the task of looking up the word in the *OED* to compare definitions. The exercise encourages them to move beyond a superficial knowledge of terminology to achieve a broader understanding of how Gothic language transmits different cultural concepts in different historical contexts. In the *OED* they find early modern definitions involving Germanic language, massive architecture, and medieval barbarity, all of which pertain to the tribe of the Goths. They also find the entries "Gothicisms" and "Gothicizing," terms coined by Walpole himself and cited from his writings. The terms refer to medieval, antiquarian things with barbarous, uncivilized overtones. That Walpole turned the adjective "Gothic" into a noun and a verb warrants further discussion in the classroom. Not only does his wordplay indicate the emerging prevalence of Gothic language in eighteenth-century discourse, it also sets up a linguistic framework for students to pay close attention to how Walpole "Gothicized" a romance story by adding "Gothicisms." From the simple philological exercise of looking up words in the *OED* students learn that Walpole's first readers associated the term "Gothic" not only with the macabre, as readers often do in today's popular culture. Rather, they associated it also with Germanic barbarian history of which the macabre was one element. Students see, then, that the reinvention of barbarian antiquity had popular appeal and provided the historical setting for Walpole's fiction.

In eighteenth-century discourse "Gothic" meant an interest in the medieval past, so the next teaching task is helping students begin to reconstruct antiquity as Walpole and his contemporaries would have imagined it. The terms "Gothicisms" and "Gothicizing" are cultural inventions that originated in the Gothic revival that the early-eighteenth-century English aristocracy conceived.

James Macaulay locates the revival between 1745 and 1845. A good place to begin explaining the historical origins of the revival is with Sacheverall Sitwell's pithy observation that it was an effort by eighteenth-century antiquarians, like Walpole, to discover the "amount of the Gothick which the Renaissance did not conquer" and to discover the "amount of the Renaissance which was conquered by the Gothick" (60). I quote Sitwell's passage in class to open up the idea that Gothic revivalism not only introduced a new vocabulary into the English cultural lexicon but also created a revolutionary alternative view to Renaissance values of ideal beauty and Enlightenment theories of rationalism.

The Gothic aesthetic invested the grotesque and the irrational with cultural value, and it came to be associated with literary fantasy, favored by Romantic writers, in opposition to literary formalism, favored by neoclassicists. As students discover, the opposition Sitwell sets up between Gothic and Renaissance can be traced back to Walpole and his contemporaries, who advanced Gothic primitivism and supernatural fantasy against the authority of neoclassical art and empirical science. Here I illustrate the opposition further by referring to Sir Walter Scott's use of Gothic language in his critical essays. Scott explains in his 1811 edition of *The Castle of Otranto* that Walpole's "Gothic style" was in "diametrical opposition to the rules of true taste" associated with Enlightenment rationality and neoclassical order (Walpole, *Castle* [Scott] vi). To add a psychological dimension to Scott's explanation of style, I mention that, in a letter to his friend William Cole, Walpole tells of inventing his irrational, antineoclassical Gothic story from a weird dream he had of a gigantic disembodied medieval hand that was wearing a knight's glove (*Letters*, letter 3/9/1765). Walpole's dream as a source of literary creativity, I explain to students, is a marker for the beginning of the Romantic period in which later writers such as Coleridge and De Quincey found creative inspiration in the dream world. To enhance this literary information I refer to *Frankenstein*, the seminal dream-induced Gothic narrative that was inspired by Mary Shelley's nightmare of warming her dead infant by a fire to restore it to life. Shelley's dream of an infant body and Walpole's dream of a body part underscore connections Gothicism makes between the nightmarish imagination and the corporeal world.

Bringing in architecture helps students advance their understanding of relations between the imaginative and corporeal dimensions of Gothic fiction. Walpole's dream fiction was born from his mythological fantasies about Gothic architecture in medieval society, but few students know that the Gothic revival in England began as an architectural fad in the early and mid-eighteenth century. Swept up in this fad, Walpole turned his estate at Strawberry Hill into a Gothic mansion, and the ancestral painting that comes to life in *The Castle of Otranto* has its creative origins in the great hall of art that Walpole built to emphasize the Gothicism of his home. Architectural information broadens students' comprehension of the development of Gothic fiction in the context of material culture, and it helps students see that the reliance of early Gothic fables on ancient architectural forms was partly a result of England's fashionable taste for medieval styles. To highlight relations between architectural and narrative forms, I cite Scott's reminder to readers of Walpole's fascination with Gothicism, which began as a love for antiquarian collectibles and medieval ruins and then developed into his writing of *The Castle of Otranto*, the setting of which is a fictional Gothic castle. Scott credits Walpole as one of the first English novelists "to give the public a specimen of the Gothic style adopted to modern literature, as he had already exhibited its application to modern architecture" (Walpole, *Castle* [Scott] xii).

I encourage students to investigate the narrative function of architecture in *The Castle of Otranto* by considering relations between Gothic buildings and Gothic stories.

Walpole's conversion of Strawberry Hill into a pseudo-Gothic palace can be explored by studying the Gothic visual designs reproduced in Macaulay's pictorial guide to English Gothic history. This guide facilitates the comparison I assign students to make between real Gothic architectural blueprints and the fictional configuration of Walpole's Otranto. Mapping out Otranto's complex design motivates students to see how Gothic narrative is rooted in material culture. Strawberry Hill was one of many contemporary aristocratic mansions popularly called "Gothic follies" because they artificially replicated medieval buildings and gardens. Lee Morrissey shows that the fabricated character of eighteenth-century Gothic follies was a forerunner to the self-conscious artificiality of postmodern architecture. I ask students to find examples of Gothic follies in their own communities: churches, old government buildings, mausoleums, and antiquated mansions. We use this visually familiar information to explore how massive ancient architecture provides concrete settings for Gothic thrillers. Secret passageways, trapdoors, subterranean corridors, and ancient crypts engulf the physical and psychological dimensions of characters as they become disoriented and lost in mazes of darkness.

I change the focus to antirationalism. At this point students have been introduced to *Gothic* as a term that privileges the imagination over reason, and they are ready to explore how Walpole uses the gloomy labyrinthine architecture of Otranto to create a fearful atmosphere that enhances the antirationalist stance seemingly taken by his narrative. They usually begin this exploration by concentrating on three or four specific scenes. Scenes that work well for discussion are the frightening adventure in the dark corridor where Isabella mistakes Theodore for the ghost of Conrad, the episode in which Theodore and Isabella escape from Manfred through a trapdoor that leads into an underground "vault totally dark," and the moment when Frederic encounters a living "skeleton, wrapt in a hermit's cowl" in a dark, isolated prayer room on an overcast evening (*Castle* [Lewis] 27, 102). While exploring these and similar scenes in which characters are enclosed in ancient walls, students should push beyond literal understandings of Gothic darkness and confusion as simply descriptive strategies intended to produce claustrophobia. They should begin to consider how, in the historical context of eighteenth-century rationalism and neoclassical aesthetics, Walpole uses the disorienting effects of Gothic architecture in direct opposition to Enlightenment values of clarity and order. Teachers might also want to call students' attention to Walpole's narrative use of dashes, a kind of stream of consciousness writing style that distorts traditional dialogue structures and often makes it unclear who is speaking to whom. As the characters lose their way in Otranto's maze of corridors, readers lose their way in Walpole's maze of dashes. The confusion he creates with gloomy architectural images and unconventional dialogue patterns, then, can be presented to students as attacks against the clarity of rational thought and rhetorical expression that neoclassicists held in high esteem.

The twelfth-century characters and events in *The Castle of Otranto* represent eighteenth-century perceptions of medieval Gothic culture. To understand these perceptions of medievalism, students should know that while Gothic novelists drew theories of fear, terror, and infinity from Edmund Burke's *The Sublime and Beautiful* (1757), it was Richard Hurd's *Letters on Chivalry and Romance* (1762) that furnished writers like Walpole with a fantastic blueprint of a medieval Gothic world in which power, war, sex, supernatural entities, and death were people's primary concerns. I encourage students to read Hurd's sections on Gothic medievalism (available in Clery and Miles), but for classroom convenience I summarize Hurd's theory that in pre-Renaissance northwestern Europe, home of the Goths, knightly militarism emerged as feudal lords battled one another for power, territory, and women. Although Gothic warriors were keen on rage and mass slaughter, they created codes of civil conduct, such as the chivalric rescuing of women held as sex slaves by lecherous tyrants. From this military context came fantastic fables of knights fighting giants, monsters, and dragons, which Hurd suggests were allegories of "oppressive feudal lords" (96). The tribal Goth imagination also invented a grotesque supernatural world of witches, fairies, and "Gothic enchanters" as a national mythology to replace the foreign mythologies of Greek, Roman, and Christian origins that had entered Germanic culture (110). Hurd elevates the wild and mysterious Gothic world as an imaginative literary subject that far surpasses what he believed to be the unimaginative ideas of Enlightenment rationality and neoclassical art.

I ask students to compare Hurd's Gothic history with the Gothicism in *The Castle of Otranto*. The comparison sharpens their understanding of how historians and novelists reinvented and popularized Gothic culture. A point of similarity that students readily recognize is between Hurd's theory of feudal tyranny and Manfred's tyranny over his subjects. The fights among Frederic, Manfred, and Theodore can be seen as representations of medieval power struggles. Also, Manfred's attempt to rape the young Isabella; his imprisoning of his barren wife, Hippolita; and Frederic's lustful pursuit of the teenaged Matilda fit Hurd's theory of Gothic male barbarity toward women. Opposed to that barbarity is Theodore, whose saving of Isabella and Matilda from danger represents Gothic male chivalry. Before leaving the subject of chivalric and barbaric behavior, I encourage students to put Walpole's critique of medieval masculinity into the context of eighteenth-century political terms. Tim Fulford's work on chivalry and masculinity is helpful here. Fulford shows that political instability and corruption in eighteenth-century England destablized traditional chivalric codes of courtesy, duty, bravery, honesty, reverence for women, and protection of the weak (1–28). His thesis is useful for generating discussion on how Walpole, who was deeply involved in politics, uses Gothic discourse to critique the English political structure that was created and perpetuated by a system of privilege that protected and sustained male corruption and oppression.

In addition to exploring masculine politics as a Gothic subject, students need to realize that, in turning Hurd's Gothic history into "A Gothic Story," Walpole accentuated supernatural elements or what Hurd identified as Gothic enchantment, thereby enlarging the meaning of *Gothic* to include paranormal occurrences. Since then, Gothicism has come to be associated less with medieval barbarity and more with supernaturalism or what modern critics have emphasized as Walpole's addition of supernatural elements to historical romance (e.g., Richter, *Progress*). One way to frame the story's supernaturalism as an eighteenth-century cultural phenomenon is to bring in E. J. Clery's account of how sensational media reports of inexplicable events, especially the appearance of the murderous Cock Lane Ghost in the early 1760s, gave rise to the entertainment value of apparition narratives (*Rise* 13–32).

To further classroom discussion of Walpole's supernaturalism, I return to my introductory point that *The Castle of Otranto* was criticized in 1765 for its "Gothic devilism." Teachers can use this criticism to generate students' interest in why supernatural Gothicism was sometimes condemned as blasphemy against God. Coaxing students to consider what Walpole's reviewer meant by the charge of devilism leads them to realize that, although the story contains ecclesiastical elements of Christianity, such as prayer and the founding of Saint Nicholas's church, it depicts a world in which God is mostly impotent if not altogether absent. In fact, godlessness is an important theme in later Gothic fiction, including Shelley's *Frankenstein,* Emily Brontë's *Wuthering Heights,* and Stoker's *Dracula.* The godless, enchanted world of Otranto troubled the reviewer, whose high religious standards of censorship will motivate even the least motivated students to seek out and analyze episodes of devilism. Walpole was acutely aware of the attacks against what he called "the visionary part" of his story, by which he meant events that contradict rationalism and empirical science (*Letters*, letter 8/22/1778). Students will have no problem finding instances of devilism and the visionary. For example, the enormous helmet on Alfonso's statue crushes Conrad, Don Ricardo's portrait comes alive, servants are terrorized at seeing gigantic hands and feet, Alfonso's statue bleeds, a living skeleton horrifies Frederic, and Alfonso's statue grows gigantic at the end of the story. By eighteenth-century Christian standards, devilism denotes evil. As students will discover, however, Walpole's enchanted figures of devilism actually work against evil as they endeavor to restore honor, morality, justice, and Christian righteousness to Otranto. Supernatural elements intercede as a surrogate God to rectify the social and political wrongs that Manfred and his male lineage have created.

Supernatural elements, students assume, render the story unrealistic and unbelievable, but Walpole's purpose was just the opposite; he used supernaturalism to create historical authenticity, believing that medieval society gave rise to superstition. To emphasize this point I quote Scott's observation that while Ann Radcliffe's Gothic novels refer supernatural events, called prodigies, "to an explanation, founded on material causes," Walpole's novel "details supernatural incidents as they would have been readily believed and received in the eleventh or twelfth century" (Walpole, *Castle* [Scott] xxiii). As the fictional translator of the first edition of *The Castle of Otranto* says, "Belief in every kind of prodigy was so established in those dark ages" and "the story is founded on truth" (*Castle* [Lewis] 4–5). The novel contains many enchanted episodes that are intended to pass for historical truth, yet at the same time they raise improbability and believability issues. Some good episodes for generating discussion about distinctions between historical truth and fiction, and between eyewitness accounts of the marvelous and skepticism, are the moment when witnesses are "thunderstruck" at "the miracle of the helmet" falling on Conrad, Hippolita's efforts to convince Manfred that "the vision of the gigantic leg and foot was all a fable," and concerns that Otranto might be "haunted by giants and goblins" (17, 35, 99).

Finally I turn to church history. This focus helps students explore parallels between sacred and secular superstition. Now that they have become conversant with Walpole's basic Gothic theory—which I have simplified to some extent by summarizing it to claim that for Walpole supernatural forces are good and that medieval people believed in them—they are ready to wrestle with the ecclesiastical questions the story raises. I suggest they study the title page and fictional preface of the first edition (ed. Lewis) to find interpretation clues. William Marshal, the fictional translator, offers readers textual evidence to explore the story's religious history, to verify its historical authenticity, and to suggest its social meaning. I encourage students to use Marshal's interpretation process for their own analyses of the narrative.

On what information does Marshal base his conjecture that the story originated in the late eleventh or early twelfth century, I ask students, and how does he figure out that it was revised and published four hundred years later, in 1529 by Onuphrio Murlato, an Italian Roman Catholic priest? Evidently a copy of the text was brought into England in the early years of the Protestant Reformation but survived Henry VIII's dissolution of monasteries and destruction of monastic archives. The most vexing historical question Marshal raises for students to ponder is, Why would a Roman Catholic priest in 1529 be interested in revising and reissuing the ancient supernatural story of Otranto? Because no original twelfth-century manuscript exists, it is impossible to know for certain what Murlato revised in the sixteenth century. Nevertheless, part of his interest in the story may have been personal, for reasons of ecclesiastical heritage. Such a theory can be deduced from the fact that, according to the title page, Murlato was a member of the Church of Saint Nicholas, and the story ends with Manfred's undergoing a spiritual conversion and making a penitential vow "to saint Nicholas to found a church" (104). It will still seem strange to students that a Christian holy man would want people to read about unholy superstitions, what students have already identified as "Gothic devilism" and "the visionary." Marshal explains that in early-sixteenth-century Italy, literature was published "to dispel the empire of superstition, at that time so forcibly attacked by the reformers" (3). Given the context of reformers' attacks against church mysteries and corruption, according to Marshal, Murlato did not reject superstition but instead wanted "to confirm the populace in their ancient errors and superstitions" by reissuing a Gothic story that "would enslave a hundred vulgar minds beyond half the books of controversy that have been written from the days of Luther to the present hour" (3–4). Marshal concedes, however, that Murlato's motives are baffling.

Marshal's uncertainty about the text's social function provides a good opportunity for students to explore their own ideas concerning Murlato's motives in relation to church history. In doing so they should keep in mind the fictive complexity of Walpole's narrative. Walpole invented Marshal, who interprets Murlato, also Walpole's invention. To help students think about ways in which Marshal and Murlato are fictive agents of Walpole's attitude toward religion and the marvelous, I quote a passage from Walpole's cynical work *An Account of Giants* (1766):

> Ghosts and witches are entirely of your own growth. Excepting the famous ghost of a sound in Cock-lane, from which the Methodists expected such a rich harvest (for what might not a rising church promise itself from such well-imagined nonsense as the apparition of a noise?).
>
> (*Works* 2: 93)

Walpole's commentary on the emerging sect of Methodism as taking advantage of the Cock Lane ghost phenomenon to scare ignorant people into joining the Wesley brothers' congregation is somewhat analogous to Marshal's historical interest in the relation between Murlato's Roman Catholicism and secular superstition. The analogy helps students consider whether or not Murlato's intention was to reinvent twelfth-century Gothic supernaturalism for purposes of scaring sixteenth-century Italians into believing they needed the church's spiritual protection against unholy ghosts. Such scare tactics make sense in the historical context of the Church of Rome's weakening under the reforms set in motion by Luther, Calvin, and others. Thus, representations of supernatural events could reinforce ecclesiastical power structures. Another angle on the topic of church history and Gothicism is Edward Ingebretsen's theory that just as supernaturalism has been artificially produced to cause psychological distress in readers, English Puritans perpetuated concepts of eternal hell to cause spiritual distress in believers and nonbelievers, thereby strengthening the need for God's salvation. My classroom instruction concludes by opening up avenues for students to undertake more studies of religious cultism as a subject of Gothic literature.

My teaching approach is designed to help students gain a broader, more appreciative, and historically accurate understanding of eighteenth-century Gothicism, which began as a fascination for medieval culture and a challenge to rationalism. *The Castle of Otranto* serves as a prototype for Gothic narrative, and it provides students with solid preparation for their studies in later Gothic fiction and theory.

Early Women's Gothic Writing:
Historicity and Canonicity in
Clara Reeve's *The Old English Baron*
and Sophia Lee's *The Recess*

Angela Wright

At the beginning of any course on Gothic fiction, if one were to ask students which Gothic texts they were familiar with, it is unlikely that they would name either of the novels that this essay addresses. They would probably mention Matthew Lewis's *The Monk*, Mary Shelley's *Frankenstein*, and possibly some of Ann Radcliffe's novels, but the works of Clara Reeve and Sophia Lee, which are so crucial to these subsequent creations, remain relatively unknown. Such omissions from students' knowledge of the Gothic are telling. They suggest that canonical judgments are still exercised on a genre that was critically neglected for so long. Despite the important position that both Reeve's *The Old English Baron* and Lee's *The Recess* occupy in the formation of the Gothic novel, they have been mostly passed over in critical discussions, and *The Recess* was for a time allowed to fall out of print. Before the 2000 edition of *The Recess*, students were obliged to read the novel on microfilm or in the one original edition that a library might hold. Thus its pedagogical uses were limited. Thankfully, this current lack of availability is now being redressed, and so teaching both these novels will become an easier task. I discuss the potential offered for studying the Gothic by both novels. My examination of them incorporates discussions of how issues of genre, gender, and canonicity can be focused through them.

Reeve's 1778 tale *The Old English Baron* was, as the author herself acknowledged, the literary offspring of *The Castle of Otranto* (3). As a novel it does, however, differ substantially from its predecessor, both in the development of plot thematics and in its correction of what Reeve saw as the violent excesses of Walpole's *Otranto*. First, in terms of plot thematics, Reeve's novel is more historically specific. She places its action in the time of Henry VI, then inserts the historical character of Richard Plantagenet, "whose pride of birth equaled that of any man, living or dead" (30). Plantagenet, leader of the house of York, claimed that he was the true legitimate heir to the throne of England and instigated the War of the Roses to substantiate this claim. His sons eventually won the throne. Such a deliberate historical placement by Reeve is not coincidental: Plantagenet's claims to the throne curiously resemble the legitimacy claim in *The Old English Baron*, where the hero, Edmund Twyford, initially portrayed in the novel as a retainer of the Lovell family, discovers that his true parents were in fact murdered and that he is the heir to the castle in which he resides as a retainer. The plot bears some small resemblance to *Otranto*, but Reeve emphasizes the importance of legitimacy, property, and honor to highlight how frivolously Walpole addressed these issues. Her use of the supernatural is situated in the motif of the murdered father returning to direct his son Edmund about his woes: this supernatural, in contrast to Walpole's more humorous use, is focused and moral.

Walpole was, unsurprisingly, outraged by Reeve's correction of his Gothic tale: he called it totally void of imagination and interest (*Yale Edition* 2: 110). In a similar vein, Sir Walter Scott later described it as a "tame and tedious, not to say mean and tiresome work" (*Lives* 207). It is, of course, entirely possible that students may share these literary judgments. To counter these easy dismissals, I argue that it is important to bear in mind that Reeve's 1778 novel paves the way for the development of the Gothic novel. *The Old English Baron* is important on three levels: first, it blurs the boundaries between the historical romance and Walpole's Gothic tales and so is important for both Lee's subsequent *The Recess* (1785) and Scott's historical romances. I indicate that Reeve's blurring of these boundaries may be partly responsible for the consequent multiplicity of definitions of Gothic and the very instability of its form.

On a second level, Reeve's foregrounding of issues of property and legitimacy was the prototype of what James Watt terms the "Loyalist Gothic romance" (42), a brand of Gothic concerned with issues of patriotism and rightful ownership in Britain. *The Old English Baron* was a crucial foundation stone for, among others, Radcliffe's subsequent narratives of usurpation in such novels as *The Mysteries of Udolpho* and *The Italian*. Although Reeve's novel all but ignores the issue of gender in property ownership (the marriage between Edmund Twyford and Lady Emma at the end appears to be more a submission to plot conventions than an exploration of gender issues), it does provide, as critics have widely acknowledged, a shift from aristocratic property beliefs to a more bourgeois, middle-class conception of property ownership. Such a repositioning in terms of class also allows for the possibility of female property ownership. Emma Clery, in *The Rise of Supernatural Fiction, 1762–1800*, has aptly described *The Old English Baron* as "Reeve's rewriting of *Otranto* as *Pamela* in fancy dress with the spice of the paranormal, an illustrative conduct-book for the proper correlation of wealth and virtue" (86). The novel paved the way for Gothic narratives of stolen and restored property, which were to prove crucial for Radcliffe's tales of young heroines reclaiming what is theirs. It also establishes a strong moral tone, providing a guarantee of "doing justice to the innocent and oppressed" (109), a theme that also clearly influenced Radcliffe.

On a third level, Reeve's novel is important to the formation of female Gothic in its development of the use of the dream. Both Sir Philip Harclay and Edmund Twyford have dreams that are connected to the injustices that have been committed on their respective friend and father. The motif of the ominous dream, to signal unease and wrongdoing, is used to increasingly greater effect in the novels of Lee, Radcliffe, and Mary Shelley, to name only a few.

Reeve's modest revision of Walpole's *The Castle of Otranto* is frequently criticized for being too derivative. Students of the Gothic will invariably withdraw such a judgment, however, when they read *The Old English Baron* under the lenses I offer above. Including a second neglected Gothic novel on a syllabus, namely Lee's *The Recess*, further focuses the issues of usurpation, historical and Gothic fusions, and dreaming. Lee's novel has been called both "the first fully developed English Gothic novel" and one of the first "recognizable historical novels in English" (Doody 551). It was influenced in particular by Prévost's historical novel *Le philosophe anglais ou Histoire de M. Cleveland*, but whereas Prévost focused his narrative on a fictional illegitimate and unwanted son of Oliver Cromwell, Lee chose to fabricate her tale around two legitimate, unknown daughters of Mary, Queen of Scots, Matilda and Ellinor, who have to be kept hidden from the politically jealous gaze of Queen Elizabeth I.

In *The Recess*, history and Gothic thematics complement each other. There are numerous Gothic tropes such as imprisonment in a subterranean cavern, hidden origins, tyrannical persecutors, insanity, and death. These tropes are, however, worked into a historical setting specific to English history, the reign of Queen Elizabeth I. While Lee was clearly influenced by Reeve's novel in terms of usurpation, dreams, and historical English settings, her work is in many ways quite different from *The Old English Baron*. Discussion of these differences can prove useful for highlighting different issues in the Gothic. The three levels of discussion for Reeve's novel that I previously highlighted are also useful to this text.

Before offering suggestions of my own on *The Recess*, I ask students what they find Gothic about this text. They raise the tropes of imprisonment and dreams and in so doing begin working toward their own definitions of Gothic. However, because this particular novel is also historically specific, unlike Radcliffe's and Lewis's, which are invariably set on the European continent, discussions ensue about its possible deviations from Gothic. The text thus provides a useful way of thinking about generic categories in a classroom situation.

The Recess, even more than *The Old English Baron*, by its resistance to one specific category forces students to think about the generic categorizations historical novel, Gothic novel, and the more recent critical term "female Gothic." As a text chronologically positioned near the beginning of any course on Gothic fiction, it compels students to consider the hybridity and instability of the Gothic as a genre. The second level of discussion that I established for *The Old English Baron* related to its recent definition by Watt as "Loyalist Gothic." *The Recess*, however, by its deviating from such a category, forces students to consider issues of political concern in Gothic texts. Lee's novel is very different from Reeve's because of its unresolved narrative of oppression. The two young sisters are hidden in the eponymous "recess" so that their existence will be shielded from Queen Elizabeth. The history of the Recess itself, once inhabited by nuns during the Reformation and also used simultaneously as a hiding place for monks, draws attention to the larger cultural oppression of Roman Catholics in England during the religious wars instigated by Henry VIII. In terms of political content, then, this novel, when juxtaposed with *The*

Old English Baron, clearly demonstrates to students the differing political and cultural aims of Gothic novelists. Such discussions are usually grounded in the difference of endings in these two novels: whereas *The Old English Baron* concludes on a happy and moral note, stating, "All these, when together, furnish a striking lesson to posterity, of the over-ruling hand of Providence, and the certainty of RETRIBUTION" (153), *The Recess* concludes with what we suppose is the death of the final narrator, Matilda. In addition, Matilda's self-identification at the beginning as "a solitary victim to the crimes of my progenitors" (1: 1–2) suggests not the resignation to Providence that Reeve's text advocates but rather a displacement of blame onto parents. Because this blame is placed on the very first page of the novel, students often find it a useful opening to a discussion of how the two novels differ thematically and ideologically.

The appearance of dreams in *The Old English Baron* was important in its move toward greater subjectivity in characterization. *The Recess*, a tale mediated uniquely through female characters, takes the trope of the dream much further. In book 2, the persecuted, insane Ellinor lucidly declares of her lover, Essex, "I have dreamt of him my whole life long!" (243). Margaret Anne Doody's "Deserts, Ruins, and Troubled Waters: Female Dreams in Fiction and the Development of the Gothic Novel," one of the first articles to concentrate on Lee's novel, foregrounds the importance of the dream in this text and its subsequent importance to other Gothic creations. As secondary reading for early Gothic, I have found Doody's essay indispensable in its establishment of dreams as the reality of many female-authored Gothic texts. As Doody states, "There is no longer a common-sense order against which the dream briefly flickers; rather, the world of rational order briefly flickers in and out of the dreamlike. There is no ordinary world to wake up in" (553).

It would be difficult to discuss *The Recess* without mentioning dreams and insanity. Similarly, no discussion of the novel can ignore the central positioning of the two female heroines who tell the story of their complex lives in the first person. This text is one of the most important examples of female Gothic, because the heroines find no refuge in the domestic space offered by the confined recess; instead, the narrow refuge is a locus of danger for them. Whereas Matilda, the primary narrator, initially perceives the recess as a "hallowed circle to seclude us from the wicked," she later conceives "an involuntary hatred" for its "silence and confinement" (1: 7, 167–68). Such paradoxes are explored to great effect by Kate Fergusson Ellis in *The Contested Castle*, where she identifies *The Recess* as an example of "Otranto feminized" (69).

Of equal importance to the novel's status as an example of female Gothic is its complex portrayal of gender. The two heroines are first portrayed as exemplary models of female virtue who read conduct books in their safe haven and exist in perfect harmony. However, they are later shown to disagree with each other's assessments of their respective lovers. This disagreement estranges them from each other and leads to a rather curious contest in the narrative for dominance. The contending first-person narratives consistently undermine the heroines' protested beliefs that passivity, resignation, and silence are the best attributes for females to possess. Similarly, the true villain of the novel, Queen Elizabeth, also evades any stereotypical categorization. She is described alternately in distinctly masculine terms of power and then as the victim of feminine emotionalism. Critics of the novel have chosen to explain this masculinization by suggesting that Elizabeth belongs to the realm of power in her desire to control everyone and everything (Roberts, "Sophia Lee's *The Recess*" 79). However, her portrayal is more complex than such a judgment allows for. When confronted by an insane Ellinor who reproaches her for depriving her of her lover, Essex, Elizabeth faints, believing that she has seen a ghost. Such complexities of plot and gender portrayal erode the conservative gendered assumptions of male power and logic, female insanity and superstition, which are evident in the novel's initial premises; the complexities underline this novel's resistance to easy ideological categorization.

This example of early female Gothic is excellent for pedagogical purposes, because it does not thrust on its readers the artificial happy closures of Radcliffe's later texts and presents a lyrical description of insanity that would only be paralleled later by Charles Robert Maturin in *Melmoth the Wanderer*. It paves the way for fruitful discussion of female Gothic that both questions and supports that term by interrogating its recent critical currency.

All students who have read *The Recess* in my female Gothic course have been struck by its differences from other Gothic texts: its resistance to a happy ending; its sympathetic repositioning of Catholic persecution, its remarkable portrayal of female insanity, the evasion of simplistic gender attributes, the lyrical quality of its prose. I highly recommend its inclusion in courses that address female Gothic and that trace the development of the Gothic novel. Like Reeve's novel, this text reflects the hybridity and conflicting ideologies of the Gothic genre.

Reeve's *The Old English Baron* and Lee's *The Recess* both relate "untold and unknown" tales from a fictional historical space, and yet these novels remain relatively unknown in terms of the literary canon. We could, of course, argue that the Gothic genre as a whole has stubbornly resisted admission into any such canon, but even in critical accounts of the Gothic, these novels have remained peripheral. But this very neglect can prove to be a pedagogical tool. Before discussing either of these novels, I ask students to consider why they do not know these texts. Their responses inevitably express that often unconscious process of canonicity that haunts university syllabi.

After students have read the novels and formed their own judgments on their literary value, I discuss canon formation with them in terms of critiques offered by writers such as Walpole and Scott and in terms of twentieth-century attempts to recuperate novelists such as Reeve and Lee. Foundational texts like Ellen Moers's *Literary Women* (which first introduced the term "female gothic") and Jane Spencer's *The Rise of the Woman Novelist* can accompany more recent studies such as Clery's *Women's Gothic* and Diane Long Hoeveler's *Gothic Feminism*. Such inclusions on secondary reading lists will help pave the way for critical discussions of canonicity. For students, to address neglected and unknown novels is ingeniously Gothic in itself: they discover and relate their own unknown and unjust stories.

Teaching the Early Female Canon: Gothic Feminism in Wollstonecraft, Radcliffe, Austen, Dacre, and Shelley

Diane Long Hoeveler

I have been teaching undergraduate and graduate courses on the Gothic, the female Gothic, and Gothic fiction and drama for the last ten years.[1] My methodology has evolved from a straightforward, historically chronological approach to the major canonical texts of the genre to a more thematic and theoretical approach that stresses the Gothic's complicity in ideological constructions of class and gender from the late eighteenth century through the mid-nineteenth century. In short, students in my Gothic courses are presented with my interpretation of the Gothic's role in reforming class attitudes, in defining appropriate behavior for both sexes, and in codifying literature's role as an ideological system that operates to shape and enforce what we now call values in society.

I begin the course The Female Gothic with selected readings from Mary Wollstonecraft's *A Vindication of the Rights of Woman* (1792), followed by her last and uncompleted novel, *Maria; or, The Wrongs of Woman* (1798). My approach to Wollstonecraft as a proto-Gothicist is not, perhaps, self-evident to the students, but they soon see that her primary literary devices—hyperbole, dramatic self-stagings, and the repeated presentation of her heroines as victims—lead directly into the atmosphere and action of Ann Radcliffe's novels, written primarily during the same decade. Given the space constraints of this essay, I can only mention here that Wollstonecraft's use of imagery, rhetoric, and patterns of victimization in *Maria*, where the heroine is imprisoned in a madhouse by her diabolical husband, is very similar to that employed by later female Gothic novelists. This similarity is explored in much greater detail in my articles on Wollstonecraft as a proto-Gothicist ("Reading"; "Tyranny").

At one time or another I have taught all Radcliffe's novels but never all in the same course. There are advantages to teaching what is generally considered her best novel, *The Italian* (1797), as it is the text that contains most clearly the depiction of the supposedly orphaned heroine, the evil monk turned false father and finally uncle-murderer, the vicious phallic mother as rival, and the full trappings of anti-Catholicism dripping for all to see in the dank chambers of the Inquisition. *The Italian* is by far the most dramatic and engaging of all of Radcliffe's novels, but I would make a case for teaching *A Sicilian Romance* (1790) as well. This text is the shortest and most concise, and, let's be honest about this, length is a factor with our students. The novel also contains in almost embryonic form all the major themes and concerns that were to develop more fully in Radcliffe's next three novels as well as in the female Gothic genre itself. When teaching *A Sicilian Romance*, I provide students with a copy of Henry Siddons's dramatic adaptation of the novel as an illustration of how popular novels were used as fodder for the masses (much as television miniseries today will adapt and further dilute for mass consumption a powerful and successful film). I inform students that during the month of May 1794, the most popular drama, playing to packed houses at Covent Garden, was Siddons's *The Sicilian Romance; or, The Apparition of the Cliff*, based on the Gothic novel published by Radcliffe (B. Evans 90–115). One of the more interesting changes in the play concerns the villain, who in the Siddons piece keeps his inconvenient wife chained to solid stone in a rocky cave in the forest, a place he visits only to feed and blame her for inflicting wounds of guilt on his heart. The Gothic villain would later metamorphose into the Byronic hero, consumed by unspeakable guilt over illicit sins, but the villain of the Siddons drama is a bit more prosaic. He simply desires to marry a younger and more beautiful woman, one who will further improve his social and political status, because his first wife, the mother of his children, has become redundant. The young woman he desires, whom we would recognize as a trophy wife, is pursued from castle to convent to cavern, her pursuit aided by the hero, the villain's son-turned-outlaw. As students soon recognize, female Gothic novels like Radcliffe's *Sicilian Romance* provided the subject matter, techniques, and literary conventions of popular melodrama, first on the stage in France, then on the London stage, and much later in Hollywood "women in jeopardy" films like *Silence of the Lambs*, which have continued the primal Gothic tradition of good or femininity triumphing over evil or masculinity (see Marjean Purinton's essay in this volume for a fuller discussion of popular dramatic adaptations of Gothic novels). This extremely polarized attitude toward gender is the first ideological strategy we recognize in the female Gothic universe, but, of course, that primitive distinction breaks down as Radcliffe develops more fully in her next novels the feminized hero and the masculinized heroine (Hoeveler, *Gothic Feminism* 65–66, xvii, 40).

Radcliffe's next Gothic novel, *The Romance of the Forest* (1791), has also proved extremely popular with my students, who are intrigued by a heroine who must successfully read the clues in her dreams in order to solve her father's murder and learn her own identity. Gothic elements come thick and fast in this text: the heroine's uncanny dreams, her rummagings in an old chest (in which she finds her father's skeleton), and her discovery of his deathbed journal and the dagger used to kill him, and students learn to decode the clues themselves as one leads to the next. Radcliffe's Gothic devices are recognized in a transformed manner when students read Austen's *Northanger Abbey* (1817), a heavy-handed satire of the excesses of *The Romance of the Forest*. Austen's novel is also interesting for its lightly humorous examination of the dense Gothic heroine who, in Austen's view, triumphs not through her own efforts, but through the loving patience and assistance of the feminized hero.

Twelve years after Siddons's play was all the rage in London, Charlotte Dacre Byrne, who published under the dramatic pen name of Rosa Matilda, presented another chained Gothic victim-heroine in the best-selling novel *Zofloya; or, The Moor* (1806). In Dacre's version, however, it is Satan, disguised as a black slave, who suggests to the Gothic antiheroine, Victoria, that they dispose of Lilla, Victoria's inconvenient rival, by chaining her to a damp stone cave, where Lilla later is murdered in a perverse sexual frenzy, a viciously protracted beating and stabbing delivered by Victoria, an aristocratic woman who functions literally in league with the devil. As a work that has been recently reissued by both Oxford and Broadview and has more in common with the male Gothic tradition than with the female, *Zofloya* was written in direct homage to Lewis's *The Monk* and can be taught most successfully in tandem with Radcliffe's *The Italian*, also written in response to Lewis's text. Placing the three novels in chronological order of composition reveals the intertextual debate that was occurring as Gothic authors each attempted to respond to and correct another's definition of the Gothic. Radcliffe wrote *The Italian* in an attempt to undo the damage she thought that Lewis's violent, misogynist text had done to her literary reputation. Radcliffe also treats anti-Catholic themes, but she redeems the family, particularly the role and status of the mother in a way that Lewis very obviously does not. Writing after both Lewis and Radcliffe, Dacre also begins her text with the mother figure, situating the entire ensuing tragedy at the feet of the adulterous mother who deserts her husband and children for a German aristocrat. As I have argued at greater length elsewhere ("Charlotte Dacre's *Zofloya*"), Dacre's novel functions as the most explicit ideological statement of gender and racism that I know from this period. Its adaptation of Wollstonecraft's theories about the role of the mother in relation to the education and moral development of her children is also interesting, as is its condemnation of the sexualized mother who forsakes her maternal responsibilities for a licentious and adulterous passion. Teaching the three novels together allows students to see how the Gothic functioned as an ideological construct that attempted to control the sexuality of women, both before and after marriage.

After reading Wollstonecraft and a choice of novels by Radcliffe, Austen, and Dacre, students are ready to begin to draw some initial conclusions about Gothic feminism or the underlying ideology operating in female Gothic novels. In my view, the typical female Gothic novel presents a blameless female victim triumphing through a variety of passive-aggressive strategies over a male-created system of oppression and corruption (alternately known as the patriarchy). The melodrama that suffuses these works is explicable only if we understand, as Paula Backscheider has recently demonstrated (*Spectacular Politics*), that a generally hyperbolic sentimentalism was saturating the British literary ambience, informing the Gothic melodramas that were such standard fare during the popular theater season. But melodrama, as Peter Brooks has demonstrated (*Melodramatic Imagination*), is also characterized by a series of moves or postures that make it particularly attractive to middle-class women. Specifically, Brooks lists as crucial to melodrama the depiction of intense, excessive representations of life that tend to strip the facade of manners in order to reveal the essential conflicts

at work and produce moments of intense symbolic confrontation. These symbolic dramatizations rely on what Brooks lists as the standard features of melodrama: hyperbolic figures, lurid and grandiose events, masked relationships
and disguised identities, abductions, slow-acting poisons, secret societies, and
mysterious parentage (3).

So what does melodrama have to do with the female Gothic and what does
the female Gothic have to do with the development of feminism as an ideology?
Following Hayden White's theory of metahistory, I read Enlightenment feminism and its successors as bourgeois ideologies that grew out of the literary discourse systems we have come to identify as the Gothic, the melodrama, and the
sentimental and sensibility traditions of virtue vindicated and rewarded. The
fact that Wollstonecraft wrote an incipient Gothic novel after she wrote *Vindication of the Rights of Woman* has not been fully understood or placed in its
broader cultural, literary, and historical context. Wollstonecraft is, properly
speaking, not the mother of feminism; she is the mother of Gothic feminism.[2]

In short, melodrama is a version of the female Gothic, while the female Gothic
provides the undergirding for one particular type of feminism as an ideology
bent on depicting women as the innocent victims of a corrupt and evil patriarchal system. Indeed, the fantasy, the ideology that seems to ground female
Gothic novels is the same one that activates this one particular (white middle-
class) type of feminism: the notion that women are victimized not simply by gender politics but also by the social, economic, political, religious, and hierarchical
spaces that bourgeois capitalism has constructed. The ideological compulsion of
the female Gothic can more accurately be read as the need to privatize public
spaces, which is the same dream that compels modern feminists to assert that the
personal is political. The motivation for the women who write Gothic novels is
both simple and complex: they aim for nothing less than the fictional feminiza-
tion of the masculine world, the domestication of all those masculine institutions
that exist to define the sexuality, not to mention the sanity, of women. The optimistic dream that concludes the female Gothic requires that juridical violence,
paranoia, and injustice, coded as the masculine, be brought to heel, punished
(and preferably beaten), and contained safely in the confines of the fantasy
home—the female-dominated companionate marriage. This triumph is essentially the same dream that today motivates one type of feminism as an ideology.
As the ideological heirs of Wollstonecraft, the middle-class, white, feminist
movement is rooted in Gothic and melodramatic tropes of female victimization.
It does not exist apart from or above history; rather, it is grounded in the history
of discourse systems like the female Gothic novel. It is a literary ideology and
cannot be understood without reading its rhetoric in the originating sources—
the Gothic novels of Wollstonecraft, Radcliffe, Austen, Dacre, and Mary Shelley.

Matilda (1820) the Gothic novella written by Shelley after she completed
Frankenstein (1818), has recently enjoyed a renaissance and is much more frequently taught than it was even five years ago. A text that depicts a father's
incestuous passion for his motherless daughter, *Matilda* is an extremely pow-

erful work both on its own and taught alongside *Frankenstein*. In fact, the voice, characters, and actions of *Matilda* are almost embarrassingly autobiographical and explain why William Godwin, her father, conveniently misplaced the manuscript when Mary sent it to him for his reaction and approval. Not published until 1957 and not well-known until the 1980s, *Matilda* is also an interesting companion text to be studied alongside Wollstonecraft's *Maria*. The echoes of a daughter rewriting the mother's work are unmistakable, and students, I have found, are particularly intrigued by reading a daughter's novels after studying the mother's. The anger, sense of loss and betrayal, and the jealousy toward the father, projected so that it is the father who desires the daughter and not the other way around, present my students with a case study in neurosis that none of us can resist psychoanalyzing. Shelley's *Frankenstein* has long been a test case for teaching the woman's romantic novel, but in many ways her *Matilda* is a better choice for that category. Unlike *Frankenstein*, *Matilda* centers on a motherless female heroine who is reunited with her father, only to find after a few months that the father is passionately in love with her. Bearing a striking similarity to the seduced maiden narratives so popular at the time, *Matilda* presents a daughter whose rejection of her father's love actually sends him to his suicide. This work, written by a woman whose father remarried all too quickly after her mother's death, can be read as a fascinatingly blatant revelation of Mary Shelley's fantasy rewrite of her own life.

Finally, I ask my students, if husbands can routinely chain their wives to stone walls and feed them the way one feeds a forsaken pet that will not die, then what sort of action is required from women to protect and defend themselves against such tyranny? Batting one's eyes and demure, docile behavior are hardly adequate protection against a lustful, raving patriarch gone berserk. According to Brooks, the Gothic novel can be understood as standing most clearly in reaction to desacralization and the pretensions of rationalism. Like melodrama, the female Gothic text represents both the urge toward resacralization and the impossibility of conceiving sacralization other than in personal terms. For the Enlightenment mentality there is no longer a universally accepted transcendent value to which one can be reconciled. There is, rather, a social order to be purged, a set of ethical imperatives to be endorsed. And, we might ask, who is in the best position to purge the new bourgeois world of all traces of aristocratic corruption but the female Gothic heroine? Such a woman—professionally virginal, innocent, and good—assumed virtually religious significance because in the discourse system so much was at stake. Making the world safe for the middle class was the goal inscribed in both female Gothic texts and feminism. But such a task was not without its perils. What I am calling Gothic feminism was born when women realized that they had a formidable external enemy—the ravening, lustful, greedy patriarch—in addition to their own worst internal enemy: their perception of their sexual difference as a weakness.

I introduce my students to theories that buttress my interpretation. First, I provide them with a copy of Freud's essay and a handout that summarizes his position in "A Child Is Being Beaten," published in 1919 and the source for much recent speculation about the contours of the female Gothic novel tradition (see essay appendix). Female Gothic novels actually encode in almost uncanny precision the three versions of the female beating fantasy as Freud has delineated them. For a girl the first and the third psychological positions are sadistic and voyeuristic ("Another child is being beaten, and I am witnessing the act"), while the second position in the fantasy is masochistic, erotic, and deeply repressed ("I am the child being beaten by my father"). For the boy the psychic transformation is less complex because of the elimination of one stage. For him the first position, "I am loved by my father," becomes the conscious fantasy "I am being beaten by my mother." Both male and female subjects—generally children between the ages of five and fifteen—appear to shift continually between these psychic positions largely through the conscious and unconscious permutations of desire and its repression (see Massé, *In the Name*; and Sedgwick, "Poem").

The struggles we see in Radcliffe's novels, for instance, between her heroines and various other women who actually take the beatings from a variety of father substitutes, suggest compulsions at work here. The Gothic feminist is a deeply conflicted subject who fends off the blows and manages to watch voyeuristically other women get punished for her projected crimes. Consider Emily, the heroine of Radcliffe's *The Mysteries of Udolpho* (1794), who is forced to witness her foolish aunt's murder by starvation in a deserted tower and then to unearth the truth about another aunt's murder by her husband and his lover (and thereby vicariously relive it in all its brutality). But Gothic heroines also witness the beatings and murders of men. Adeline, the heroine of Radcliffe's *The Romance of the Forest*, effectively masculinizes herself when she solves her father's beating and murder at the hands of his younger brother, the evil uncle now incestuously romancing his own niece. Not to be overlooked, Matilda dreams her father's death and then hears that it happened exactly in the manner she feared/wished. And, of course, Victor Frankenstein watches every other child in his family get beaten. The beatings that fill female Gothic novels suggest the ambivalent construction of gender that lies slightly below the surface of these texts. Gothic feminist authors appear to be very angry, while their heroines are pointedly controlled and strategically not annoyed. These heroines are characterized, unlike their creators, by repression and silence, by acceptance or at least the pose of complacency. They are what I have called "professionally feminine" (*Gothic Feminism* xv–xvi), while the projected anger of their authors can be detected only in the violence that just happens to plague anyone foolish enough to stand in the heroines' way.

The final theoretical paradigms I consistently introduce into the classroom concern the construction of the novel as a middle-class discourse system designed to condemn the aristocracy as it lauds the values of the growing bourgeoisie, the class for which the novels were written. I have designed a series of handouts that explain the theories of Norbert Elias, Mikhail Bakhtin, and

Michel Foucault, all of whom are concerned in different ways with explaining the invention of the bourgeoisie or what Elias calls the civilizing process. Elias's work traces the creation of what he calls *homo clausus* during the early modern period, an individual who will professionalize his gender and make total biological control of himself a private matter. Such an individual experiences the culturally imposed rising threshold of shame and embarrassment about bodily functions as an endorsement of increasing personal restraint, as "the institution of a wall, of something inside him separating him from the outside world" (259). According to Elias, it was the newly created and controlled public body that was given validation by bourgeois society. This public body distinguished itself from the lower social classes by its aping of the courtly value of self-control, along with its acceptance of shame as the secret sin at its bourgeois heart. It was through the imposition of such behaviors that the modern state could come into existence. Civilizing the urban space meant that educational and recreational activities were now controlled by moral censorship, while the new sensibilities made physical violence, dueling, hunting, and public displays of bodily functions all abhorrent and grossly unacceptable (126–29).

Bakhtin privileges the carnivalesque body of the early modern period. This body enacts its essentially antibourgeois values through intense releases of emotions, destroys authoritarian strictures, and challenges and inverts imposed political and religious systems. The lower classes, of course, are freest to indulge in such communal dances, while the obverse of this harmless activity would be the carnage and mob violence of the French Revolution. The struggle between these two bodies—*homo clausus* and the carnivalesque—can be seen as one locus of meaning in the female Gothic novel, although ironically the carnivalesque possibility is generally associated in these works not with lower-class women but with aristocratic practitioners of adultery, gossip, slander, and dueling or poisoning as a way of settling one's scores. A woman like Radcliffe's Emily in *The Mysteries of Udolpho* is advised by her father to conform, to conceal, to privatize, while the carnivalesque possibility is always open to her, luring her into the history of the rampaging maenad Signora Laurentini, aka Sister Agnes, the woman who poisoned Emily's aunt. These two bodies and the warfare between them characterize the shifting personae of all the polarized women in Radcliffe's works as well as of Victoria and Lilla in Dacre's *Zofloya*.

The middle class founded its status—its economic and political power—on *homo clausus*, the retentive, controlled, and concealing body. Such a body was usually coded as male and gained its power through the ability to distance others, to refuse engagement, and to mimic the scientific values of objectivity and rationality. The female body, meanwhile, was associated in this formula with diffuse energy, subjectivity, and emotionality. As Gary Kelly has observed, the construction of both the sentimental and the reasonable woman during the late eighteenth century was part of a larger ideological project, the creation of a professional middle-class discourse system that would supplant the aristocracy at the same time it gained control over and coopted the lower classes. A woman in this cultural enterprise was crucial as a pawn in the issues of property, children, and inheritance; finally she constituted a certain technology of the self that we now recognize as "virtue" and "reason" (*Women* 3–5).

The female Gothic novel, in other words, assisted in the bourgeois cultural revolution by helping to professionalize gender, by collaborating in the construction of the professionally middle-class woman and the professionally bourgeois pater familias. Women who did not conform to appropriately coded bourgeois norms—who reminded the reading audience of long discarded and disgraced aristocratic flaws like adultery, gossip, slander, and physical violence—became the targets of unlucky accidents throughout the novels (Madame Cheron is starved to death by her husband, the evil Montoni, in *The Mysteries of Udolpho*; Bertha Mason Rochester meets a fiery death in *Jane Eyre*; and there are many more such examples). Men who are coded as aristocratic, like Valancourt in *The Mysteries of Udolpho*, are allowed to survive only after they have been subjected to shootings or stabbings and thereafter effectively renounce their flawed and anachronistic tendencies.

I would claim that the Gothic feminist becomes a heroine when she establishes a new domicile with her ritualistically wounded husband, a quasi-sibling who, like her, has barely survived his brush with the oppressor and emerged chastened and appropriately and professionally gendered. When critics puzzle over the final castrated status of Rochester, blinded in one eye and missing one hand, they reveal that they do not appreciate the long heritage of wounded and feminized Gothic heroes that foreground Rochester's history. I ask my students to explain why, for instance, Valancourt receives two gunshot wounds in *The Mysteries of Udolpho*, one of them delivered supposedly by accident by his beloved's father, the mild St. Aubert. Beating fantasies emerge in the real wounds that virtually every Gothic hero is forced to endure in the female Gothic canon, and it is tempting to explain these stabbings or worse as symbolic wounds, as Bruno Bettelheim has. But Gothic heroes and heroines suffer this abuse, humiliation, and harassment from evil parental figures, and in the receiving of the wounds it is as if they have earned the right to overthrow their father and establish a new companionate family and a redeemed class—a bourgeoisie that has learned to tame its excesses and perfectly balance reason and the emotions.

I attempt finally to show my students that Gothic feminism participates, as do sentimentality and Romanticism as intellectual movements, in the broad cultural project of Enlightenment ideology—that is, making the world a safe place for feminized men and masculinized women. For Foucault, the bourgeoisie distinguished itself from both the aristocracy and the lower classes by making its sexuality and its health a primary source of its hegemony. Whereas blood was the source of the aristocracy's power, sex and its control and regulation became the predominant characteristic of the middle class, both men and women. According to Foucault, it was Sade and the first eugenists who advanced the transition from "sanguinity" to "sexuality" (*Introduction* 148). But Foucault fails to reckon with the female Gothic novelists, whose works chart in increasingly graphic detail this very shift from status and class based on blood claims to the regulation and control of one's sexuality. In their triumphant overthrow of the aristocracy and a patriarchy based on aristocratic values, most Gothic feminists finally do battle with that ultimate patriarchal family—institutionalized Christianity. The Gothic feminist usually becomes a heroine and professionally middle-class when she confronts, outwits, and destroys a terrifically corrupt monk or priest. I am thinking here of the ferocious struggle against Schedoni that occupies both Ellena and her beloved throughout the text of *The Italian.* In destroying Schedoni and Vivaldi's aristocratic mother, his evil accomplice, Ellena not only redeems her inheritance, her economy, her world, she also creates a home and companionate family that installs her and her long-lost mother as female quasi-deities. In this sense, she invents the middle-class family.

The female Gothic protagonist as cultural heroine has triumphed precisely because she brought to birth a new class—the bourgeoisie—shorn of the excesses that characterized the aristocracy and that had come to make it unfit to preside over a new, industrialized society. But in destroying and supplanting the aristocracy, the Gothic feminist accomplishes nothing less than the resacralization of her world. She excavates the buried body of her real or metaphoric mother and by doing so reinstates a fictionalized feminist fantasy: the matriarchy. In redeeming her mother, as Ellena does in *The Italian* or as Julia does for her long-imprisoned mother in *The Sicilian Romance,* or as Emily manages to do for her long-murdered aunt in *The Mysteries of Udolpho,* the Gothic heroine reasserts her inheritance in a long-lost female tradition. This act is typically represented in the texts as the rediscovery and reanimation of the mother's supposedly dead body. Further, these texts posit the end of the discourse as located in the rediscovery of a sort of female-coded epistemology embodied in the stories that these women tell one another, the lost narratives about mad nuns and bleeding mothers. The biological heritage of suffering and wounded women is transformed through this ideology into a saga of heroic triumph; the Gothic feminist text tells us that the world will be reborn and purified through the mother's—not the son's—blood. Gothic feminist heroines discover their own bodies and voices only after they redeem their mothers, and they speak in a discourse that we have come to recognize as feminism spun with Gothicism. But that voice is considerably more complex and conflicted than has previously been recognized—largely, I would claim, because its origins in Gothic and melodramatic texts have not been fully recognized.

NOTES

[1]All course syllabi, handouts, and instructional materials related to these courses can be found on my home page: www.marquette.edu/dept/engl2/faculty_pages/hoeveler.html.

[2] I am well aware that using a term like *feminism* is a complicated and controversial issue. I am also aware that feminists like Audre Lorde, Barbara Smith, et al. define their views as diametrically and explicitly opposed to bourgeois ideology. But, as bell hooks has noted, there is no one feminism, only an unending series of critiques, dissents, and renegotiations. See her "Thinking past Censorship" 4.

APPENDIX
A Summary of Freud's "A Child Is Being Beaten"

Female Version of the Beating Fantasy

Stage 1: "My father is beating the child whom I hate."
  Voyeuristic, sadistic tendencies
  "My father loves me more than this other child/rival."
Stage 2: "I am being beaten by my father."
  Deeply repressed, masochistic, erotic
Guilt over incestual attraction to father is motivating factor ("My father loves me" is transformed through guilt into "My father is beating me").
Stage 3: "A child is being beaten by a representative of my father"; "A woman is being hurt" (a teacher, authority figure).
  Voyeuristic, sadistic
  Child being beaten is usually male.
  Observer is part of a crowd watching act.
Michelle Massé, *In the Name of Love*: Freud's third stage—"'A woman is being hurt' remains the manifest arena of the Gothic" (61); an essentially dyadic relationship becomes triadic through the imposition of a voyeur, an onlooker, a reader.
Eve K. Sedgwick, "A Poem Is Being Written," observes that in the beating fantasy, the display of trauma can serve as a "free switchpoint for the identities of subject, object, onlooker, desirer, looker-away" (*Representations* 17 [1987]: 115).

Male Version of the Beating Fantasy:

Stage 1: "I am loved by my father."
State 2: "I am being beaten by my mother."
"The boy's beating-phantasy is therefore passive from the very beginning, and is derived from a feminine attitude towards his father. . . . In both male and female cases the beating-phantasy has its origin in an incestuous attachment to the father" (17: 198).

Suffering through the Gothic:
Teaching Radcliffe

Cannon Schmitt

> O ye! whom misfortune may lead to this spot,
> Learn that there are others as miserable as yourselves.
> —Pierre de La Motte,
> in Ann Radcliffe's *The Romance of the Forest*

Readers working their way through Ann Radcliffe's *The Romance of the Forest* more than two centuries after its initial publication in 1791 may well experience a shock of ironic recognition on encountering the lines that stand as my epigraph. Cut into the wall of a ruined abbey, these lines are a ruse meant to deceive soldiers pursuing Pierre de La Motte (on the run from creditors and the law in Paris) into believing he has fled to another place of hiding, leaving only a verbal testament to the misery he has endured. But the vocative "O ye!" speaks not so much from the wall to passing soldiers in the fiction as from the page directly to readers outside the fiction. Several chapters into a novel that wanders from the now unconvincing terrors of banditti and ghostlike birds to effusions on the beauties of tame deer and mists at sunrise, readers can hardly be blamed for identifying with those unfortunate souls addressed by La Motte. Such, at any rate, is the response students often have to *The Romance of the Forest* and other Gothic novels from the 1790s. Those who associate the term *Gothic* with the macabre lushness of Anne Rice or Stephen King are certain to find the productions of Radcliffe and her contemporaries disappointingly restrained. Those who expect from the British novel the high seriousness of George Eliot or Joseph Conrad may view these novels' engagement with the aesthetic, political, and philosophical issues of their day as clumsy and dilettantish. In fact, when invited to comment on the experience of reading 1790s Gothics, students initially tend to speak of it as one of estrangement. Apparently led to this spot not so much by "misfortune" as by professorial whim, they derive solace from voicing their reactions and learning that in their classmates they can indeed find others as miserable as themselves.

For teachers, of course, such a response is Gothic in its own way, the stuff of pedagogical nightmare. But in this essay I want to demonstrate that, particularly in the case of the Gothic, student resistance is worth acknowledging and even dwelling on. Itself a spectacularized form of suffering (exasperated student to sympathetic roommate: You won't believe what we have to read this week!), that resistance can readily be parlayed into a crucial realization about the Gothic: namely, that scenes of spectacular suffering are its stock in trade. Attending to a variety of such scenes in Radcliffe's *A Sicilian Romance* (1790), *The Romance of the Forest*, *The Mysteries of Udolpho* (1794), and *The Italian* (1797) provides a useful rubric for making sense of those texts. At the same time, it allows for the introduction of larger questions about generic expectations and historical context. Finally, that similar scenes recur not simply in other Gothic novels but also in more canonical texts from the same period, including William Wordsworth and Samuel Taylor Coleridge's formative *Lyrical Ballads* (1798, 1800, 1802), reveals a continuity between early Gothics and the literary movement known as Romanticism.

To students who express some difficulty in making it through Radcliffe's novels (and even to those who prefer to keep their distress to themselves), it will be apparent that, as painful as the experience may be for them, it is much more so for the novels' protagonists. Julia, the heroine of *A Sicilian Romance*, provides a case in point: raised by her stern but dissipated father from the time of her mother's (supposed) early death, forced by her father's second wife to sleep in a room regularly subject to nocturnal disturbances in the form of hollow moans and communicating by a hidden door to a long-closed and vaguely menacing section of the family castle, Julia suffers from the beginning of the novel almost until its end. In love with Hippolitus but destined by her father for marriage to a duke whose unfortunate first two wives, "subjected to his power, had fallen victims to the slow but corroding hand of sorrow," Julia herself gives in to despair when the date of the dreaded marriage is set: "At length [her father] informed her, that the nuptials would be solemnized on the third day from the present; and as he quitted the room, a flood of tears came to her relief, and saved her from fainting" (57, 60). If "flood" at first appears hyperbolic, repeated deluges reveal its simple accuracy. A partial inventory of the tears and bouts of sobbing referred to over merely the next few pages reveals that Julia's "tears flowed" (60); she "could but speak with her tears," then bravely attempts "smiling through her tears" (61, 63); "tears sprang in her eyes, and it was with difficulty she avoided betraying her emotions" (65). Finally, after fainting away, Julia, "on recovering her senses, found herself in a small room . . . with her maid weeping over her" (68). This exorbitant lachrymosity—together with the sighing, swooning, trembling, and fainting that accompany it—marks Julia as a stock character: the Gothic heroine. Like Adeline in *The Romance of the Forest*, Emily in *The Mysteries of Udolpho*, and Ellena in *The Italian*, she figures as a victim whose tribulations are registered on her body, signaled by its displays of uncontrollable anguish (see Chard; Cottom). How can we account for these convulsively and compulsively tearful female characters in the Gothic? And what does their suffering tell us about our own?

Anna Laetitia Barbauld, reviewing the history of the novel in the introduction to her fifty-volume collection entitled *The British Novelists* (1810), offers one answer to those questions with somewhat rhetorical questions of her own: "Why is it that women when they write are apt to give a melancholy tinge to their compositions? Is it that they suffer more, and have fewer resources against melancholy?" (44). In asserting a connection between the gender of a novel's author and the nature of a novel's affect, Barbauld gives early voice to an approach that would prove particularly enduring for making sense of the

Gothic and its ubiquitous imperiled heroines. Because many Gothics published in the 1790s were written by women and most feature a central female
character, it has been common to think of them as constituting a gendered
genre, what Ellen Moers terms "female Gothic." In *Literary Women* (1976),
Moers follows Barbauld's lead by dwelling on women's suffering; she views the
travails undergone by Gothic heroines as a displaced version of the realities of
life for late-eighteenth-century women (see also Fleenor). Since Moers, many
other critics have extended this interpretation. Michelle Massé, for instance,
claims that the Gothic plot, as unrealistic as it may seem, is "not an escape from
the real world but a repetition and exploration of the traumatic denial of
[women's] identity found there" ("Gothic Repetition" 688; see also her *In the
Name of Love*). And Daniel Cottom writes of the Gothic heroine that "[h]er
melodramatic situations are distillations of the fears and dangers uppermost in
the society of her time, especially as that society appeared to women" (66).

To show students how such distillations work in Radcliffe's novels, a teacher
might well ask them to turn back to *The Romance of the Forest* and consider
another moment in which, as in La Motte's inscription, misery is proclaimed
and sympathetic identification requested: "O! ye, who may hereafter read what
I now write, give a tear to my sufferings: I have wept often for the distress of
my fellow creatures!" (132). Thus the as-yet-unknown author of a manuscript
found and secretly perused by Adeline, an author who by novel's end is
revealed to be her father. Here he asks for readers' tears in response to the
details of his abduction, imprisonment, and impending execution. Adeline
meets his appeal with a declaration of sympathy that metamorphoses into a
recollection of her own afflictions: "Wretched, wretched victim! . . . O that I
had been near! Yet what could I have done to save thee? Alas! nothing. I forget that even now, perhaps, I am like thee abandoned to dangers" (140). The
analogy she suggests between a man wrongly imprisoned and incapable of
escape and a young woman without protection constructs womanhood itself as
a state of captivity and imminent peril. That peril is at once literal and figurative. Adeline faces actual dangers: the unwanted attentions of the marquis de
Montalt, one of the many depraved aristocrats who walk the pages of the
Gothic. At the same time, her vulnerability and powerful imagination combine
to suggest danger everywhere, possible betrayals in every countenance (see
Schmitt, *Alien Nation*). The suffering she undergoes, then, may be read as a
displaced version of what Radcliffe and her contemporaries knew or feared
about being a British woman in the 1790s.

This reading of *The Romance of the Forest* and, by extension, of Radcliffe's
corpus in its entirety must acknowledge, however, that in her novels neither sex
holds a monopoly on suffering. If we return to Adeline's response to her father's
request for sympathy, for instance, we realize the possibility of reading the analogy it proposes in reverse, as a rendering of the apparent frailty of men that
works by comparing their state to that of a young woman subject to unjust and
inexorable persecution. For what this episode exhibits is not simply a helpless

daughter but also a helpless father, himself victim of the rapacity of others, in this case of his half brother, the very marquis de Montalt who later pursues Adeline. Indeed, students encouraged to keep a running list as they encounter characters who suffer in Radcliffe's novels will discover that a great many men are, like Adeline, victims. More surprisingly, perhaps, given current notions about the limits of acceptable masculine emotionality, they will also discover that those men respond to victimization with their own elaborate displays of crying and trembling. To take merely one example among many, note that Valancourt in *The Mysteries of Udolpho* possesses a fount of tears easily equal to his beloved Emily's: "Convulsive sobs again interrupted his words, and they wept together in silence, till Emily . . . summoned all her fortitude to utter a last farewell" (159).

In *Equivocal Beings*, Claudia Johnson reads what she calls the "egregious affectivity" of both male and female characters in Radcliffean Gothic as one aspect of a political and cultural crisis in the 1790s, combining a sophisticated analysis of gender with another influential tradition of interpreting the Gothic that places it in connection with the British response to the French Revolution (1). One possibility for continued pursuit of the meaning of suffering in Radcliffe's novels would be to turn to some of the many studies that suggest its relation to the tribulations across the English Channel undergone by victims of the ancien régime and of the Revolution that toppled it (see M. Butler, *Romantics*; Paulson, *Representations*; Punter, "Social Relations"). At this point, however, I would propose a way to focus on spectacles of suffering in the Gothic that allows students to make connections not so much between literature and history as between two types of literature: the Gothic novel and Romantic poetry. From enumerating scenes of suffering and evaluating the degree to which they are gendered, students may proceed to an examination of the spectacular structure all such scenes share—a structure that finds a place in Romantic literary production at least in part by way of Wordsworth and Coleridge's *Lyrical Ballads*.

For suffering in the Gothic is a spectacle. Victims take center stage; their victimization never occurs in the absence of an audience. In *The Romance of the Forest*, even Adeline's father gains an audience, however belated, in his daughter. Further, he anxiously proclaims his status not only as a sufferer but also as a responsive witness of suffering himself: "[G]ive a tear to my sufferings: I have wept often for the distress of my fellow creatures!" Adeline, reading this years after it is written, weeps for a man who has wept for others, even as she demands sympathy for herself. This tableau and others like it assume the form of a *mise en abyme* in which suffering and sympathy, the twin marks of incontrovertible virtue, are endlessly repeated. Of course, like all Radcliffe's works, *The Romance of the Forest* contains frequent and pointed caveats about the dangers of succumbing to sentiment. The novel's final words recommend a careful balance between reason and feeling, noting of Adeline and Theodore's fortunate children that they "rejoiced . . . in parents whose example impressed upon their hearts the precepts offered to their understandings" (363). But if restraint and rationality are the novel's "precepts," its more powerful "example" is sentiment: again and again, onlookers take note of and weep over the sufferings of others, all the while, as in the sentimental novel, establishing their own claim to readerly interest.

It is by way of this spectacular structure that the Gothic can be connected to Romanticism. Although they both belong to the period around the turn of the century, these two types of literature are sometimes taught as if they have nothing to do with each other. Wordsworth in particular tends to be presented as the least Gothic of poets. Indeed, he writes in explicit opposition to and protest against Gothics, which figure in the "Preface" to *Lyrical Ballads* as those "frantic novels" that, together with "sickly and stupid German Tragedies, and deluges of idle and extravagant stories in verse," corrupt the common reader (Wordsworth and Coleridge 249). Like Radcliffe, though, Wordsworth is especially interested in the human mind under duress or, as he writes in the "Preface," "the manner in which our feelings and ideas are associated in a state of excitement" (247). More important still, he deploys the very structure of suffering and sympathy found in the works of Radcliffe and her Gothicizing contemporaries.

First appearing in 1798, a year after the last of Radcliffe's novels to be published during her lifetime (*The Italian*), *Lyrical Ballads* might well be included following one or more Radcliffean texts on a syllabus for a course in British literary history. Encountering Wordsworth and Coleridge's volume after a reading of any of Radcliffe's novels such as that outlined above, students should immediately recognize that Wordsworth's contributions nearly all turn on scenes of suffering and victimization. "The Female Vagrant," "Poor Susan," "The Last of the Flock," "Simon Lee," "The Mad Mother"—each poem features a central figure who, with a greater or lesser degree of eloquence and intensity, echoes the lament of Martha Ray in "The Thorn": "Oh misery! oh misery! / O woe is me! oh misery!" (78). Moreover, when asked about the position of the speaker in these poems, students familiar with Radcliffean Gothic will be able to enlist their knowledge of its characteristic structure of suffering and sympathetic response in the service of demonstrating that the Wordsworthian speaker's distinctive feature is an insistence on his feelings of compassion for those in pain (see C. Jones; Pinch).

For classroom purposes, a productive way of beginning such an analysis requires nothing more elaborate than moving back and forth between an excerpt from Radcliffe and a poem by Wordsworth. Many poems from *Lyrical Ballads* would serve, but "Michael" is especially suited to such a treatment, insofar as the incomplete sheepfold in that text occupies the same position as Adeline's manuscript in *The Romance of the Forest* or the various miniatures that circulate throughout the pages of *A Sicilian Romance*, *The Mysteries of Udolpho*, and *The Italian*. As a first step in approaching "Michael," students who have read *The Mysteries of Udolpho* might be asked to look again at a passage from the second chapter of the first volume of the novel, where Emily witnesses her father,

M St. Aubert, shedding tears over a collection of letters and a "miniature picture" that was "that of a lady, but not of her mother" (26). Refusing the palpable temptation to construe his behavior as a sign of past infidelity to her mother (or present infidelity to her mother's memory), Emily feels for her father in the throes of unaccountable sorrows—an interpretive generosity whose soundness is borne out hundreds of pages later, in the seventeenth chapter of volume three, when she learns that the miniature depicts her aunt and the tears it occasioned were those of a brother crying over a long-dead sister (660). At first glance the miniature functions as a touchstone of character, allowing Emily to enact a victory of sympathy over suspicion. It also, however, serves as the repository for a history of suffering whose details emerge only at the end of the novel: St. Aubert's sister's murder at the hands of her husband and his Italian mistress (a mistress, it should be mentioned, whose "only indulgences" during a period in which she was abandoned temporarily by the object of her affections were "to sigh and weep over a miniature" of him!) (656).

Moving from Radcliffe to Wordsworth, students directed to note any similarities between "Michael" and these episodes from *The Mysteries of Udolpho* will see at once that the unfinished sheepfold in the former functions like the miniature of Emily's aunt in the latter, that is, as a concrete embodiment of and marker for a tale of woe: Michael's loss of his son, Luke, to the dissipations of the city (or perhaps to his own unwillingness to divide the patrimonial lands he has worked for so long to make his own). As Emily's predilections and experiences teach her correctly to interpret the tale told by the miniature, so the speaker of "Michael" instructs readers in the proper way to understand the sheepfold they may encounter should they turn their steps "from the public way" (line 1). Moreover, while it involves no crime of violence, the spectacle of victimization of which the sheepfold stands as material remnant nevertheless and in good Gothic fashion provides the Wordsworthian speaker (who is also the Wordsworthian spectator) with an occasion for demonstrating the sympathetic response that makes him who he is: "this Tale . . . / . . . Led me on to feel / For passions that were not my own" (lines 27–31).

Our response, of course, also makes us who we are. Radcliffe's and Wordsworth's texts provide a model for the relationship between sufferer and witness that amounts to a model of reading. (It is, after all, a manuscript and not a dungeon that prompts Adeline tearfully to exclaim, "Wretched, wretched victim!" [140].) If the displays of suffering that appear in Radcliffe evoke from us an apparently inappropriate response—estrangement, boredom, even amusement—we and our students are not for that reason bad readers, merely readers with a different set of expectations from those of Radcliffe's contemporaries.

I have suggested that teachers can use the "suffering" we may endure reading 1790s Gothics as a point of entry, an experience in some way parallel to the trials and tribulations in the novels themselves. But more useful still may be the pronounced difference between the reaction we have and the reaction that (given the models presented to us) we are supposed to have. For that difference points up the historical specificity of generic conventions and, in doing so, brings us closer to a sense of what we mean when we refer to the Gothic. If the suffering represented in Gothic novels no longer enlists our sympathy, that fact alone goes some way toward advancing our understanding.

Teaching the Male Gothic:
Lewis, Beckford, and Stevenson

Scott Simpkins

While references to the female Gothic have become commonplace, the genre's male correlative still receives scant attention. (Kate Ferguson Ellis, Eve Kosofsky Sedgwick, Anne Williams, and Joseph Andriano are among the few to talk about the "masculine Gothic" [K. Ellis xv].) But given the large number of male Gothic writers and the ubiquitous male characters who populate the genre, classroom discussion can benefit substantially by considering its men and their often troubled versions of masculinity.

Feminist critics have clearly played a major role in demarginalizing the female subgenre of the Gothic, and their models provide fruitful inspiration for identifying a male counterpart. In effect, if feminists had not discovered the female Gothic, the male version would probably still be considered the genre's default and not gendered in its own right. In addition, feminist methodologies highlight a difficulty regarding criteria: What should be identified as significant generic markers? The author's gender? Formal components (plot, story, etc.)? Themes? The characters' gender? Gender relations? We spend the semester debating the benefits and shortcomings of these and related criteria, and students are encouraged to embrace those that seem of greatest use.

To construct a working definition of a male Gothic, we draw extensively on typological formulas such as those Anne Williams proposes in *Art of Darkness*. Williams offers especially useful formal considerations such as author identification (real names versus pseudonyms), focalization (multiple versus single points of view), narrative ends (uncertainty versus closure), plot (tragic versus happy endings), character development ("spiritual inoculation" [104] versus epiphany), emotions (horror versus terror), and "assumptions about the supernatural" (supernatural that is real versus supernatural that is explained away) (102). We then ask if features based on simple dichotomies misrepresent the more subtle distinctions between these two subgenres, or if they in fact identify characteristics that could lead to useful generalizations about the Gothic and gender.

We consider what is frequently viewed as a female clinamen (as Moers identified it in the 1970s ["Female Gothic"]) that appears to have taken place with the Gothic. In the light of the common Gothic practice of presenting the victimization of vulnerable figures, it is no surprise that female characters figure so prominently in the genre, and their treatment may well depend on an author's gender. We entertain author-based distinctions made by critics such as Juliann Fleenor, who contends that "while a male Gothicist might use incest and rape to unite good and evil, female Gothicists . . . adapted this division, modifying it into a dichotomy not between the evil man and the good woman but between the good and evil woman" (11). I use this and related critical observations on a specifically female Gothic as a springboard for identifying the difference of a male version.

My students familiarize themselves with the critical commentary on the Gothic, sampling representative (and, again, presumably nongendered) criticism along with criticism that specifically explores the Gothic's female aspects. Susan Wolstenholme's *Gothic (Re)Visions*, Diane Long Hoeveler's *Gothic Feminism*, and Ellis's *The Contested Castle* are representative of the recent scholarship that has effectively gendered the Gothic novel.

I also prompt my students to craft their own versions of a male Gothic in relation to theoretical discussions of masculinity. Works by R. W. Connell (*Masculinities*), Mary Crawford (*Talking Difference*), David Graddol and Joan Swann (*Gender Voices*), Paul Smith ("Vas"), Tim Fulford (*Romanticism and Masculinity*), Judith Lorber and Susan Farrell (*The Social Construction of Gender*), and Marlon Ross (*The Contours of Masculine Desire*) help them provisionally theorize male identity and its concomitant problems. This reading is important, because undertheorized assumptions about gender yield only blunt conclusions about the Gothic. My students are often quick to embrace those critics who needlessly assign gender attributes—so that, for instance, an overly sensitive male is feminized rather than merely inhabiting one of numerous masculine positions. By considering a host of possible masculinities, the class uncovers much more sophisticated and nuanced distinctions.

Through a conceptually thematic as opposed to historical arrangement, we sample many Gothic novels that facilitate this inquiry: Jane Austen's *Northanger Abbey* (1818), Ann Radcliffe's *The Italian* (1797), Charlotte Dacre's *Zofloya* (1806), Percy Bysshe Shelley's *Zastrozzi* (1810) and *St Irvyne* (1811), William Godwin's *Caleb Williams* (1794), Mary Shelley's *Frankenstein* (1818) and *Matilda* (1820), and Mary Wollstonecraft's *Maria; or, The Wrongs of Woman* (1798). After establishing a context for the genre, we focus extensively on three novels: William Beckford's *Vathek* (1786), Matthew Lewis's *The Monk* (1796), and Robert Louis Stevenson's *The Strange Case of Dr. Jekyll and Mr. Hyde* (1886). These three offer spectacularly conflicted depictions of masculinity as they cap our discussion of the vexed presence of men in the Gothic. They truly offer "a dramatization of conflicts between opposing ideals of masculinity" (K. Ellis 151). An issue shared among them is the problems that specifically heterosexual men face. Homosexual panic in an arena dominated by compulsory heterosexuality becomes prominent, but more prominent are the difficulties involved in successfully performing an estimable male role in a decidedly fragile, even asymmetrical, terrain that seems booby-trapped at every turn.

Our discussion of *Vathek* considers a larger (cosmic) framework of male-male opposition: that of a supreme being versus his nemesis. The activities of the male characters who strive against each other portray yet another layer of conflict, whose presence is deferred textually. By drawing on this late information first in class, we highlight the ways in which gender concerns often manifest themselves on different cognitive levels at different times, making it difficult for men to negotiate their way through social interactions. On the brink of arriving at his goal (Eblis's palace), Vathek receives one last warning from an attendant of Mahomet who had pleaded with Mahomet to save Vathek from perdition. This "good Genii" tells Mahomet that Vathek is being deceived by "his enemies" (240), not those of Mahomet specifically, but it is clear whom these enemies are really attempting to irritate by seducing this human. In fact, when Mahomet responds with "an air of indignation" to the Genii's request, his anger is directed not only at Vathek.

At the palace, Vathek and his companion in debauchery, Nouronihar, are welcomed by the Giaour, who exclaims ("with a ghastly smile"), "Ye are welcome! . . . in spite of Mahomet and all his dependents" (245). Clearly, the Giaour has been endeavoring to please Eblis by effecting the downfall of the misguided Vathek. We discuss downfall in the broader context of the Gothic economy and the dysfunction that often attends the motivations of male (and related female) characters. In his address to Vathek, Eblis even makes a point of denigrating the presumed supremacy of his opponent, additionally highlighting his previously hidden agenda.

Student debate then centers on the obvious heterosexual male components of the novel—Vathek's competition for Nouronihar against the noncompetitive, effeminate Gulchenrouz, as well as Nouronihar's desire (like that of Carathis) to gain a foothold in patriarchy's hegemony. In this dynamic, we consider Beckford's use of character design in relation to gender. Like many overcompensating men, Vathek is hyperbolically masculine yet repeatedly hampered—if not crippled—by this self-defeating investment. Gulchenrouz appears to be a caricature in the opposite direction: disablingly feminine, he is disempowered and receives a questionable reward of perpetually residing in "the pure happiness of childhood"—a point made all the more emphatic by appearing as the last words of the novel (255). The two female characters are equally disempowered, receiving eternal and severe punishment for sharing Vathek's "restless ambition" (254). Classroom commentary frequently returns to considering how these four characters are marred by their extreme positions in different gender orientations influenced by a reigning heterosexual masculinity.

We approach *The Monk* similarly, beginning with an incarcerated Ambrosio awaiting his impending death and desperately weighing his options. Debating which male to align himself with figures prominently in his thoughts. After halfhearted attempts to give himself over to Lucifer, Ambrosio finally abandons hope for redemption, and the fallen angel draws attention to the apostasy that attends this alliance. "Dare you embrace my cause?" he asks Ambrosio. "Are you prepared to renounce him who made you, and him who died for you?" (433–34). Lucifer's competition with God continues even to the last moments of the novel, when Ambrosio, facing his fate at Lucifer's mercy, is about to make a pathetic final attempt to appeal to God, an action that so infuriates Lucifer that he hastens his punishment of the monk. As this perspective reveals in class, in many respects the entire action of the novel hinges on this ostensibly gendered competition between God and Lucifer.

The local, noncosmic male conflicts in the novel, like those in *Vathek*, also receive a great deal of consideration in class. For instance, Lucifer points out (again at the end) that he played on Ambrosio's decidedly human—and arguably male—vulnerabilities to seduce him into abandoning God. That Ambrosio's initial sensual appreciation for Matilda cools dramatically and is displaced by a fervent longing for the unreachable Antonia demonstrates further that Ambrosio is ensnared in a self-defeating conception of heterosexual masculinity.

The subplot between Don Lorenzo and Don Raymond / Alphonso provides another point for discussion as they enact a triangulated dynamic centered on Agnes. (A similar triangle is the bid by the Baroness Lindenberg for Don Alphonso, which requires him to remove his own love interest, Agnes.) Like Carathis and Nouronihar, Donna Elvira and (at least seemingly) Matilda appear as women unfortunately caught up in a masculine economy fraught with contradictory codes of conduct. Given the prominence in recent scholarship of gender and sex issues, we inevitably focus on Ambrosio's incestuous act and Lewis's use of cross-dressing through the Rosario/Matilda figure assumed by "a subordinate but crafty spirit" (440) from Lucifer's realm, two developments with considerable significance in relation to the conflicted vortices of masculinity.

In keeping with this classroom approach, the final section of *The Strange Case of Dr. Jekyll and Mr. Hyde*, "Henry Jekyll's Full Statement of the Case," is our point of entry with its substantial information about what has already occurred. We see the full revelation of events reconfigured by a closing development and speculate on the import of this Gothic deferral in relation to masculine practices of concealment—a prominent issue itself in Jekyll's own practices, as he recounts them.

In Stevenson's novel, Jekyll is not a pawn between two superpowers but instead is pitted against his two selves and the strictures of masculine propriety, as is reflected in his interactions with his male friends. His friends face the same strictures: their investment in propriety makes it increasingly difficult for them to consort with Jekyll since they would risk contact stigma (as is also seen in Wilde's *The Picture of Dorian Gray*). In his "Statement," Jekyll discusses his struggle with his "two natures" (79) in a manner that superbly dramatizes the potentially disabling manifestations of masculinity that men frequently face and, more important in Jekyll's case, feel they must hide from other men. We ask: What is Stevenson suggesting about men and their discontents in this statement? Can men find secure expression only under secretive conditions that prevent them from interacting with others? Does the threat of disclosure outweigh the possibility of communal bonding? And, as with Jekyll's friends, is even bonding of this nature itself a threat to masculine (and necessarily autonomous) individuation?

Jekyll's account of the vibrant joy he experiences through his Hyde self ties these three novels together, for the euphoric liberation that Hyde feels is undeniable, serving to open new vistas of subjecthood for Jekyll that he had denied himself in order to maintain sufficiently heterosexual, manly gravity. By transforming himself, Jekyll notes, he discovered "a solution of the bonds of obligation" (82), a freedom that provides an outlet for far greater self-fulfillment. But the attendant cost of this transformation is great, and our classroom discussion centers on the attraction-repulsion that Jekyll faces in the course of his experiments, and on the implication that male fulfillment comes at the loss of one's more limited, social self. We consider whether, by embracing a dissonantly multiplicitous self, Jekyll/Hyde somehow becomes more complete as a man, or whether to the contrary Stevenson is suggesting that the residual dichotomies of masculinity cannot be happily melded into a homogeneous self because their oppositions are inherently polar. The same polarity holds for Vathek and Ambrosio, figures of great achievement who nevertheless cannot find satisfaction through a lesser, single-faceted self and are thus driven to self-destruction as a consequence. Yet, like Jekyll, it appears that they too are the most engaged in their lives when they are stridently violating the public images of manhood they have embraced, by pursuing what Jekyll refers to as "the lethal side of man" (83).

We emphasize this last point in relation to heterosexual masculinity insofar as it can be freighted with many usually unremarked difficulties. This is initiated in class by exploring several masculinist critics. David Rosen's commentary on "role stress" in *The Changing Fictions of Masculinity* provides a handy concept for classroom discussion along these lines. Rosen argues that masculinity is often conceived in conflicting ways, so that each man striving to perform manly behavior may well experience "abrasion" as a result (xiii). Since all men are presumably vulnerable to this gender dissonance, it is easy to imagine how it could lead to disastrous consequences for their interpersonal relations.

Perhaps the most empowering component of gender studies is the opportunity it offers for readers to draw on personal experience. Even better, I have found through class exchanges, is the possibility of imaginative imputation of gendered responses as an extension of one's own experience. We also explore essays such as Jonathan Culler's "Reading as a Woman" at this point, along with Norman Holland and Leona Sherman's "Gothic Possibilities," to prompt commentary about strategies for reading as a man. Gothic novels themselves provide numerous invitations to speculate in this fashion. Indeed, if Anne Mellor was correct by suggesting (in 1993) that "our current cultural and scholarly descriptions of that historical phenomenon we call Romanticism are unwittingly gender-biased" (*Romanticism* 1), the classroom is a good place to try to thicken these descriptions.

Teaching the Homosocial in Godwin, Hogg, and Wilde

Ranita Chatterjee and Patrick M. Horan

In our current climate of teaching theory to savvy or politically aware students, questions of gender, sexuality, class, and race inevitably arise in discussions of the Gothic novel. As numerous recent critical works by David Punter (*Literature*), George Haggerty (*Gothic Fiction*), Kate Ferguson Ellis, Michelle A. Massé (*In the Name*), Anne Williams, and Judith Halberstam have variously suggested, if the Gothic novel is the preeminent genre of libidinal desires, it is also an intensely political genre. By displaying the simultaneous attraction and repulsion of eroticism—its desire and anxiety—Gothic novels expose the contradictions inherent in society, contradictions that strike our undergraduate students, whether in British Romanticist, Victorian, modernist, or critical theory classes, as especially contemporary and relevant to their own lives.

Although Eve Sedgwick has notably defined Gothic fiction as inherently paranoid and homophobic because its subject matter by definition is heterosexuality (*Between Men* 116), teaching the novels of William Godwin, James Hogg, and Oscar Wilde together intimates something else. In discussing the signature works of these three writers, students can explore the diverse spectrum of what might be called masculine Gothic fiction, ranging from the suggestively homoerotic world of political intrigue in Godwin's 1794 *Things As They Are; or, The Adventures of Caleb Williams*, which is neither clearly homophobic nor heterosexual; to the psychologically lurid and religious scenes of class conflicts in Hogg's 1824 *Private Memoirs and Confessions of a Justified Sinner*, which is located in the specifics of Scottish nationalism; and to the significantly modern homosexual and aesthetic concerns of Wilde's 1891 *The Picture of Dorian Gray*, whose thematization of same-sex relationships is not only powerfully attractive but also potentially salvific, as critic Claude Summers notes (21). All our students, whether they identify as homosexual or heterosexual, are usually able to recognize both the Gothic elements and their inextricable connections to eroticism, politics, and aesthetics in these works. Indeed, we have found that those students who are not openly gay or lesbian particularly appreciate these three writers' need to express their sexuality or that of their characters in a guarded fashion. Although in this essay we primarily discuss the two novels that we teach regularly, *Caleb Williams* and *Dorian Gray*, Hogg's text does serve as a useful bridge to explore the role of male paranoia in homosocial relations, a bridge between its implicit expression in Godwin's novel and its explicit expression in Wilde's. For a richly layered discussion of homoeroticism in Hogg's work, we refer readers to Sedgwick's important analysis in *Between Men* (97–117).

While we discuss *Caleb Williams* as a fictional version of Godwin's Enlightenment critique of the sociopolitical system of 1790s Britain, what captures the imagination of students is the novel's themes of surveillance and forbidden curiosity, especially in the ambiguously homosocial relationship between Ferdinando Falkland and the eponymous hero. We begin by asking our students to consider the genre of Caleb's tale (biography, autobiography, confession): Why does Caleb need to vindicate his character in the face of Falkland's false charges? As a first-person narrator, how reliable is Caleb? Why does he describe his patron both as a desirable and worthy individual and as the most heinous representative of the tyranny of the upper classes? Since Godwin wrote two conclusions for his novel, which are provided in one volume in David McCracken's edition, we also ask students to write an essay justifying their preference of ending. They are asked to discuss either how the original, unpublished conclusion (in which Caleb descends into madness) affects their view of Caleb as narrator or how the published ending (in which Caleb, though able to extract Falkland's confession of murder, does so with guilt, remorse, and self-deprecation) affects their understanding of Caleb's desire for Falkland.

This first assignment enables us to discuss the complicated relation between Caleb's desire and the Gothic narrative that he authors. We point out that at the heart of Caleb's story is Falkland's confession that he is the "murderer of Tyrrel" and the "assassin of the Hawkinses" (135). Students rightly observe that while this revelation confirms Caleb's worst fears about his employer, it does not entirely justify Falkland's relentless persecution of Caleb. We ask students to consider why Falkland is so persistent in his tyrannical surveillance of Caleb's actions, considering that Caleb's disfranchised position in society makes him a far less credible person than Falkland, whose social status empowers him to use the available political and juridical structures to his advantage.

To foreground the homosocial dynamics of the male relationships in the novel, we also get students to sketch out the role and function of the female characters in Godwin's novel. Students generally notice that although women are remarkably not portrayed in their traditional Gothic roles as pure maidens in distress or evil seductresses, neither are they desirable victims or lovers. This insight can be used to encourage students to consider the narrative position of Caleb: How does Emily's interest in Falkland parallel that of Caleb for his master in the second half of the novel? Why does Caleb describe Emily's tale as "those incidents in which my own fate was so mysteriously involved" (79)? A close reading with students can further reveal that the similarities between Emily's and Caleb's position relative to Falkland may point to Caleb's superiority to Emily as an object for Falkland's affections.

Like the other female characters, Emily is less than attractive and serves more to justify the relations among men—in her case to connect Tyrrel to Falkland—than to be an object of desire for either man. As students note, her passion for Falkland, which leads to her death, foregrounds in the absence of any other male-female couple the fact that female desire must be brutally sacrificed for the exploration of male desire in the political economy of Godwin's narrative. This section of the class discussion can then be productively connected to the earlier one on genre by our noting that Godwin's inclusion of Emily's romantic tragedy as an embedded episode in the narrative of Caleb's desire for Falkland further indicates that Godwin could portray female desire and sexuality only as a figure of sympathy and cautionary instruction for male desire. It is in Caleb's recollections of Mr. Collins's memory of Emily that we hear about her failed romance and pathetic death. Emily, then, becomes according to Alex Gold a "prophetic emotional 'double'" in Caleb's eyes (141–42).

Once students appreciate how *Caleb Williams* can be read as a homosocial narrative, we turn to specific problematic incidents and scenes that suggestively point to the queer dimensions of Godwin's political Gothic novel. Some of the most compelling moments to consider are the garden scene, in which Caleb experiences an orgasmic rush of passions on confirming that Falkland is a murderer (129); the fire scene, in which Caleb is caught by Falkland's gaze furtively checking the contents of Falkland's private trunk (132); the parodic scene of conjugal consummation shortly afterward, in which Falkland confesses to the murder and tells Caleb he shall "always hate" him until "death or worse" (136); and the published ending, in which Caleb's desire for Falkland seems to be fulfilled in the narration of the embrace between the two men. An analysis of these scenes still meets with resistance from some students who have difficulty with the potential homoerotic aspects of Caleb's narration. Thus we usually leave the discussion of Falkland's earlier association with the vulgar Barnabas Tyrrel, and particularly his relationship with Emily, for later class discussion. We suggest to students that they reconsider the changes in Tyrrel's attitude to Emily and the reasons behind his increasing hostility toward her.

As students begin to realize, the real interactions in Godwin's novel occur between men: between Falkland and Count Malvesi; between Falkland and the poet Mr. Clare; between Falkland and Tyrrel; between Tyrrel and his agent of destruction, Grimes; between Tyrrel and his steward of injustice, Barnes; between Tyrrel and his tenant, Hawkins; between Falkland and Hawkins; between Falkland and his henchman, Gines; and finally between Falkland and Caleb. Not only do these male-male pairings mirror and reinforce one another, but they also replicate the tropes of homoerotic anxiety.

A queer reading of Godwin's *Caleb Williams*, then, leads students to explore two crucial issues: the foregrounding of the fictional autobiographical genre of Caleb's story prompts students to discuss why his ostensible narrative of vindication indulges in depicting male homoerotic moments, and a close attention to Godwin's use of language raises the question of how Caleb's narrative contains and yet stimulates the suggestive potential of homoeroticism with the prohibitive controls (and Gothic staples) of fear, punishment, and dread.

Like Godwin's novel, Hogg's *Confessions of a Justified Sinner* places its main characters in a homosocial environment that presents opportunities for same-sex relationships. Teaching *Confessions* as an example of the devil's (Gil-Martin's) influence over a young man (Robert Wringhim) ignores the fact that Robert's attraction to Gil is more than a Gothic fascination with evil and subsequent struggles to resist the devil. Teaching *Confessions* as a satire on the extreme forms of Calvinism infecting Scottish society is also relevant. Fanatical Calvinism actually had its historical and theological source in one branch of Antinomian belief, while the Antinomians themselves were a sect that in the early 1500s believed that children of grace would be saved regardless of how evil they acted (an extreme interpretation of Paul's biblical injunction that we are saved by grace alone [Eph. 2.8–9]). A more interesting approach for students is to examine Hogg's story as an example of how homosocial environments are powerfully seductive but potentially unsettling for those who are ambivalent about their sexuality.

As in *Caleb Williams*, suggestive scenes (although perhaps much less suggestive and certainly less obvious than in *Dorian Gray*) point to the queer dimensions of Hogg's narrative. After Robert meets Gil-Martin, we learn that he comes to despise and abhor the beauty of women and eventually finds the idea of an amorous relationship with a woman absurd. We also see Robert become more and more captivated by Gil, almost to the point of obsession; consequently, he willingly obeys Gil's wicked commands. Although *Confessions* is not primarily a love story, obsession and desire figure in the narrative. Our students, especially those questioning their sexual orientation, are understandably intrigued by the obsessive attraction that these two young men share.

Like Robert, the title character of Wilde's *Dorian Gray* becomes drawn to (and more obviously sexually attracted to) a dominant male character who both fascinates and frightens him. When we discuss *Dorian Gray* in our literature classes, students clearly see that modern themes are presented in this typically Gothic narrative, which includes melodramatic characters and supernatural occurrences. Interestingly, as he did in his plays and short stories, Wilde chose a conventional form to express radical ideas.

Even though the principal gay male characters in *Dorian Gray* are often melodramatic, our students, whether homosexual or heterosexual, usually identify with at least one of them: the beautiful but manipulative Dorian, the cleverly witty but subversive Lord Henry Wotton, or the sensitive but priggish artist Basil Hallward. Our students do not, however, identify with the characters in the 1945 film version, which sentimentalizes Wilde's novel, underplays the homosexual relationships, and fabricates additional heterosexual romantic entanglements for Dorian. Nonetheless, we show students this film because it illustrates the narrative's Gothic elements and because its weaknesses help reveal the strengths of Wilde's original work. We view the film only after class lectures and discussions have encouraged close readings of the narrative.

Our class lectures usually lead up to Wilde's theme that homosexual relationships share essentially the same frustrations and fulfillments as heterosexual ones. In class discussions, therefore, we inevitably compare the heterosexual romance between Dorian and Sybil Vane with the homosexual partnerships that he shares with Lord Henry and Basil. As in Godwin's and Hogg's narratives, homosocial attraction is excitingly dangerous, because it is not socially sanctioned and inevitably leads to fascination and near obsession with male-male desire. Ultimately, the homosexual partners are bonded intellectually rather than physically, which is understandable given that physical relationships between men were not only socially taboo but also illegal in Victorian society. Lord Henry and Basil are mesmerized by Dorian's beauty in much the same way that the young man idealizes Sybil. To a certain extent, their attraction and consequent intellectualizing recall Caleb's interest in Falkland and Robert's obsession with Gil-Martin.

Our students inevitably remark that these intellectualized homosexual relationships are much more communicative (and thus emotionally healthier) than the conventional heterosexual marriages. Lord Henry continually converses with Dorian (in fact, the most witty and perhaps the most memorable sections of the narrative are those chapters in which Lord Henry relates to Dorian his philosophy of life), yet he cannot share his thoughts with his wife. Tellingly, Lady Wotton tells Dorian that she hears her husband's views only from his friends.

Promoting same-sex relationships as communicative and emotionally healthy seems oddly out of place in the Gothic. Yet our students quickly recognize that Basil, the artist, and Dorian, the model, are united in their shared homosexuality; this union helps explain why Basil's painting reveals the soul of the artist as well as the model. Moreover, our students appreciate Claude Summers's observation that Wilde presents Basil Hallward as the most obviously homosexual character and also the most morally sensitive, which counters the stereotyped notion that homosexuality is decadent (21).

Fear of being condemned by homophobic peers is as real for many of our students as it was for Wilde, causing them to empathize with Basil, the repressed homosexual, who worries that he will be punished for his desires. Many of our closeted bisexual students no doubt empathize with Dorian, who lives a double life; like him they must want to explore their homosexuality but also fear being ridiculed for their sexual orientation. Therefore they most likely understand how Dorian can associate with male prostitutes and at the same time flirt with the eligible women of his social milieu. Even some heterosexual students (especially those from repressive home environments) appreciate his ambivalence toward his sexuality and his need to pass as a heterosexual.

Since our homosexual and lesbian students are all too often ridiculed for their sexual orientation, we teach *Dorian Gray* to help validate their sexuality and to help educate heterosexual students about the naturalness of same-sex relationships. Inevitably we talk about how brave Wilde was to present such radical issues and how clever he was to promote homosexuality in the popular genre of the Gothic novel. His narrative, like *Caleb Williams* and *Confessions*,

is exciting to teach because the Gothic elements keep even the most unmoti-
vated students interested, while the underlying same-sex attractions presented
in the homosocial environments of these very different novels challenge
inquisitive and analytic students both to assess their own sexuality and to
appreciate sexual diversity in others.

Teaching the Gothic Novel
and Dramatic Adaptations

Marjean D. Purinton

The British stage and novel of the late eighteenth and early nineteenth centuries promulgated the Gothic in fascinating and interconnected ways—"incestuous ways," to use a term often associated with Gothic relationships that the reading and theatergoing public of the Romantic period would have enjoyed. Stories of supernatural fiction were dramatized, and the mechanisms, tropes, and characters of Gothic fiction became the elements of Gothic drama and melodrama. Although E. J. Clery's analysis of the Gothic locates the place of supernatural fictions in the "reading revolution of the day" (*Rise* 1–10), the theater revolution was equally significant in the production, popularization, and commercialization of Gothic. For us to read Gothic fiction and drama dialogically, as they operated culturally, opens new pedagogical and critical spaces. Reading Gothic novels through the lens of Gothic drama informs our reading, helps us make sense of it and perceive the historical and cultural pressures of the Romantic period that generated Gothic forms. One approach to teaching the Gothic novel is therefore to read it in tandem with Gothic drama, an approach that also helps explain why the Gothic was so popular and continues to fascinate us today.

In addition to being an actual site where Gothic stories were staged, the theater functioned as a culturally defining metaphor for Gothic material. In other words, the elements that came to be generally recognized as Gothic appeared in fiction in theatricalized terms. Mary Wollstonecraft asserts in the preface to *Maria; or, The Wrongs of Woman* (1798) that great misfortunes impress readers because of their "*stage-effect*" (6). During one of her visits to Paris, Wollstonecraft may have witnessed a stage performance with phantasmagoria, a magic-lantern show developed by Philippe Jacques de Loutherbourg that produced optical illusions, for she uses it as a metaphor for memory in her novel (Clery, *Rise* 146). The theater functioned as a politically charged metaphor in much French revolutionary discourse, drawing on the ways in which actual political events were theatricalized as spectacles (see, e.g., Bruhm, *Gothic Bodies* 63–73; J. Cox, "French Revolution"; Carlson 30–62).

The theater further served as a structuring device for Gothic fiction. We can read each woman's story in Wollstonecraft's *Maria* as a dramatic vignette delivered in soliloquy. Maria, in fact, sees herself in theatrical terms. Recalling how her uncle introduced her to some literary society, she remarks:

> The theatres were a never-failing source of amusement to me. My delighted eye followed Mrs. Siddons, when, with dignified delicacy, she played Califta; and I involuntarily repeated after her, in the same tone, and with a long-drawn sigh, Hearts like our's were pair'd not match'd.
> (76)

Paul Ranger notes that many of Henry Tilney's descriptions of picturesque scenes in Jane Austen's *Northanger Abbey* (1818) are cast in language that replicates the structural features of the Georgian stage (25). Interrogations about the performative nature of gender and identity are played out in the rehearsals of Elizabeth Inchbald's *Lovers' Vows* (1798) at the center of Austen's novel *Mansfield Park* (1813), which, although not an ostensibly Gothic novel, includes Gothic elements. Joseph Litvak claims that the novel is about the theatricality of everyday life that can only be repressed, not eliminated (1–26). Much Gothic fiction can be read as drama, structurally defined by production devices particular to the stage.

Novels Adapted for Drama

Playwrights were quick to appropriate plots of Gothic novels for their work. These adaptations in turn created a larger demand for Gothic fiction. Although numerous Gothic novels were recast as dramas, a few adaptations are particularly suited for classroom use. Horace Walpole's *The Castle of Otranto* (1764) was dramatized as *The Count of Narbonne* in 1781 by Robert Jephson. Matthew Lewis wrote the drama *Raymond and Agnes* (1809), based on the ghost-of-the-bleeding-nun episode of his novel *The Monk* (1796). Another dramatic adaptation of *The Monk* was James Boaden's *Aurelio and Miranda* (1798). Lewis's novel was also staged as a ballet, *Raymond and Agnes; or, The Castle of Lindenbourgh* (1797). Boaden's play *Fontainville Forest* (1794) was adapted from Ann Radcliffe's novel *The Romance of the Forest* (1791) and offered what Jeffrey N. Cox claims was the most famous ghost scene before the one at the ending of Lewis's Gothic drama *The Castle Spectre* (1797) (Introduction 33). Boaden's play *The Italian Monk* (1797) was based on Radcliffe's novel *The Italian* (1797). James Robinson Planché wrote a Gothic stage version of John Polidori's story " The Vampyre" (1819). Planché's *The Vampire; or, The Bride of the Isles* (1820) was set in Scotland because his acting company had a wardrobe of kilts that they needed to use (MacDonald 292).

Teaching texts of these dramatic adaptations are accessible. *The Castle Spectre* is included in Cox's *Seven Gothic Dramas, 1789–1825*, a collection that also contains Richard Brinsley Peake's *Presumption; or, The Fate of Frankenstein*. Steven Cohan's facsimile edition of *The Plays of James Boaden* includes *Fontainville Forest*, *The Italian Monk*, and *Aurelio and Miranda*. Donald Roy's edition of *Plays by James Robinson Planché* includes *The Vampire; or, The Bride of the Isles*.

Mary Shelley's novel *Frankenstein; or, The Modern Prometheus* (1818) was made popular by stage versions by Robert Brinsley Peake, *Presumption; or, The Fate of Frankenstein* (1823); by Henry M. Milner, *Frankenstein; or, The Man and the Monster* (1826); and by John Atkinson Kerr, *The Monster and Magician; or, The Fate of Frankenstein* (1826), among the numerous dramatic adaptations of the novel in England and in France (see Steven Forry's anthology of the dramatizations of *Frankenstein*). Godwin accompanied Mary Shelley to a performance of Peake's *Presumption* in 1823, and in a letter to Leigh Hunt she comments about the theatricalization of her story, about T. P. Cooke's portrayal of the monster, and about the audience's reaction to the melodrama:

> But lo & behold! I found myself famous. Frankenstein has prodigious success as a drama and was about to be repeated for the 23rd night at the English opera house. . . . The story is not well-managed—but Cooke played ———'s part extremely weak, his seeking as it were for support, his trying to grasp at the sound he heard, all indeed he does well imagined and executed. I was much amused, and it appeared to excite a breathless eagerness in the audience.   (*Letters* 378)

Because these plays constitute the basis for subsequent cinematic adaptations of Shelley's novel, they are an important link between *Frankenstein* as novel and as film that most students do not know.

The Gothic Stage

Describing to students the Romantic-period theater and the conditions under which Gothic plays were staged helps them visualize how Gothic took on public, collective, material, and popular forms and helps them read dramatic adaptations of Gothic novels. The theater of the late eighteenth and early nineteenth centuries was especially well suited to staging Gothic. It literalized the Cartesian mind/body dichotomy, sensationalizing the dynamic of corporeality/mentality at the core of Gothic fiction. On the stage, Gothic takes on a potentially dangerous, and perhaps even subversive, physicality. Its excesses of pain and pleasure, instruction and delight, horror and allurement are made material, enhanced by the optical effects and production strategies of the theater. Confounding gendered private and public spaces, theater makes public those private experiences fiction renders individually to its readers. In the auditorium, reactions are shared collectively, and the audience itself becomes a player in the Gothic performance.

From 1837 to 1843, the Licensing Act created three patent theaters, Covent Garden and Drury Lane during the regular season (September through June) and the Haymarket Theatre during the summer. Dramas produced at these theaters were regulated, and therefore censored, by the lord chamberlain (John Larpent and then George Colman the Younger as examiner of the plays from 1778 to 1836), who determined what was appropriate for the stage. Dramas that included sensitive religious, political, and sexual subjects were frequently rejected. No references to female body parts could be made; no obscenities were allowed to be uttered; no sacrilegious topics were permitted. Political material that might excite riots, uncontrollable behavior, and revolutionary thinking was carefully monitored. Gothic that could not pass the censorship of the lord chamberlain was often staged in the minor theaters, which were not so closely scrutinized but which were not permitted to perform drama that was only spoken. In other words, dramas performed at the minor theaters had to include music, opera, pantomime, farce, and spectacle. Furthermore, censorship could occur at several levels; scripts could be altered by theater managers, actors, and even the audience after being licensed by the examiner of the plays.

Students should be aware of the staging location and history of the Gothic drama they read. They also need to understand that as a performance medium, Romantic drama can sometimes be found in more than one version: the play submitted to the examiner, the censored and revised play licensed for performance, the prompt scripts, and the published drama. The censorship instituted by the Licensing Act makes a fundamental difference between Gothic read as fiction and Gothic staged in the theater. Students need to be alert to material that might have been censored, altered from the novel, or cleverly disguised and made latent in a play. These differences between the private venue of the Gothic novel consumed by the individual reader and the public site of Gothic drama performed for a collective audience are important considerations in teaching dramatic adaptations of Gothic novels. For discussions of censorship and theatrical legislation, direct students to L. W. Conolly, Joseph Donohue (8–56), Marilyn Gaull (81–95), and Jane Moody.

Because the theater was a popular social experience and event, students might want to explore how Gothic was staged and how the theater's physicality, staging machinery, stylized acting, and audience responses affected the action and dialogue. For this information I direct them to Ranger (42–89), Donohue (105–26), and Richard Leacroft (118–219). Audience attention was generally divided between the onstage performance and offstage activities (eating, drinking, picking pockets, talking, flirting). Spectators frequently provided immediate criticism by shouting at the performers and throwing things onstage. Stories featuring physical extravagance in plots and spectacular scenic effects secured audience attention. Students might investigate the special effects used to stage Gothic drama, the scenography, Loutherbourg's Eidophusikon, the panoramas and dioramas, and James Planché's Vampire Trap, for example (Ranger 90–105; J. Heller 11– 27). Performers adopted acting styles to accommodate the larger acting spaces and to overcome unruly, inattentive audiences. They used ranting and bombast in the delivery of speeches and relied on a codified body language to portray recognizable postures. The cult of stardom evolved from the Romantic stage. A Gothic favorite, T. P. Cook dazzled audiences in various monster and comic roles, including Frankenstein's creature and Planché's vampire (see Donohue 57–83; Gaull 95–101; Backscheider, *Spectacular Politics* 189–233). The stereotypes of Gothic and melodrama were inherently theatrical; conversely, the stage gave life to the characters of Gothic fiction that functioned in performative roles.

Pedagogical Strategies

When students read passages out loud, they can hear the dramatic nature of the language in the novels, or in some instances the language lifted from the novels. I encourage them to read in character and with special vocal effects (creaking doors, whispers, screams) so that they can discuss the theatricalized scene as rendered on their mental stage by the novel. The scene between Aurelio and Miranda in act 4 of Boaden's play *Aurelio and Miranda* is an excellent one to read aloud. The rescue scene (5.3) can even be enacted in the classroom and then compared with the ending of the novel. Another way for students to see the inherently theatrical or dramatic nature of Gothic fiction is to ask them to select a scene from a novel and rewrite it for performance. In addition to letting them perform their little drama, I ask them to identify what scene they selected, what changes they made to the novel and why. Students often have to restructure fictive scenes that incorporate multiple narrators. A popular group activity among both undergraduates and graduate students, this conversion simulates for them the actual adaptation process of Gothic writers, and it makes them more aware of the differences and similarities between the two genres.

One way for students to perceive the interconnectedness of Gothic fiction and drama is to perform a comparative textual analysis of excerpts from Shelley's novel *Frankenstein* and Peake's melodrama *Presumption*. I ask them how our perceptions of the monsters vary as a result of the two presentations and how the familial relationships operate differently in the novel and play. Their responses inform the reading of the creature's birth passage in the novel (the very beginning of 1.5) and the play (1.2). In both accounts, Victor is the speaker. I divide the students into teams, encourage them to read each passage aloud, and ask them to respond to the following questions: In what ways are the two passages similar and different (e.g., the ordering of the narrative, the adjectives Victor uses to describe his creation and himself, the major rhetorical passages, the tone)? Which account gives readers more interpretative freedom? How does seeing an audience affect the presentation? Are the creatures depicted similarly? How is Victor characterized? In which passage does Victor seem less human, more like the monster?

I ask students to present evidence that Peake read or used Shelley's novel, then I ask in what ways his adaptation changes the language, the effect of the novel. I ask them to consider what differences might be expected by going from one genre to the other. I ask them whether the gender difference between the writers might account for textual differences. They generally find it curious that Shelley allows the women no direct voice and little agency in the novel, with the possible exception of Safie. They point out that Peake's women are not especially strong and independent, that they are in fact rather stereotypically feminine. My students note how the relationships among the characters are changed significantly in the melodrama, and we discuss the political and social implications of those changes. Finally, I let students pick the passage they find more engaging and ask them why. Peake's drama has influenced various film adaptations of the novel and so has helped ensure the enduring popularity of the monster and its creator. *Mary Wollstonecraft Shelley: Frankenstein, the Making of the Monster* (1994), a fifty-minute video made by Films for the Humanities and Sciences, provides an excellent introduction to the comparative analysis activity. It includes excerpts from Milner's 1826 melodrama *The Man and the Monster* that shows students the stage lighting and exaggerated acting styles that would have been used for productions of Peake's *Presumption*.

Boaden's adaptation of Radliffe's *The Romance of the Forest* was performed at Covent Garden on 25 March 1794. Its elaborate staging and its ghost made it a huge success. According to Cohan, the major dramatic transformation of the novel is that there is no rational explanation for the corporeal presence of the ghost onstage. When Adeline returns to the secret apartment to read the manuscript that reveals her father's murderer, the ghost of her earlier dreams actually appears and speaks to her. The ghost, claims Cohan, is not a projection of overworked female fancy but a "real" specter (x–xv). While Boaden says in the play's epilogue that he does not "give up the ghost" for the stage production despite pressures to do so (*Plays* 69), I am not altogether convinced that the ghost scenes in the two versions have to be seen in absolute terms of mental or physical projections.

The appearance of the ghost to Adeline in the drama and the novel makes for another project of comparative analysis, but this time I ask students to consider the gender-specific implications of both accounts. Do spectators of Boaden's drama imagine Adeline as a hysterical woman, there being no rational explanation for her seeing the phantom? Are readers of Radcliffe's novel convinced that the specter is merely a figment of Adeline's overactive imagination? How much of our reading of text/body is conditioned by our cultural understandings of psychology, medicine, and epistemology? What critical baggage would Radcliffe's and Boaden's readers/spectators bring to bear in the reading of Adeline (as text/body)? How much of her reaction in the drama is performative, imitative of stereotypically female responses to Gothic? How does the narrator's interpretation shape readers' responses in the novel? Such questions lead to an examination of the ways in which both Gothic fiction and theater confound and explode the binary relations of masculine and feminine, private and public, body and spirit.

The optical and special effects of the stage challenged spectators to imagine the absence of substance or body even as, in some productions (such as Boaden's), the ghost's stage appearance requires a visibility (even physicality) that it seeks to deny. Boaden explains how he sought to solve this staging problem: "The great contrivance was, that the spectre should appear through a blueish-grey gauze, so as to remove the too corporeal effect of a live actor and convert the moving substance into a gliding essence" (*Memoirs* 117). Perhaps,

I challenge students, the possibility of alternative spaces imagined as Gothic is best perceived when we consider them in the contexts of both fiction and drama; perhaps we might not be able to see them at all if we consider one genre at the exclusion of the other.

Another issue I have raised with Radcliffe's and Boaden's Gothics involves the influence of scientific activities that rendered what I term "techno-Gothic grotesques and ghosts" (135), Gothic conventional forms infused with new significations by the scientific and medical discourses and experimentation (technologies) of the late eighteenth and early nineteenth centuries. My argument is that the spectacular staging of science may, in fact, explain the predominance of Gothic and melodrama as dramatic genres during the Romantic period (Purinton). While Gothic drama was often associated with cultural hysteria as a response to political turbulence following the French Revolution, the psychological and pathological responses of Gothic females, like Adeline of Radcliffe's novel, can be seen as instances of medicine theatricalized in Boaden's drama. That is, madness and hysteria may relate to the politics of the day, but they may also reflect ways in which cultural preoccupations about science are being staged. Some students see how the techno-Gothic drama complicates with new explanations the novel's unnatural phenomena and forbidden passions.

In a graduate course on Romantic drama and theater, I directed students to the scientific studies of Anton Mesmer, Thomas Beddoes (whose son, Thomas Lovell Beddoes, wrote Gothic dramas; see Beddoes and Watt), Thomas Trotter, George Cheyne, and Jane Marcet, who all were exploring the medical and biological bases for the conditions enacted by Gothic heroines on the stage. I also asked students to investigate the prevailing explanations of ghosts, both scientific and imaginative (e.g., Samuel Taylor Coleridge [*Biographia*, esp. ch. 23 in vol. 2], Charles Lamb, Thomas Love Peacock). Students consider how playwrights might use techno-Gothic strategies of staging science to deflect censorship of content that novelists could discuss more explicitly. Other Gothic dramas featuring spectacular ghost scenes are Joanna Baillie's *Orra* (1812), Margaret Harvey's *Raymond de Percy; or, The Tenant of the Tomb* (1822), Charles Robert Maturin's *Bertram; or, The Castle of St. Aldobrand* (1816) and *The Castle Spectre* (1797).

Reading Gothic fiction and drama dialogically not only replicates the conditions under which both were produced and received during the late eighteenth and early nineteenth centuries but also emphasizes the ways in which Gothic functions as a theoretical and interpretative paradigm, a cognitive and cultural structure that responds to historical and societal pressures. This comparative approach helps students move beyond the window dressing of Gothic tropes and explore the real issues and tensions that Gothic cloaks in fantastic terms.

Teaching Irish Gothic:
Big-House Displacements
in Maturin and Le Fanu

Mark M. Hennelly, Jr.

With the recent publication of Margot Gayle Backus's *The Gothic Family Romance: Heterosexuality, Child Sacrifice, and the Anglo-Irish Colonial Order*, the first book-length study of "Irish Gothic," it seems more apparent than ever that the concept is riddled with problems, paradoxes, and possibilities. Illustrating David Lloyd's general suggestions about "the social significance of genres" and that "Accounts of the nineteenth-century Irish novel are troubled by the need to explain its perceived inadequacy in relation to British and continental models" (153, 128), an Irish subgenre of Gothic fiction implies that the critical touchstone of the castle or house of British Gothic—as dominant genre—has imperiously colonized and usurped Irish home rule. Students need to realize, however, that a different, homemade architectural trope may define Irish Gothic in the indigenous figure of the Anglo-Irish big house with its attendant colonial concerns of unhomely displacement, ambiguous hybridity, and border violence.

An effective way to teach a unit on Irish Gothic consequently involves establishing the architectural similarities between English and Irish forms and then asking students to consider the possibility that traditional big houses in Irish literature significantly displace and deconstruct English Gothic values and replace them with a very mixed bag of Anglo-Irish ascendancy conflicts. As Marjorie Howes describes these conflicts:

> The Anglo-Irish were a local ruling class whose pretensions to aristocracy belied their profoundly middle-class character, and whose imaginative construction of an authoritative, aristocratic political and cultural tradition belied their dependence on English centers of power for their strength and legitimacy in Ireland. (165)

The big houses in Charles Maturin's *Melmoth the Wanderer* (1820) and Sheridan Le Fanu's *Uncle Silas: A Tale of Bartram-Haugh* (1865) can comparatively and constructively help one teach such Irish conflicts.

As outlined in "Framing the Gothic: From Pillar to Post-structuralism," my introduction to Gothic fiction always begins with an examination of reproductions of architecture, slides of cathedrals and castles, in addition to prints from Piranesi's *Carceri*, in order to stress Gothicism's perverse poetics of space. I later schedule student seminar reports on Gothic architecture as analyzed in John Ruskin, Norman Holland and Leona Sherman, Linda Bayer-Berenbaum, and Allison Milbank's three essays ("Doubting Castle," "Haunted House," and

"Through a Glass"; and more generally in Bachelard; Knapp; Vidler; and Wigley). After studying this architectural archetype throughout the semester in novels like Horace Walpole's *The Castle of Otranto* and Matthew Gregory Lewis's *The Monk*, students can consider the possibility of Irish variations and violations of British Gothic space in *Melmoth* and *Uncle Silas*.

In his survey of Irish Gothic from Edmund Burke to Elizabeth Bowen, William McCormack states that the concept itself seems as insubstantial as bog mists in the Celtic twilight: "the idea of a coherent Irish Gothic fictional tradition . . . is doubtful" ("Irish Gothic" 135). Irish writers like William Butler Yeats in *The Celtic Twilight*, however, repeatedly and revealingly stress endemic motifs that conjure things Gothic: "In Ireland this world and the world we go to after death are not far apart" (100). In exile after his infamous trial, Oscar Wilde even assumed the alias of Maturin's famous Gothic hero/villain, illustrating *Melmoth*'s enduring Irish Gothic legacy if not Julian Moynahan's claim that "early nineteenth century Ireland *is* a living Gothic" ("Politics" 47). Michael Begnal further argues that Le Fanu's "protagonists seem to follow in almost a direct line from" *Melmoth* (31), while Elizabeth Bowen adds that *Uncle Silas* reads like

> an Irish story transposed to an English setting [because] the hermetic solitude and the autocracy of the great country house, the demonic power of the family myth, fatalism, feudalism and the "ascendency" outlook are accepted facts of life for the race of hybrids from which Le Fanu sprang.   (Introduction 8)

Considering "the great country house," Devendra Varma recalls, "One of the most recurrent of the weird dreams that haunted [Le Fanu] . . . was of a vast and mysterious crumpling old mansion—of the type which he had often recounted in his tales—threatening imminently to fall upon and crush him" (Introduction ii). In fact, such big-house nightmares haunt most Irish Gothic writers and prove far more significant than the general "monument and ruin" that David Punter has recently emphasized in the genre ("Scottish Relations" 105).

Teaching the big house, classically located in Maria Edgeworth's *Castle Rackrent* (1800), against the grain of the British model of archetypal architecture makes "a coherent Irish Gothic fictional tradition" much more clear for students. In *Castle Rackrent*, as Backus writes, "the projective capacities of the Gothic family romance allow for figurations of colonialism that, like the Rackrents, simultaneously embody both the colonized and the colonizer" (132). I schedule reports on the big house and relevant (literary) colonial history, as collected in the "Historical Perspectives" (15–57) of Jacqueline Genet's pertinent anthology *The Big House in Ireland*; Bowen's "The Big House"; Backus (21–47, 171–215); Janet Madden-Simpson; Patricia Kelly; Terry Eagleton; Declan Kiberd; and Moynahan (*Anglo-Irish*). I also schedule reports on biographical studies of Maturin's and Le Fanu's hybrid nationalistic leanings as documented in Moynahan, "Politics"; Victor Sage, "Irish Gothic"; Dale Kramer (11–25); Ivan Melada (1–12); and James Cahalan (31–34; 70–76). Students thus learn to question whether Irish writers oedipally appropriate or contest specific structures from "Father Walpole" and "Mother Radcliffe," especially ruined mansions ruled by primogeniture, vertical tensions between towers and vaults, liminal entrances, secret recesses, labyrinthine passageways, flying buttresses, stained glass, art objects, and cloistered gardens and graveyards.

Students can then explore how the big house displaces uncanny Irish troubles like a decaying and colonized homeland and even the question of home rule itself, rebellion against the Anglo-constructed "Irish Frankenstein" (Malchow 34) and the monstrous parasite-host relationship with the British Empire, exile and the hyphenated burden of being Anglo-Irish and thereby blurring insider/outsider boundaries, the related metaphysical borders between Celtic folklore and Christian faith, and finally the crucial role of art in preserving the original Irish Beauty (from the Irish-constructed British Beast). This forlorn Beauty is often personified in either an imprisoned or a homeless female figure like Yeats's Cathleen Ni Houlihan, who wanders in exile because "too many strangers [are] in the house" (*Collected Plays* 53) of Ireland. Teaching such Irish Gothic motifs through the architecture in *Melmoth* and *Uncle Silas* can thus prove to be an enlightening exercise in teaching the conflicts and also in exemplifying the treacherous borderlands between colonial and postcolonial fiction, since, as Judie Newman puts it, "Gothic motifs are exceptionally prevalent in postcolonial fiction, even from very different locations" (85). Homi K. Bhabha's analysis of the terrifying unhomeliness "inherent in [the liminal] rite of extraterritorial and cross-cultural initiation" is even more to the architectural point:

> The recesses of the domestic space become sites for history's most intricate invasions. In that displacement, the borders between home and world become confused; and, uncannily, the private and the public become part of each other, forcing upon us a vision that is as divided as it is disorienting. (*Location* 9)

It is not very difficult to lead a class through specific instances of Gothic big-house architecture in both Maturin and Le Fanu. It is more difficult to teach the abyssal ambiguity of the big house, the values of which often depend on whether the authorial authority is an Anglo-Irish outsider inside the house or a native Irish insider outside the house. Sometimes the house projects dilapidated Irish values, sometimes domineering British ones—as reflected, for instance, in the Irish nickname for the Monarchy, "the Castle." The major classroom task, though, becomes Gothicizing Genet's thesis and testing it through this architecture: "The Big Houses of Ireland contain the myth of the Anglo-Irish Ascendancy. They offer an explanation of that class, its style and manners; they set out its relation with its environment and culture, and they plot its eventual disintegration and decomposition" (ix).

Now let me suggest how one might take students through the relevant architectural motifs in *Melmoth* and *Uncle Silas*. Following Moynahan and Sage, one should first stress the uncanny resemblances between Maturin and Le Fanu. As Sage compares them, both were

> with family connections in the Irish Church, both curiously learned, self-conscious writers, absorbed by their Calvinist heritage and its relation to aesthetics, psychology and politics, and both with an irresistible attraction to effects of terror and horror. There is something, perhaps, about the Hugenot refugee heritage which gives these writers, perched with varying degrees of discomfort inside a dominant class, a particular sensitivity to the darker implications of a fractured society.   ("Irish Gothic" 81)

Melmoth begins and ends in "the waste and ruin" (11) of its big house, Melmoth Lodge in County Wicklow, which Backus sees as a site of "settler colonial pathologies" and conflicts "between the interests of the native Irish and those of the Anglo-Irish" (113). In between occur frequently displaced descriptions of "vast masses of ruined architecture" (*Melmoth* 243) like "the architecture of the Roman and Moorish ruins" featuring vertical extremes: "the remains of fortresses, embattled, castellated, and fortified from top to bottom" (22). Such ruins imply the cultural condition of "discordant unison" (9)—a repeated phrase in *Melmoth*—that (still) plagues self-divided Ireland's separatist/unionist tendencies. This culturally conflicted ambivalence toward the big houses (and the represented British houses of fiction that the Union Jack built) suggests both the dreaded and the desired power of the colonial oppressor. In fact, the last word of *Melmoth* is "home" (412), recalling the uncanny motifs of the "secrets of the house" (116) and the "alienated quest of what is called Hospitality" (21) in an Ireland held hostage by parasitic England, which has paradoxically become the home host in the big house. Students must consider whether the domestic "persecution of children, who are sexually and ideologically appropriated, cannibalized, and ultimately destroyed within literal or symbolic families, [thereby] suppl[ying] an allegory for the experiences of the settler colonial child," is peculiar to unfamiliar Irish Gothic, as Backus argues (6), or whether Irish Gothic simply imitates the more familiar Gothic Romance in general, typified by Ann Radcliffe. As Monçada tells young Irish Melmoth, "Romances have made your country, Sir, familiar with the tales of subterranean passages, and supernatural horrors" (148).

Newman relevantly concludes that "postcolonial Gothic" situates itself at the threshold and "is therefore Janus-faced. At its heart lies the unresolved conflict between the imperial power and the former colony, which the mystery at the center [here, the big house] both figures and conceals" (86). When Sir Roger, descended "from the age of the Norman Conqueror," dies in Mortimer Castle, Maturin makes it clear that his mysterious "passing with a light and lofty step from a narrow entry to a spacious and glorious apartment" also signifies that

Janusian and boundless Celtic twilight zone or "dark and rugged threshold that lies between" life and death (344), if not between Irish rebellion and British rule—a zone also liminally figured in Yeats's play *The King's Threshold* (*Collected Plays*). To modify Bram Stoker's description of this traditional Gothic mytheme in *Dracula*: no British demon may "enter anywhere at first, unless there be someone of the [Irish] household who bid him to come" ([Modern Lib.] 264). Students should also consider how such liminal motifs clarify Immalee's "painful initiation into the mysteries of a new existence" (*Melmoth* 236), since in her Spanish role as Isidora "the sleeping beauty" (385), she personifies (like Cathleen Ni Houlihan) Ireland's embodiment of paradise lost and possible promise of being regained. Ireland's mythic origins—fleetingly remembered as Immalee's edenic island—are now dismembered by both the Eurocentric corruption of her father and the Anglo-Irish domination of Melmoth himself. In this Janusian sense and with the visual aid of Henry Fuseli's *The Nightmare*, students can appreciate the significance of different Irish versions of the hybrid Sleeping Beauty/Beast fable.

Like the Janus-faced threshold, the external joints of flying buttresses and the stained-glass windows further blur the Anglo-Irish boundaries between inside and outside values and thus can help students grapple with the colonial implications of Gothic *mise-en-âbime* antistructures. Vijay Mishra locates this abyssal archetype in the (political) unconscious, "the place of the uncanny (and of the sublime), . . . the labyrinthine site of the *mise-en-âbime*, of images that constantly regress and reduplicate, of compulsive repetitions into which the entire human history is locked and from which the subject speaks" (78). Although buttresses do not literally appear in most works, the violently explosive, fugitive significance of their Gothic exoskeleton figuratively haunts almost every novel. In *Melmoth*, this figure appears when the traitorous parricide helps Monçada flee outside the Inquisition walls only to have a rebellious mob "dash [the parricide into] a mangled lump of flesh right against the door of the house" inside which Monçada hides. This narration and violent conversion experience confirm the disturbing overlap between colonial escape and involvement, Monçada and the parricide, and the contextual demonic rabble and the extratextual disturbed reader: "The drama of terror has the irresistible power of converting its audience into its victims" (196–97).

In order to show how images of stained glass help us understand what I call the Gothic gaze, my students read the writing-on-the-wall passage from the Book of Daniel (5.25–31) and Plato's allegory of the cave wall in *The Republic*. We compare and contrast the apparitional, apocalyptic, and aesthetic implications of each piece, supplemented with Lacanian insights involving the "stained scopic field" and "anamorphosis" from Jacques Lacan's "Of the Gaze as Objet Petit a." In Irish Gothic, such visual staining seems to transport, or abject in Julia Kristeva's sense (*Powers*), the visionary back to some maternal and cultural imaginary in the Celtic twilight, besides foreshadowing that the future days of the Irish kingdom (or contrarily, British hegemony) are apocalyptically numbered. In "the ruined monastery" in *Melmoth*, for example, where the Wanderer and Isidora are married by the spectral monk, the window's "broken and discoloured . . . stained glass" sheds the light of "a faint and watery moon-beam . . . on [surrounding] objects." Isidora then regressively experiences an "instinctive feeling of her former existence" as the prelapsarian (i.e., Irish) Immalee/Eve when "she had once imagined the moon was her parent, and the stars her kindred" (301–02).

Other architectural images—secret recesses, art objects, and hybrid gardens and graves—seem to overlap in their links to what I call the Gothic gnostic quest for occult knowledge of the past and thus power over the present, in both *Dracula* and *Melmoth*. For Ireland, the knowledge sought again involves a questionable quest for its original green age, what Yeats's Cathleen Ni Houlihan laments as her once "beautiful green fields." The subsequent power involves either union with the Anglo-Irish landlord or the overthrow of that landlord: Cathleen's "hope of getting my beautiful fields back again; the hope of putting the strangers out of my house" (Yeats, *Collected Plays* 53, 55). Students must learn to tease these Anglo-Irish possibilities from the texts by understanding that what Oscar Wilde's *The Picture of Dorian Gray* calls the hybrid "horror and misshapen joy . . . lend[ing] to Gothic art its enduring vitality" ([1973] 134) does not answer questions. It questions pat answers by evading the binary "Manichean allegory" (138) of colonially oppressed and colonial oppressor, which, as Lloyd argues, plagues so many colonial readings of Irish fiction.

Cathleen's stranger in the house, the Wanderer, figuratively appears as some monstrous Gothic gargoyle but more often is associated with a mysterious recess housing ancestral secrets represented in a portrait like that at Melmoth Lodge. Imprisoned Monçada even reflects on the "recesses" of "my heart" (80). Like the novel *Melmoth*, Melmoth's mysterious portrait provokes gnostic curiosity about the fearfully fascinating "original of the picture" (407). Further, the "garden of death" at Melmoth Lodge previews the Wanderer's reprise of "the first mortal sin—a boundless aspiration after forbidden knowledge" that would result from eating "the fruit of the interdicted tree" (380, 408, 380). Thus like "homeless" Leopold Bloom believing the "Irishman's house is his coffin" (Joyce, *Ulysses* 110), wandering Melmoth (and wondering Silas) becomes a version of the hybrid Irish Jew "driven from . . . the region of [Celtic] paradise, and sent to wander among worlds of barrenness and curse forever" (*Melmoth* 408).

Moving to *Uncle Silas*, students should note that its subtitle features a big house, Bartram-Haugh, and that somewhat like Monçada, Maud references the British tradition, linking Radcliffe's architecture with Bartram as she identifies with Adeline in *Romance of the Forest* during her explorations of "the actual decay of the house" (198–99). Thus she perhaps even illustrates Milbank's claim in "Doubting Castle" that Le Fanu represents female, Maturin male Gothic (108). As in *Melmoth*, repetition compulsion again uncannily prevails, since Le Fanu's plot begins and ends at the same big house, Knowl, which as McCormack argues provides a displaced domestic double of demonic Bartram: "the world of Bartram is the post-mortem recreation of Knowl" (*Sheridan Le Fanu* 168). Both Gothic manses also house recessive family secrets and uncanny versions of the family romance; the Ruthyns, in fact, "are a very secrete family" (419). And just as Maturin's architecture suggests that the Melmoths have "*an odd story in the family*" (17), so too the "irregularly shaped" room associated on Le Fanu's very first page with Ruthyn odd family lore repeatedly plays a major Gothic role in unlocking those family secrets.

Students should consider whether such a conventional architectural trope in British Gothicism has more of what "the Irish . . . call blarney" (79) than banshees about it in *Uncle Silas*. Or does it crucially pit the hybrid, promiscuous values of colonized Ireland, where native and Anglo-Irish interbreed, against Silas's Anglophile defense of (sterile) "Ruthyn blood—the purest blood, I maintain it, in England" (318)? Such a reading perhaps reverses Howes's relevant discussion of the colonial context of *Uncle Silas*: "Since most nineteenth-century Anglo-Irish Gothics were narratives of internal corruption and decline, they usually revolved around collapsing the distinction between the corrupt house and the apparently pure lineage" (175). Like Isidora's father, Silas attempts to enforce an endogamous union between first cousins Maud and his debased son Dudley, illustrating the English landlord's kidnapping of an [Irish] heiress" (Rudd 33) if not Backus's generality about "unconscious collusion between parents and the forces of imperial domination" (131).

Recurring threshold, flying-buttress, and stained-glass motifs also riddle Le Fanu's novel. Swedenborgian Silas experiences entranced "hoverings between life and death" (261); more important, Maud repeatedly faces liminally monstrous "spirit[s] of evil" who terrify her "on the threshold" (97). Still more important, her beauty is doubled by that other damsel in distress Meg, appropriately nicknamed Beauty, who like some Joycean female personification of Ireland characteristically stands on the "threshold" or "doorway of the cottage, withdrawn into the shade" (368–69). In fact, Bartram-Haugh's "great fantastic iron gate" dramatically emphasizes the big house's "impressive gateways barred by high wrought-iron double gates" (Mac Aodha 21) as it liminally "bar[s the] passage to the enchanted castle" (*Uncle Silas* 185), imprisoning the Irish Sleeping Beauty. *Uncle Silas* also internally references the external joints or flying buttresses of the Gothic exoskeleton when Dudley enters Bartram through the trick window and then bludgeons Madame de la Rougierre, whom he mistakes for Maud. The observing Maud herself had been attempting to flee when his "scrunching blow[s]" prompt "a horrible tremor quivering through the joints and curtains of the bedstead—the convulsions of the murdered woman" (426), much like those of Maturin's parricide, violently doubling those of Maud and the reader. Windows in the novel are not specified as having stained glass as they are in *Melmoth*, but the disorienting effect on Maud is the same as on Immalee when Maud sits "in admiration of the moonlighted scene" by "the great drawing-room window" at Knowl: "Fancies and regrets float mistily in the dream, and the scene affects us with a strange mixture of memory and anticipation" (12). Later, after her father's death, "through each window in the perspective came its blue sheet of moonshine," which prophetically projects a hybrid version of Daniel 5 and Plato: "a gigantic and distorted shadow upon the ceiling and side-wall. . . . The mind is a different organ by night and by day" (123–24).

Even more than Melmoth, Silas appears architecturally as an avuncular gargoyle: "one of those demon grotesques we see in the Gothic side-aisles" (339); and again like the Wanderer, this "living original" is associated with a mysteriously recessive chamber housing his "shadow . . . which hung on canvas" (178). Like young Melmoth, Maud is also affiliated with such ancestral-cultural secrets as she "coiled [herself] up in the inner-most recess of [her] little chamber" (80). And like Melmoth's symptomatic *Heimweh* or longing for a Celtic paradise lost, Maud's portentous Swedenborgian vision in "the Dutch garden" also references the original "Home [which] we can only reach . . . through the gate of death" (13–15)—as in the case of the Faustian Melmoth and Silas, through imitating the curiosity of exiled Eve: "The serpent beguiled her and she did eat" (285). At Knowl, Maud may even suggest to students that Gothicism precedes Foucauldian discourse when she insists that such "Knowledge is power." But Irish Gothic also revises such discourse by adding that colonial "power of one sort or another is the secret lust of human souls" (11).

In sum, students of Irish Gothic need to understand the way big-house architecture signals riddling yet revealing ambivalence about colonial issues like unhomely displacement, ambiguous hybridity, and border violence. Maturin realizes that Cromwell's attack on Cloghan Castle during his "Irish campaign" wielded such "a two-edged sword," in fact, a "double exercise of the sword and the word" (*Melmoth* 342), which he repeatedly displaces on other differently colonized big houses: "All Spain is but one great monastery" (143). Le Fanu raises the cultural stakes and synecdoche even further as Bartram's "forlorn character of desertion and decay, contrasting almost awfully with the grandeur of its proportions and richness of its architecture" (185), ultimately gives way to a cosmic big house: "This world is a parable—the habitation of symbols—the phantoms of spiritual things immortal shown in material shape" (436). In either case, as Yeats later advises in his Irish Gothic drama *Purgatory*, students should "Study that house" (*Collected Plays* 430).

Fear of Furniture:
Commodity Gothicism and the
Teaching of Victorian Literature

Tricia Lootens

A commodity appears, at first sight, a very trivial thing,
and easily understood. Its analysis shows that it is, in
reality, a very queer thing, abounding in metaphysical
subtleties and theological niceties. . . . So soon as [a
table] steps forth as a commodity, it . . . evolves out of
its wooden brain grotesque ideas.

—Karl Marx, *Capital*

The bourgeois interior of the [eighteen]sixties to the
nineties, with its gigantic buffets, overrun by carving, its
sunless corners where the palm tree stands . . . , provides
adequate housing only for corpses. "On this sofa, the
aunt can only be murdered.". . . The bourgeois living
space . . . trembles for nameless murder.

—Walter Benjamin, *Einbahnstrasse*

"Who can say," asked Samuel Butler's *Erewhon* in 1872, "that the vapour
engine has not a kind of consciousness?" (199). Who can be sure, for that matter, that one's furniture isn't issuing secret accusations of wage slavery—or
panting for prey? Such questions came to haunt The Victorian Gothic, a mixed-
genre undergraduate topics course I recently taught at the University of Georgia. Through thematic constellations that juxtaposed well-known Gothic novels
with expository prose, personal narratives, short stories, and poetry, the course
attempted to explore Gothicism's involvement in conflicts over the powers of
art and the politics of race, gender, nation, and empire (see essay appendix).
From King Solomon's mines to the mines of northern England, from the passages of aristocratic estates to the streets of London's East Side or the clutter
of suburban middle-class parlors, Victorian culture has increasingly entered
recent criticism as a world of Gothic spaces. In many ways, The Victorian
Gothic set out as a sort of quick tour of those spaces. In a few weeks, however,
our exploration of the multiple agendas of Victorian Gothicism began to take
an unexpected turn toward the creation and use of Gothic objects—and thus,
perhaps inevitably, toward what Karl Marx's *Capital* terms "the Fetishism of
Commodities and the Secret Thereof" (*Marx's* Capital 31).

After a series of brief lectures, paired with excerpts from criticism of the
Gothic and from early works such as Ann Radcliffe's *The Mysteries of Udolpho*
and Matthew Gregory Lewis's *The Monk*, the class moved into a section on

Gothic art, opened by Alfred Tennyson's "Palace of Art" and John Ruskin's discussion of Gothicism in *The Stones of Venice* ("Second, or Gothic, Period"). As we worked through a series of poems centered on painting or paintings, we asked to what extent such texts employed the motifs, issues, and rhetorical strategies of Gothic literature as we understood it. The readings both illuminated and complicated questions of genre. Gothic approaches to the dramatic monologue, for example, highlighted the uncanny, often metaphorically violent processes whereby that quintessentially Victorian genre implicates readers in the workings of devious or deranged minds. Analysis of the disturbing ekphrastic poetry of Michael Field resonated suggestively with readings of the more notoriously seductive terrors of "La Gioconda" in Walter Pater's *The Renaissance*. Because early classroom discussions centered on poetry, students eager to prove a point concerning, say, relations between sexual and aesthetic anxieties or between the unspeakable and the unpaintable, felt compelled to offer highly detailed readings. Short response paper topics pushed them to extend such concentrated analysis to selected passages in works of prose. Progress was halting; but as students ceased to skip or skim descriptive passages, they also began to move beyond fully plot-driven or character-centered readings. As one class member put it, "I'm trying to read everything as if it were a poem"—which is to say, as if every word counted. This development was more or less planned. What was not planned was how often students found that the materiality and salability of art objects, or links between the creation of art and the exploitation of labor, lent strange new force to the familiar trope of the haunted painting. Whether through the bitterness of May Probyn's "The Model" or the parody of Dickens's "The Ghost of Art," the class began to see in the faces of literary paintings the forces of what I have come to call commodity Gothicism.

With its Crystal Palace, department stores, and novels awash in consumer items, the Victorian period notoriously marks the development of commodity culture—a development dependent on the process of abstraction. Abstraction, whose workings bear suggestive analogies to the more overtly Gothic psychological process of abjection (see Anne Williams's essay in this volume), transforms objects into commodities by occluding their physical materiality and precise social origins. As we replace objects' use value with exchange value, Marx argues, we put "out of sight both the useful character of the various kinds of labour embodied in them, and the concrete forms of that labour" (*Marx's Capital* 5). Commodification sets aside the "plain, homely, bodily form" of a table, for example, to render that table a mere "mirror" of abstract value (13, 24). Abstracted, a piece of wood becomes "something transcendent": it assumes "a social relation" to "the whole world of commodities," a fantastic realm in which human productions not only appear as "independent beings endowed with life" but also seem to "rule" their "producers instead of being ruled by them" (31, 24, 32, 35). No wonder, then, that Marx's table "not only stands with its feet on the ground, but, in relation to all other commodities, . . .

THE HAUNTED LADY, OR "THE GHOST" IN THE LOOKING-GLASS.

Madame La Modiste. "WE WOULD NOT HAVE DISAPPOINTED YOUR LADYSHIP, AT ANY SACRIFICE, AND THE ROBE IS FINISHED A MERVEILLE"

"The Haunted Lady; or, 'The Ghost' in the Looking-Glass." *Punch* 4 July 1863. Reproduced with permission of Punch Ltd.

on its head"; no wonder it "evolves out of its wooden brain grotesque ideas, far more wonderful than 'table-turning' ever was" (31).

Enter commodity fetishism's modulation into commodity Gothicism—a process that may well emerge most brutally through Victorian plays on the trope of poisoned clothing. In July 1863, for example, *Punch* published a cartoon entitled "The Haunted Lady; or, 'The Ghost' in the Looking-Glass" (Walkley 36–54). At left, a sharp-faced female figure in an elaborate bonnet looks on, while a beautiful—and beautifully gowned—central figure leans toward a mirror at the right. Reflected there, we see the lady's skirt; but above, where her face should be, appears a haggard, once-beautiful female corpse. It is as if, having attained commodities' symbolic endowment of life, the lady's dress and mirror unveil the terrible secrets of those very origins that commodification seeks to put "out of sight" (Marx 5). Refusing to "mirror" one another as abstract commodities (24), such rebellious objects lay bare human beings' terrifying vulnerability to relations between things. For the ghost in the looking glass does more than expose the horrifying material origins of the lady's dress: she also metaphorically reflects the status of the lady's incompletely abstracted, abjected body as a fleshly commodity. Flanked by darkness as well as by the

"A Shroud as well as a Shirt." *Punch* 1848. Reproduced with permission of Punch Ltd.

sharp features of the cruel modiste and the dead seamstress, the white breast and dress of the faceless, haunted lady stand frozen at the center of a grim triptych. "We would not have disappointed your Ladyship, at any sacrifice," begins the caption, in the voice of "Madame La Modiste."

"It is not linen you're wearing out, / But human creatures' lives!" (Hood 305). Read attentively, as it was by the Victorian audience that rendered Thomas Hood's 1843 "The Song of the Shirt" among the most celebrated of all Victorian poems of social criticism, the assertion of Hood's exploited seamstress is quintessentially Gothic. It seeks to make one's very clothing creep with suffering, to call up the sense of dying bodies clinging to one's very skin: "It is not linen you're wearing, but human creatures." One of the poem's many popular illustrations, an 1848 *Punch* cartoon, exposes a pretty child's smock as inscribed by skulls and the price "2 1/2d"—the price identified as the scandalous going rate for ten hours' sewing. The cartoon's title, drawn from Hood's poem, "A Shroud as well as a Shirt" (Walkley 67; Hood 305), suggests that distressed needlewomen may not be the only ones killed by such clothing.

Where did it come from? How much did it cost? Such questions, posed of objects whose cost refuses to be calculated solely in terms of exchange value, helped students make sense of a wide range of texts. After reading excerpts from the 1842 Children's Employment Commission parliamentary reports on child labor in the mines (esp. the first 44 pp.), we discussed how middle-class reformers, apparently intent on exposing mines as the sites of secret nakedness, sexual license, and gross human exploitation, implicitly threaten to align readers with those figures the students themselves found most frightening: that is, with mine owners or managers who implausibly denied knowledge of who was working—and how—to provide consumers with coal. From 1843 parliamentary reports on child labor in the trades and manufacturing (Horne, "Report" and "Evidence"), we moved to Elizabeth Barrett Browning's "Cry of the Children" (53–59). In its deployment (and partial reversal) of sentimental tropes of childhood; its nightmarish, incantatory evocation of factory wheels; and its culminating promise of divine retribution against a bloody-robed England, this poem draws explicitly on the 1843 reports, providing a fine counterpoint to Friedrich Engels's equally Gothic, prophetic use of the same material.

Studying Engels prepared students to approach "Cry of the Children" in terms of cultural discourses. Analyzing poetic repetition in Barrett Browning grounded later debates over the ethics and stylistic effectiveness of repetition in parliamentary and journalistic prose. Dickens's *Oliver Twist* would work well with such readings. So too did a poem devoted to that most vicious version of commodification, slavery. Originally paired with "Cry" in Barrett Browning's 1850 *Poems*, "The Runaway Slave at Pilgrim's Point" (160–70) helped students think about intimate, problematic connections among Victorian Gothic accounts of women's oppression, "wage slavery," and enslavement of Africans.

Revelations of the secret and terrifying origins and transformations of commodities helped us connect a wide range of less overtly reformist texts as well. In some respects, it was an easy step from the dehumanized strange fruit that is called up, embodied, and restored to human voice by the Runaway Slave to the seductive, fatally luscious wares of Christina Rossetti's eerie "Goblin Market"—or even, for that matter, to the overwhelming, sensuously described material objects of Oscar Wilde's *The Picture of Dorian Gray*. (As this novel opens Dorian abandons his volunteer cultural work in the East End.) From the early moments when Dorian's portrait begins inscribing itself with the materiality and mortality, as well as the viciousness, of its specific origins to the final, apparently ineluctable process whereby the painting achieves abstraction by writing Dorian's hideousness back onto his dying flesh, Wilde's novel may be taught as an irresistible exercise in commodity Gothicism. (The famously bizarre catalog of luxuries in chapter 11, for example, inspired a final paper connecting "poisonous books" to deadly interior decoration.) *Lady Audley's Secret* works equally well. Like the prostitute who is "saleswoman and wares in one" (Walter Benjamin, qtd. in Bowlby 10), Mary Elizabeth Braddon's charming villainess sells herself to a wealthy older husband, reigning happily among her husband's other possessions until his nephew Robert and Robert's friend George secretly penetrate into her private chamber. In that gorgeous, semi-private commodity spectacle (Richards 13), the men find an unfinished painting whose flaming, fleshly Pre-Raphaelite beauty lays bare both Lady Audley's potential demonic force and her identity as George's "dead" wife. Toward the novel's close, however, the trapped, murderous Lady Audley arises as the ghost in Robert Audley's mirror. She confronts him with those very maternal, material origins that he, like the commodification process itself, has most eagerly "put out of sight" (Marx 5): that is, her physical vulnerability to pregnancy and maternal madness, her childhood poverty, and her abandonment by Robert's best friend George. In so doing, she exacts a commodity vengeance.

I can now imagine using fear of furniture to open up Gothic themes in a range of Victorian novels. Where my students once looked to characters and geographic locales as guides for mapping the intricate symbolic and narrative webs of Charles Dickens's *Bleak House*, for example, they will soon look to material objects as well. Once we have reached the secret of Esther Summerson's birth, we will turn back to William Guppy's outburst before Lady Dedlock's portrait at Chesney Wold. "I know her! Has the picture been engraved, miss?" (82). Unable to explain the painting's familiarity by virtue of its reproduction as a cheap popular commodity, Guppy must learn instead to read this aristocratic possession (and symbol of possession) for its betrayal of commodified, albeit insufficiently abstracted, female flesh. For the image he recognizes, which is already "imprinted on his art" (397), reveals another sort of reproduction altogether: it is that of Esther Summerson, Lady Dedlock's illegitimate child.

When art and flesh meet in the *Galaxy Gallery of British Beauty* portraits that adorn the walls of Tony Jobling's grim room at Mr. Krook's, the result is a perfect occasion for addressing Gothicism's grisly intersections with comedy. Dickens does not show the nauseating smoke from Mr. Krook's spontaneously combusting body as it congeals on Lady Dedlock's engraved figure. He does not have to. He need only strand Guppy and his friend in Jobling's "suicidal" room, allow them to praise Lady Dedlock's ironically presented picture on the wall, and wait a page or two before showing Guppy launch from queasiness into horrified panic: "See here, on my arm! . . . smears, like black fat!" (396, 398). Fog, moral corruption, disease, sexual transgression and commodification: all coalesce in the linguistically absent yet imaginatively inescapable vision of Lady Dedlock's fouled image hanging on the walls of the room in which her former lover died.

Disturbing undercurrents of abjection and commodification run throughout the novel, from Mr. Krook's early bragging about his sacks of ladies' hair, through Sir Leicester's pride in Lady Dedlock, to John Jarndice's pleasure in giving Esther away in marriage. Focusing on material objects not only helps us address such strains but also informs larger readings. After all, raised as she has been by a censorious aunt, in ignorance of her origins, Esther Summerson seems to fear her own being as a kind of Gothic object—a fear that is altered but scarcely allayed by the passionate joy of secret reunion with her mother. For much like Lady Dedlock's portrait, Esther's body constantly threatens to betray its origins. No wonder, then, that when Esther finds herself haunting

Chesney Wold's "Ghost Walk" at night, she is "seized" with what she terms "an *augmented* terror of myself" (454; emphasis mine).

Wilkie Collins's *The Moonstone* offers equally fascinating possibilities. Wrested from an Indian shrine, and bearing with it the curse of a murdered priest, Collins's fabulous yellow diamond is not only a genuine fetish but also an imperial Gothic object par excellence. In its effect on the Verinders, the moonstone dramatizes how the brutality of imperial rule and the fear of retaliatory violence may saturate an apparently peaceable English family. Like other objects of commodity Gothicism, the moonstone betrays the human suffering associated with its past. As a plundered sacred object, it carries the threat of vengeance and forcible repossession by Indian priests; as an heirloom left to young Rachel Verinder by a vicious and embittered uncle, it may well act as a token of personal vengeance for familial rejection. Whether as an Indian sacred object or a British heirloom, however, the diamond is incompletely commodified. Huge, flawed at the heart, the intact stone is priceless—which is to say, among other things, hard to sell. In order to gain full access to the realm of exchange value, the stone would have to be split: this destruction alone could divest the gem both of its unique materiality and its historical claims on religious and familial loyalties. Both literally and metaphorically, such annihilating abstraction is precisely what Godfrey Ablewhite, the novel's villain, seeks.

Past students have quickly noted that Rachel's acceptance of a Gothicized spoil of empire seems to implicate the Verinders in continuing struggles of violent expropriation. Through focusing on actual or potential Gothic objects, I hope that my future students will gain a deeper understanding of the extent to which the moonstone's presence lays bare, rather than creates, the family's engagement in such struggles. Why, we will ask, does so much of the novel's mystery revolve around a paint smear from Rachel and Blake's interior decoration project—a project that the good-humored steward Gabriel Betteredge, one of Collins's more sympathetic narrators, compares to the "cruel nastiness" of other bored gentry who amuse themselves by impaling spiders and torturing frogs (55)? Why does Collins insist on the existence of an Indian cabinet, which stands in one of the most intimate spaces of the Verinder household even before the moonstone invades the house? Suggestively located in Rachel's bedroom, that chest might be a Gothic object. Instead, it serves as an eroticized metaphor for Rachel herself: it houses her jewel, which her true lover Franklin Blake, in his drugged wanderings, seeks to protect—and which her mercenary suitor, Godfrey Ablewhite, cold-bloodedly steals and vainly attempts to destroy. As the family's household furnishings suggest, then, mercenary violence, empire, and the Verinders' domestic comforts cannot be easily disentangled. For all the novel's orientalist Gothicism, true danger in *The Moonstone* very often comes from within—whether it be England, the family home, or the psyche itself.

All this is not to say, of course, that commodity Gothicism is the key to all Victorian Gothic mythologies. Lucy Westenra's mother may well doom herself by interfering with her doctor's flower arrangements, but this point is scarcely the most interesting thing one can say about Bram Stoker's *Dracula*. Still, fear of furniture may offer Gothic access points even to such apparently unlikely novels as George Eliot's *Middlemarch*. What dooms Lydgate, after all, is that the "distinction of mind which belonged to his intellectual ardour, did not penetrate his feeling and judgment about furniture, or women" (103). Though it is the cost rather than the character of Lydgate's literal household furnishings that helps doom him, there is something truly Gothic in Eliot's account of this man, who begins by marrying a woman in great part for her decorativeness and ends by comparing her to Isabella's pot of basil, which "flourished wonderfully on a murdered man's brains" (575).

Even as focusing on Victorian Gothic objects suggestively linked Victorian texts and recent studies of Victorian culture, it also encouraged the class to think about long-term developments in the meaning of Gothicism itself. In most contexts, to say "Gothic" is to conjure up simultaneous fantasies of objects, architectural styles, narratives, and modes. Dark, crooked, irregular settings—be they the wildly disorienting passages of a medieval cathedral or the sewers of London—tend to appear as direct hypostatizations of nightmarish power, perfect physical incarnations of the half-hidden, unspeakable viciousness of fathers or women, aristocrats or monks; of science, mortality, sex, or the mind itself. What happens to such associations in the face of the Victorian Gothic revival? Students raised this question in our second week: in *The Stones of Venice*, they noted, architectural Gothicism triumphantly embodies an organic, fully human aesthetics. Ruskin's prose style may well mimic the tortuous movement, crucial detours, and not-so-dead ends of the Gothic edifices in Lewis or Radcliffe, as one student remarked; yet others responded that in Ruskin's own terms such parallels could only be read as signs of vitality and health. Here, irregularity, crudity, and imperfection evoke not terror but nostalgic utopianism. Granted: in practice, nineteenth-century Gothic interior decorations were no less vulnerable to the workings of commodity culture than any other style of decoration (Crosby 112–14). Even gargoyles, if they are mass-produced, may waste workers' strength. Still, as celebrated by Ruskin, the rough, dark wildness of Gothic creativity gives rise to exuberant envisionings of moral and social revival.

As Gothic style is revalued, materializations of guilt, corruption, terror, and half-hidden secrets of origin take on new forms. In Ruskin as in Benjamin, a strong, comfortable mass-produced sofa, rightly read, pants for corpses—and not merely because its origins lie in the soul-killing "racks" of "wage slavery." Created in the attempt "to banish imperfection" through mechanical production, such furniture embodies a corrupting aesthetics whose values act to "destroy expression, to check exertion, to paralyze vitality" (Ruskin, "Second" 203–04). Gothic revivalism's explicit, theorized transfer of the terrors of Gothic architecture to the proud, mechanized perfection of orderly late-nineteenth-century middle-class interiors finds counterparts elsewhere, as students noted. One need only turn a suspicious eye toward Emily Brontë's Thrushcross Grange; or toward the hideous, fatally sterile symmetry of George's childhood home in *Lady Audley's Secret*; or even, on a different level, toward Tennyson's "Palace of Art" to see how sunny, orderly domestic spaces may begin to house Victorian terrors.

Poised as it is between Horace Walpole's *The Castle of Otranto* and Shirley Jackson's *We Have Always Lived in the Castle*, Victorian Gothic writing suggests that frightening furniture may not be the worst form of interior decoration. When works of commodity Gothicism urge Victorian readers to read their shirts, their walls, or their "good and strong" furniture for secret signs of terror (Ruskin, "Second" 193), the even deeper fear they may leave unspoken is that commodities will not, in fact, attain rebellious life and resist abstraction—that they will not tell us what we need to know. It is surely not accidental that by the end of the term, my students had turned the hall outside our classroom into an organizing site for a student-run street-theater protest against sweatshop production of university paraphernalia. (The resulting parodic performance was aptly named the "Fashion Show of Horror.") Literature, too, is a commodity; and as citizens, as well as students and teachers, we still have grounds to be unsettled by Victorian texts' complex and painful negotiations between "moral condemnation" of commodity culture and "implication in what they oppose" (Andrew Miller 9).

APPENDIX
Primary Texts for the Victorian Gothic

Gothic Art

Ideals and Terrors
   Alfred Tennyson, "The Palace of Art"
   John Ruskin, excerpt from "The Nature of Gothic," in *The Stones of Venice*

Modeling
   Charles Dickens, "The Ghost of Art"
   May Probyn, "The Model"
   Christina Rossetti, "In an Artist's Studio"
   Elizabeth Siddall, "The Lust of the Eyes"

Painting
   George Eliot, "The Lifted Veil"
   Robert Browning, "My Last Duchess"

Wicked Renaissance, Wicked Aesthetes
   Robert Browning, "Andrea del Sarto"
   Walter Pater, "La Gioconda," from *The Renaissance*
   Michael Field, "La Gioconda," "A Portrait: Bartolommeo Veneto"

Oscar Wilde, *The Picture of Dorian Gray*
Vernon Lee, "A Wicked Voice"
Robert Browning, "A Toccata of Galuppi's"

Gothic Law

"Wage-Slaves" and the Poor
Parliamentary Papers—Children's Employment Commission
Friedrich Engels, "The Great Towns," from *Condition of the Working
Class in England*
Elizabeth Barrett Browning, "The Cry of the Children"
William Booth, from *In Darkest England*
G. W. M. Reynolds, from *The Mysteries of London*
Frances Power Cobbe, "Wife-Torture in England"

Slavery
Elizabeth Barrett Browning, "The Runaway Slave at Pilgrim's Point"
Mary Prince, from *The History of Mary Prince*
Fanny Kemble, from *Journal of a Residence on a Georgian Plantation*

Hanging in the Panopticon
Oscar Wilde, "The Ballad of Reading Gaol"
Rudyard Kipling, "Danny Deever"
Coventry Patmore, "A London Fete"

Haunted Landscapes and the Horrors of Home

Emily Brontë, *Wuthering Heights*
Margaret Oliphant, "The Open Door"
Robert Browning, "Childe Roland to the Dark Tower Came"
Alfred Tennyson, "Maud"
Mary Elizabeth Braddon, *Lady Audley's Secret*
Henry James, *The Turn of the Screw*

Alien Nations: Humanity and Beyond

Alfred Tennyson, *In Memoriam* excerpts
Mary Seacole, on cholera, from *The Wonderful Adventures
of Mrs. Seacole*
Bram Stoker, *Dracula*
Christina Rossetti, "Goblin Market"
Algernon Charles Swinburne, "Faustine," "Dolores," "The Garden of
Proserpine," "After Death"
Rosamund Marriott Watson, "Werewolf Ballad"
Robert Louis Stevenson, *Dr. Jekyll and Mr. Hyde*
Rudyard Kipling, "The Mark of the Beast"

Henry James, "The Beast in the Jungle"
H. G. Wells, *The Island of Dr. Moreau*
Charles Dickens, "Branch Line: The Signal-Man"
Samuel Butler, "The Book of the Machines," from *Erewhon*

Hearts of Darkness:
Teaching Race, Gender, and Imperialism in Victorian Gothic Literature

Tamar Heller

He cried in a whisper at some image, at some vision—he
cried out twice, a cry that was no more than a breath:
"The horror! The horror!"
            —Joseph Conrad, *Heart of Darkness*

Written in the closing years of the Victorian era, Joseph Conrad's important modernist text *Heart of Darkness* is quintessentially Gothic. Although their meaning is famously ambiguous, Kurtz's dying words can be read as referring to his European horror at the otherness of Africans and—even more terrifying—his recognition that he has become one of "them." His words thus express an anxiety characteristic of nineteenth-century imperialism, the fear of going native that Stephen Arata has dubbed "reverse colonization" ("Occidental Tourist"). In its images of the fine line between the civilized self and the atavistic one associated with native peoples in nineteenth-century racist thought, the ideologeme of reverse colonization is classically Gothic in expressing terror at the permeability of the boundary between self and other. One could thus classify Conrad's text as a type of what Patrick Brantlinger has called "imperial Gothic," which he defines in his reading of fin de siècle adventure fiction as a genre expressing "anxieties about the ease with which civilization can revert to barbarism or savagery" (*Rule* 229).

The affiliation of Gothic other and colonial other, well established by the time of Conrad, may be seen as early as Mary Shelley's *Frankenstein*, where the monster created by an imperialistic scientist identifies with the colonized people he hears about in Volney's *Ruins of Empires* (see Malchow 9–40 for an extended reading of the monster as racial other). Starting with *Frankenstein*, an entire tradition of texts illustrates the affinity of the Gothic to representations of race in nineteenth-century literature. This tradition reveals the genre's fearful fascination with otherness, which makes the Gothic an ideal vehicle for expressing cultural anxieties about the instability of racial and cultural categories that Victorian taxonomies sought to separate and place in an unquestioned hierarchy of higher and lower, civilized and barbaric. What one could call the Gothicization of the racial other in nineteenth-century fiction is a sign of anxiety about the hybridization of white and black, colonizer and colonized. This anxiety is also frequently entangled in an anxiety about sexual hybridization—the dissolution of boundaries between domesticated and sexualized women and of the very categories of male and female in the era of the rise of the new woman—that reflects the insistent association in Victorian culture of racial and gender discourses and the analogous position in such discourses between woman (conceptualized by default as white) and the racial other.

In this essay I discuss strategies for teaching nineteenth-century Gothic that engage discourses about the racial other in the context of the course Race, Gender, and Imperialism in Victorian Gothic. While the syllabus, which ends with *Heart of Darkness*, includes fin de siècle works—Arthur Conan Doyle's *The Sign of Four* (1887), Bram Stoker's *Dracula* (1897), and H. Rider Haggard's *She* (1887)—I begin with an earlier text, Wilkie Collins's *The Moonstone* (1868), one of the most explicit treatments of colonialism in nineteenth-century fiction. Collins's novel shows, too, that nineteenth-century Gothics are not univocally racist; one might, indeed, point to *The Moonstone* as a liberal (though not anti-imperialist) critique of nineteenth-century racist discourses.

In teaching the history of race and imperialism, instructors can find it useful to consult, and to put on reserve or excerpt for students, selected texts from the now burgeoning library of critical and historical sources on these topics. Works I have found particularly helpful are Edward Said's *Orientalism* and *Culture and Imperialism*; Arata's *Fictions of Loss in the Victorian Fin-de-Siècle* and "The Occidental Tourist: *Dracula* and the Anxiety of Reverse Colonization" (a good, concise text for students); and two indispensable books: Brantlinger's *Rule of Darkness: British Literature and Imperialism, 1830–1914* (containing the chapter "Imperial Gothic") and H. L. Malchow's *Gothic Images of Race in Nineteenth-Century Britain*. Chapters 2 and 3 of Stephen Jay Gould's *The Mismeasure of Man* describe the formation of nineteenth-century anthropological and racist thought; his brief essay "Bound by the Great Chain," which discusses the ideas of Charles White, an important voice in the evolution of nineteenth-century views of racial superiority, is a particularly succinct discussion of these issues to give to students. Because I stress the analogies between nineteenth-century theories of race and those of gender, I also recommend chapter 2 of Cynthia Eagle Russett's *Sexual Science*, "Up and down the Phyletic Ladder," which links nineteenth-century views on women with racist taxonomies, and the introductory chapter of Anne McClintock's *Imperial Leather: Race, Gender, and Sexuality in the Colonial Contest*. Two books that focus on gender and imperialism are Susan Meyer's lucid *Imperialism at Home: Race and Victorian Women's Fiction* and Deirdre David's *Rule Britannia: Women, Empire, and Victorian Writing*. Sander Gilman's "The Hottentot and the Prostitute: Toward an Iconography of Female Sexuality" shows how a fear of female sexuality undergirds both racist and sexist discourses of the nineteenth century.

In introducing students to a selection of this material (which can be done in a few classes at the beginning of the course), it is important to show them how the construction of race as a taxonomic category in the nineteenth century justified the ideology of imperialism and to emphasize how such categories were based on concepts not just of difference but also of a hierarchy of difference, placing white people on the top and black people lower on the "phyletic ladder"

—a hierarchy that resembles that of male and female in nineteenth-century gender ideology. It is important to remind students, too, that the concept of race applied not only to people of color but also to groups considered other during the nineteenth century, such as the Jews and the Irish (the Irish a European colonized people). A crisp way of demonstrating this point is to bring into class images of the Jew from Gilman's *The Jew's Body* and the cartoon labeled "The Irish Frankenstein," which can be found in Malchow (36).

These introductory classes set the stage for turning to the course's touch-stone text, *The Moonstone*, a novel that requires several types of historical con-textualization. The instructor can point out to students that the hinge on which the novel's plot turns—the theft of the moonstone from a Hindu temple dur-ing the 1799 Siege of Seringapatam—refers to a crucial moment in the history of the British imperial domination of India. *The Moonstone* also responds to two important contemporary incidents regarding race: the Sepoy Rebellion or so-called Indian Mutiny of 1857 and the Eyre Controversy of 1866 (two years before the novel was written), in which an insurrection of Jamaican blacks was brutally suppressed by the governor of the colony.

The Indian Mutiny provoked national hysteria about the uprising of demo-nized others. Instructors might refer to, and put on reserve, Brantlinger's chap-ter "The Well of Cawnpore" in *Rule of Darkness* and Nancy Paxton's work on images of chivalry and rape in mutiny fictions ("Mobilizing Chivalry" and *Writ-ing under the Raj*). These sources emphasize the Gothicism of the fears the mutiny generated about the overthrow of English authority, fears epitomized in images of the rape of white women by natives. To situate Collins in this cultural context, it is worth pointing out his differences from his friend and mentor Dick-ens, who took a virulently racist position on both the mutiny and the controversy over whether Eyre should be punished. While Collins collaborated with Dick-ens on such postmutiny adventure stories as *The Perils of Certain English Pris-oners* (Dickens and Collins), his own views on race, as Lillian Nayder (*Unequal Partners*) and Audrey Fisch have shown, were far more nuanced and less hys-terical. Moreover, as Jaya Mehta has pointed out, by setting the main action of *The Moonstone* before the mutiny, in 1848–49, Collins sidesteps the worst types of pandering to postmutiny hysteria (618). At the same time, his references to the revenge of Indians bent on retrieving their lost jewel (the image of the jewel was often used in the nineteenth century to refer to India), and the theft of the gem from the bedroom of a virginal English girl while the Indians lurk outside, echo mutiny-era images of the dangerous and rebellious native.

What is notable about *The Moonstone*, however—and what makes it so rewarding to teach—is the complexity with which Collins treats what could have been an unreflectively racist iconography. I ask students whether the Indians are treated at all sympathethically; what they notice is the negative por-trayal of English rapacity, in the prefatory narrative about the Siege of Seringa-patam, and the depiction of the theft of the jewel, stolen from a hitherto "inviolate deity" (2), as itself an act like rape. Though Collins's portrayal of a

crucial historical act of imperialist expansion in India does not explicitly critique the colonial enterprise—and though the portrayal of the disguised Indian
priests in pursuit of the gem is unabashedly orientalist—he considerably complicates the racism of imperialist ideology by paralleling the dark-haired Rachel
Verinder (a name that suggests "true Indian") with the Indians of the Seringa-
patam siege as victims of a similar violation by Englishmen. For that is the
major twist of Collins's plot: in his Gothic, it is not the Indians who invade the
Englishwoman's bedroom but an Englishman, Franklin Blake, Rachel's suitor,
who is revealed to have stolen the gem in an opium-induced trance.

In speaking about Blake's complex position, I introduce the concept of
reverse colonization and ask students to what extent it is a theme in *The Moonstone*. Images of going native abound in the text: Blake himself (whose name is
similar to "black") is seen as a disturbing miscegenation of Continental identities by the butler Betteredge, a devotee of the imperialist fiction *Robinson
Crusoe*. There is also the sinister Colonel Herncastle, the thief of the gem from
the Indian temple, who becomes an opium-addicted outcast, and the Indian
explorer Murthwaite, a "long, lean, wiry, brown" man modeled on Victorian
explorers like Richard Burton, who, like Murthwaite, passed as native in pursuing the imperialist adventure of "penetrat[ing] in disguise where no European had ever set foot before" (65). Significantly, these characters are
hybrids—mixtures of the imperialist Englishman and the racial other. As such,
they point to the permeability of racial boundaries calculated to be disturbing
to mainstream imperialist ideology that relied on segregating colonizer and colonized.[1] (The prevalence of opium in the plot—Herncastle is an opium addict
and Blake steals the diamond under the influence of the drug—is another sign
of the infiltration into English life of Eastern practices, associated with violence and repressed primal urges.)

To complicate a reading of the novel as simply being about reverse colonization, the instructor can ask to what extent Collins criticizes English greed
and desire for power. While Herncastle might seem to be a prime example of
going native, he is also an image of imperialist aggression, much as Kurtz will
later be in Conrad's novella. The aptly named Godfrey Ablewhite—a hypocrit-
ical philanthropist revealed as the true villain, the one who tries to sell the
jewel once he takes it from Blake—is also ambiguous in this sense. Murdered
by the Indians, he dies in blackface (disguising himself as an Indian), becoming, like Herncastle, another terrifying example of what it means to go native,
but also representing an implicit indictment of imperial theft (Able-white's
authority [i.e., the authority of the able white man] is undercut when he is
revealed to be not a God-fearing missionary but a thief with a double life).
Blake's own motive for stealing the jewel turns out to be remarkably complex:
while the act is one of symbolic sexual violence, he claims he takes the diamond
because he wants to protect Rachel from the violence of the Indians lurking
outside. Does the revelation of this motive exonerate Blake, or—in a novel
filled with unconventionally strong-willed women—does it point to a disturb-

ing duplicity on his part, since the rhetoric of imperialism was similarly two-faced, promising protection for those who supposedly could not take care of themselves even while overpowering them? In this sense, does Collins subtly question the ideological justification for imperialist aggression?

Indeed, so sympathetic is Collins's portrayal of types of marginalized others that, as I have argued in my reading of the novel (*Dead Secrets*), one can emphasize the text's ambivalence and see the main plot about the privileged white man Blake subordinated to what initially appear to be subplots about types of oppression (142–63). I always ask students to note how the paralleling of the imperialist and domestic plots raises questions about the status of women as well as racial others. The evidence pointing to Blake as an example of the misguided imperialist is strengthened by his attitude not only toward Rachel but also toward Rosanna Spearman, a servant who kills herself because he will not notice her. The novel's main symbol for the suppression of the other—the Shivering Sand, the quicksand that is the site of Rosanna's suicide—is, significantly, racialized, described as an eerily Gothic "brown face" (25) that represents both the suppression and resistance of types of others in the novel: women, the lower classes, and colonized races.

In giving students the tools to negotiate the ideological complexity of Collins's portrayal of race, gender, and imperialism, I think it useful to introduce an important term from postcolonial theory, *hybridity*. Hybridity, or the mixture of racial or national characteristics, is a significant theme in *The Moonstone* in the portrayal of characters like Herncastle, Murthwaite, and Blake, but the term is especially useful when applied to the character I would argue is central to the novel, Ezra Jennings, the mixed-race doctor's assistant who solves the mystery by figuring out how Blake was given opium.

Jennings is the most extravagantly Gothic figure in the novel, his remarkable piebald hair in which "[a]t one place, the white hair ran up into the black; at another, the black hair ran down into the white" (319), announcing the miscegenation of his origins ("My father was an Englishman, but my mother—" [366]). Possibly the most remarkable mixed-race character in nineteenth-century British literature, he has multiple hybridities: describing himself as being a combination of male and female (411), he is a man of Western empiricism (who proves Blake's moral innocence in a scientific experiment) but also an opium addict, associated with the seduction of the East, and the town pariah disliked and mistrusted, not least because of his signs of racial difference (e.g., his "gipsy" complexion [319]). Jennings's role as detective is also ambiguous: it is his duty to whitewash Blake's culpability and restore domestic order at the end of the novel, yet he is also associated with images both of uprisings of oppressed people in *The Moonstone* and of their suppression (Tamar Heller, *Dead Secrets* 156–63). As such, like the Shivering Sand, he represents the oppression and resistance of the racial other. Thus, while embodying Collins's authorial strategy of containing what is most subversive about his social critique, he recalls Homi Bhabha's definition of hybridity as that which "disturbs

the visibility of the colonial presence and makes the recognition of its authority problematic" ("Signs" 34).[2]

In disturbing imperial authority as much as it does, *The Moonstone* is to my
knowledge unique among nineteenth-century British texts. Later nineteenth-
century works that portray colonialism are, as scholars like Brantlinger and
Arata have noted, more racist than Collins's. While Collins portrays hybridity
in a complex and even sympathetic way, hybridization is the catalyst for Gothic
terror in fin de siècle imperial romance. Tracing this transformation in the
classroom, I have found it useful to pair *The Moonstone* with a text heavily
influenced by its tale of an Indian curse, Doyle's *The Sign of Four*. This juxtaposition of texts not only reveals the significance of imperialism as a theme in
the development of the mystery genre but also underscores the growing conservatism of late-nineteenth-century depictions of race.[3]

As students compare *The Moonstone* and *The Sign of Four*, instructors will
want to help them identify many repeated elements, in particular the tale of a
curse on stolen Indian treasure and the invasion of an English landscape by the
oriental realm. When I ask students to compare the two narratives' representation of race, they notice immediately that the Indian Mutiny (recalled as the
uprising of "two hundred thousand black devils let loose," in the words of
Jonathan Small [Doyle 187]) is portrayed in a much more overtly racist way
than are images of otherness in *The Moonstone*. Unlike the mournful dignity
of the Indian priests at the end of Collins's novel or the sympathetic portrayal
of the mixed-race Jennings, the depiction of the pygmy Tonga (the Tonto-like
servant of Small who turns out to be the murderer of Sholto) is a textbook
example of nineteenth-century representations of blacks as atavistic savages: "a
little black man . . . with a great, misshapen head and a shock of tangled,
dishevelled hair. . . . Never have I seen features so deeply marked with all bestiality and cruelty"(177–78). Images of reverse colonization are rife in *The Sign
of Four*, with the Englishmen who conspire to steal the treasure being associated with regression to Tonga's "bestiality and cruelty." (Instructors who want
to examine further the going-native theme in Doyle may wish also to assign the
Sherlock Holmes story "The Man with the Twisted Lip," in which a respectable
white man lives a double life as a beggar who hides in an opium den.) The figure of Holmes himself is a more morally nuanced version of hybridity; in a
rewrite of Ezra Jennings, he is both a man of science and a dreamy drug addict
with a feminized bohemianism. His role, though, like Jennings's, is a double
one, at once skirting the margins of respectability and containing this other self
in order to shore up imperial power by vanquishing criminalized racial others.[4]

The pattern of domination in *The Sign of Four*, of a white male homosocial
group of detectives allied against the invasive racial other, reappears in *Dracula*, which can be read as a central fin de siècle text about race and imperial
Gothic. *Dracula* is a classic example of nineteenth-century Orientalism, with
the shadowy Eastern European realm of Transylvania the site of vampiric
otherness, and Dracula with his "aquiline nose" ([ed. Ellmann] 282), as both

Judith Halberstam (86–106) and Malchow (149–65) have persuasively argued, linked to stereotypes of the Jew. Teaching the imbrication of *Dracula* with images of race, it is worth underscoring that vampire fictions draw on anxieties about blood, a common nineteenth-century signifier for race and cultural anxieties about its purity.[5]

In contrast to the homosocial Holmes mystery, in *Dracula* femininity is not marginalized but central and moreover associated with the theme of racial contagion. One can see in *Dracula*, indeed, the same topoi that one finds in postmutiny images of white women threatened with violation by the lustful male other (the scene where Dracula forces the angelic Mina to drink his blood in front of her disempowered husband [282] is a prime example of this iconography). Many critics have commented on how the sexual voraciousness of Lucy following her infection by vampirism is a coded representation of the threat of the new woman (see, e.g., Showalter, *Sexual Anarchy* 180–81), but it is also important to place this representation in the context of the tradition Gilman refers to in "The Hottentot and the Prostitute" that compares the potentially threatening sexuality of the white woman with that of the black woman. I bring to class a passage from an important predecessor text, Sheridan Le Fanu's "Carmilla" (1872), another tale of an orientalized Eastern Europe in which a lesbian vampire attempts to infect a virginal girl with the contamination of sexual knowledge (for more on this reading, see Tamar Heller, "Vampire"). The passage I show students describes how, as the vampire appears for the first time—a delicate if exotic white woman—spectators notice in her coach a "hideous black woman, with a sort of coloured turban on her head, . . . with gleaming eyes and large white eyeballs, and her teeth set as if in fury" (286). Such images of the demonized racial other lurking beneath the surface of the apparently civilized white woman resonate throughout *Dracula*, as Lucy and Mina both embody a terrifying hybridity—a hybridity not just of the sexual and the domestic woman but also of the white Englishwoman and the implied degeneracy of the orientalized Jew.

This mingled sexual and racial hybridity is also central to the classic imperial Gothic *She*. Waiting to meet Ayesha, Haggard's passionate antiheroine, the English narrator wonders if he will see "some naked savage queen, a languishing Oriental beauty, or a nineteenth-century young lady, drinking afternoon tea" (141). The narrator's initial confusion is significant; although her body is repeatedly described as "white" (e.g., 142, 154), Ayesha is, like Mina and Lucy or Le Fanu's vampire Carmilla, a hybrid, an orientalized woman ruling over a native African people, the Amahagger, who mirror the new woman–like power of She by being a matriarchal culture in which "the weaker sex has established its rights" (89). Comparing *She* with *Heart of Darkness* as depicting another imperial quest into Africa, Sandra Gilbert and Susan Gubar see the novel, with its foregrounding of male anxieties about female power, as one of the nineteenth century's "literary turning points, a pivot on which the ideas and anxieties of the Victorians began to swivel . . . into the modern" (*Sexchanges* 21). Although Gilbert and Gubar disappointingly avoid the issue of race in their reading, the

setting of this fable of female aggression, the heart of Africa, is far from accidental. If one emphasizes Ayesha's racial hybridity as well as the miscegenation
of gender roles she embodies, one can see how her vision of overthrowing the
British Empire (256) evokes the Victorian ideologemes of both the revenge of
the racial other and the erotic contamination of the white woman gone native,
a contamination that suggests the threat of female sexuality to the male enterprise of empire building.

Following *She* with *Heart of Darkness* as a last text in the class underscores the
works' similar themes while enabling us to circle back to *The Moonstone*, since
both Conrad's and Collins's fictions can be seen as ambivalent portrayals of imperialism. That Conrad's novella has inspired such a variety of responses—some
critics seeing it as racist and others as an indictment of imperialist aggression (see
Brantlinger, *Rule* 255–74)—recalls *The Moonstone*'s complex balancing of sympathy for oppressed people and fearful images of going native. Yet, despite the
similarities between *The Moonstone*'s portrait of imperial rapacity and Conrad's
Gothic catalog of colonial atrocities, *Heart of Darkness* is less an interrogation of
racism than a text obsessed with anxiety about reverse colonization, an anxiety
significantly portrayed through iconic images of black and white women. The
"savage and superb" black woman whom Marlowe sees as he leaves Kurtz's plantation—an eerie Gothic "apparition" who is apparently his mistress (76)—is the
mirror opposite of the refined white "Intended," Kurtz's fiancée. Both, however,
represent an emasculating threat to white male subjectivity. As Johanna M.
Smith argues, the black woman embodies the vampiric embrace of the Dark
Continent that transforms Kurtz into a savage (184), while the white woman represents the threat of a contaminating ideological duplicity, of telling lies that
undergird both the domestic and imperial projects and entrap men in the "horror" of a shattered selfhood. In this sense, *Heart of Darkness* suggests not just the
centrality of anxieties about racial and sexual identity to the development of
modernity but also the importance of the Gothic as a genre ideally suited to
express these anxieties.

NOTES

[1]For another reading of the breakdown of racial boundaries in the text, see Carens.
See also Nayder's discussion of race and reverse colonization in the novel in *Wilkie
Collins* 115–25.

[2]I am indebted to Piya Pal-Lapinski for bringing to my attention this definition of
hybridity and for helping me see its usefulness to Collins; see her "Chemical Seductions."

[3]For an excellent discussion of *The Sign of Four* as a conservative rewrite of *The
Moonstone*, see Mehta.

[4]For a discussion of *The Sign of Four*, imperialist ideology, and Victorian "criminal
anthropology," see Thomas, "Minding" 242–49. Thomas's essay, like Mehta's, juxtaposes
The Moonstone and *The Sign of Four*.

[5]Given the history of Irish colonization, the instructor can also consider the significance of Stoker's Irishness to his portrayal of race. Several readings of *Dracula* look at this topic (see Schmitt, "Mother Dracula"; Moses). Joseph Valente, who recently published a book-length study of *Dracula* as "metrocolonial Gothic," *Dracula's Crypt,* contextualizes Stoker's portrayal of Irishness in a particularly useful way in "Double Born" (see esp. 633 for a discussion of Stoker's own hybridity).

Surveying the Vampire in Nineteenth-Century British Literature

Daniel Scoggin

The problems one faces in teaching a literary survey course become even more apparent when one addresses a genre as amorphous as the Gothic. For instance, in organizing a survey of the nineteenth-century British Gothic, how can one begin to sketch connections between two of its most noted representatives, Mary Shelley's *Frankenstein* and Charles Dickens's *A Christmas Carol*, or between, say, either of those two texts and Bram Stoker's *Dracula*? In this essay I suggest that an effective course on the development of the genre in the period can be organized around the subject of living-deadness. While the eighteenth-century Gothic exhibits a central fascination with horrific artifacts—the labyrinthine mansion-castle, corrupt priests, feudal tyranny—much of the nineteenth-century Gothic concerns the character of a modern economic parasite. Much of the usefulness in surveying the vampire stems from that considerable, topical gap between John Polidori's description at the opening of the nineteenth century of a feudal vampire-lord "strangling young ladies for the miserable purpose of surviving" (Moretti 84) and Stoker's definitive portrayal at the end of the century of a "rational entrepreneur who invests his gold to expand his dominion: to conquer the City of London" (84).

James Twitchell in his *The Living Dead: A Study of the Vampire in Romantic Literature* argues convincingly that vampire overtones are discernible in a wide range of Romantic works: Coleridge's "Christabel" and "The Rime of the Ancient Mariner," Percy Shelley's "The Cenci," and Keats's "La Belle Dame sans Merci" (4–5). Yet Mary Shelley has the distinction in *Frankenstein* (1818) of being the first to incorporate an ancient Continental tradition (both oral and literary) of the vampire into a Gothic text. As such, her novel stands as the first item on our course syllabus. In an epiphany only second to the monster's initial awakening, Victor recognizes that his progeny still lives and is, moreover, responsible for the death of his brother:

> I considered the being whom I had cast among mankind, and endowed with the will and power to effect purposes of horror, such as the deed he had now done, nearly in the light of my own vampire, my own spirit let loose from the grave, and forced to destroy all that was dear to me.
>
> ([Penguin] 74)

Shelley makes use here of a basic vampire trait gathered from lore: "it was thought that the vampire's first victims would be his closest friends and relations" (Twitchell, *Living Dead* 8). Furthermore, it is quite appropriate that Victor labels the vampire his own, since it is his distorted will that breathed life into a collection of dead body parts. In addition, then, to the number of powerful critical readings that an instructor should employ to explain the complex relationship between Victor and the monster, an attention to the vampiric ties between the two will provide a class with familiar access to some of the novel's more subtle themes.

Thanks to the enduring popularity of the vampire narrative in literature and film, students are already aware that a vampire is a reanimated corpse who "sustains its immortality by feeding on blood, and, in doing so, drains the victim's life force and transforms the victim into a likeness of itself" (Margaret L. Carter, qtd. in Senf, *Vampire* 13). By stopping to consider the force of Victor's use of the term, a class will be better prepared for the violent yet symbiotic duel of the second half of the novel (which often seems needlessly excessive to first readers). Although neither monster nor father are literal bloodsuckers, they will preside together over a family of death; master and slave will often uncannily double each other in their mutual pursuit of revenge.

Any discussion of *Frankenstein* would be remiss without considering its famed genesis in the bout of storytelling among Mary, Percy, Byron, and Polidori on the shores of Lake Geneva in the summer of 1816. (It is fascinating to note that we can largely attribute what Twitchell calls the "monster diptych" of the vampire and the Frankenstein monster, each completing the other in British literature ["*Frankenstein*" 44], to this one fertile summer.) In her 1831 introduction to the novel, a fascinating account that should also be included on our syllabus, Shelley recalls how the group's interest in German and French ghost stories compelled them to produce their own chilling narratives (7). Some of these Continental stories must have addressed the subject of the vampire, since two out of the four works subsequently offered by the group (Byron's and Polidori's) primarily concern this type of monster. As such, it is worthwhile for any class studying the vampire in British fiction then to compare Byron's "Fragment" with Polidori's more developed narrative, "The Vampyre: A Tale" (in the Penguin edition of *Frankenstein*, both are offered complete in the appendices). The close ties between the two works serve as an excellent example of literary influence; Polidori claimed in a letter to the *New Monthly* that "though the ground-work of his tale is certainly Lord Byron's," the development, at the request of a lady, is his own (234), an admission that corresponds to the former intimacy between the two men and their subsequent falling-out. As in Shelley's novel, both short stories outline a coercive relationship between a worldly father figure and a more innocent novice, a point that gives credence to Eve Kosofsky Sedgwick's provocative thesis regarding the homosocial origins of the British Gothic (see her *Between Men*). This threatening plot of coercion will be expanded on throughout the century, becoming a map for the subject's powerlessness against new economic and cultural forces.

Byron's "Fragment" is so brief as to make sense only when read alongside Polidori's effort. Polidori's work may not figure as great or compelling literature, but it lays the foundation for a number of more polished vampire tales that were to follow in its wake. Unlike the first English Gothic novelists a generation before, who often set their stories back in the Middle Ages, Polidori selected an ordinary setting more or less of his own era. In his story, the aristocratic Lord Ruthven (an extension of Byron's Darvell) is described only later as a physical parasite; he is presented from the start as a notorious, upper-class gambler in modern-day London. The villain quickly emerges as a debtor whose embarrassed affairs force him to flee England and seek out the resources of the affluent and fashionable youths of several European cities. Ruthven easily converts others to his disease of bankruptcy and destitution, a death by insolvency that only he seems to be able to survive (238–39). Polidori's story of how Ruthven employs Aubrey's honor as a tool to infiltrate his family and destroy his sister's virtue sets the stage for vampire fiction throughout the century. Polidori is not only the first author to present the vampire as an aristocratic threat to the domestic circle; he also foreshadows how subsequent authors will portray the monster as seeking an erotic bond with his or her victim. The tale thus adds to the identity of the vampire gathered from folklore by making him a topical monster, suggesting that his consumption of a victim's means of life extends far beyond the taking of blood. Students are fascinated by the reading of the vampire as a symbol of upper-class excess, and the monster serves well as an introduction to the social tensions of burgeoning capitalism. Carol Senf has suggested that

> not only does *The Vampyre* take a crude character from folklore and make it complex and interesting, but also it anticipates . . . the way that more skilled writers, including the Brontës, Dickens, and Eliot will incorporate Gothic details into realistic fiction.
>
> ("Polidori's *The Vampyre*" 197)

Roxana Stuart points out that there were a number of vampire plays introduced on the English stage in the 1820s and 1830s that loosely followed the model of Polidori's story of Ruthven. Interestingly enough, those adapted from Polidori often shared a double bill with a stage production of the conflict between Victor and his monster (Twitchell, "*Frankenstein*" 61). However, these dramas are difficult to teach, having largely fallen out of print (on this topic, see Marjean Purinton's essay in this volume).

An instructor can next direct the class to a number of mid-century vampire narratives, a series of short readings that could be photocopied and with copyright approval gathered into a course reader. A good place for this collection to begin is with selections from the most popular of mid-Victorian British thrillers or penny dreadfuls, James Malcolm Rymer's *Varney the Vampire; or, The Feast of Blood.* (A word on the now obscure *Varney* would be helpful here. It was printed by Lloyd twice in the 1840s and then reprinted in 1853 in penny parts. The 1847 work was reprinted by Dover in 1972 and is now available in most academic libraries.) Since each number of *Varney* was meant to be somewhat self-sufficient and later numbers dramatically repeat the circumstances of earlier ones, a class can quite successfully obtain a firm sense of this first full-length fictionalization of the vampire (almost nine hundred pages) by reading selectively. The following chapters are especially significant in their attention to Varney's monstrous career: 1–5, 12–15, 20, 32, 48, 51, 61, 72–82, 88, 171, 214–20. They provide the reader with a sense of how the text refines and extends Polidori's and Shelley's treatment of the vampire.

Varney not only describes a myriad of vampiric reanimations and ritual killings; in a Frankensteinian gesture, the novel also cultivates sympathy for the monster. Furthermore, the author provides a scientific explanation for the existence of the undead by clarifying how Varney is no more than an executed gambler and murderer. (Elsewhere in *Varney*, however, we are told that the vampire has existed since the reign of Henry IV, and later that he became a vampire during the Restoration for killing his son. This internal inconsistency suggests that more than one writer might have had a hand in the story.) After being hanged, Varney's body was given by the hangman to one Dr. Chillingworth, who employed the latest galvanic principles to bring life back to the corpse indefinitely. Varney awakens on the doctor's table proclaiming, "Death, death, where is the treasure?" After the doctor flees the house, terrified that the monster will discover "to whom it was he was indebted for the rather questionable boon of a new life" (1: 330), Varney unwillingly returns to his former career of exploitation in order to survive. Just as he interprets his inability to die as a magical revision of his previously mortal and uncontrollable compulsion to gamble (351), he comes to acknowledge that accumulated money and status are to him a new form of "life-blood" circulating in his "shrunken veins" and allowing him to cling to vitality (149). Ken Gelder observes that in *Varney* "vampirism is certainly connected to the accumulation of capital: he [Varney] hoards treasure, like Dracula, hiding it away" (21). The vampire, in turn, employs his wealth to establish his claim as a pretender among the living:

> How frightful an existence is that of Varney the Vampire! . . . considering the strange gift of renewable existence which was his. . . . And who shall say that, walking the streets of giant London at this day, there may not be some such existences? Horrible thought that, perhaps seduced by the polished exterior of one who seems a citizen of the world in the most extended signification of the words, we should bring into our domestic circle a vampyre!   (Rymer 2: 734)

As in Polidori's story, the vampire may establish himself as a civilized man of the modern city. Yet Varney's polished exterior serves as a thin cover for a threat to the family and what was also the plight of *Frankenstein's* undead outcast. This precarious opposition between a seemingly living, social exterior and a dead essence, an opposition central to what makes vampirism horrifying, will be returned to with added force in late Victorian Gothic narratives such as

Robert Louis Stevenson's *Dr. Jekyll and Mr. Hyde*, Oscar Wilde's *The Picture of Dorian Gray*, and, of course, *Dracula*.

The course reader I have compiled turns from *Varney* to portions of other mid-century texts that extend Polidori's interpretation of the vampire by employing the monster as a social metaphor. Twitchell and Senf have both discussed how the vampire was used selectively by realist writers to project a pessimistic vision of modern life, ranging from draining relationships to horrific class exploitation. Telling references to the monster can be found in Charlotte Brontë's *Jane Eyre* (358) and Emily Brontë's *Wuthering Heights* (280).

Above all, Dickens was a master at incorporating Gothic elements into realist fiction. The course reader should contain chapter 60 of his *Bleak House*, in which the author makes precise use of the vampire to critique the financial and political corruption inherent in the English legal system. Esther Summerson describes the lawyer Vholes, with his "long black figure," as greedily consuming both his client's inheritance and health: "So slow, so eager, so bloodless and gaunt, I felt as if Richard were wasting away beneath the eyes of this advisor, and there was something of the Vampire in him" (720). Dickens's fascination with the theme of undeath is most apparent in his last complete novel, *Our Mutual Friend*. By examining the detailed (yet isolated) descriptions of villains such as Silas Wegg, Lammle, and Old Harmon, the class can obtain a sense of how Dickens converts the formerly supernatural figure of the vampire into a sign of the deathly truncation of the human spirit at the hands of greed and intense worldly competition. In an important sense, *Our Mutual Friend* completes a fascination with living death that Dickens had exhibited as early as his first Christmas book, "A Christmas Carol." In that story Marley's ghost warns Scrooge, "It is required of every man . . . that the spirit within him should walk abroad among his fellow-men, and travel far and wide; and if that spirit goes not forth in life, it is condemned to do so after death."

Finally, students should note that George Eliot was adept too at selectively using the predatory image of the vampire to achieve a "heightened realism," providing the reader "with a glimpse into the darkness that lies within the most prosaic characters" (Senf, "Vampire" 87). In *Middlemarch*, she repeatedly refers to the avaricious banker Bulstrode as a kind of vampire, "not because he is openly violent, inhuman, or irrational like the vampire from folklore, but because he is a morally and emotionally incomplete person, a 'dead' man who preys on others" (87–88). Overall, a class should consider at least a few of these mid-century, transitional references to the vampire, because they serve as a touchstone for the growing complexity and depth of the figure and help dispel the notion that there is a pronounced gap between the first and second generation of vampire stories.

Students can learn that nonfiction writers were apt to use the figure of the undead to characterize the more ruthless subjects of the Victorian economy. As is well known, Karl Marx, in a fascinating chapter of *Capital* (1867) titled "The Working Day," employs the figure of the vampire to identify the coldhearted capitalist's exploitation of his workers: "Capital is dead labour, that vampire-like, only lives by sucking living labour, and lives the more, the more labour it sucks" (*Capital* 342). And in his *Speculative Notes* (1864), David Moirer Evans, an influential writer on economic issues, devotes an entire chapter, titled "The Great Enigma" (about twenty pages), to describing the career of one Count D——, a foreigner with "jet hair," an "aquiline nose," and "burning dark eyes," who periodically visits England at the first hint "of any fresh current of speculation setting in" (198–99). That Evans intended this Count D——to be read as a vampire figure is quite clear. In what is very like a short story, the narrator describes the count, the worst of economic parasites, as staying youthful beyond the memory of several generations of people. Also, the count has secretly infiltrated the highest circles of society and caused several scandals that ruined some of London's best families (198–99), an account that recalls Polidori's story of Lord Ruthven. Marx's and Evans's application of the vampire to characterize an economic threat prepares us for how Bram Stoker will closely align, as Judith Halberstam puts it, the interference of "the natural ebb and flow of currency" with Count Dracula's manipulation of "the ebbing and flowing of blood" (102).

One cannot examine the cultural significance of the vampire without pausing to observe that Rymer, Evans, and, at the end of the century, Stoker, all employ what would can be read as anti-Semitic images in their vampire narratives. Rymer's Varney possesses "dark, sombre eyes" and a hook nose (61); Evans's Count D—— has an "aquiline nose" and "burning dark eyes"; and Count Dracula has a "very marked physiognomy" of massive eyebrows with a strong aquiline face with "peculiarly arched nostrils" (28). Halberstam goes so far as to suggest that modern anti-Semitism is in itself Gothic, "because, in its various forms—medical, political, psychological—it, too, unites and therefore produces the threats of capital and revolution, criminality and impotence, sexual power and gender ambiguity, money and mind, within an identifiable form, the body of the Jew" (95).

In the last nineteenth-century vampire narrative, Stoker's *Dracula* (1897), the monster is, among other threats, the incarnation of Slavic foreignness as well as an aggressive and mysterious investor in England's future; he both hoards ancient estates and "must be restricted precisely because he moves money so easily through many nations" (Gelder 16). Count Dracula, then, resembles the Jew of anti-Semitic discourse not only in his "very marked physiognomy" but also in "his relation to money/gold, his parasitism, his degeneracy, his impermanence or lack of allegiance to a fatherland, and his femininity" (Halberstam 92). As the "prototype of the wanderer," the "stranger in a strange land," he "reflects the way that homelessness or restlessness was seen to undermine a nation" (98).

Sheridan Le Fanu's short story "Carmilla" stands as the last entry in a course reader on mid-nineteenth-century vampire fiction. Referred to in his day as an Irish Wilkie Collins (Punter, *Modern Gothic* 203), Le Fanu brought his mastery of suspense and mystery to bear on the vampire tale, which he inherited from Polidori, Rymer, and his Victorian associates. "Carmilla" also served as a key source for Stoker both in its catalog of vampiric conventions—how one kills a vampire, how one becomes a vampire, what are the vampire's physical limitations, et cetera—and in its juxtaposition of Western, rational science with the Eastern threat of the supernatural. Significant characteristics of Le Fanu's proof-gathering Doctor Hesselius and the mystical Baron Vordenburg can be seen in Stoker's principal vampire fighter, Doctor Van Helsing.

Le Fanu's tale is particularly important as a predecessor of *Dracula* in its alignment of vampirism with a dissolution of traditional gender identity through transgressive female sexuality. Critics have commented on how the female victims of the male vampire in *Dracula* can themselves be seen as images for the new woman, stereotyped as the embodiment of a threatening female sexuality (see Showalter, *Sexual Anarchy* 180–82). This theme has its origins in "Carmilla," which has been called "the first lesbian vampire story" (Case 7) and which showcases the sexually aggressive Countess Mircalla Karnstein, also known as Carmilla, like Ruthven a voracious predator who preys on beautiful young ladies. Laura, one of Carmilla's (or Mircalla's) victims, describes the power of the vampiric gaze:

> Sometimes after an hour of apathy, my strange and beautiful companion would take my hand and hold it with a fond pressure, renewed again and again; blushing softly, gazing in my face with languid and burning eyes, and breathing so fast that her dress rose and fell with the tumultuous respiration. It was like the ardour of a lover; it embarrassed me; it was hateful yet overpowering; and with gloating eyes she drew me to her, and her hot lips traveled along my cheek in kisses; and she would whisper, almost in sobs, "You are mine, you *shall* be mine, and you and I are one for ever."   (588)

This passage, and others like it in the story, will help an instructor introduce the challenging question of the intended audience of vampire fiction. What group of readers would be the target of such an erotic account? What, in particular, would be the imagined response of the female reader, who in many ways takes the position of the naive Laura experiencing the attempted—and in disturbing ways attractive—seduction of the female vampire? How is the depiction of the vampiric act suited to the narrative requirements of an author who hopes to imply the most invasive of penetrations while deflecting accusations of licentiousness by apparently ascribing sexual knowledge only to a monster who can be killed off? Such questions can prepare a class for similar questions in Stoker's *Dracula*, where female victims are in a similar ambiguous position to Le Fanu's Laura, more affiliated with illicit sexuality than they are supposed to be (and Lucy, who becomes a mirror of the wicked Carmilla once she enters on her vampire career, is an example of how fine the dividing line is between innocent and sexually voracious women).

Before closing their surveys with a study of *Dracula*, instructors will wish to consider how the vampire informs two major late Victorian texts at the center of the Gothic revival: Stevenson's *Dr. Jekyll and Mr. Hyde* and Wilde's *The Picture of Dorian Gray*. Both novels describe a Frankensteinian relationship between a master-creator and a rebellious progeny, a relationship that is built equally on the exchange (or sharing) of blood and an attempt to overcome the barrier between life and death. In Stevenson's story, Jekyll, like Victor Frankenstein, uses a scientific process to create a new life. While Jekyll hopes to escape moral accountability through Hyde, he soon discovers that his ascendant creation hopes to use his blood and name against him. Jekyll finally comes to understand that Hyde is no longer just the inheritor of his estate but "co-heir with him to death" and that this "insurgent horror [is] knit to him closer than a wife." To the extent that Jekyll reads that other portion of his consciousness (and conscience) as an unholy other—the "slime of the pit seemed to utter cries and voices," he exclaims, "the amorphous dust gesticulated and sinned" ([1886] 95)—he himself figures as undead, one alive in sin although dead to the world and himself. In the end, the blood relationship between Jekyll and Hyde can be resolved only by a ritual killing, the execution of the vampire's host by the host.

In Wilde's *Dorian Gray*, a wealthy and protected protagonist also discovers a furtive method by which to avoid judgment for sin. Under the vampiric influence of Lord Henry Wotton, who "conveys his temperament" into Dorian "as though it were a subtle fluid" ([1982] 34), Dorian Gray makes a fabulous wish regarding the portrait that Basil Hallward has just painted of him, a work of art that reveals to Dorian the extent of his own beauty. "If it were I who was to be always young, and the picture that was to grow old! For that—for that—I would give everything! Yes . . . I would give my soul for that!" (26). Art and aesthetics, instead of science, will be the catalyst that allows Dorian to engage in an utterly duplicitous life. In turn, he employs his diseased immortality to corrupt an entire generation of wealthy young men and women. Reminiscent of the career of Polidori's Ruthven, Dorian, as Basil remarks, corrupts "everyone with whom [he] become[s] intimate and it is quite sufficient for [him] to enter a house for shame of some kind to follow" (132). In the novel's closing scene, the still beautiful Dorian vainly stabs at the picture, the only living sign of his soul's corruption, and in so doing destroys himself. Unforgiven, he falls, as vampires do, into immediate decay.

Stoker's *Dracula* completes our survey because the novel consolidates and refines the features of its predecessors, while it also has irrevocably stamped our own period's interpretation of how a vampire should appear and behave. At the risk of not doing justice to the range of criticism sparked, in part, by the centennial of this most influential of Gothic narratives, I close by briefly referring to several interpretations of the vampire that might be of special interest to students and instructors who have followed the undead's career throughout the nineteenth century. As well as being "a corpse (an 'it') as well as an animated humanoid (apparently a 'he')" (Hogle, "Introduction" 4), Count Dracula is the colonization of Christian Britain by Eastern foreignness (see Arata, "Occidental Tourist"); an anti-Semitic image of the speculative and avaricious Jew (Halberstam); a sign of the threat made to the middle-class by an outdated aristocracy (Moretti); an enactment of the crisis of the liberal subject at the hands of the rapidly expanding natural and social sciences (Glover); a haunting figure of modern, domestic consumption (Wicke); the antithesis of that topical Victorian phenomenon, the new woman (Senf, "Dracula"); a Victorian model of female sexuality and the oedipal mother who threatens by being desirable (Roth); the frightening source of a sexual longing that fails to adhere to "prohibitions against polygamy, promiscuity, and homosexuality" (Senf, *Dracula* 99; see also Craft); and an enemy of science and rationalism who is finally defeated by their more inclusive organization (Jann).

One could go on. The diverse body of critical work on the vampire provides students and instructors with a wide choice of intellectual frameworks by which to explore how the quintessential Gothic figure can serve as an expression of modern anxiety, a "(s)he/it" that threatens "the socioeconomic distinctions of its author's culture with complete dissolution" (Hogle, "Introduction" 5). The fascinating, central horror of *Dracula*, that the monster (as in *Frankenstein*) may spawn an apocalypse and a new race of deadly beings, is renewed in our age's seemingly endless reproductions on film of the count's career (see Roberts in this volume). Many of these progeny, from Murnau's *Nosferatu* to Coppola's *Bram Stoker's Dracula*, might be employed strategically in the course sketched above, although they are quite deserving of a course of their own.

Teaching Contemporary Female Gothic:
Murdoch, Carter, Atwood

Susan Allen Ford

A required course in literature can become a Gothic experience in and of itself: a young and naive protagonist, cut off from the familiar comforts of high school, under the tyrannous authority of the university, must penetrate dark and obscure verbal labyrinths, braving the terrors of incomprehension, exploring the codes of those texts as well as the mysteries of self and other that lie at the center of the maze. The regional university at which I teach requires of all students six hours of composition and six hours of literature, dividing its sophomore literature sequence into two courses defined around genre: one on poetry and drama and the other on the short story and novel. Each semester, then, offers a course in how to read, how to understand and interpret the conventions of literary expression, even as it offers students an opportunity to experience a range of texts from a variety of periods, nationalities, perspectives. For the last few years in the course on fiction, I've begun with a consideration of different versions of Little Red Riding Hood (Perrault's versus the Grimms') in order to introduce students to the ways narratives—specifically, plots, characters, settings, imagery—can be shaped to different effects. After a few weeks of introducing students to basic fictional techniques in a range of writers, the remainder of the semester focuses on the Gothic.

Why do I do this? What are the benefits of such a course? The Gothic as a mode of fictional experience clearly, even ostentatiously, marks its tactics as artful, as both derived from and productive of some kind of meaning. Its plots, characters, settings, and imagery are repetitive and at some level familiar to students, providing a nicely distorted looking glass through which to study how writers explore and attempt to enclose fears and anxieties derived from both internal and external sources. Even as the Gothic heroes and heroines explore labyrinthine spaces of castle, home, and psyche, readers explore the complicated narrative designs that lead to an interrogation of the dimensions of power and desire that construct (and deconstruct) elements that students, at first, often assume to be immutable and essential: culture, family, and self.

"We live in Gothic times," wrote Angela Carter in 1974 (Afterword 460). What Carter meant, of course, is that the Gothic is peculiarly appropriate to mapping the psychic, emotional, and cultural labyrinths of our world, our selves. Indeed, when students consider writers like Mary Shelley, Edgar Allan Poe, Nathaniel Hawthorne, Bram Stoker, and William Faulkner, they are invited to chart out those forces that convert family, community, identity, as well as all rational systems of scientific inquiry into the imprisoning, institutionally defined structures characterized by oppression, repression, and guilt. As my students and I explore nineteenth-century and modern versions of the Gothic, we also test out a number of the formulations of the Gothic by critics such as Ellen

Moers, Claire Kahane, Sandra Gilbert and Susan Gubar, Judith Wilt, William Patrick Day, and Valdine Clemens. Culminating the course with fictions by contemporary women practitioners of the Gothic provides students with an opportunity to foreground issues of gender central to the Gothic as well as to move deeper into those fictional worlds in which ontological questions are essentially unresolvable. As Fred Botting has remarked of twentieth-century Gothic fiction,

> In a century that has become increasingly sceptical about the values and practices associated with modernity and perceives these values as powerful fictions or grand narratives, new and yet familiar terrors and horrors emerge to present the dissolution of all order, meaning and identity in a play of signs, images and texts. One of the principal horrors lurking throughout Gothic fiction is the sense that there is no exit from the darkly illuminating labyrinth of language.   (*Gothic* [1996] 14)

The works of Iris Murdoch, Angela Carter, and Margaret Atwood illuminate the varied ways in which postmodern women writers explore and transform Gothic conventions. Teaching Murdoch's philosophical Gothic, Carter's tales, and Atwood's more realistic novels provides various opportunities to explore fictions that interrogate the very generic boundaries that threaten to enclose them. All these writers create, in Atwood's phrase, "Gothic[s] gone wrong" (*Lady Oracle* 232), fictions that provoke unease by discovering the terrors of the contemporary landscape, of the female body, of patriarchal systems of power, of the boundaries of the self, and of generic definitions, while simultaneously playing with a reader's often suppressed desire for security, for definition, for narrative closure, even for affirmation of patriarchal systems.

Although Murdoch resisted being considered in feminist or gendered terms, her novel *The Unicorn* (1963) offers a challenging introduction to the contemporary female Gothic, placing the familiar Gothic conventions in the service of fable, of allegory. Marian Taylor, a young woman waiting for her life to begin, arrives at Gaze Castle, a decaying house in a barren landscape of terrifying sea and dangerous bog, as a governess to Hannah Crean-Smith, a woman who has been imprisoned for seven years. Murdoch's employment of the feminine carceral aspect of the Gothic (as explored by Gilbert and Gubar, Moers, and Kahane) presents the figure at the center of the labyrinth as a feminized and infantilized being whose time is spent playing with clothes and jewelry, studying French, and waiting for the return of her husband. The castle's name indicates the novel's allegorical dimension as well as its emphasis on vision and interpretation, and students can quickly generate examples of characters who gaze and are gazed at.

Instead of highlighting plot, the novel emphasizes the attempts of the characters in and around Gaze to determine the meaning of Hannah and her suffering as well as to define their own roles in the story. As students participate in the attempts of those characters to make meaning, to search for significance, they must consider for themselves the ideas of suffering, love, God, and the good that the novel develops. Robert Scholes argues that Murdoch is teaching us to read allegorically through the process of this novel, "allow[ing] us to discover that this work is 'Gothic,' like a cathedral in which every spire and every gargoyle is packed with meaningful allusions to an invisible world" (60). Murdoch's allegory, however, unlike the allegory of earlier times, is, as Scholes points out, "full of meanings but devoid of Meaning" (56), an instructive experience in searching for significance but resisting certainties. Further, although Murdoch's perspective may not be avowedly feminist, her use of the Gothic does raise for students issues of gender. How significant is it that the figure on whom these meanings would be projected is female? To what extent is she peculiarly available to and to what extent does she finally resist the readings that define her? And how do we understand the novel's conclusion, in which Murdoch's other heroine, Marian Taylor, resists the conventional Gothic conclusion of marriage to the damaged hero, instead returning to the world from which she came to dance at the wedding of her former lover?

While Murdoch's use of the Gothic invites a consideration of sexuality and of the ambiguous power of the suffering Christ figure (in this case a suffering woman), *The Unicorn* does not overtly underscore the gendered aspects of suffering and power. It seems, somehow, to gaze beyond or through those concerns. Like the allegorical strategies it employs and subverts, *The Unicorn* gestures outward in a search for a new kind of literary and symbolic language, one that invites our questions of gender and sexuality even if it does not explicitly articulate those questions.

In the work of both Carter and Atwood, however, those issues of gender are brought into focus. Carter's "The Bloody Chamber" (1979), her revision of Charles Perrault's "Bluebeard," like Murdoch's work uses the Gothic in the service of fable though to very different purposes. In her afterword to *Fireworks* (1974), Carter talks about the concentration of meaning possible within the "limited trajectory of the short narrative" in which "[s]ign and sense can fuse to an extent impossible" in a longer one (459). That concentrated fusion—with the distractions of formal realism minimized—encourages students to consider how the tale functions, what it might reflect. Carter suggests:

> The tale does not log everyday experience, as the short story does; it interprets everyday experience through a system of imagery derived from subterranean areas behind everyday experience, and therefore the tale cannot betray its readers into a false knowledge of everyday experience.
> (459)

"The Bloody Chamber," then, propels students into the fabulous world of fairy tale, Gothic, and romance, into "the unguessable country of marriage" (111). Carter's naive, seventeen-year-old heroine leaves her mother's home and ethical world as she marries a sophisticated but beastly bridegroom (a connoisseur of pornography) for the money, power, and knowledge he seems to offer. What he awakens in her is a sense of self as passive, erotic, even pornographic spectacle in opposition to the creative and self-sustaining musician whom her mother has tried to educate.

Students can chart the images of women against and by which the heroine is defined: throughout the narrative she constructs herself and is constructed through analogy to Gothic heroines, martyred virgins, the receptive women of romantic and pornographic literature. Reading Perrault's version before Carter's, students discover her inversions and complications of the relatively simple ironies of his tale. In Perrault, the heroine's transgression, as when she uses the key to enter the castle's only forbidden room, is defined as simple curiosity, "a charming passion but . . . very, very expensive" (41). Moreover, that curiosity, as Marina Warner has demonstrated, is often defined and illustrated in erotic terms and remains essentially unpunished, "a version of the Fall in which Eve is allowed to get away with it, in which no one for once heaps the blame on Pandora" (244). In Carter's version, however, that transgressive curiosity is presented as moving through and beyond the erotic, a necessary step in the moral and psychological development of the heroine. Indeed, in Carter's tale, the heroine's true transgression is her denial of the values imparted by her mother's example: of self-directed action and the importance of love over the lure not of the erotic but of power and money. That transgression, of course, ends in imprisonment.

But is the story's reworking of "Bluebeard" as simple as it at first appears? Students might find the ending, for instance, problematic. The triumphant resolution of the mother-daughter plot, seen in the bride's rescue by her mother rather than, as Perrault's version has it, by her brothers, seems an assertion of feminist power. But as students will also argue, the story's excessively conventional dénouement is so formulaic as to call attention to its artifice: the linkage of tyrannical bridegroom and father; the heroine's strange passivity as she prepares to meet her death; her salvation through and reunification with her mother; her renunciation of ostentatious wealth while retaining enough for economic independence (the establishment of a music school); marriage to the characteristically Gothic damaged hero, the blind piano tuner who could not intervene to save her; the curious emphasis on the heroine's "shame" (143) as the story's final word. Carter might almost be writing to Diane Long Hoeveler's Gothic definition:

> Although she has all of the considerable forces of the patriarchy aligned against her . . . the young, innocent, naive heroine manages to gain her rightful inheritance, usually by besting an evil uncle (read: displaced father figure). And to make matters perfect, the heroine further triumphs over the patriarchy by creating an alternative companionate family, marrying a "feminized" man who promises, if not in word then through his sheer incompetence, to be completely malleable.
>
> (*Gothic Feminism* 6–7)

What are we to make of this absolute fidelity to a generic design? In her excessive adherence to these Gothic conventions, Carter seems perhaps to be sending them up in a kind of Irigarayan mimicry. Hoeveler's formulation can be helpful here:

> Women can undo the effects of phallocentric discourse only when they act out and hyperbolize those same codes. To break out of the masculine imaginary that went under the name of the Gothic required a new discourse system, the hyperbolic female Gothic, a miming of the mime, a mimicry of the gigantic mirror we call the Enlightenment or sensibility cultures. (12)

Carter's fable suggests another strategy for resisting the seductive fixities of meaning—this time the fixities, the narrative forms, through which we construct our notions of gender and the plots that might attach to them.

Atwood's fiction looks even more markedly at the notion of the construction of the female self through narrative and at the ways the Gothic might be both imprisoning and liberating. Her *Lady Oracle* (1976), a comic novel about a Gothic poetess and writer of costume Gothics, demonstrates and reinvents Gothic conventions through parodic excess. From its first sentence—"I planned my death carefully; unlike my life, which meandered along from one thing to another, despite my feeble attempts to control it" (3)—whose simple and controlled first section is immediately undercut by the three clauses that succeed it, the novel's excesses both fulfill and parody its Gothic definitions. Through its accumulation of names, identities, and narratives to explain them, the novel offers students an exploration of postmodern fragmentation and indeterminacy. Who is this character, really? One clue is offered by a fortune cookie, given not to the heroine but to her seemingly more competent other: "*It is often best to be oneself*, whispered the small crumby voice, like a conscience. But which one, which one?" (230).

The novel's circular structure seems to allow no way out of the labyrinth of self. Particularly interesting is the representation of the spectral Gothic mother, as Kahane has defined her, "a dead-undead mother, archaic and all-encompassing, a ghost signifying the problematics of femininity which the heroine must confront" (336). Here the heroine's mother—whose presence at significant moments is explained by a kind of ectoplasmic rubber band that allows her to roam—is at least initially presented as the Gothic villain. The mother-daughter struggle is waged over whether the narrator will be defined as her mother's product or her own creator. Atwood's novel raises the question for students of whether these multiple selves represent the affirmative power of the artist to create self or signify the fragmentation of self that seems to be at the heart of the contemporary Gothic. Students are asked to consider the creative and destructive powers of self, narrative, the very heart of the Gothic mode.

Even the novel's self-conscious use of the Gothic—its tricks with mirrors, mazes, ghosts—raises more questions for students than it resolves. One of the Gothics in the Gothic, the narrator's book *Lady Oracle* is "a Gothic gone wrong. It was upside down somehow. There were the sufferings, the hero, the flights, the looming death, the sense of being imprisoned, but there was no happy ending, no true love" (232). For students, the questions the novel raises define its comic and artistic mystery. Which narrative here is the truest? the most valuable for the character's discovery of self? the most accurate reflection of the world? Does the key lie in the divergences from generic definitions or in their fulfillment? Lost in the mazes of her own narratives, the heroine finally emerges through an act of (mistaken) violence that seems as if it will bring her to a sense of self and unite her with the conventional damaged hero ("there is something about a man in a bandage" [346]). Or does she emerge? The novel's conclusion suggests that even the story we have received might be Joan's narrative *as told to* that injured reporter "without any lies. Well, not very many" (344–45). *Lady Oracle's* Gothic parodies offer students a playful challenge to straightforward notions of narrative resolution and generic definition.

While *Lady Oracle* charts Joan Foster's wild scrambles into one version of self after another, the seemingly more realistic narrative mode of *Alias Grace* (1996) provides a subtler exploration of issues of the construction of the self and of the carceral institutions that define criminality, sexuality, sanity, identity. The novel is based on a Canadian cause célèbre, the 1843 conviction and twenty-nine-year incarceration of the sixteen-year-old Grace Marks for murder. Its Gothic interest in the past and its assemblage of documents and narrative perspectives provide for students a clear connection to other multiply constructed narratives such as *Frankenstein* and *Dracula*. Indeed, the tension between the framing masculinist associations of "real" historical incident and the unstable, feminized content of repressed memory and split personality within (the stuff of talk shows) leads to a central question of the postmodern female Gothic: Where, if anywhere, does meaning lie?

Atwood's focus again is on the construction of the heroine, whose story is told partly through historical documents; partly through her narratives told to a doctor of the mind, partly through her memories, dreams, visions, and projections of what she might say. In a letter to the reader posted on Amazon.com ("Letter"), Atwood explains that for a number of years

> Grace Marks continued to wander around in my head. . . . More time passed and she kept insisting on being given a fuller hearing, so I began to write this novel. Was Grace Marks the cunning female demon many considered her to be—or was she simply a terrorized victim?

Even by the end of the discussion of this novel, my students find themselves divided as to who Grace is and what the nature of her guilt might be. The reasons for that division are interesting. Grace seems to exemplify Hoeveler's notion of "professional femininity": "a cultivated pose, a masquerade of docility, passivity, wise passiveness, and tightly controlled emotions" (*Gothic Feminism* xv), a concept students are interested in exploring. They see that Grace's power derives partly from her apparent acceptance of her fate and partly from her lack of anger, approaching even masochism. Is she victim, victimizer, or somehow both? Atwood asks.

Atwood's construction of characters so that all the female characters—including again mother and daughter—are foils for one another and most of the male characters simply replaceable (even down to their initials) suggests the narrow range of possible identities in this world. Indeed, that mask of professional femininity that Grace must adopt to be interesting, to be rescued, is what makes her surface so difficult to penetrate. Those notions of penetration put teacher and students seeking to understand her in uncomfortable alliance with the doctor Simon Jordan, a version of Victor Frankenstein, who, like the reader, would pluck out the heart of Grace's mystery. While some students find themselves frustrated at the lack of certainty the novel provides, others are intrigued, even exhilarated, by the novel's seductive shift in focus to an examination of the readers' habits as readers—fixing and defining meanings and by doing so exerting power over characters and text. Perhaps this resistance to the imprisoning fixity of meaning, of identity, and even of generic definition is at the very heart of the contemporary female Gothic.

The Gothic wings of the house of fiction provide a diverse and pleasurable labyrinth for exploration by introductory literature students, and among those corridors contemporary female Gothic writers provide both accessible and challenging experiences. The familiar dimensions of these Gothic constructions can be measured, of course, against other models, encouraging attention to genre, to fictional forms. But beyond and through these issues of genre are other concerns, the reasons behind the sometimes obsessive replications of the forms. If the Gothic works as a mirror for our fears and anxieties, how do Murdoch's Anglo-Irish, Carter's English, and Atwood's Canadian labyrinths reflect one another's anxieties or our own? How do the clarifying distortions of these writers create intersecting labyrinths recognizable to those outside the national habitations and names that define each fictional world? In the center of the Gothic maze, students can come face to face with other and with self. From there they might begin their own journeys.

Historicizing the American Gothic: Charles Brockden Brown's *Wieland*

Teresa A. Goddu

In teaching the Gothic, I take a historical approach, beginning my classes on the American Gothic by introducing the notion of "cultural work"—the quotation is from the introduction to Jane Tompkins's *Sensational Designs* (xv)—and arguing that the Gothic is a historical mode, intensely engaged with its culture's concerns. Instead of being an escapist genre, it registers its culture's contradictions, presenting a distorted, not a disengaged, version of reality.

At the outset, students often have a bias toward reading the Gothic psychologically. While this approach has many useful applications, it can reinforce a stereotype of the Gothic as a transhistorical mode that is peculiar in its portrayal of extreme psychological states and hence not integral to an American national or literary identity. Edgar Allan Poe, the main author through whom students are exposed to the American Gothic, exemplifies this problem: typically taught as a psychological misfit and a hack writer, he is portrayed as an aberrant figure in American literature. To challenge students' understanding of the Gothic as a marginal genre—both in its psychological content and its popular-sensationalistic form—I provide a brief history of its origins and development and disclose the canonical investments inherent in generic classification. Once it is placed in a canonical as well as a historical context rather than simply classified by its conventions, the Gothic becomes a dynamic mode that undergoes historical change rather than an essential category with static literary value. Moreover, a historical approach shows students that the Gothic is not only troubled by the terrors of its cultural moment but also central to the way national identity and a national literature are defined and formulated.

Charles Brockden Brown's *Wieland* (1798) is an excellent place to begin such a project. *Wieland* works well as the opening text for a course specifically on the American Gothic or as a representative example of the Gothic in an American literature survey course. It can serve as the foundational fiction for introducing the Gothic in many different types of courses. I position *Wieland* in two ways: as a national narrative and as a reflection on the nature of language and of writing itself. Both these points rely on a cultural reading of the text, and both show how Brown's Gothic—in both content and form—crafts a national-literary identity.

I begin the discussion of *Wieland* by giving students background on Brown. If Poe is often pathologized in students' popular mythology, Brown is usually, and usefully, a blank slate. He is an unknown yet significant figure: although he influenced such later writers as John Neal, Poe, and Nathaniel Hawthorne, he remains largely unread outside the academy. When we situate him in the cultural context of the early national period and in terms of his adaptation of the British Gothic tradition and its translation to the American scene, he becomes crucial in the development of an American literary identity. Students respond to *Wieland* rather flatly on their first reading. The story has all the sensational elements of a good read (murder, incest, sexual passion, spontaneous combustion), but its convoluted plot and eighteenth-century prose often leave students bewildered and bored. Once they understand *Wieland* to be a critique of post-revolutionary American society, they become more interested. However, given limited class time, the problem of providing them sufficient historical context along with the tools for a cultural reading remains difficult. This difficulty is one reason that the Gothic continues to be taught mainly as a psychological mode: such an approach is just more user-friendly.

If making cultural criticism accessible in the classroom is a challenge, some strategies are successful. A modern connection, for instance, helps bridge the distance between Brown's time and the present. The film *The Sixth Sense* (1999) can teach students to read the Gothic through a historical lens and to understand how issues of national identity are integral to the Gothic. The film takes the same imaginative landscape as Brown's text: the haunted city of Philadelphia. By reading their own cultural moment first, students not only read Brown's novel better but also learn to interpret popular culture critically instead of just imbibing it.

The film can be easily summarized for those who have not seen it: it is a ghost story about a boy who sees dead people and about the psychologist who tries to help him. Short clips can also be shown. I begin by quickly going through one possible psychological reading of the film (one that the psychologist, played by Bruce Willis, provides for us). The boy, abandoned by his father, is delusional and perhaps paranoid. His psychological wound can be healed only by a surrogate father (the psychologist) who helps him face his fear; in the end, the boy, in the role of Arthur in a class play, gains his manhood and his peers' acceptance by pulling a phallic sword from the rock. I move on to a cultural reading of the film, asking students to make sense of the film's setting: a gray and dreary Philadelphia depicted as much by its modern skyline as by the architecture of its historical past. The ghosts that haunt this place are similarly from the recent present (a battered wife, a teenager shot with his father's gun, a daughter killed by her mother who suffers from Munchausen by Proxy Syndrome) and from the distant past (indentured servants, courthouse hangings); all have died violent deaths. The film makes Philadelphia, once the capital city and the cradle of liberty, a synecdoche for the nation and its ideals. Its haunted space represents the national psyche, showing how violence is at the heart of our culture—in terms of both our violent beginnings (the nation was built through bloodshed, the film argues as the camera lingers on a close-up of a statue of an Indian) and the violence that permeates modern life and destroys its children. The surprise ending suggests that the violence that our culture perpetrates on its children will come back to kill that culture. More than just a scary movie, *The Sixth Sense* is a serious reflection on the roots and destructive potential of a nation built on violence. *The Sixth Sense* thus gives students a quick lesson in reading a text historically. Moreover, by doing the psychological reading first, they learn how different critical approaches result in different insights. Finally, by linking the film back to *Wieland*, they recognize that the Gothic has a long tradition of interrogating the myths of national identity by providing a nightmarish vision of the American experiment gone awry.

Wieland not only describes the same haunted landscape as the film but also takes up the theme of a national identity built on violent and irrational impulses. The text figures the Wieland family as representative of the nation, as reenacting its history. Father Wieland, who immigrated to the United States to flee religious persecution and convert the Indians, becomes wealthy through cheap land and slave labor; his children, Clara and Theodore, who turn their father's religious retreat into a temple to the Enlightenment, represent ideal republican citizens. The "transformation" of the title—*Wieland; or, The Transformation: An American Tale*—refers to the specter of the American Revolution that has yet to happen in the novel's chronology and that haunts the author's postrevolutionary culture.

Having students read the letter that Brown sent to Thomas Jefferson along with *Wieland* (Clark 163) emphasizes the novel as a national narrative. This document paired with the advertisement of *Wieland*, in which Brown describes himself as a "moral painter" (8) and insists on the instructive nature of his text, underscores the cultural work he intended his novel to perform. Once students understand the text as a serious interrogation of the nation's postrevolutionary moment, they can proceed to a specific critique, which may take a variety of forms—from a discussion of the text's analysis of the limits of Enlightenment empiricism and Lockean theory to its examination of religious enthusiasm.

I focus on the social anarchy that threatened the new republic. By showing the negative side of the American Revolution's transformative potential,

Wieland warns of the precarious nature of the postrevolutionary order. Father Wieland's death by spontaneous combustion signifies the loss of authority and raises central questions: How can the new nation succeed if its citizens are powder kegs of passion rather than rational beings? How can the nation reinstitute authority in a body that can self-destruct? One need only invoke Benjamin Franklin (and in the survey course I often pair *Wieland* with Franklin's *Autobiography*) for students to see how Brown is exploring the irrational side of Franklin's self-made man and exposing the destructive power hidden at the center of the rational, republican self.

After setting up *Wieland* as a cultural critique in the first class, I turn in the second to a discussion of the novel's analysis of the postrevolutionary period through its narrator, Clara. We look at how Clara represents the ideal republican citizen and discuss why the female body is potentially the most terrifying place to locate the transformations occurring in Brown's culture. Focusing on Clara and the double-voiced nature of Brown's text allows for some broader comments about the role of women—both as authors and characters—in the Gothic. By tracing Clara's sexual self-combustion through close readings of several parallel scenes that occur in her bedroom (her discovery of a voice issuing from her closet, her dream in the summer house, her subsequent suspicion that Theodore is in her closet, the murder of Catherine in Clara's bed, and the final confession), the threat to the woman-house-family-nation is revealed not to be coming from without—in the form of the alien other, Carwin—but from within: through both Theodore and, more important, Clara herself.

Wieland's use of the Gothic convention of doubling shows how the novel collapses boundaries between self and other to disclose that the enemy is the self. The doublings of Carwin and Theodore and Catherine and Clara, as well as the important mirroring of Theodore and Clara in the confession scene, reveal that not only Theodore but also Clara has destructive impulses. By the end of the novel, Clara is transformed into a savage who thirsts for Carwin's death and whose hands are sprinkled with her brother's blood. Her final collapse into a ferocious frenzy is anticipated throughout the novel by her sexual passion. Her "affection more than parental" (35) for Louisa Conway, her passionate prose, and her incestuous longing for Theodore (who loves her with a "passion more than fraternal" [211]) all manifest uncontrollable desires. The plot locates these desires in her long before Carwin arrives to ignite them.

Time is needed to discuss the incest in the novel, since students often do not pick up on it on their own, and to address how Brown uses incest as a cultural metaphor. Students are surprised to hear that brother-sister incest is a dominant motif in early American literature. When I ask them to interpret incest as a social model—one that signals a closed social circuit (in Lévi-Strauss's sense) or a dangerous narcissism—they begin to see how incest signifies the Wieland family's social withdrawal.

The novel's conclusion, which places Clara back in proper sexual bounds through the socially sanctioned love of Pleyel and the institution of marriage, makes clear the conservative nature of the novel's cultural critique: that without strong institutional controls the nation, like Clara's house consumed by flames, will self-combust.

I spend the third and final class discussing narrative form. *Wieland*'s highly wrought form is a good example of the self-conscious artifice of the Gothic, and the novel's narrative technique intersects its cultural critique. Once again, historical context—in this case the intimate connection between language and social order in the early national period—is necessary in order to establish this link. When one teaches *Wieland* in a survey course, this context is relatively easy to provide, since a number of texts from the period exemplify how language served as a tool for social stability or change. Franklin's textualized self, whose errata can easily be amended; the Declaration of Independence, where the nation is literally written into being; or excerpts from the Alien and Sedition Acts, where language is legally regulated, are just a few examples. I provide excerpts from Noah Webster's preface to *An American Dictionary of the English Language* along with sample words from the dictionary. For instance, *duty*, which Webster defines in part as "obedience to prince magistrates and the laws" by "every citizen and subject," suggests conservatism. Through Webster's dictionary, students see how language was believed to constitute political and cultural unity and how Webster's definitions of words were part of a larger project of social control. Students now quickly understand *Wieland* as commentary on the power of language to destroy the social order. The novel's central metaphor for that dangerous power—ventriloquism—shows how easily language can create reality and the disruption that occurs when words are separated from their source of authority. Carwin's ventriloquism begins the destruction that eventually consumes the Wieland family. Instead of embracing Theodore's republican belief in the purity of language (Theodore spends his time restoring the purity to Cicero's text), the novel represents a world where words, like the rational citizens who use them, spin out of control.

The novel's obsessive representation of its own tale telling mirrors its fascination with the impurity of language. When the many written narratives are listed—Clara's letter (the novel itself), her journal, her father's manuscript, her brother's confession—as well as the many competing and conflicting accounts given, the text becomes visible as a conglomeration that lacks a unified authorial voice or a single script. Insistence on the novel's written nature suggests that no definitive history of events can be told—even after the fact. With its emphasis on imperfect, mangled tales and its statement that "the clearest narrative will add nothing to [our] present knowledge" (140), the novel argues that language does not clarify events but further complicates them. In *Wieland* there is no truth, only tales. By writing his novel in an imperfect way, Brown enacts his point. In a society that has overthrown traditional forms of authority, the author (both Clara and Brown) also loses control. In this reading, Brown is not a writer who wrote too hastily; instead, *Wieland*'s loose ends are integral to his purpose.

I conclude by discussing *Wieland's* ending as a restoration of social as well as linguistic order: the madness of Clara's Gothic tale is replaced by a sentimental story where she moralizes about virtue. Like so many Gothic tales, *Wieland* seems to end by conservatively containing the subversive forces it has unleashed. But terrors continue to trouble the ending. What does it mean for Clara, the representative American, to retreat to Europe and for Carwin to become a yeoman farmer and the author of a "faithful narrative" (240)? How does the Maxwell story disprove Clara's claim of being cured? What about the threat of another transformation, the French Revolution? The ending reinforces the central theme: that the nation harbors the potential for self-destruction despite strong social regulation. Writing itself, *Wieland* suggests, may do more to destroy than to reform society. Brown abandoned writing in favor of a career in commerce, retreating from the revelations that his Gothic fictions exposed.

Through our discussion of *Wieland*, I hope to give students a critical approach to the Gothic as much as a reading of the novel: that the Gothic is haunted by the horrors of history and that it intervenes in rather than escapes the cultural moment. By showing the Gothic to be at the core of national identity and the starting place of a self-consciously American literary tradition, *Wieland* provides a springboard from which to explore the Gothic's centrality to nineteenth- and twentieth-century texts. One can turn to Poe after having taught *Wieland*, because Poe often haunts discussions of Brown (almost as if the literary influence between them worked in reverse). Excerpts from Toni Morrison's *Playing in the Dark* (1992) as well as historical texts (like newspaper descriptions of Nat Turner's uprising) help demonstrate that the terror of Poe's tales are not of the soul but of society. By reading their blackness and whiteness in terms of race and by historicizing them in terms of slavery ("The Black Cat" works especially well [*Great Short Works* 390–401]), the argument can be developed further: that slavery and its attendant horrors lie at the core of the American Gothic. Frederick Douglass's slave narrative can then be used to show how the Gothic operates in a realist form and how an African American author transforms its conventions not only to unveil slavery's horrors but also to haunt back. *Beloved*, Toni Morrison's masterful rewriting of the slave narrative in the form of a ghost story, is a wonderful text with which to close this argument. Whatever texts one chooses, however, it is important to emphasize the different ways the Gothic responds to its cultural moment and how different authors adopt and transform its conventions. Once historicized, the Gothic should not always look or act the same. Whether serving as the gateway to more specific units on the Gothic or as the representative Gothic text itself, *Wieland*, read historically, not only discloses the Gothic's connection to national identity but also sets its multiple manifestations in motion.

Using Narrative Form
to Teach Poe's Gothic Fiction

Richard Fusco

One of the major goals of an instructor of English is to have undergraduates see continuities among literary texts produced at different times and by different authors. With Gothic fiction, I exploit narrative form to establish links among short stories with a particular commonality. Since my approach depends on the recognition of patterns, I have found that a short-fiction syllabus allows me to present enough examples to convince students of the theory's validity.

The structural similarities of madman narratives—first-person monologues by insane characters—can guide students in achieving the following insights: (1) to dissect the plot construction of individual texts; (2) to demonstrate how two seemingly contradictory readings can be based upon one text; (3) to examine variations of this plot formula within an author's oeuvre; (4) to link a variety of authors who employ this formula, stressing how they imitate past models while still personalizing their texts; (5) to demonstrate how Gothic writers— British, American, and Continental—explored aspects of abnormal psychology before Freud; (6) to observe trends in how the form was refined throughout the nineteenth century; and (7) to see how this literary device was used in texts not usually regarded as Gothic. My aim is to alter students' perception of Gothicism as solely a literary tradition. I want them to see it as a dark impulse ever present in the human psyche.

To establish the interpretive foundation of my approach, I ask students to read chapters 10, 11, and 16 of Aristotle's *Poetics*, which I put on reserve in the library. In these passages, Aristotle defines and explores *anagnorisis*, the textual point at which a tragic protagonist makes a devastating discovery. In the discussion that ensues, I have students apply this concept at two levels in interpreting a story (such as Edgar Allan Poe's "Ligeia" [*Great Short Works* 175–93]): (1) to locate and explore the significance of a discovery point from the protagonist's perspective and (2) to do the same from the reader's perspective. Students soon realize that in such texts readers usually see the truth of a situation before the narrator. Thus, rather than dictate a textbook definition of dramatic irony, I have students develop their own working theories.

I propose that these "reader discovery points" can map various plot sequences in short fiction. The location and number of sites where the author intends readers to see a turning point in the plot can define a variety of short-story structures. I list seven plot formulas in my book *Maupassant and the American Short Story: The Influence of Form at the Turn of the Century*. One of these schemes, which I call a "descending helical" (49–63), maps out the usual progression of a madman's narrative. Often in first person, descending helicals trace the oscillations of a self-destructing mind. I suggest that this structure, used by many Gothic writers, mediates the relationship between a text and its audience.

Using a Socratic approach, I ask questions designed to point out the fascinating dimensions in the plot structures of madman narratives. I invoke Poe's tales to lay the foundation for discussing the works of other authors. A good tactic is to have one student read selected paragraphs from "The Tell-Tale Heart" (*Great Short Works* 384–89). (The passage where the narrator stalks his victim nightly works well.) Students will see the simple consequences of employing a first-person narrator. The psychological trick of the repeating word "I" draws readers into the mind of an insane murderer, a technique that achieves Poe's agenda of having them realize these innate propensities in themselves. Subsequent discussion often leads to an interesting debate over the human inclination for violence, revenge, and irrational behavior. Occasionally, a student will contribute insights derived from a course in psychology. (Once, a junior invoked Konrad Lorenz's *On Aggression.*) Discussion invariably arrives at the insight that these Gothic tales present extreme manifestations of unpleasant but common human instincts.

Early in the course, I instruct students to read in class the first passage of a Poe text not yet assigned for homework, a text most are not familiar with. (Recently I used "The Cask of Amontillado.") After they complete the first paragraph or two, I ask them to close their books and speculate about how the story will turn out. A few creative students will go so far as to construct their own stories. Most, however, talk generally about how the writer has preformed their expectations of the denouement. The clues, both psychological and metaphoric—that we should doubt the sanity of the narrator and therefore the truth of his narrative—are conspicuous from the first sentence, allowing us to see what he cannot admit. I ask students to make a psychological model that will predict the narrator's behavior. When they have read the rest of the tale, they are surprised by the accuracy of their model. They discover that, in shaping their preconceptions, the initial passage heightened their reading skills and manipulated their conceptions as they completed the story.

Next I outline how I think such maniacal narratives dilate the reader's discovery point to the length of the entire text and thus become an initiation into the processes of a decaying mind and deepening irrationality. One vital question I ask is, Why do Gothic writers avoid story structures that value the decisive impact of one instant on a life in favor of a form that advocates discovery as a gradual process? Some students eventually speculate that Gothic writers have tapped into an insight about the human experience, that no single event can induce insanity in a person. Instead, it is an array of misfortunes that takes a toll upon rationality. Clinical aspects of abnormal psychology often enter our discussion.

At this point, I invite suggestions about how to describe the pacing of these narratives. I begin this session with a few useful metaphors. Poe himself proposed an interesting metaphor in "A Descent into the Maelström" and its literary ancestor, "MS Found in a Bottle." With its slow beginning, its gradual acceleration, its ebbs and flows, the maelstrom parallels the degradation in a haunted mind. The circularity of plot movement calls attention to the egocentric focus of insanity. The descent parallels the motion away from rationality, safety, and civilization toward irrationality, death, and chaos. I draw the descending helix of a maelstrom on the blackboard, accentuating the slow concentric movements in a large circle at the top, picking up the tempo as the spiral descends, and ending up in a furious crescendo as the drawing funnels at the bottom, which signals the threshold of absolute madness (and sometimes of death as well).

In recent classes, students have suggested parallel metaphors. At first they usually respond with other types of weather phenomena: whirlwinds, tornadoes, and hurricanes. The notion of the eye at the storm's center is particularly useful in interpreting how such stories end. Another related example is water gurgling down a drain. One student interested in and knowledgeable about recent advances in astrophysics traced parallels with black holes. Another drew parallels to world economic history: she recounted the vicious cycle of how during the 1920s the United States lent money to Germany so that Germany could pay war reparations to Britain so that Britain could repay its war loans to the United States, a financial morass that contributed significantly to the collapse of the world economy at the end of the decade. Such free-ranging discussion reinforces the notion that these Gothic writers have tapped into a basic pattern in nature, in individual behavior, and in civilization itself. To dramatize this descending helix, I sometimes play a version of the old Jacques Brel song "La Valse à mille temps." (One of the English translations, entitled "Carousel," recorded by Elly Stone during the 1960s, is particularly effective.) The song begins with a slow, airy, delightful, ingenuous account of riding on a carousel. As it progresses, however, the tempo gradually increases. The repeated lyrics assume a more disturbing tone as the piece reaches breakneck speed with obvious maniacal overtones.

I follow the Brel song with a recitation of "The Bells." Poe's poem has strong parallels with his madman tales. Each of the four stanzas represents a stage of mental dissolution. I read the first stanza slowly and easily, accentuating its innocent tone. Each of the next three stanzas increases in length, relies on repetition for effect, and becomes desperate in tone. Therefore, as in the Brel song, I accelerate the rate of my recitation. The innocent words of the first stanza sound frenetic by the last. These raving repetitions approximate a rare occurrence among schizophrenics in which victims rage continually until they drop dead from exhaustion.

After asking the class to interpret several such tales, I show how a descending helix presents perceptual problems for readers. I recapitulate a story such as "Ligeia" strictly as a madman's narrative. Then I ask students to look at it strictly as a supernatural tale. Events such as the ruby drops that find their way into Lady Rowena's goblet can be seen by the reader as either (1) the narrator's subconscious dissociating itself from his poisonous act or (2) the presence of the ghostly Ligeia preparing the way for her fantastic resurrection. Students soon discover what a difficult position an unreliable narrator puts them in. They speculate on the Gothic writer's interest in tenuousness of perception. To demonstrate this duality visually, I show a drawing of the old gestalt puzzle, the white vase formed by the juxtaposition of two black silhouettes. As readers, we participate in the creation of the story by making interpretive choices based on our prior experiences and prejudices.

Once I have established the egocentric, depressive, increasingly frenetic movement of the plot, I deal with the acutely perceptive subtleties in such short-story structures. The rate of mental decline does not accelerate steadily. There are ebbs and flows, moments of creeping insanity and moments of respite from it. Examining texts more closely, students note the variations in the pacing of events. Almost any Poe tale will do in this exercise. Such evaluation confirms the psychological realism of Gothic texts. In effect, these tales, while not true to a reality ruled by physical laws, do faithfully represent the human mind's capacity for violent extremes.

Reinvoking the metaphors of the eye of the storm and the inescapable core of a black hole, I ask students why Gothic writers end their stories when a character reaches the very center of insanity. Different writers elicit different responses. Students offer the theory, for example, that Poe had the ability to understand and describe going insane but lacked the knowledge of what lies beyond the brink. Some students believe that such stories attack Romantic individualism; thus, absolute trust in imagination produces chaos and an intellectual void. At the opposing end, one student suggested that in succumbing incrementally to madness these characters eventually achieve an intellectual level so rare that it cannot be explained to the rational world. Poe's disciple, Guy de Maupassant, occasionally ended descending helical tales with the narrator's announcing his intention to commit suicide. Death as a solution to the horror of madness inspires a variety of sincere personal philosophical responses from students.

We study how other writers used the descending helix to achieve some aspect in their literary, political, or social agendas. It is intriguing to compare these goals. I like to compare Poe's "The Tell-Tale Heart" (1843), Maupassant's "The Horla" (1887), and Henry James's *The Turn of the Screw* (1898). Poe's tale shows the devastating consequences of madness for both the individual and society and reveals the potential for self-destruction in us all. Maupassant imitates Poe's model but focuses his story more on the consequences for the individual. He presents life as a continual but ultimately losing battle against irrationality. Following Maupassant to some extent, James nevertheless refuses to have any character succumb totally to madness. The ability of a person to reflect made such an outcome unthinkable for him. Instead, through the governess's self-revealing narrative in his classic ghost story, James suggests that the human mind can confront whatever exasperating misfortune life has to offer.

Students are quick to note structural similarities between Poe's and James's tales, but they are quicker to pick out the differences. I list their observations on the board and ask them to look for and analyze the patterns in this evidence. They discern a component of each author's insight into human psychopathology. Some even see evidence that these Gothic texts contain insights into the workings of the human mind that anticipated the emergence of twentieth-century psychology. Certainly, the authors' inclination to explore the dark recesses of the soul and the willingness of their audiences to read such narratives evince the fundamental Jungian principle that we can best control threatening impulses by recognizing their existence and reflecting on them.

These descending helical texts also construct contrasting definitions of schizophrenia, the cause of which theorists have debated vigorously throughout the twentieth century. This controversy is reflected in a dozen articles in Benjamin B. Wolman's *International Encyclopedia of Psychiatry, Psychology, Psychoanalysis, and Neurology*. Several times during a semester, I assign a student to present one of the definitions. I then use the concepts from that report as the starting point for that day's discussion.

When I get the opportunity, I demonstrate how a descending helical plot, with its thematic and philosophical import, appears in works not usually regarded as Gothic. I have used stories by writers as diverse as Ivan Turgenev ("Clatter of Wheels"), Kate Chopin ("A Vocation and a Voice"), James Joyce ("The Dead"), Sherwood Anderson ("The Philosopher"), Katherine Mansfield ("The Garden-Party"), and William Faulkner ("Pantaloon in Black"). Most of these writers used not Poe's egocentric narrative voice but the third person. In varying degrees, however, they retained the descending helix's concentric movement toward relatively greater psychological instability. The reward of interpreting these texts is that students eventually realize that Gothicism is not just a literary tradition but also an impulse omnipresent in the human condition.

On occasion, I have applied the notion of the descending helix to interpret novellas and novels. Stephen King's *Carrie* works well when readers link each level of the protagonist's growing psychokinetic powers with each stage of her emerging paranoia. Looking at such narratives from a less apocalyptic, Jamesian point of view (in which characters suffer a mental decline but do not descend into utter madness), I find that texts such as Joseph Conrad's *Heart of Darkness*, Kate Chopin's *The Awakening*, and James Joyce's *Ulysses* inspire interesting conversations. In *The Awakening*, for example, Chopin places Edna Pontellier in increasingly exasperating dilemmas that eliminate her social options one by one. The pace of Pontellier's psychological decline is not as frenetic as that experienced by one of Poe's mad narrators, but the direction is the same, emphasizing the inevitably escalating assaults on individual sanity that pervade existence.

I have used this approach in a variety of pedagogical contexts while teaching eighteenth- and nineteenth-century American, British, and Continental short fiction. I do not make it the sole or even the primary focus of a course. Instead, I integrate it with other sorts of literary investigations. This search for form becomes a way to link texts across a syllabus and to unify a course. Ultimately, students see Gothicism as more than a literary tradition or a set of fictional symbols and devices. The continuities of psychological themes among overtly Gothic texts reshape the sensibilities of readers so much that they begin to look for descending helical patterns in other sorts of narratives.

Gothicism thus migrates from the boundaries imposed by its traditional literary associations to the expanded horizons granted by its psychological universality. A madman's narrative by Poe allows us to examine our own bizarre possibilities of personality with an insight so acute that it sometimes approximates that of a psychiatrist. Poe's depiction of behavioral extremes creates so indelible a pattern that we automatically begin to look for it in subtler textual contexts, such as in a novel by Joyce or Conrad. Since many students tend to personalize their reading experiences, some may eventually include this Gothic pattern of perception in their view of the world. Studying Gothic narrative form will then construct an intellectual framework on which they can articulate their insights about abnormality and differentiate them from other ways of looking at human behavior.

Teaching the Doppelgänger in American Gothic Fiction: Poe and James

A. A. Markley

One of the most effective ways that I have found to approach Gothic literature in the classroom is by arranging the texts that we read and analyze in units that are linked by a particular theme common to a broad array of Gothic fiction—that of the doppelgänger or double. Variations on the doppelgänger motif abound in English and European literature of the nineteenth and early twentieth centuries, and they tend to exhibit the best of what Gothic fiction offers in terms of terror and suspense. By their very nature doppelgänger tales raise issues of identity and relationships with others; thus such works tend to be rich catalysts for class discussion on these topics. The approach to the American Gothic tradition suggested here concerns the doppelgänger motif in the fiction of Edgar Allan Poe and Henry James. Beginning with a time-honored set of conventions in this genre, both Poe and James developed the motif in a new direction with a specific focus on psychology and the unconscious mind. In the hands of each of these authors the doppelgänger became a tool for exploring the multiple and often pathological manifestations possible in a character's psyche.

Before one addresses in the classroom how Poe and James depart from tradition, it is important that students understand how the motif functions in earlier examples of Gothic fiction. I usually present the tradition characterized by two strands: stories that focus on emotional bonds between characters by emphasizing profound similarities between their personalities and stories in which one character faces the terrors of demonic temptation by a strangely familiar other.

I approach teaching the doppelgänger as an exploration of emotional bonding by beginning with Joseph Conrad's *The Secret Sharer*, a tale of two characters who share a host of uncanny similarities. Students tend to be intrigued by the fact that *The Secret Sharer* lends itself to a wide variety of critical interpretations, and they enjoy debating the merits of various critical readings of the work. Like some Conrad scholars, some students choose to interpret the narrator's secret companion Leggatt as a figment of his imagination, born of his sense of isolation and his intense longing for companionship in the insecurity of his first stint as a captain over a crew with much more actual sailing experience. Others insist that Leggatt is real and cite textual evidence requiring such an interpretation. Perhaps the best reading of the text is reached when the class becomes comfortable acknowledging the symbolic aspect of Leggatt's presence on the ship without insisting that this aspect be carried to the ultimate degree—accepting the irreconcilable aspects of Conrad's use of the symbolism of the double allows realism to exist alongside allegory.

The inevitably spirited debate over interpreting *The Secret Sharer* can lead smoothly into a study of other novels where character doubling is used to emphasize emotional bonds. In this context, I have often taught William Godwin's *Caleb Williams* and Mary Shelley's *Frankenstein*. The love/hate relationship between Victor Frankenstein and his creature, the conflicted and distorted aspects of their relationship as parent and child, and their alternating roles of pursuer and pursued closely resemble the relationship that William Godwin depicts between the overly curious Caleb Williams and his aristocratic employer, Ferdinando Falkland.

Mary Shelley provides a perfect segue into a study of the second strand of the doppelgänger tale—the tale of demonic temptation and of the struggle between good and evil. After our work on *Frankenstein*, I often assign her humorous short story "Transformation," in which the narrator describes how he was persuaded to exchange bodies with a mysterious dwarf with supernatural powers in a scheme to win back his estranged fiancée. Students particularly enjoy this story because of its lighthearted parody of the very Gothic conventions used seriously in *Frankenstein*. Shelley's most direct source for her plot was Lord Byron's unfinished Gothic drama *The Deformed Transformed*, a highly Faustian play in which Byron's deformed protagonist, Arnold, is tempted by a demonic spirit to trade his misshapen form for that of the beautiful Greek warrior Achilles. With many similarities to Byron's unfinished play, James Hogg's *The Private Memoirs and Confessions of a Justified Sinner* provides perhaps the best example of a novel in this tradition. In Hogg's tale the devil, who here calls himself Gil-Martin, gradually destroys a religious and highly self-righteous Scottish nobleman, Robert Wringhim. Using his powerful gift for subtle persuasion, Gil-Martin gradually maneuvers Wringhim into committing a series of ever more insidious crimes. At certain points in the story, he adds to Wringhim's mounting confusion, and to the community's mounting distrust of Wringhim, by taking on the young man's appearance and committing misdeeds in his victim's guise.

Studying these two aspects of the way the doppelgänger motif manifested itself in early-nineteenth-century English fiction lays a firm foundation for classroom discussion of the emergence of the motif in Poe and James. Byron's play leads naturally to a discussion of Poe's well-known doppelgänger tale "William Wilson" (*Tales and Sketches* 422–51), for which it was an important source. In Poe's story the narrator describes the uncanny experience of encountering a peer at school who shares his appearance, his name, and even his birthday. The unlikely similarities between these two characters often make students suspicious from the outset; and the manner in which the double begins to appear to the narrator in order to admonish him for bad behavior may suggest to them that the double is a projection of the narrator's conscience. Students gradually realize that the narrator's double represents the narrator's own ability to distinguish between good and evil and that his mounting hostility and ultimate violence against his double merely chronicle the stages of his madness.

In "William Wilson" Poe draws on aspects of the doppelgänger tradition to depict what seems at first to be a highly conflicted relationship between two characters who are linked to each other to an unusual degree. But, not interested in exploiting the conventions merely to create suspense and terror, Poe takes the motif in a new and even more haunting direction as the story gradually reveals itself to be concerned not with two independent characters but with merely one—a dissolute confessional narrator who experiences trauma in attempting to reconcile a pattern of licentious behavior with an aberrant perception of his conscience. In Poe's hands traditional elements of the doppelgänger motif are put to work in the service of intense psychological exploration, a preoccupation that characterizes much of his fiction as well as that of many writers of the late nineteenth and early twentieth centuries whose works reflect an emerging fascination with human psychology.

Writers influenced by Poe's use of the doppelgänger as psychological exposé continued to develop the idea of the double as a manifestation of a personality split—a split usually characterized as a division between good and evil halves of the human personality. Robert Louis Stevenson's *Dr. Jekyll and Mr. Hyde* and Oscar Wilde's *The Picture of Dorian Gray* fall into this tradition, where the doppelgänger is specifically used to illustrate the psychological terror and the real danger of a human psyche characterized by distinct multiple personalities. From this context, students can be led into a productive analysis of how James was also to develop this theme in his own unique way.

In his story "The Private Life" (*Complete Stories* 4: 58–91), James carefully unfolds a chilling tale in which the narrator, amid a group of acquaintances on vacation on the Continent, gradually begins to suspect that one of his friends, the famous writer Clare Vawdrey, "the greatest of our literary glories," leads a double existence (58). At first the narrator is unable to reconcile Vawdrey's lackluster social presence with his brilliant literary endeavors. When Vawdrey is unable to quote lines from a play that he insists he has composed, the narrator becomes even more suspicious. His suspicions are finally confirmed when he leaves Vawdrey's company among his other friends and steals into Vawdrey's hotel room without knocking. There he finds an unresponsive double of Vawdrey, lost in deep concentration on his writing. The story takes a humorous turn when it is likewise discovered that another among the party, Lord Mellifont, a man renowned for his exceptional public bearing, leads no private life whatsoever but literally disappears from the face of the earth when left alone.

Although "The Private Life" is said to have been inspired by Robert Browning, whose public manner struck many as inconsistent with the passion and depth of his poetry, the story clearly can be read as an expression of the author's own anxieties about the disparate energies required to maintain both a public, social existence and a successful, private, literary life. James would refashion the doppelgänger motif in a similar way several years later in his story "The Jolly Corner" (*Complete Stories* 5: 697–731), in which his fifty-six-year-old narrator, Spencer Brydon, returns to America after many years of living in Europe.

Gradually Brydon's obsession with his ghostly, now empty childhood home, "the Jolly Corner," grows into a fixation on the idea of what he might have become had he chosen to stay in America and live a life more in line with his family's expectations. Brydon begins to perceive this projection of his personality in an alternate life as having a physical presence of its own. He becomes more and more convinced of the physical presence of this second self in the house and pushes himself to the point of psychological breakdown in a climactic confrontation with his double. The existence of his other self is uncannily affirmed by his former love, Alice Staverton, who has likewise perceived the presence of Brydon's double.

The psychological implications of Poe's treatment of the doppelgänger motif, and indeed of comparable treatments in such works as *Dr. Jekyll and Mr. Hyde* and *The Picture of Dorian Gray*, reflect a concern with the distinctively good and evil potentialities of the human personality. James, however, is concerned less with moral behavior than with a much broader conception of personality development, and with the power we each possess to make life choices that then shape us. In "The Private Life," he explores how people are forced to create a public, professional persona distinct from that of their private life. "The Jolly Corner" is a much more profound exploration of how the choosing of one's path in life—what one does for a living, where one lives, and who one lives with—literally constructs personality and character. James raises questions about both the conscious and unconscious consequences of such choices, about the struggle that inevitably ensues as we are forced to come to terms with the irreversible choices we have made as time goes by. Do these choices have moral implications? Of course they do. But James moves beyond these considerations, expanding the capacity of the doppelgänger motif for psychological exploration by experimenting with the idea that the personality can be developed not merely in two but in countless directions.

Both Poe and James also draw heavily on the suspenseful, symbolic, and sexual aspects of ghostly character doubling in, respectively, the highly Gothic "The Fall of the House of Usher" (*Tales and Sketches* 392–422) and *The Turn of the Screw*. Roderick and Madeline Usher can be interpreted as doubles in the sense that Poe artfully develops their shared physical and emotional characteristics and their shared demise along with their highly Gothic family home. The ghost figures of James's *The Turn of the Screw*, Peter Quint and Miss Jessel, likewise double the figures of the children, Miles and Flora, accentuating the peculiar nature of the bond between the children and their ghostly counterparts.

In teaching Poe's and James's Gothic stories, I introduce students to the terminology that Wayne Booth has applied to *The Turn of the Screw*—the concepts of "straight," "ironic," and "mazed" readings (169; a mazed reading allows for both straight and ironic interpretations simultaneously), which let students decide on their own interpretation of exactly what is happening in these narratives. Booth asks us whether the ghosts in *The Turn of the Screw* actually exist or are to be interpreted merely as figments of the narrator's imagination. In a straight reading, James's narrative is taken at face value and the ghosts are interpreted as literal manifestations. An ironic reading of the story, of which there are many good ones, sees the governess's visions of the ghosts as representations of conflicts in her own sense of self, her sexual awareness, her anxieties concerning her responsibilities. Finally, a mazed reading has the author attempting to do both things at once—that is, to provide us with a straight narrative in which the ghosts may or may not be real and also to encourage us to think about the psychological implications of the characters', and particularly the narrator's, beliefs and behaviors.

Booth's paradigm works beautifully in providing students with a simple way to approach a host of complex readings of particular texts. Are there really two characters named William Wilson in Poe's story, or are we to interpret the tale as that of a madman? And how are we to interpret the story's ending? Exactly who, if anyone, has been destroyed? Similarly, is James's Clare Vawdrey really possessed of two distinct physical entities, or is James simply offering us a parable for the different roles that life demands of us? Does a hardened, American version of the ex-patriot Spencer Brydon actually exist in his abandoned childhood home, or is Brydon merely obsessed with considering how he might otherwise have chosen to live his life? In each of these cases, student debate of the merits of both straight and ironic readings invariably leads to an appreciation of a mazed reading—that is, that a story can do and mean many things at once. This exercise is a particularly fruitful one for encouraging undergraduates to embrace the idea that different critics can argue for different interpretations of a text and that while one or two may seem stronger than others, each can offer a valuable point of view.

The doppelgänger motif in literature naturally lends itself to psychoanalytic interpretations, and students often find it interesting to compare the development of this highly symbolic aspect of psychological realism in Poe, James, and other authors with modern developments in the field of psychology. There are a variety of ways to approach the motif from this standpoint. In an anthropological-psychological approach, Otto Rank associated the idea of the double with early cultures' belief in the existence of an immortal soul distinct from the human body. Rank was also intrigued by the implications of the motif in literature as a symbol of the disintegration of the modern personality (*Beyond Psychology* and *Double*). In his essay on the *unheimlich* ("Uncanny"), Sigmund Freud described the phenomenon as a manifestation of the return of the repressed or as a representation of the development of the conscience. Both Rank's and Freud's theories can be useful for a discussion of "William Wilson."

Carl Jung defined the double as an archetype of the collective unconscious, thus allowing for richer explorations of the double figure in literature as distinct from the self ("Aion" and *Archetypes*). A Jungian may tend to focus on the import of the double as a culturally recurring figure—for example, in its many reappearances as the demonic entity of the temptation narrative. Building on Freud, Jung also developed the idea of the shadow of the unconscious, which

represents hidden and repressed desires, motivations, and other traits of a protagonist's personality—or, indeed, undeveloped or unlived aspects of the protagonist's life or personality. This aspect of Jung's work is particularly applicable
to James's exploration in "The Private Life" of the ability to develop refractions
of one's personality. Jungian theory is even more relevant to "The Jolly Corner"
in terms of one of the main questions the story raises: While the many decisions
we make in life clearly shape us into distinct individuals, what are the unconscious consequences of the potential we possess for moving in other directions
and making other choices? Studying these works alongside works of psychoanalytic theory offers students the opportunity to see the close relation between
literature and the development of larger ideas in the history of Western culture.

Each of the works discussed in this essay employs a variety of conventions
that are typical of Gothic fiction throughout the nineteenth and early twentieth centuries, and all exemplify the potential that the Gothic has to thrill, hor-
rify, and entertain readers as well as to stimulate critical thinking. I have found
that organizing texts along the lines of a single theme such as that of the doppelgänger is a successful way to introduce students to the conventions of
Gothic literature and that the relations and differences among these texts
engender productive class discussions and student writing projects. The psychological concept of self and identity can always be relied upon as a catalyst
for passionate student discussions and intense critical analysis in nearly any
classroom setting, and it has the added benefit of making Gothic fiction seem
more real and more relevant to students' lives today.

The Fall of the House of the Seven Gables and Other Ambiguities of the American Gothic

Laura Dabundo

When teaching American Gothic fiction in undergraduate classes in fiction, Romanticism, American literature, and the Gothic, instructors need to provide students with a definition of the genre, even if it can be elastic in its applications. A useful starting point is the psychological approach taken by Joyce Carol Oates, as outlined in the introduction to her collection *American Gothic Tales:*

> How uncanny, how mysterious, how unknowable and infinitely beyond their control must have seemed the vast wilderness of the New World, to the seventeenth-century Puritan settlers! The inscrutable silence of Nature—the muteness that, not heralding God, must be a dominion of Satan's; the tragic ambiguity of human nature with its predilection for what Christians call "original sin," inherited from our first parents, Adam and Eve. When Nature is so vast, man's need for control—for settling the wilderness—becomes obsessive. And how powerful the temptation to project man's divided self onto the very silence of Nature.   (1)

According to Oates, American literature has responded to the challenge of the landscape its earliest settlers discovered by creating and sustaining a nightmare literature fraught with the psychological implications of the perils of pioneer life. In tracing this development in two important novelists—Nathaniel Hawthorne and Herman Melville—students have the opportunity to follow several threads that will educate them in reading literature critically and in exploring literary history. In particular, they can learn to situate these writers in their own time and see them as heirs to a developing tradition of American literature; this process will give students a broader understanding of the Gothic in general. At the same time, they can be introduced to the ways that Hawthorne and Melville actively engage each other in the construction of their works. Students can explore expectations and surprises frequently contained and encountered in Gothic plots and learn to evaluate literary failures and successes on aesthetic and other planes. Finally, they can be brought to a unique definition of the Gothic, which acknowledges its wide lineage yet also focuses on a period of American Romanticism during which the Gothic was developed in specific ways. The most important word in Oates's introduction may be "ambiguity"—ambiguity between good and evil, between order and disorder, and between European and American. It becomes the chord that again and again resounds in these novels.

In the middle third of the nineteenth century, two of America's greatest writers crafted novels shadowed by a Gothic impulse, probably inherited from Brockden Brown, Washington Irving, and Edgar Allan Poe but also reflecting the transatlantic influences of Ann Radcliffe, Charles Robert Maturin, Mary Shelley, and other English and Irish Gothic predecessors. Hawthorne's *The House of the Seven Gables* (1851) and *The Marble Faun* (1860) and Melville's *Pierre* (1852) utilize Gothic conventions to explore psychosocial dramas in a context of superstition, criminality, and psychopathology, which, as Fred Botting has noted in his book *Gothic*, was already popular with reading audiences of the period. Similarly, in ways not unlike a "lyrical dialogue," to use Paul Magnuson's characterization of the conversation conducted by Wordsworth and Coleridge through their poetry earlier in the century, Hawthorne and Melville use their fiction to comment on each other's interpretation of the Gothic, as can be demonstrated in teaching these three works. The beginning of this conversation can be seen in Melville's correspondence with Hawthorne at the time of the writing of *Moby-Dick*. Unfortunately, Hawthorne's responses and rejoinders have not been preserved, but students can consult online what Melville wrote (*Melville's Letters*).

American college students are likely to be familiar from high school or before with Poe's short stories and perhaps with "The Legend of Sleepy Hollow" and "Rip Van Winkle" by the time they encounter the greater complexities of these later writers. Thus, when undergraduates begin to study Hawthorne and Melville, they should be ready to consider the sophisticated applications of the Gothic manifest in these novels and discover ways that the Gothic frequently mirrors personal and private reality in fictional accounts haunted and chastened by past civilizations and established mores as the American empire struggled to emerge into sunlight and transcendence (the roots of transcendentalism?).

Of the three novels, *The House of the Seven Gables* probably poses the fewest challenges for undergraduates, so it is a good place to begin. Moreover, to respect the chronology of composition, in addition to rewarding students who toil through the hyperbolic, prolix longueurs of *Pierre*, the Melville work should be considered before *The Marble Faun*.

Students respond positively to the notion of the cursed family, the mysterious stranger, the scientist figure, and the interventions of technology in the earlier Hawthorne work, which sets such established Gothic conventions in an American frame and American context. The characters are two-dimensional in E. M. Forster's vision, and the plot is straightforward if not predictable. The most obvious issue for students to debate involving the Gothic might be the appropriateness of the resolutely sunny outcome. That is to say, the novel proceeds to vanquish its shadows and sense of horror, not just by a wedding and a happy ending but by the entire defeat of all possible suggestion of the ghostly or cursed avatars that animated much of the plot. There is a sense of renunciation at the end, not as in Radcliffe or other British Gothic writers—whose works also end happily because of hardship overcome, good vindicated, or mystery unveiled, a feature that students should learn is part of the baggage of the Gothic—but from the denial or destruction of the conventions of the novel.

The conclusion of *The House of the Seven Gables* seems to sabotage the Gothic in the American pantheon of literary tropes. Youth and innocence have triumphed in light and goodness.

In his famous letter of 16 April 1851 to Hawthorne, Melville emphasizes the dark and Gothic in *The House of the Seven Gables* by declaring, "There is the grand truth about Nathaniel Hawthorne. He says No! in thunder: but the Devil himself cannot make him say *yes.*" This characterization, however, is what Harold Bloom might later term a "misreading" of the precursor (*Map*), in which Melville finds what he wants to in the book, casting his formative antecedent in his own image instead of acknowledging the truth of the narrative preceding him.

Accordingly, in contrast with Hawthorne's ultimately sunny tale, *Pierre* is a study in despair, with a tragic and sorrowful ending that places the eponymous hero in prison (also to be the fate of one of the promising young men of *The Marble Faun*, young Donatello). But before attaining that point, Melville's work clearly begins where Hawthorne's *House* has left off, and that transition can be helpful to students lost in the morass of Melville's prose, especially the early parts, when the sentimental novel collides with the realistic and both tangle with the genres of Gothic and satire. Melville seems aware that he is being derivative, as when he writes, somewhat defensively, such explanations as this one:

> In general terms we have thus decided in asserting the great genealogical and real-estate dignity of some families in America, because in so doing we poetically establish the rich aristocratic condition of Master Pierre Glendinning, for whom we have before claimed some special family distinction. And to the observant reader the sequel will not fail to show, how important is this circumstance, considered with reference to the singularly developed character and most singular life-career of our hero. Nor will any man dream that the last chapter was merely intended for a foolish bravado, and not with a solid purpose in view.   (12)

Students can appreciate the notion of a struggling author whose story keeps getting away from him, as they also notice that larger issues are afoot. It is obvious from this passage that Melville wishes for the Glendinnings the same deeply rooted, early colonial heritage, the same strains of nativist American identity and value vouchsafed to Hawthorne's Pyncheons in a satire of European and Gothic forebears. Here, however, the curse and Gothic shadowing, which Hawthorne has attempted to expunge from the American heritage, will assert themselves. Melville seems to want to secure validity for the Gothic, which Hawthorne dispels in *The House of the Seven Gables*, but the ambiguities of his writing overwhelm him.

The Pyncheons' curse is famously in and of their blood. Therefore when the name and line die out with childless Clifford and female Phoebe, the curse is ended. In fact, all the major characters end up being related to one another by the close in this fantasy of familial reconciliation and reconstitution, so that the curse gets swallowed up and erased in relationship. In contrast, the Glendinnings bring about their fatality as they wander from their proper destiny, and a curse is triumphant and relationship ends. That Pierre's father dallies and fathers a child leads ultimately to the exile of the legitimate child and heir from his legacy, from the love of his mother, from acknowledgment by other relatives, from his fiancée, and into destitution, death, and the end of the line. The tragedy thus has its own curious familial strophe and antistrophe. As William Spengemann observes:

> Pierre calls his mother "Sister," takes his sister (if that's what Isabel is) to wife, and makes a cousin of his jilted fiancée. A nameless orphan, Isabel makes Glendinning her father, makes the guitar her mother. . . . Throughout this labyrinth of untethered kinships stalks the specter of incest. (*Pierre* xii)

Incest, in some ways, is the least of the narrative's Gothic moves, but students can be asked to speculate on the narrator's view of family and relationship and the meaning of incest for the novel and its literary milieu. For Melville, honorable behavior is as doomed as evil. Incest in this topsy-turvy world becomes a positive value for Pierre and his mother, Pierre and his bride, Pierre and his intended wife. Certainly, when given a moral choice, Pierre opts for sin every time. Whereas the Hawthorne of *The House of the Seven Gables* seems to say that in optimistic, urbanizing American daytime the old-fashioned, more agrarian Gothic night has no lasting sway in the face of nineteenth-century industrial prosperity, for Melville and the Hawthorne of *The Marble Faun* the implication is that Americans are a doomed people, destined to bring catastrophe on themselves, a conclusion echoing and amplifying the tone struck by Oates at the opening of this essay. The venue is the same, whether in the city or the country, for both *The Marble Faun* and *Pierre* contain frightening and surreal scenes of urban horror that seem straight out of the Wordsworthian St. Bartholomew's Fair (book 7 of *The Prelude*, published in 1850). In all three of these books, then, there are a number of themes students enjoy tracking; the dichotomies of city versus country and urbanity versus innocence; the questions of lineage, family loyalty, and responsibility; and the meaning of heredity. These issues have important literary and Gothic resonances, especially in the psychology of the family romance, which accords with the line of argument Oates develops and which students can usefully investigate.

If Melville's response to Hawthorne's dispelling of the Gothic is the ambiguous *Pierre*, then Hawthorne's rebuttal with *The Marble Faun* emphasizes ambiguity even more. In fact, after the initial publication and baffled reception of the novel, Hawthorne attaches a postscript to the next edition: "There comes to the Author, from many readers of the foregoing pages, a demand for further elucidations respecting the mysteries of the story" (463). However, he remains coy and noncommittal, even to the extent of impersonal distance and third-person reference:

> He reluctantly avails himself of the opportunity afforded by a new edition, to explain such incidents and passages as may have been left too much in the dark: reluctantly, he repeats, because the necessity makes him sensible that he can have succeeded but imperfectly, at best, in throwing about this Romance the kind of atmosphere essential to the effect at which he aimed. He designed the story and the characters to bear, of course, a certain relation to human nature and human life, but still to be so artfully and airily removed from our mundane sphere, that some laws and proprieties of their own should be implicitly and insensibly acknowledged.   (463)

In other words, I shall tell you this much but no more. Hawthorne embraces the ambiguous, whereas Melville seems to have stumbled into it and been unable to extricate himself or his novel. Again, students can see the self-conscious artifice of narrative construction beneath the architecture of the novel, and this insight leads directly to explorations of definition and genre.

Hawthorne, in general, is clearer on the subject of his craft, denominating all four of his novels "romances," and this latest one, partaking as it does of the Gothic, provides an opportunity for classes to consider the definition of the term offered in "The Custom-House," the introduction to *The Scarlet Letter,* in which he likens the power of the imagination to the radiance of moonlight and its shapings and shadowings of "the Actual" in interesting and new forms. From that, students can consider whether all three of these American novels are romances as a unique genre or as a subspecialty of the Gothic (or something else altogether!).

In *The Marble Faun,* Hawthorne turns to the Old World, the source of the Gothic in the first place, to confront if not finally to exorcise that demon from American literature, a task that evidently *The House of the Seven Gables* did not accomplish. There are heights and depths held in common with *Pierre*; in both novels characters inhabit aeries, high-tower dwellings apart from the rest of humanity that emblematize difference and superiority. All three novels are cognizant that theirs are at the same time fallen worlds, successors to Adam and Eve's transgression, desperately trying to make their way back to paradise, redemption, and home. America's Puritan forebears posited the country as Eden, but instead it became as soiled and sinful as the homeland of its European progenitors. In *The Marble Faun,* Hawthorne offers deliverance and renewal to his American characters but finally reveals that the mysterious Miriam, whom mostly the narrator lumps in with the American characters, is actually half English, half Italian, and so she is denied, along with her Italian suitor Donatello, American rebirth.

The enigmatic, evil Italian monk in this novel is straight out of Radcliffe, and we have a Radcliffean imprisonment of a heroine in a convent and all the rich paraphernalia of English Protestant anti-Catholicism, here adopted, enlarged, and not to be gainsaid, so that Hawthorne's reach swoops back to the earliest Gothic in order to enrich his story and to make it definitive and final in its renunciation.

Robert Martin and Eric Savoy suggest that "gothic cultural production in the United States has yielded neither a 'genre' nor a cohesive 'mode' but rather a discursive field in which a metonymic national 'self' is undone by the return of its repressed Otherness" (vii). For Hawthorne and Melville, the other who haunts the heart of the Gothic, the image in the mirror that gestures and mocks and yet is true begins as American innocence versus European decadence in anticipation of Henry James, of course, but rapidly takes specific form, for each, literally as the other writer. Accordingly, they create complex characters, exploring identity and relationship in what become psychodramas of inner horror and dramatized nightmare. In June 1851, Melville imagines "the eternal times that are to come" for him and Hawthorne united in "Paradise," clearly regained but forever for them "some little shady corner by ourselves." The shady Gothic shadows in these writers' hands, as a result, can become for college students a vehicle for profound investigations into American literature, to understand its legacy from the Continent and its own defining moments and ideals.

Supernatural Transmissions:
Turn-of-the-Century Ghosts
in American Women's Fiction:
Jewett, Freeman, Wharton, and Gilman

Kathy Justice Gentile

By teaching the eerie short fiction of Sarah Orne Jewett, Mary Wilkins Freeman, Edith Wharton, and Charlotte Perkins Gilman in a class on the American
or female Gothic, an instructor has the opportunity to review the oral and written tradition of the ghost tale and to engage students in a study of cultural-
historical contexts for the reemergence of the ghost story in the 1890s, while
examining the stories as supernaturalized commentaries on gendered fin de
siècle anxieties. As with other historically bound literary genres, one cannot
apprehend themes, conventions, allusions, and ideologies without some knowledge of the sociocultural background that frames each author's writing of a
story. Two questions I ask students to consider over the course of the semester
are why there was a resurgence in the ghost tale at the turn of the century and
why so many prominent realist women writers turned to the form at this time.
As Alfred Bendixen points out, the 1890s and early 1900s marked "a period
when the feminine ghostly tale attracted the talents of the finest women writers in America and resulted in some of their most powerful and most intriguing work" (Introduction 2).

The ghost tale, of course, has a long history preceding this gendered literary flourishing. Students are intrigued to learn that ghost stories may be one
of the oldest forms of oral tale, as old as humankind's belief in and fear of the
unseen and unembodied imaginary. I point out that spirit manifestations
adumbrate biblical tales, as in the stories of Job and the Witch of Endor (1
Sam. 28.7–14). While Hamlet's father is Shakespeare's best-known ghost, spirits appeared in other Elizabethan and Jacobean tragedies, and ghost tales and
ghost sightings were an integral part of community lore well into the eighteenth century. However, not until the nineteenth century did the ghost story
emerge as a literary genre in the Irish tales of Sheridan Le Fanu and Fitz
James O'Brien and the American Gothic of Washington Irving and Edgar
Allan Poe, who eerily transformed oral conventions of the unquiet, vengeful
spirit and the haunted mansion.

In teaching the ghost story to undergraduates at the beginning of the third
millennium, an instructor may have to overcome modern rationalist resistance
to ghostly manifestations. I begin our consideration of the ghost story by having students air their prejudices and expectations toward the supernatural,
which generally turn out to be more complex than mere skepticism. Invariably,
some students concur with a statement in Edith Wharton's preface to her own
ghost stories: "No, I don't believe in ghosts, but I'm afraid of them" (1). With

this acknowledgment of the conflict between mind and feeling, we might move to a discussion of the aesthetic rewards of suspending one's disbelief and vicariously enjoying the sensations evoked by the text—an exercise, I suggest, that we undergo in reading any literary text, not just scary stories, for pleasure.

Even before the development of the ghost story as a distinct literary form, Enlightenment challenges to popular and theological belief in apparitions as proof of the immortality of the soul attempted to characterize ghost sightings as either deceptions or hoaxes or as the product of a disordered individual psychology (Castle, "Phantasmagoria" 161–63). The exponential increase in scientific knowledge in the second half of the nineteenth century further undermined public credulity. Despite this increasingly rationalist intellectual climate, students may be fascinated to learn of a countertrend, the rise of American spiritualism. I give a brief history of the spiritualist movement, as outlined in Howard Kerr's *Mediums, and Spirit-Rappers, and Roaring Radicals*: its beginnings with the Fox sisters' claims of spirit rapping in 1848; the increasing public fascination with seances, mesmerism, and spirit autobiographies; and the exposure of several hoaxes, which marked the movement's decline before the end of the century. Most relevant for our purposes is the association of spiritualism with women and radical social movements, including those advocating women's rights. Women's roles in spiritualism were cited by some male writers and scientists as evidence of woman's inherent inferiority, their emotionalism and ethereal, unscientific natures (Dickerson 3). Against this climate of conflict over women's roles and rights to equality, some of the most prominent women writers in this country, most of whom had established reputations as staunch realists, chose to experiment with the supernatural tale. As an alternative or supplement to lecturing, I sometimes have students do group reports on the history of the ghost tale, the spiritualist movement, and women's issues at the fin de siècle. Depending on the background and sophistication of the class, an instructor may encourage enterprising students to seek out primary sources on the spiritualist controversy, including newspaper and other accounts of spirit manifestations, for example.

In the last two decades of the nineteenth century, the pursuit of spirits became a more intellectually respectable exercise under the auspices of Societies for Psychical Research on both sides of the Atlantic. Not only did members attempt to verify claims of spirit manifestation but they also studied the psychology that motivated such claims (see Kerr 207). I suggest that the class constitute itself as a literary society for psychical research and study the spirit manifestations in the assigned stories in order to gauge the validity of each ghost, attempt to decipher its message, and examine the psychological attitudes and conflicts that foster or culminate in supernatural happenings. Our findings will lead to broader applications; for example, students may come to recognize a ghostly presence as an indication of a malady or canker in the body of late-nineteenth-century American society.

Jewett's novel *The Country of the Pointed Firs* and many of her short stories are haunted by the memory of times past and the permeability of this world to the world beyond. In situating most of her tales in a rural Maine in economic decline after the heyday of the fishing and shipping industries and the abandonment of family farms and in writing about characters in the middle or late stages of life, Jewett envisions a future not of mind and body but of spirit. Romance and marriage, notably subordinate themes in her fiction, do not tend toward procreation. Captain Littlepage, an old sea captain who relates his adventures to the narrator of *The Country of the Pointed Firs*, obsesses about a reported mass spirit sighting near Greenland. His preoccupation reflects his increasingly shadowy presence as a village citizen, for he drifts between fantasy and reality, between this life and intimations of the next. While long-lived characters in the short stories "A Sorrowful Ghost" and "Lady Ferry" appear to endure beyond the temporal realm, I usually assign "The Foreigner," Jewett's only tale of actual spirit manifestation, written after *The Country of the Pointed Firs* although concerned with the same characters and setting of Dunnet Landing.

Students should know that Jewett's fictional world bears the imprint of the doctrines of Emanuel Swedenborg, a Swedish theosophist and spiritualist who influenced a number of American writers at the turn of the century. Swedenborgian illuminations, "correlation[s] between the microcosm and the macrocosm, between this realm 'here below' and that realm beyond" (Donovan 101), are espoused poetically throughout the text of *Country of the Pointed Firs* and its related episodes. Some feminist critics have interpreted Jewett's transcendentalism as a "feminized Christianity" (Easton xii) or a female-centered, communally based spirituality (Ammons 58). Of the writers I assign, Jewett probably comes closest to affirming spiritualist beliefs in her fiction.

As psychic investigators we begin with the appearance of the ghost, which occurs at the end of "The Foreigner." Most students agree that the ghost is a benevolent spirit—of Mis' Cap'n Tolland's mother, who is waiting for her daughter to cross over from life to death—and that its message is comforting, offering assurance that we may reunite with our mothers after death in a benign spiritual home. The mystery and complexity of the story, students may then discover, lie in the nonlinear, protracted narrative structure and the significance of the title. Why does Mrs. Todd end the tale twice, first with Mis' Tolland's death and funeral and second with the accidental burning down of her house, before providing us with the third and final revelation that Mrs. Todd witnessed the appearance of a maternal ghost in the doorway soon before Mis' Tolland's spirit passed through that door to her death? Is Mrs. Todd wary that her listener will be incredulous, or, in the manner of a master storyteller, does she defer the scariest and most profound aspect of her tale until her audience (including the reader) is wrought up to a proper frame of mind?

When I ask students to explain the title, they assume first that the foreigner is Mis' Tolland, "a stranger in a strange land" (233), having been exiled to an unsympathetic Maine fishing village from her native French-speaking island.

But if we think of the foreigner in conjunction with the appearance of the ghost, students quickly see the foreignness of the visitor from the other world or possibly the foreignness of Mrs. Todd as the worldly witness of a spirit-world transaction. The reunion after separation promised by the spirit manifestation standing in the door to the next world is verified by the reliable Mrs. Todd, "You know plain enough there's something beyond this world; the doors stand wide open. There's something of us that must live on; we've got to join both worlds together an' live in one but for the other" (245), the last statement quoting the old village doctor, thus placing a scientific stamp on a supernatural doctrine.

Reading Freeman's supernatural tales in her collection *The Wind in the Rose Bush*, originally published in *Everybody's Magazine* in 1902–03, students will find an order of ghost different from the benevolent maternalistic spirit in Jewett's story that finds its material echoes in her pastoral female community. Except for the curiously inept "The Vacant Lot," each of these stylistically spare, plainly wrought stories introduces students to ghosts who signal, to other characters and the reader, sinister family secrets and horrific crimes. A class can examine the significance of the spirit manifestations by identifying the major conflicts in the story, conflicts that always occur in domestic space and center on the perverse constraints of women's roles or of family and gender relations.

The girl ghosts in the title story and "The Lost Ghost" appeal to students' sympathies and sense of outrage because they bear witness to the tragic result of maternity gone horribly awry in the hands of abusive, murderous mother figures. In "The Lost Ghost," a woman's self-sacrifice in leaving this world to accompany and care for the motherless child in the land of the dead demonstrates the opposite—maternal responsibility—and the conflict between the pursuit of selfish desires and the extinguishing of self for another. Analyzing the role and message of the ghost child helps illuminate for students Freeman's ambivalent view of motherhood. A child bereft of maternal love cannot flourish and develop the substantiality of personhood, but a mother who devotes her life and spirit to her children risks becoming an unsubstantial ghostly self.

The class will be interested to learn that "Shadows on the Wall," which features a ghost who tells of a Cain-and-Abel conflict, was televised in an old *Twilight Zone* episode, an episode that I have been unable to locate but that, if located, might be an effective teaching tool in spookily vivifying the contemporary relevance of Freeman's psychological study of guilt. Typically, students discuss the ineffectual role of the three sisters who bear witness to the playing out of the conflict between the brothers but cling to one another on the sidelines and demonstrate little power to intercede and prevent the tragedy. In these three stories, Freeman innovatively reconstructs, in terms of family and gender relations, the convention of the unavenged wrong that the ghost brings to the attention of the living.

The ghost in "The Southwest Chamber" provides the most intriguing and challenging case study for my student psychic researchers. In this chilling tale, the ghost of Aunt Harriet terrorizes anyone who dares to invade her room, the private space she continues to inhabit in death. Freeman's exploration of the psychology of fear and the tyranny of possession fascinates students, because the text suggests that anyone can be terrorized if the stimulus of terror is directed to the person's weaknesses and susceptibilities. Doubting students find themselves in the position of each character and inhabitant of a boarding-house, formerly the family home of Aunt Harriet, who enters Harriet's room. They may feel tremulous, like the frailer niece, Amanda, and the timorous grandniece, Flora, or they may be brave and scornful of superstition, like the more stubborn and practical-minded niece, Sophia; the widow; and the preacher. Each character is routed by the malign spirit of Harriet, who haunts in a manner most calculated to unhinge and frighten. Her haunting culminates in the attempted possession of Sophia's mind with evil thoughts of Sophia's aunt, a device that gives us insight into Harriet's motives but does not mitigate her triumph over the living.

Identifying the central conflict as the struggle between the living and the dead; between the malign spirit of Harriet and her living, decent descendants; or between the power of the supernatural and New England empiricism and common sense, students may be unsettled by this story, because the evil ghost proves impervious to decency, reason, and Christian faith. Harriet's machinations demonstrate nothing less than a "refutal of all laws of reason" (153), some accursed evil power at work, of which modern faith and modern science know nothing," as the vanquished minister admits (159). Along with the emphasis on the home as site of supernatural disturbance, Freeman uses the convention of the haunted chamber, a mainstay of female Gothic, as the setting for her assault on New England literal-mindedness. Limited to the private domain of her room, a woman becomes so perversely possessive of this territory that she over-throws natural law to retain it. Spirit and material realms occupy the same space and contend for ownership in Freeman's stories, as female energies that are balked and banked in the separate-sphered world of late-nineteenth-century New England may be unleashed in a less restrictive afterlife and employed in plaguing and baffling those living characters whose visions and energies are limited by the here and now.

At some point in our spirit investigations students begin to understand how these women writers' choice of the ghost-story genre enables their signification of the spirit world as a salient metaphor for the difficulties of women's lives in the real world. By the time we are ready to read *The Ghost Stories of Edith Wharton*, they are excited to realize that these stories aren't merely calculated to frighten and entertain but have social and ideological relevance to their own lives. Wharton, who turned intermittently to the ghost story from the early 1900s to the 1930s, used the form as she did her realistic fiction, to project the horrors of institutional repression and disfiguring social expectations. Reading the stories I assign from the collection, students quickly surmise that the institution Wharton subjects to the most critical scrutiny is marriage.

In her first ghost story, "The Lady's Maid's Bell" (1904), Wharton employs the Gothic conventions of the isolated country manse and the villainous husband to dramatize women's ghostlike, and relatively powerless, status in patriarchal society, a condition emblemized by the ghost of Emma Saxon, the former lady's maid. Woman's passivity and servility in the face of male sexual abuse and drunken brutishness, as exemplified in the person of Mrs. Brympton, the lady of the house, have rendered Emma sick unto death. The role of the ghost in "Afterward" (1909), who appears before the disappearence of Mary Boyne's husband from their English country estate, is for a long time inexplicable to Mary, because she has long been shortsighted about her husband's business affairs and corrupt, selfish nature. By the story's conclusion, Wharton seems to indict the wife, because of her cultivated ignorance, as complicitous in her husband's nefarious dealings—in his death too, for she unwittingly delivered him up to the avenging ghost. However, through the power of supernatural agency, both stories investigate and indict the evils of gender imbalance in the material world of business, property, and law.

"The Pomegranate Seed," a later story (1931), is perhaps Wharton's finest and most elusive. When she wrote the preface to her ghost-story collection in 1937, she complained that modern technology had atrophied the imaginative faculty in readers and hindered their ability to actively engage a story of the supernatural—an observation that can generate a lively class discussion. "The Pomegranate Seed" is another supernatural treatment of the conflicts and secrets in marriage: Charlotte, the second, living wife, competes with Elsie, the first, dead wife, for the love and soul of the husband, Kenneth Ashby. A woman's worth is measured by her ability to hold or maintain power over a man.

When I explain the myth of Persephone and its relevance to the title, students quickly see the story as a gender reversal of the characters in the myth. Elsie becomes a Pluto figure trying to drag Kenneth down to the underworld, while Charlotte, who in the end combines her energies with Kenneth's mother, is Demeter, trying to keep her daughter-husband with her in the land of the living. Because Kenneth has already eaten the pomegranate seeds (his first marriage and allegiance to Elsie), the class wonders if Charlotte's struggle to keep him is doomed from the start.

Students also see the conflict between the outside world of the twentieth century, "skyscrapers, advertisements, telephones, wireless, airplanes, movies, motors . . . and on the other side of the door something I can't explain, can't relate to them. Something as old as the world, as mysterious as life" (225). A recurring symbol in the stories we read, the door demarcates the barrier between the familiar, the real, and material progress, on the one hand, and, on the other, that which remains unresponsive to science and reason: death, the spirit world, psychic communication. In the same vein, the Kenneth that Charlotte knows and loves covers a concealed, repressed self in thrall to the past and the dead. It is a theme in Wharton's supernatural stories of marriage that the wife is partially sealed off from her life partner and can never really apprehend or break through to his true, darker nature.

Noting that we do not have an actual ghostly presence in this story, only let-ters delivered by an unseen hand, students may see these barely decipherable letters to Kenneth as a metaphor for the continued hold that the memory of his imperious former wife maintains over him, for his inability to let go of the past and live in the present. Charlotte and her mother-in-law marshal the forces of the modern industrial state (the police and the telephone) to find the missing husband at the end, but Charlotte's comment, "as if we thought it could do any good to do anything" (253), suggests that their real-world efforts will be pow-erless in the face of "[s]omething as old as the world, as mysterious as life." In Wharton's last ghost story, the supernatural persists into the modern age as a force to be reckoned with.

The instructor may choose to include Gilman's hallowed story *The Yellow Wall-Paper* as a culminating textual experience in ideological ghostliness. The work is more often taught as a realist critique of the misguided sexist treatment of mental illness and postpartum depression at the turn of the century. Although the myth that it was misunderstood by early readers as a simple ghost story has been dispelled by Julie Bates Dock (16–18), recent feminist readings emphasize the Gothic qualities of the story (Owens; DeLamotte, "Mysteries"). Teaching this story, an instructor may ask students to consider first its Gothic or ghostly qualities before analyzing Gilman's social critique. At some point, I suggest to the class that the unnamed narrator is herself a ghost, rendered insubstantial by her husband and the medical authorities who recommend the rest cure. She is a ghost, because she is effectively disembodied—forbidden to mother, cook, write, or interact significantly with others and ordered to render herself unconscious through sleep and effectively immobile through inactivity. No wonder that she begins to see her ghostly presence behind the wallpaper and secretly works to free her ghost (herself) from the wallpaper-bars of patri-archal prescription. She sees the necessity of shredding the wallpaper and free-ing the ghost, who frightens her husband into a faint. Seeing the patterns and consequences of her imprisonment enables her to "creep," to work subver-sively to verify herself as an embodied and able individual. Discussing the end-ing, students will want to consider the issue of the narrator's sanity, and some will argue that the story is a realistic study of mental illness. At this juncture, the instructor may initiate a discussion of the relation of mental illness to the experience of the supernatural. Is the ability to see or sense ghosts an accident of circumstance, a special power, or a sign of delusionary illness?

Including the ghost stories of these women writers in a course on American Gothic, female Gothic, the ghost story, or in a broader course on late-nineteenth- and early-twentieth-century American literature, can train students to be spirit investigators and textual sleuths. Teaching these stories can also provide them with an enhanced understanding of a significant literary genre, an appreciation of its particular aesthetic rewards, and a knowledge of the historical and meta-phoric links among spirits, spiritualism, and gender constraints.

Teaching the African American Gothic: From Its Multiple Sources to *Linden Hills* and *Beloved*

Jerrold E. Hogle

African American Gothic fiction is by now rich and extensive enough that it can be the subject of an entire college course and certainly a segment (I use it as a culmination) of a wider-ranging class on Gothic writing. In either case, if the Gothic qualities in such works are to have any importance for students, instructors face a dilemma: how to balance a thorough understanding of the ways these texts rework fundamental Gothic motifs with a grasp of how and why the texts still manifest cultural fears and quandaries distinctive to African American life. True, many of the most Gothic of these novels are relatively recent, as are the examples I propose using here, Gloria Naylor's *Linden Hills* (1985) and Toni Morrison's *Beloved* (1987). Even so, the complex cultural visions in these and similar books become most visible to students, in my experience, only if the books' many symbolic roots in Gothic fictions as old as *The Castle of Otranto* are revealed to be unusually apt for symbolizing African American history—and to be connected to it today with extraordinary force. I therefore want to sketch out a teaching method that encapsulates the features of the Gothic tradition most essential to African American history and then helps students see how African American uses of those features, epitomized by *Linden Hills* and *Beloved*, produce cultural transformations so distinctive that they end up using the Gothic tradition to turn it on its head.

A class about the Gothic from Horace Walpole on, of course, can be organized to establish the key motifs before students reach the African American Gothic of recent years. But even if a course is about African American writing alone and brings in Gothic fictions only some of the time, it is possible (and, I would argue, necessary) to provide students—through handouts, reserve lists, or online examples, including references to specific older texts—with thoughtful descriptions of the Gothic genre since the 1760s. Whatever the lead-in, the Gothic motifs that should be most emphasized for later reference are these: (1) the haunting of an antiquated, often *falsely* antiquated, space by the monstrous specter(s) of a hidden primal crime, which can be discovered only by probing through layers of memory, documentation, or buried physical evidence; (2) the connection of both that setting and the crime to the class-climbing and property-seeking drives in the major characters and their middle-class readers, which draw both characters and readers into conflicts within themselves about the true grounds for their constructed identities and for their guilt over what these repress; (3) the repression of primordial feminine origins—often in the form of a sequestered or distanced mother figure—

to shore up a patriarchal hierarchy whose counterfeit grounding is increasingly exposed; (4) the employment of such repression in the fabrication of a rising middle-class suburban community caught between the receding past of the country estate and a capitalist future of individual, though actually city-based, free enterprise (as in Ann Radcliffe's *The Mysteries of Udolpho* or Oscar Wilde's *The Picture of Dorian Gray*); and (5) the middle-class throwing off or throwing under—the psychological and cultural "abjection" in Julia Kristeva's *Powers of Horror*—whereby all that class climbers strive to free themselves of (dependency on the feminine, connections to working-class hard labor, desires for aristocratic decadence, mixed racial origins, nonstandard sexual longings, roots in supposedly less evolved conditions, great economic uncertainty, dysfunctional families, etc.) is projected onto spectral or monstrous others, which seem to reside more in the past or on the margins than in the present or at the center of society, where they haunt us nevertheless (see Punter, *Literature*; Hurley; and Hogle, "Gothic and the 'Otherings'").

Once these enduring elements of Gothic tales are clear to students, anchored by examples that they already know or that have been provided in discussion, they should be helped to see that such elements have long been bound up with race and racial otherness. Vivid examples from Anglo Gothic works, which students should be given the chance to generate, can include the Negro characters in Matthew Gregory Lewis's *The Castle Spectre* (1797; in J. Cox, *Seven Gothic Dramas* 149–221) set alongside his later account of owning slaves in the West Indies (Lewis, *Journal*); the use of a Moor as the primary villain in Charlotte Dacre's *Zofloya* (1806), as the title character who intensifies the vaguely foreign darkness of previous Satanic, Wandering Jew, or oriental figures in Ann Radcliffe, Lewis, and William Beckford's *Vathek* (1786); and the African slave–ish and several other nonwhite qualities in the creature of Mary Shelley's *Frankenstein* (1818), many of which refer to British writings of her time specifically about the abolition of slavery and the black subjects of British imperialism, as H. L. Malchow has shown (parts of his *Gothic Images* can be copied for students online while the book is placed on library reserve).

As these examples unfold, students should be asked to articulate the underlying cultural fears that such Anglo creations embody and why Gothic monstrosities are so suited to arousing them. One fear will surely be the combined guilt and terror among whites that half admits a dependence on, even an attraction to, a vaguely known black culture while at the same time feeling a repugnance toward any prospect of racial mixture or black proliferation that might bring down mythical constructs of white purity, priority, or supremacy. Few literary forms are as obsessed as the white Gothic, students should realize, with the Anglo vacillation across a wide continuum between extreme abolitionist and racist attitudes toward black people of African descent—a spectrum in which many abolitionists are racists too—partly because Gothic specters and monsters so readily combine the attractive and the repulsive, the deeply familiar and the unfamiliar (Freud's "uncanny") in one symbol.

Students should soon realize, however, that this persistence of racial black-ness in the Gothic is especially pronounced in American writing, well before the works of Naylor, Morrison, and their contemporaries. Anglo-American writers from Brockden Brown to Poe to Hawthorne and Melville to Stephen Crane (most blatantly in his story "The Monster") often

> work against [the] dominant text of [emerging white American history, the surface narrative in most of these tales,] to recall the anxiety over race in [nineteenth-]century America, writing a countertext of guilt and endless expiation in the midst of [what often seems] a narrative of redemption.
> (Martin 130)

Morrison herself is quite eloquent about this complex history in the second chapter (29–59) of her critical study *Playing in the Dark* (1992), which an instructor can make available for student use by placing the work on reserve. Examples of this tangled web readily accessible to students are Poe's "Ligeia" (see Dayan) and "The Black Cat" (see Ginsberg). There is also the early scene in Hawthorne's *The House of the Seven Gables*, where Hepzibah Pyncheon sells a gingerbread Jim Crow to a customer in the shop on the old house's ground floor, thereby revealing the many "dark" foundations that help haunt the "fam-ily estate" (see Hawthorne, *House* 58–60; Martin 130–39). No wonder the southern white American Gothic, culminating most forcefully in William Faulkner's fiction from the 1920s through the 1940s (especially *Light in August* and *Absalom! Absalom!*), concentrates so much on racial oppression and mix-ture as the primary ghosts or monstrosities recalling the past and presents these as intimately bound up with such classically Gothic obsessions as fears about illegitimate ownership, forbidden sexual attractions, and the conversion of bod-ies and labor into reified objects of exchange (in a sense, ghosts of their former selves). This complex, all parts of it chaotically interrelated, is "what the domi-nant culture cannot incorporate within itself" in mainstream white America, the students should now understand, and thus what must be spectralized or mon-sterized, and hence abjected, as "the return of the unsuccessfully repressed" in the Anglo-American Gothic as it has just been redefined (Savoy 4–5).

The emphasis of this preliminary survey, however, should be on the African American writing, much of it by women from an early point, that parallels and complicates the white American Gothic. To be sure, throughout American his-tory there are significant Gothic texts by black male writers to which the stu-dents should be directed, many of which are notable short stories ranging from "The Mulatto" (1837; in Gates and McKay 287–99) by the expatriate Victor Sejour (1814–74) to "Po Sandy" and "The Sheriff's Children" (both 1899; in Crow 341–59) by Charles Chesnutt (1858–1932). But Kari J. Winter has dis-covered (*Subjects*) some remarkable parallels between, on the one hand, the parts of the Radcliffean Gothic that point to the archaic confinement of women and, on the other, nineteenth-century American slave narratives by freed black women, best epitomized by Harriet Jacobs's *Incidents in the Life of a Slave Girl* (1861; see Jacobs 9–158), not to mention the most Gothically charged moments in Harriet Beecher Stowe's *Uncle Tom's Cabin* (1852). Students should be exposed to several of these either in copies of Winter's opening chapters or in excerpts from slave narratives duplicated from Web sites or handouts. Students should also be led to the occasional Gothic passages in *Our Nig* by Harriet E. Wilson (1859), the first novel-memoir published by an African American woman of the north, "Showing that Slavery's Shadows Fall Even There" (a Gothic image) and including echoes even of Charlotte Brontë's *Jane Eyre* (iii, 55–57). Most of all, students should at least sample the influentially semi-Gothic fiction of Pauline Hopkins at the turn of the last century. Her novel *Contending Forces* (1900) has "hidden connections" among characters and "unspeakable secrets in [the] background" (the words of Richard Yarborough introducing the work [xxxi–xxxiii]) that are sometimes uncovered in Gothic moments of "mental vision," as when a character gazing at an urban carnival suddenly "beholds in all its hideousness the cankering sore [of racism] eating into the heart of republican principles and stamping the lie upon the Constitution" (202).

African American Gothic, then, should be perceived by students not only as already established and deeply rooted by the twentieth century but as deliberately articulating profound social horrors. The horrors persist in both white and black America, especially in or near the modern city, to the point where all attempts to leave slavery and racism behind only reconfront the unresolved and visceral hauntings by an abjected past, already linked to race, that Gothic specters incarnate. Now students are prepared to analyze recent African American Gothic novels down to their most fundamental concerns and unsettling suggestions in a process that considers both their many Gothic elements and the complexities of African American history especially visible in them. Once I have reached this stage with a class, I find students genuinely galvanized with excitement when I ask them to start reading Naylor's *Linden Hills* and to specify all the Gothic features of it. They recognize immediately, giving many specific examples, that this book reenacts all the five Gothic motifs listed above, and some can even link those motifs to earlier African American writing that has already reshaped the Gothic.

Students readily see *Linden Hills* as about the creation and inner decay of the exclusive black suburban community of the title, with all its members torn between the quasi-aristocratic hope for a purified, wealthy blackness that seems inherited (though its pedigree is always fake) and the acquisitive, class-climbing desire to possess the lives of upper-middle-class white suburbanites. The underlying psychological hells and hauntings that doom this world to the state of a grim inferno—so much so that Dante's *Inferno* is echoed often, especially in the descending circles of streets by which this hillside community is developed over decades (see Ward; Homans, "Women")—have the depth and range they do because of Naylor's particularly skillful reworking of the Gothic primal crime alongside the Gothic burial of the primordial feminine by patri-archal power plays.

Once their reading of the novel is well along, I ask students to specify what the original sin buried in the past actually is, both for Luther Nedeed, the descendant of the community's founder who still runs the family funeral busi-ness from his cellar in the lowest circle of Linden Hills, and for all the residents we see as having sold their souls in various ways (down to selling their very blackness, which I ask the students to specify in each case) in the character sketches we are given in flashbacks as the temporary handymen / aspiring poets Willie and Lester (Naylor's Dante and Vergil) arrive at their several doorsteps between 19 and 24 December. Most students who have read with care soon focus on all the residents' efforts from the start, described in the book's pro-logue and confirmed near the end by the historian Braithewaite, "to forget and make the world forget their past" in a "black power" restyled "in white capital letters" that is so dominated by the "Almighty . . . *will* to possess" of their white models that they "forget what it meant to be black" in many ways (10–11, 16–17). The Gothic's penchant for haunting bourgeois Anglo culture with "the hidden violence of its present social structures" (Punter, *Literature* 418) is now employed to define the threat to African Americans of their attraction to the surfaces of those structures.

I now ask the students to note that Naylor topographically places this original sin alongside Luther Nedeed's imprisonment of his submissive wife in his fune-real cellar, ostensibly because she gave birth to a white-looking child, which Luther leaves to die with her in the sort of burial alive often experienced by Gothic heroines and mothers. What does it mean, I ask, that this book's primal crime is so connected to the burial of the silenced feminine and maternal, which keeps interrupting the flow of the novel with interior monologues and finally erupts on Christmas Eve with a bursting of woman and child from the cellar much like the encrypted sister's emergence in Poe's "Fall of the House of Usher"? What does Naylor's most buried woman embody? Class discussion, focused on Willa Nedeed's monologues, should finally reveal that this figure physically symbolizes a culture's self-negation when it suppresses the primacy of woman in Western *and* African American history. Linden Hills is most haunted and fissured, the students should see, by the contradictions in a recast Madonna and child into which several anomalies of African American experience have been abjected. Meanwhile, black male desire pursues power through a coun-terfeit white capitalism that drains black people of their origins, their color, and (Willie discovers) their poetry and multiplicity; this Gothic quest for identity ultimately denies them the power they seek.

Having analyzed *Linden Hills* in this fashion, students are more attuned to recognizing the extraordinary achievement and meaning of Morrison's *Beloved* as both a Gothic novel and an African American masterpiece. Even before I ask, they note the Gothic qualities of this book, again finding the five key motifs thoroughly reused, which they are less able to see if their wider context is only the 1998 film version. Such students move rapidly beyond the demon-filled house on Bluestone Road near Cincinnati and ghostlike title character who finally appears bodily in 1873–74 (the main time of Morrison's novel). They find that a complex memory of southern slavery—which the characters involuntarily recall even as they strive to forget it—Gothically haunts the black suburban community of southern Ohio (Morrison's own birthplace and a key borderland between North and South during the Civil War) in a series of intrusive flashbacks not unlike the musings of Naylor's Willa that gather together the histories and enslavements of three previous Mrs. Nedeeds.

Students will readily see that this kind of haunting extends a Gothic element in Wilson's *Our Nig*, Hopkins's *Contending Forces,* and the slave narratives that *Beloved* recalls in its many flashbacks, all of which are indebted as well to the Anglo tradition of Gothic retrospection. But students should equally be urged to discover echoes of the Gothic in the efforts of a class-climbing community, even one composed of former black slaves, to avoid their memories and the many abasements abjected into them. They avoid them partly by isolating the main character, Sethe, and her family shortly after she escapes from Sweet Home plantation in 1855 and joins her mother-in-law, Baby Suggs, on Bluestone Road, having already sent three of her children ahead, freeing them from slavery before she frees herself. The character Beloved, students will soon conclude, haunts a whole community as well as Sethe with layer upon layer of what its members strive to repress in their history. Some of these layers can be clarified in a visual chart that places all the recalled events linearly from 1850 to 1874 and incorporates key parallel facts on which *Beloved* depends—ranging from the United States Congress passing the Fugitive Slaw Law in 1850 (allowing owners in slave states to recover their escaped property) to federal troops leaving the defeated South in 1876, two years after the novel concludes.

When this community-focused recasting of the Gothic is clear, the time is right to ask students to probe into the full import of the primal crime in *Beloved.* Most by now will say that the crime, visible in the scars on Beloved's neck in 1873, is Sethe's 1855 killing of her "crawling already" third child (93), when Schoolteacher, the Sweet Home overseer who has ruthlessly reduced slaves to ciphers in a notebook (37), invades Bluestone Road to claim all his escapees under the Fugitive Slave Law (148–58, 163–65, 171). At this point I reveal that Morrison is fictionally expanding on an 1856 abolitionist article in *American Baptist* that told of an escaped slave, Margaret Garner, who slashed her children, one of them to death, because (in her words) she would "rather kill them at once [than] have them taken back to slavery, and be murdered piece-meal" (qtd. in Winsbro 131).

But Beloved, in part as the "crawling already" child risen from the dead, symbolizes and abjects far more than this one incident. She haunts the whole community both with myriad memories of slavery and with suppressions of a past that includes the community's turning against Sethe before and after the killing—for example, its failure to warn her as Schoolteacher and his party approached Bluestone Road. Referring to specific passages in the novel not explicable by the Margaret Garner story (64–66, 114–17, 133–34, 210–17), I ask students to list all the fears and anomalies cast by Sethe; by her youngest daughter, Denver; by her lover, Paul D; and by the Ohio community onto Beloved in her role as a Gothic spectral monster reconceived in an African American way. I note that Morrison has invested this figure with an "African religious belief in the behavior of the living dead" (Winsbro 133), wherein a dead family member, now wrongly unremembered, is seen as having entered a "state of collective immortality" as "one of [a] myriad of spirits" who haunt their descendants with a collective racial unconscious and not just personal qualities (Mbiti 162; indeed, students can here be directed to Mbiti's *African Religions and Philosophy*).

Students should now be able to articulate Beloved's abjection and embodiment of an extensive collective memory among African Americans, ranging from the loading onto women of greater subjugations in slavery itself all the way back to the original loss of Mother Africa in the voyage across the Atlantic in the bowels of the ships that first brought black captives to the New World. After acknowledging how a Gothic specter can encapsulate a primal crime that is really the whole history of slavery, students will see that the haunting power of Morrison's book confronts the novel's black community and all Morrison's readers with an unavoidable choice: to continue the repression of the past and the destruction of the human community pursued in the isolation of Sethe and Beloved or to embrace that past with the determination to draw the community back together in a forgiveness and reaching out that reaccepts Sethe and Denver while at least partially facing up to all the losses and desires that Beloved has incarnated by the time she vanishes from sight (see Scruggs).

Ultimately students who work through this process should be able to see how the African American reshaping of the Anglo Gothic, a tradition of reshaping that has its own history of over two centuries, has wrought a profound change in the genre. For Horace Walpole, the monstrous specters haunting old castles or abbeys were primarily fragmented disembodiments of earlier crimes and suppressions. These ghosts faced the rising middle classes with their guilty fears in walking effigies and pictures that were more floating signifiers than full-bodied people (see Walpole, *Castle* [Lewis and Clery] 21–27). Radcliffe continued that pattern in her obviously painted backgrounds and spectralized characters presented to readers mostly as ghostly thoughts rather than sexualized bodies (see Castle, "Spectralization"). If Shelley tried to return the body to the Gothic in *Frankenstein*, she did so in a patently artificial creature and presented the body of woman, from the title character's male point of view, as a complex reality so fearsome up close that his female creature had to be destroyed before she was completely made (*1818 Text* 162–71).

African American Gothic, starting from early short stories and portions of *Our Nig* and slave narratives, works powerfully to recover the fullness of the black body, especially the body of the African American woman taken from her primal Mother Africa and alienated into Western slavery. It calls attention to that body—and brings it forth into greater awareness—in the very specters and monsters of the Anglo Gothic tradition that once suppressed it. The teaching of the African American Gothic should convey most of all to students that this mixed genre at its best is not a distortion of African American life by white symbols; it is rather a resurgence of the African American body in an originally Anglo discourse that once refused to face that body and has now been reshaped to recover it from repression.

Making the Case:
Teaching Stephen King and Anne Rice
through the Gothic Tradition

Bette B. Roberts

Designed for undergraduate, upper-level English majors, our undergraduate course Gothic Fiction is open to nonmajors as well. The students bring avid reading experience in modern Gothics with them but little formal background, so this survey class introduces the history and conventions of the genre through readings intended to enrich their appreciation and assessment of it as a literary tradition. Since a chronological approach seems to work best for establishing a historical context and tracing the powerful social-psychological appeal of the Gothic, we begin with Ann Radcliffe's *The Mysteries of Udolpho* and Matthew Lewis's *The Monk*; move on through a selection of nineteenth-century classics: Mary Shelley's *Frankenstein*, Edgar Allan Poe's stories, Emily Brontë's *Wuthering Heights*, Robert Louis Stevenson's *Dr. Jekyll and Mr. Hyde,* and Bram Stoker's *Dracula*; and finally cover modern representatives, *'Salem's Lot* by Stephen King and *The Tale of the Body Thief* by Anne Rice. Ending the course with novels by King and Rice is particularly appropriate, since their works culminate our discussion of Gothic conventions all semester and suggest future directions of the genre.

Indeed, given the phenomenal success of both writers with the popular audience and the lively, prolific academic attention they are receiving in book-length critical studies and in collections of essays, articles, and reviews, it is difficult to imagine teaching a Gothic fiction course without including their work. Even Harold Bloom, for whom popular appeal is hardly the arbiter of literary merit, has introduced a recent collection of King criticism and acknowledged the archetypal power of King's images (Introduction 3). Underlying our coverage of King and Rice are the efforts not only to place them in the mainstream Gothic tradition but also to understand the reasons for their appeal: their adaptations of Gothic conventions, especially those of vampire fiction; their blend of low, sensational plots with higher philosophical, social, and psychological issues; and their allusions to other literary works and myths that enrich and deepen their narratives. Students soon discover that King and Rice are conscious artists, aware of the traditions in which they are writing, and that both comment extensively on the nature of their art and its hold on the imagination. Tracking down their intentions (especially in interviews) offers a special advantage in showing how Gothic writers who are themselves moved by the power of the Gothic can experiment with conventions and revitalize its appeal for a new audience. At the same time, bringing the history and reading experience of classic Gothic forerunners discussed earlier in the semester to the novels of King and Rice helps students appreciate the extent of their influences.

While I would enjoy teaching a special-topics course focusing on King and Rice, in this class we can discuss only one work by each, so the first challenge is to choose the texts. Any rationale for selection involves distinct advantages and disadvantages. Intent as I am on describing the Gothic tradition and establishing King's and Rice's places in it, I enjoy comparing and contrasting their work with Bram Stoker's *Dracula* because the vampire tradition is so well established that it provides a most effective way of illustrating blends of old and new conventions. Vampires are not common subject matter in King, so the choice is easily limited to 'Salem's Lot; but this early novel is a fine example of his talent in achieving a delicate balance of the real and the unreal, the ordinary and the terrifying, so characteristic of his Gothicism. Rice is well represented here, since her six novels thus far in *The Vampire Chronicles* are most of her canon. Like those of other highly successful novelists writing under the demands of enormously lucrative publishing contracts, King's and Rice's overall canons are uneven, with some novels well worth including and others sensibly avoided, so consulting reviews and criticism is another factor in the selection, as is the issue of whether or not to discuss film versions of the novels. While different rationales will lead to different choices, depending on the objectives of a course, the vampire tradition provides a structured and concrete approach not only to focus the discussion but also to explore common denominators in King's and Rice's creative departures that enliven the Gothic tradition and show its continued impact on contemporary readers.

Efforts to assess King and Rice suggest another rationale important to me in selecting novels to teach. In an article on Rice's *The Tale of the Body Thief*, Joseph Ceccio comments on the influence of literary traditions on her work: "Knowing an author's sources or inspirations—and seeing how well an author shapes and transforms those materials to a new or higher purpose—is surely one important measure for evaluating an author's achievement" (163). Since this course is also an opportunity to defend the seriousness of the genre, to discuss significant issues related to best-sellers and classic texts, and to explore bases of popular appeal and academic assessment, *The Tale of the Body Thief* (1992) is my pick of her *Chronicles*, with *Interview with the Vampire* (1976) as an alternate. The *Interview* is startlingly original in its compelling portrayal of the tormented Louis, whose inability to find meaning establishes Rice's sympathetic vampires questing for meaning in the fin de siècle climate of our time, which echoes the decadent 1890s climate of Stoker's *Dracula*; the *Interview* is also contemporary with King's 'Salem's Lot (1975). However, *The Tale of the Body Thief* shows not only Rice's continued ingenuity with the tradition but also her artistic maturity; her interweaving of literary allusions into a sensational plot deeply enriches the text. As in Charles Dickens's later novels, the result is a layering of fictional elements that attract both popular and academic audiences, who may find reading pleasure on different levels. Identifying and understanding these references enable students to explore ranges of appeal, from the erotic and sensational to the psychological and philosophical. This line of inquiry also compares well with tracing King's allusions to Stoker in *'Salem's Lot,* the novel he has identified as his tribute to the achievement of *Dracula,* an attempt to play "literary racquet-ball" by bouncing the ball of his novel against the wall of Stoker's (*Danse* 38).

Class time for King and Rice consists of four seventy-five-minute periods (or two classes for two weeks), beginning with a general discussion of students' initial responses to their reading of each novel. We then focus on comparative topic questions (see the appendix to this article) designed to help students write short essays of three to four pages that become oral presentations, in which students highlight the main points of their papers and share them with the class. (I assign at least one student to cover each topic question.) The starting point, of course, is to determine what King and Rice do with the vampire tradition. In a three-way comparison of *'Salem's Lot, The Tale of the Body Thief,* and *Dracula,* students are quick to realize that Rice's departures are much more radical than King's. We put a list on the board of all pertinent similarities and differences, starting with major adaptations and moving gradually down to more superficial ones; then we step back to synthesize the parts in relation to the whole and to examine the larger implications.

The overall role of the vampire in the action reveals the most startling distinctions between King's and Rice's handling of the tradition. King's plot remains essentially faithful to Stoker's moral struggle of good human protagonists— King's Ben Mears, Mark Petrie, and others—pitted against the evil vampire Barlow and his human enabler Straker. Yet the two surviving protagonists are not beautiful young women like Mina but a writer and a child, Ben and Mark. They are the prototypes of many later characters whom King uses to develop his theme of the imagination and innocence as means of survival and antidotes to the rationalism, deadness, and corruption of modern life, especially in rural America. As James Egan points out, most of Barlow's victims, with their souls wrapped up in consumerism, are metaphorically dead before the vampire takes them (57). As a result of the moral battle that Ben and Mark win (with some major losses of allies, including Ben's love interest, Susan), Ben comes to terms with his own childhood or exorcises "all the demons," as he says (424), and finds a meaningful relationship as a father to Mark to replace his lost wife, Miranda.

In complete contrast to Stoker's and King's conflict between good human beings and bad vampires, *The Tale of the Body Thief* demonstrates Rice's focus on a large community of humanized vampires in the *Chronicles* series, from which Rice isolates individuals in different novels to tell their stories of quests for meaning and survival. Threats to their existence come from within, from despair and alienation, rather than from humans. Lestat's relationship with David Talbot, his need to justify his existence as a vampire, and his coming to terms with his predatory nature through an epiphany in the rain forest loom as far more significant than the overt effort to recover his body from Raglan

James. Discussion tends to zero in on the fascinating ramifications of the fact that feelings of belonging and family life are central determiners in both King and Rice. For example, the personal victories of King's human protagonists, like Stoker's, depend on their faith in and loyalty to each other in conquering the vampire; the survival of Rice's vampire characters results from their making deep bonds in their own community and from their retaining human feelings to endure immortality. In different ways, both King and Rice continue the tradition of the Gothic in expressing threats to family structure and protests on domestic issues, as discussed by critics such as Eve Kosofsky Sedgwick (*The Coherence of Gothic Conventions*) and Kate Ferguson Ellis (*The Contested Castle: Gothic Novels and the Subversion of Domestic Ideology*).

While references to *Dracula* are virtually nonexistent in Rice's novel, students enjoy tracing allusions to Stoker's conventions in *'Salem's Lot* and seeing both how they respond to *Dracula* and how King modernizes them for his own fictional realities. Barlow is a clear descendant of Dracula, with his close physical resemblance to Stoker's villain, his appropriate choice of residence in the ever-ominous Marsten House, his vulnerability to crucifixes and holy water, and his diabolical cleverness with numerous hidden coffins that Ben and the others must ultimately locate in the root cellar of Eva Miller's boardinghouse. Students also recognize the branding of Mina behind Callahan's burned hand when he tries to enter the church door; the destruction of Lucy behind Ben's staking of Susan; the committee-like effort of Mina, Van Helsing, Jonathan, and others behind the plotting of Ben, Matt, Jimmy, and Mark; and the suspenseful journal entries behind King's short chapters that shift rapidly from one set of victimized characters to another. King even keeps Barlow offstage through most of the novel, a brilliant device that he thought Stoker used to maintain suspense in *Dracula* (*Danse* 72).

When we analyze the most suspenseful scenes, however, we realize the ingenuity of King's adaptation and see the characteristic themes that empower his Gothicism, especially with American readers. Toward the end of the novel is a showdown, of sorts, between Barlow and Father Callahan, the representative of the church, who could have destroyed Barlow if only he had summoned the courage. The reader has already seen, however, an alcoholic priest weakened by his loss of faith in the established church, given its accommodation to real social evils: "bombers over Cambodia, the war in Ireland and the Middle East, cop-killings and ghetto riots, the billion smaller evils loosed on the world each day" (303–04). In Father Callahan's mind the church's role in the battle with evil has been totally incapacitated by social and psychological theories, which complicate and confuse our courses of action, and by human beings' total lack of belief in the supernatural. Frustrated in his desire to be a real spiritual crusader, Callahan simply lacks Van Helsing's moral strength and determination that defeat the vampire; as a result, Callahan is an unworthy opponent of Barlow, who tells him that the child (Mark) is worth ten of him (355).

Admitting that his novel is "very much a product of the nineteenth century" set in the twentieth (*Danse* 38), King reveals an American scene characterized by its own real demons: the breakdown of family life, adultery, child abuse, ignorance, and poverty. Dropping Dracula into the present exposes the emptiness of lives far more secularized and disconnected from society than those of the Victorians, who despite the transition to modernism apparent in Stoker's novel still manage to overpower their enemy because of their unity of spirit, sense of duty, and capacity for sacrifice. As Edwin Casebeer puts it, King's novels are not just escapist fiction; the realism of his social dilemmas urges "readers to confront squarely and disturbingly the horror in their own lives" (208). The scene between Callahan and Barlow shows students King's blend of traditional Gothic suspense and terror with his distrust of social institutions, especially the church and legal authorities, where individual vision and leadership are buried in the mire of bureaucracy; it also shows his Romantic faith in the innocence of children and the imagination of the writer, who keeps his distance from mainstream culture. Many critics associate King's convincing portrait of American life with the dystopian theme in American literature of the loss of innocence, depicted in novels like *Huckleberry Finn*.

Instead of grounding the supernatural in the gritty reality of American life, Rice moves the narrative conflict away from a moral struggle between good human protagonists and evil vampires to vampires as first-person villain-heroes, whose conflicts are deeply psychological. Commenting on her preference for the marvelous and the supernatural over the real and ordinary in fiction, she sees her vampires as metaphors for human beings, the vampiric condition intensifying their struggle for meaning. Susan Ferraro observes in her explanation how the immortal and human traits complement each other to create a powerful impact on the reader; Rice's vampires are trapped, "lonely prisoners of circumstance, compulsive sinners, full of self-loathing and doubt. They are, in short, Everyman Eternal" (67). Rice humanizes her vampires by giving them different personalities, ages, dialects, hair colors, tastes in clothes, travel experience all over the globe (with a special preference for New Orleans and San Francisco), and emotional needs. Students explore her modifications of traditional vampiric traits to create sympathetic characters. For example, in her existentialism, she discards Stoker's religious icons as a method of vampiric destruction but evokes them to underscore vampiric spiritual thirst and the deep communion of blood. She also minimizes the violence of vampire attacks on human beings and maximizes the eroticism and intimacy of blood exchanges between vampires. In fact, when discussing Rice's charged blood-drinking scenes, students see the restoration of eroticism evident in Dracula's attacks on Lucy and Mina. King either omits or downplays this eroticism when Barlow takes his victims. While Stoker's eroticism derives from a more traditionally based heterosexuality, the sexual intensity of Rice's vampires transcends conventional gender roles; same-sex blood exchanges between vampires and human beings are equally passionate.

Invariably, provocative questions (many addressed in the oral reports) come up and lead to lively conversation. Students wonder how far writers can go in

modifying or adapting conventions and still be considered as writing in the tradition. What characteristics must a vampire absolutely have to be a vampire?
Can we just sympathize with a vampire, or do we also have to fear it? If a cru-
cifix or other religious item cannot destroy vampires, do they still have to drink
blood and stay out of the sun to survive? For some purists in the class, Rice
goes too far in adapting conventions (though her vampires keep these last two
characteristics); they wonder what difference it makes whether her characters
are vampires or human beings. What I hope students realize is that Rice's less
derivative handling of conventions differs from King's in her departure from
reality and immersion into the supernatural; however, the psychological depth
of these vampires enables Rice to explore compelling human conflicts that are
just as powerful as those experienced by King's realistic characters.

Knowledge of Stoker's novel clearly enhances students' appreciation of 'Salem's
Lot, as does some familiarity with other references sprinkled throughout the
text—to Poe's "Haunted Palace" and "The Masque of the Red Death," Shirley
Jackson's The Haunting of Hill House, and Wallace Stevens's "The Emperor of Ice
Cream." In The Tale of the Body Thief, Rice alludes most often to the Faustian
myth (historically important to the Gothic) and Blake's "The Tyger" poem in order
to highlight philosophical questions on the origins of evil in the universe. After
students identify these sources, they can see how Rice twists and turns the Faustian myth so that its application has multifaceted dimensions and ironies.

Lestat is the main Faustian figure in his daring to assume human form and
testing the boundaries of vampiric existence, but even David and Raglan James
can be viewed as tempters and overreachers who end up paying a hefty price
for their pleasures. In Rice's ironic inversion, Gretchen is connected solely with
Lestat's journey toward salvation, which is affirmed by Lestat's embracing evil
instead of repenting his sins. The import of Blake's tiger underscores Lestat's
renewal in the rain forest, when he realizes that his predatory nature has its
own beauty and belongs in the universe; in other words, his vampire existence
possesses a "fearful symmetry." Rice follows through this awareness with
Lestat's supreme evil act in the novel, his betrayal of David Talbot by transforming him into a vampire. Students now see the plot unity, the links between
David's identity with the tiger's victim in Lestat's dream at the beginning of the
novel and Lestat's renewed capacity for evil in the end. They should also
explore other, less prevalent but revealing allusions connected with the Faustian myth in Yeats's "Sailing to Byzantium" and in Lestat's story of Rembrandt,
who was ultimately forgiven by God for selling his soul to the devil to become
a great artist (Ramsland, Vampire Companion 354). Taking the time to explain
these references and to point students in the right direction of criticism that
analyzes them further (such as Katherine Ramsland's The Vampire Companion
and Bette Roberts's Anne Rice) is well worth the effort, not only in encouraging discussion but in seeing students experience the real pleasure of recognizing literary influences and how they operate in a text.

Comparing and contrasting King and Rice in the vampire tradition of

Stoker's *Dracula* shows students the novelists' debts to the Gothic conventions established before them and the serious contributions they make in modernizing the tradition—in King's juxtaposing the horrors of the vampire with those at the heart of American life, in Rice's linking the vampires' survival with psychological quests and existential realities that broaden the horizons for future vampire novels. Analyzing King's and Rice's modern Gothicism in comparison with Stoker's Gothicism, students see how the social threats and dehumanizing forces that caused the Victorians' fears are intensified and perhaps more keenly felt by the shift into a new century and new millennium. As apparent in media coverage during 1999 and the well-publicized fears of Y2K, people tend to take stock of where they are now and question what the future might bring. While the particulars obviously differ (Darwinism evolves into genetic manipulation and cloning, industrialism into high technology, economic reform into consumerism), the widespread response expressed by modern Gothicism is one of unease, confusion, helplessness, and the sense of insignificance—human fears that make us receptive to the experience of Gothic fiction. The power of King's and Rice's versions ensures them a permanent place in the tradition of the genre—and certainly a vital place on my Gothic Fiction syllabus.

APPENDIX

Comparison-and-Contrast Essay Questions for
Stephen King's *'Salem's Lot* and
Anne Rice's *The Tale of the Body Thief*

How do King's comments about *Dracula* and his own intentions in *'Salem's Lot* and Rice's statements about her vampires shed light on their use of the vampire as a literary device?

What are the implications of their titles?

What do King's and Rice's vampires have in common with Dracula, and what distinguishes them?

What roles do human characters play in *'Salem's Lot* and *The Tale of the Body Thief?*

How do the sources of suspense and fear in these two novels compare with those in *Dracula?*

How do King and Rice modernize Stoker's settings?

Apart from the vampire figure, what else do you see as the most important influence(s) of Stoker's *Dracula* on these novels?

What larger aesthetic and moral issues are involved in King's and Rice's departures from Stoker? (You may focus on one variation here.)

To what extent are gender issues important elements in understanding King's and Rice's treatment of the vampire tradition?

If you focus on one similar short passage from Stoker, King, and Rice, such as a description of the vampire's drinking blood, how do the language and style of the authors differ?

Teaching the Gothic in an Interdisciplinary Honors Class

Sandy Feinstein

In small colleges where English departments have been whittled down to four instructors (or fewer!), literature offerings are inevitably limited. Consequently, if one is intent on teaching a specialized course such as Gothic literature, one must find roundabout ways to do it. One means I have found is through general education and honors classes. Traditionally, English faculty members at small colleges are expected to provide or administer classes in composition and introductory literature; increasingly, however, colleges and universities have reconceptualized general education to emphasize interdisciplinary courses. As a result, fewer and fewer lower-division majors courses fulfill general education requirements while serving as prerequisites for the major. The demand on English teachers as service providers has increased at the expense of the major, whose numbers, we are reminded, keep dwindling. Being director of an honors program and a professor of English, I faced the double challenge of providing a greater variety of English classes and developing interdisciplinary courses that fulfilled the goals of the general education program. Since Honors has no budget for hiring faculty members, I knew that to help establish the program and create a distinct identity for it, I would need to develop a number of the classes. It was in this context that I designed my Gothic course.

A course on Gothic literature would add a genre course to the English curriculum yet also meet the goals I had defined for the honors program: community service, experiential learning, and research. By providing an integrative or interdisciplinary approach, the course also met the expectations of the core curriculum, of which Honors forms a small component. Moreover, the class was likely to draw student interest: Gothic is in, a fact I exploited when I omitted the word *literature* from the title in the course schedule. The community-service component of the class may also have piqued interest: I suggested students consider giving blood. The course paper was intended to develop both writing and research skills integral to education in general and English in particular. The experiential structure, modeled on science laboratories or field courses, provided a means of addressing scientific issues and concerns in the texts as well as providing an interdisciplinary approach that included characteristic methodologies of specific fields. Gothic literature proved ideal for fulfilling these goals and one more: that students in Honors engage in an education of risk.

The Gothic course I developed for the honors program involved reenacting the literature's setting. To reinforce the importance of time and place in the literature, its conventions and character, as well as to subvert the notion of what constitutes class space and time (and work space and time), the hour of class meetings was understood to be changeable: sometimes we met at the published time of 7:00 to 9:30 p.m.; often we met later, at least once running until midnight, a particularly significant hour in the literature. This flexibility was not merely a symbolic gesture or a test of conservative assumptions about education but also a practical necessity: I had to adjust to the schedules of those who would contribute their time or space to the class.

Classroom location as well was subject to change. Although we gathered every week at the assigned room, I would lead the group to another location, one intended to represent some aspect of a text's landscape or an issue that the landscape foregrounded. Since our destinations were as much fictional constructions as the texts, these journeys also served to complement another convention of the genre: travel as a process of discovery, as both physical act and psychological experience. In short, changing the class time and locales drew attention to key aspects of Gothic: suspense, mystery, and terror as reflected in setting; it also demonstrated how authors adapt the landscape they know to describe the landscape they do not. My students may be familiar with the Kansas Flint Hills and Ann Radcliffe with the cliffs of Dover, but neither she nor they ever set foot in Italy, where much of her *Mysteries of Udolpho* is set. The appropriation of a local setting to enact a text actively demonstrated the role landscape plays in the genre as sensibility, metaphor, idea, even character.

Since the class met only once a week, I could not afford to waste a day. On the first day, therefore, I began to define the genre and provide background for it. I asked students to do a five-minute freewrite listing their associations with the word *Gothic*. They read their definitions aloud, and we put some key words and images on the board. I supplemented the key words with those used by John Ruskin to define Gothic architecture—"savageness," "changefulness," "naturalism," "grotesqueness," "rigidity," "redundance"—and I showed slides of Gothic cathedrals. Then I provided excerpts from various precursors of the

Gothic: Homer's figure of Discord, Vergil's figure of Fame. I asked the students which of their definitions or Ruskin's could be associated with the classical figures. The basic distillation was of a scary character who creates chaos in an evocative landscape.

From the first day, we demonstrated the truth of Jerrold Hogle's comment that

> "Gothic" has been a misnomer that has enabled the projection of certain associations on a group, figure, and/or artistic style—all of which are made more archaic and "primitive" than they really are—for very definite ideological purposes, however much the associations and purposes have shifted over the years.   ("Introduction" 2)

After Homer and Vergil, we looked at sections from Dante (the monster Geryon), Shakespeare (the ghost scenes in *Hamlet* and *Macbeth*), and Milton (the scene in *Paradise Lost* involving Sin, Death, and Satan). To prepare students for their first on-site reenactment of the literature, I asked them to underline what they thought were Gothic images or actions, then be prepared to read a tercet or more of Dante aloud in their best imitation of a Gothic voice. We identified and discussed Dante's images, motifs, themes, and word choice in *The Inferno* that could be associated with the Gothic: the Great Tower, marsh, two horns of flame, swamp vapors, red mosques, moat, sepulcher, rocky levee, dark cliff; supernatural actions, the journey through hell itself, the bizarre and monstrous inhabitants, including the mad steersman Phlegyas, disembodied voices from darkness (the shade of Filippo Argenti), ghosts, Geryon; specific words that are literally translated, like "dark," "evil," "hell-dog," "slime," "shadow," "curse," "black word," "pack," "howling"; animal similes, for instance the scorpion's stinger; and God and the absence of God.

Slides of medieval Gothic architecture reinforced students' awareness of Dante's architectonics and demonstrated the relation of his poetic landscape to the architecture of the period. As the students had noted the Gothic characteristics of the poetry, they also identified the key characteristics of the architecture: pointy spires and dramatic arches, dark stones, gargoyles and grotesques, stone-carved animals, and leaded stained-glass windows. I tried to get them to make connections between the visual and the verbal, between Ruskin's definition and their own. By way of contrast, I provided slides of eighteenth-century art, Jean-Honoré Fragonard's and François Boucher's whimsy as well as the artificially constructed Romantic landscapes seen in architecture books of the time and later used by Tom Stoppard as a symbolic structure in *Arcadia*.

Classes scheduled to last nearly three hours benefit when an instructor varies the activities and pedagogical approaches, while still building on the learning objective for that day. My intention was to build on background and definition. For this purpose, I even used break time. Though the classroom structure changed from a focus on individual responses to collaborative group work, the intention remained the same: to add to our evolving definition of Gothic by examining specific texts. My last in-class reading assignments for the first day, from Milton and Shakespeare, were presented through performance. Groups were formed, parts chosen; the break was the journey to the performance space.

We walked up the hill to the administration building, proceeded to the third floor, where we came to a sign on the men's bathroom: Reserved for Gothic Class. I had obtained all the necessary permissions for my various field trips, and the college indulged my first request: to let me hold class on the roof of the building, the access to which is through the men's bathroom. An extension ladder had been set up, and a campus security guard stood waiting at the top of the stairs. He helped students through the small rectangular opening that led to the roof. On the way to the rooftop stage, I pointed out another stage outside, which I had prepared with candles (not yet lit), in case anyone feared heights. It was there I sent two students who, though they tried, could not make it to the roof. On the roof, with its barbican crenellations, three groups performed rampart scenes from act I of *Hamlet,* another performed the banquet scene from *Macbeth.* We discussed the relation between performance and text, site and text, and what it all had to do with the Gothic.

Three students dropped the class for various reasons: the demands of the reading, open-ended class time, and the experiential approach (though discomfort was never actually admitted). Interestingly enough, the two students who did not climb the ladder to the roof were not among the three who dropped. By the end of the semester, both would be faced with another climb, and both would surmount the challenge and describe the experience in their journals as an achievement and a personal way of understanding the literature: they realized that by both accepting and conquering fear, they had reenacted a situation faced by a number of Gothic heroines. The sixteen remaining students were excited about this approach to reading, and only one missed any classes.

Not all the field trips required students to climb or crawl. The second trip, for example, provided the set for Horace Walpole's *The Castle of Otranto:* we walked to the most Gothic church in town, an Episcopal church. The site seemed appropriate to represent the distortions of Catholic worship and ritual created by the Anglican Walpole. On the way to the church, students formed groups whose members assumed the roles of specific characters in order to dramatize the actions and interactions of characters—trying to escape from one another, discerning possible hiding places on the way to the church, and identifying lurking threats analogous to Gothic constructs in the text.

These field trips and the many that followed taught me something important: I not only learned what the community had to offer, which I and my students had vastly underestimated—its natural resources, its architecture, its history—but I also learned about the people who lived there. I learned how willing people are to make a contribution, no matter how eccentric the request might seem. Everyone wanted to know what I was doing, not out of suspiciousness so much as curiosity. When they learned what I was about and why, they went out of their way to help me give shape and form to a verbal landscape I had reimagined locally: from the college's supporting my request to teach on the roof to the Episcopal minister's leaving his church open after 7:00 p.m. so I could use it at an "appropriate time." I had no particular leverage: I was not a member of his congregation, nor am I even Christian, which he knew. This experience made me aware of another advantage of involving the community: the Gothic may have an ominous ring in rural, Christian communities; it is too easily associated with Satan worship and radical teens wearing black. By my identifying the specific texts that would be read in a particular place, one corrective to these associations was provided.

On another of the evening field trips, we met at a local bed-and-breakfast where two of my colleagues provided entertainment, eighteenth-century music on recorders (the B and B serving as the pump room of *Northanger Abbey*'s Bath). Later that same night the old Carnegie Library, now a dance studio, served as an English ballroom, and students were given a lesson in eighteenth-century dances. These entertainments, like everything else, had more than one purpose: contextualizing the genre, demonstrating how culture informs behavior, and providing a window into the fictional universe and the daily life that Jane Austen delights in satirically contrasting. Computer technology enabled me to make period invitations to the ball, which were delivered by hand; the invitations were modeled on actual eighteenth-century invitations, though mine reminded the recipients to "dress appropriately." The students responded in kind: four ladies had a page deliver the RSVP, a gentleman handwrote his RSVP, and all came dressed for the occasion. Though I had not defined "appropriate dress," a number of students had contacted the theater department, which obliged by providing tails for the gentlemen and white gowns and gloves for the ladies. Just as the formal invitations elicited formal responses and assumptions regarding what to wear, the fancy clothing changed behavior, as the students themselves remarked. Their awareness of how dressing up affected their movements, conversation, and self-image made them conscious of how clothes affect behavior and manners and demonstrated the importance of clothing in the texts. It was not only the students who accessed Austen by dressing up: the personnel at the Marland Mansion in Oklahoma, which the following week served as the abbey itself, prepared for my class by reading the novel, researching eighteenth-century clothing, and then dressing accordingly (one woman made her dress for the occasion!). A groom met our cars; the mansion agreed on a late arrival (after 8:00 p.m.), led us with torches (candles) through secret tunnels (which I knew wasn't part of the usual tour), and filled their eighteenth-century japan cabinet with "secret" papers—because, to my greatest surprise, they were permitting the students to explore the antique in a staged re-creation of Catherine Morland's surreptitious investigation of a similar piece of furniture.

The most unlikely field trip of all also involved tunnels with a professional guide: the deputy warden of the state prison, located in town, agreed to give the class a tour of the prison's underground tunnels. This venue was for *Dracula*. This time, teacher and students alike felt a fear that was real and palpable. The experience highlighted the difference between what Michel Foucault calls the Gothic's "whole fantasy-world of stone walls, darkness, hideouts and dungeons" (*Power/Knowledge* 153; qtd. in Miles, "Eye" 12) and the real world of incarceration and punishment. After we were checked in by security, three officials guided our group through two different secret passageways. Before getting started, however, the warden asked the students what Gothic was and what tunnels had to do with their reading. The students answered in a rush, identifying the tunnels in *Dracula* but also mentioning their presence in Matthew Gregory Lewis's *The Monk* and Walpole's *The Castle of Otranto*. He couldn't keep from smiling at their enthusiastic explanations, though eventually he cut them short to begin the tour. When I bumped into the warden two months later in a drugstore, I asked him if he remembered me. He asked if I was kidding, then added that he and the assistant deputy warden who had accompanied us had found themselves describing actions by the inmates or specific environments at the prison as Gothic. The ways this course touched those who were not students in the class struck me time and again.

Since I had modeled the structure of the class, to some extent, on that of a field biology class, I knew I wanted scientists to contribute to shaping students' access to the literature and its concerns. To demonstrate how scientific methodology and discoveries have informed Gothic fiction, I asked three of my colleagues in science if they would be willing to offer "labs" for two books, *Frankenstein* and *Dracula*. A chemist agreed to create a lab in which the students experimented with "chloral," the formula of which appears in *Dracula* (111); a biologist discussed bats (he provided many skins to examine and then joined us for an on-campus bat walk, though not to the "bat cave," where we discussed *Dracula* later that same night); and a biochemist constructed an experiment that engaged students in both biological and ethical issues with a "life-creating" DNA experiment. She also joined us in a night walk to the cemetery intended to recall the graveyard scenes in both *Dracula* and *Frankenstein*. This walk was used to extend the discussion of ethics to assumptions about propriety, prompted by our being at a cemetery after hours, the discomfort of which led in turn to an examination of the importance of transgression in the construction of the Gothic. An optional anatomy lesson on an actual corpse followed the walk among the buried dead. For those who, like me, did not relish the thought of dissecting a corpse, I had prepared a creative writing exercise as a substitute; I was stunned that only three students demurred from the anatomy lesson. These experiments emphasized the increasing role of science in the literature, a role represented as problematic progress, as a threat both potential and actual that had to be exposed, addressed, debated, and explored for good or ill.

Because we brought the genre into the community, asking people to contribute to the re-creation of scenes, the Gothic was demystified; town and gown united for the purpose of education, and both students and residents benefited by learning about the place they lived and about one another as well as about an unfamiliar literature. If in a town of ten thousand founded in late-nineteenth-century Kansas it is possible to find Gothic locations, then I suspect that few instructors at even very small institutions will have difficulty doing the same. The students' enthusiasm for being surprised—as the Gothic requires of its characters—affected how students perceived and read the texts. Moreover, it kept them invested in both the literature and the course, making them active readers: they are afraid not to read the books all the way through, afraid to miss class, because they think they really will miss something. They enjoy trying to figure out which landscapes from the books will be re-created, for they do not know in advance what local site will serve as the fictional place. With Gothic literature paralleling the rise in the role of science and its perceived significance—specifically biology and experimental chemistry—offering the Gothic as a field course does more than integrate the disciplines. It enables students to experience the disciplines actively while provoking them to consider how both literature and science contribute to our perception and understanding of the world.

Involving Resistant Readers: Exploring the Gothic through Role-Playing and Identity Writing

Mark James Morreale

Students often find the task of critical reading daunting because of a natural resistance to the unfamiliar. They fall prey to this defensive posture especially when confronted with the Gothic for the first time. A few students, as one might expect, initially react to these texts by calling them weird or some such unsophisticated term. Other students typically find the language and the allusive nature of the texts difficult, because they mistakenly read the novels as examples of realistic fiction and because the literary conventions of the Gothic disorient many people born in the last quarter of the twentieth century. I have therefore found that my students need to do various prewriting and even prereading activities before they can successfully compose a close reading of that genre. In this way they will better understand what writers like Ann Radcliffe or Mary Shelley or Horace Walpole have accomplished. A prewriting exercise gives students greater rhetorical and critical competence in the process and helps them overcome their initial reticence. Role-playing makes the genre their own.

A Rationale for Role-Playing

In my experience, focused exercises overcome milder forms of student resistance to eighteenth- and nineteenth-century texts. For instance, I have given students photocopies of selected chapters and the table of contents pages of conduct manuals and then, after a discussion of this material, required them to compose their version of a chapter not photocopied from the conduct manual. (This exercise works particularly well with works influenced by conduct manuals, such as Austen's *Northanger Abbey*.) However, these solutions seemed clearly inadequate for a particular group of resistant undergraduate readers enrolled in my upper-level course The Age of Satire and Sensibility, since renamed Eighteenth-Century England and the Colonies.

An assignment I call the Gothic Epistolary Novel Project, developed out of my students' resistance to Walpole's *The Castle of Otranto* and William Beckford's *Vathek*, did much to overcome this problem. The class composed an epistolary novel based on Gothic themes with the premise that it would eventually be published on the Web. Over the course of a week, students composed over a hundred letters using the scenario and characters I had created (see below). This exercise stimulates student speculation. By examining what they have done, students begin to see how male and women writers represent women differently

notice how, in the Gothic context, men and women might write about different subjects

pay closer attention to the fate of the heroine, the question of victimization, the depiction of the body

become aware of patterns of patriarchal subversion in women's but not in men's texts

If handled deftly, the exercise prompts class discussion along these lines.

The Epistolary Novel Project Explained

The following exercise, when considered as a template or model, may be adapted to several different pedagogical circumstances, hence its strength. This Gothic scenario for a class of twenty-five works especially well for non-majors. Students better comprehend the Gothic when the instructor shapes the initial plot with elements characteristic of the genre. These elements should represent fantastic or supernatural events (statues coming to life, castles moving location, hauntings by murdered children), Gothic landscapes and settings (dark forests, moors, threatening weather, forbidding mountains, dungeons, abandoned castles, graveyards), grotesque or typically Gothic characters (dwarfs, hunchbacks, a mysterious necromancer, alchemists, mad monks). Here is an abbreviated version of the assignment I give to students after breaking them up into groups of an appropriate size for the scenario:

> Each group has been assigned a character cluster. [See appendix 1 of this essay.] Each cluster has several correspondents, all of whom play a role in that "famous, but now unfortunately lost" Gothic novel by Ann Fitz-Allen Forster, *Pemberton Manor.* (Just in case you were wondering, there never has been such a novelist, or such a novel, lost or otherwise.) YOUR TASK: (1) read the material for each character cluster; (2) select a character from your own assigned cluster; (3) write your correspondence based on the plot outline applicable to your group and character. (Each correspondent should direct his or her first two letters toward a particular correspondent with a particular topic in mind. After that, you're on your own.) By the end of class today, complete and "deliver" your first two letters and have at least one in hand to respond to. All letters should be identified by place, date, and time and signed by the correspondent. (Each group should provide me with a list of who's taking on what role. Don't be afraid to take on a role of the opposite sex.) Dame Fortune (yours truly) will occasionally add a proverbial twist of fate to the plot. These events may take the form of intercepted correspondence, stolen journals, newspaper scandal sheets, anonymous letters, fantastic events, et cetera. They may also take the form of instructions that must be obeyed. . . .

As a final step, I will distribute copies of the entire "novel" to the class. Students must then write an assessment of their contribution to the project, explaining both their intent and the effectiveness of their contribution to the whole, and critique the results of the class project.

Developing a Skeletal Plot and Character Sketches

First, the instructor needs to develop a skeletal plot. It should be suggestive but brief, detailed yet open to alteration and expansion. The following sketch illustrates the type of plot that might be created:

> We begin our story sometime in the late 1790s. The refined and aristocratic Beverly family, owners of the ancient country estate called Pemberton Manor, has longed reigned over their baronial holdings with a less than benevolent hand. The poor cottagers and tenant farmers live in deplorable conditions and are regrettably susceptible to disease and alcoholism. Some are restless. It is during the time of the French Revolution. Romanticism can be sniffed in the air. Rebellion too. The county seat, Pemberton, is a pleasant little village, nestled between hills and surrounded by rolling farmland and well-kept woods. From one of these hills one can see the ruins of an old castle, a place that has generated much local legend. [Such rumors could include tales told by the ignorant peasants about the Beverly family's ancestors: a dismembered wife who haunts the moor; a ghoulish midwife hung as an abortionist; a giant man-wolf, snatcher of virgins, who inhabits the castle's dungeons. These rumors may easily be introduced as the scenario begins to percolate.] A millstream (Pemberton Rill) cuts right through the village and is crossed in the middle of town by an ancient, moss-covered stone bridge. The brackish stream itself acts as a border between the less well-off part of the village and its more fashionable section where many small shops are located. The whitewashed Anglican Church of St. Michael's dominates the green at the town's center. The Beverlys have bestowed St. Michael's living upon a poor clergyman, one Pastor Barnstable, distantly related to Mrs. Beverly.
>
> The Beverlys' closest relations, the Wilkinsons, live in London. The two families, although once very close, have grown apart of late, due to Lord Beverly's constantly vacillating will. (He is the elder brother of Mrs. Wilkinson.) No one knows who will inherit the Beverly fortune, given Lord Beverly's fragile health and occasionally unstable mind. He has oscillated between several potential heirs: Horace (his estranged elder son); Lawrence (his unacknowledged bastard); and his sister's eldest son, Jerry (whom he apparently detests), although it is said this nephew is his favorite choice for heir at present.

Step 2 concerns character development. One character should be developed for each member of the class, the professor taking on the role of Fickle Dame Fortune. (See appendix 2 of this essay for examples of her intervention.) Students in small groups could reasonably develop characters on their own, but the first time I offered this exercise, I gave the class guidelines. If students do create the characters, they must be cautioned about the necessity of being true to the time period (in this instance the late eighteenth century), of staying within the plot, and of having their various characters' traits be reasonable. In other words, they need to keep in mind the aesthetic conventions of the eighteenth century—that is, questions of probability and plausibility and how the Gothic either adheres to or violates those conventions.

Step 3 builds on what has now been established by explaining whom correspondents should initially write to and what topics they should initially address. A select group of students, with guidance by the professor, should establish an equitable distribution of letters and responses; each character should both receive a few letters and write a few letters. In my experience the rest of the correspondence takes care of itself. Here is an example of such correspondence instructions:

> Horace, the eldest remaining son (estranged and twice disinherited), is the family's black sheep. A Cambridge grad, he is very literate and likes to quote from the popular poetry of the day. Fancies himself a lady's man. He has been living in France these past few years and has sunk into debt from gambling and womanizing. Scandal seems to follow him everywhere, yet he is a likable soul and not malicious at all. His problem is that he is impulsive, imprudent, passionate, and rebellious. INITIAL CORRESPONDENTS AND TOPICS: (1) *Margaret Beverly,* his young cousin. He will speak of love and other such nonsense to turn her head. His father has banished him to France for nearly ruining her virtue with his reckless behavior. Their correspondence is therefore secret, he having bribed one of his father's servants as a messenger; (2) *Molly Filcher,* a village woman with whom he has previously "had an understanding."

Applying Technology

The application of computer technology can occur on a number of different levels. For example, instructors may create a class e-mail conference or chat room accessible only to class members. Instructors would then send each student, through the student's personal e-mail account, a character description as well as the initial correspondents the student would need to respond to. (Obviously all e-mail addresses need to be distributed to the class.) The correspondence then occurs through the e-mail conference. I prefer the exercise to occur through actual letter writing in or out of class. The letters can easily be organized, converted to HTML, and posted on the Web after the creation of needed transitional and explanatory letters, a table of contents, a preface, and even perhaps a dedication. This task can be performed by a group of interested students willing to make it their semester project. For an example, see my home page at library.marist.edu/Faculty-Web-Pages/Morreale/Morreale-Index.htm, and click on "Student Projects."

The exercise has two related goals: to develop students' deeper engagement with the material and to improve their written responses to texts. Students learn best by hands-on experience and write best when their imaginations become engaged. An important facet of this experience manifests itself when students cross-dress: male students will need to think about how an eighteenth-century woman faced with certain situations in a Gothic plot might behave, just as women students enacting the role of a man have to figure out how best to handle and portray that character. Students also need to consider the differences that would occur if one were of a lower class or a person of color. I find the women in the class generally more adept at cross-dressing than the men. Men playing women tend to make their characters more empathetic, even sentimental, especially if the character is a victim. (Are they overly sensitive to how their depiction might be perceived?) Women playing men often make their characters thoroughly despicable if the men are villains and more antihero than hero if the men are initially conceived as good.

How women are victimized also tends to differ along gender lines. The class noted that male letter writers in the class were less likely to put the women they portrayed in sexual peril but more likely to make them victims of other types of assault. Women playing women tended to give their characters—victim or not—greater depth and to make them less idealized and less fragile. This circumstance might lead to a discussion of how male Gothic writers idealize women characters, especially when victimized, and why women Gothic writers victimize their heroines, idealized or otherwise.

Women playing men tended to portray their characters more or less realistically. Female villains were truly villainous in female hands but not in an over-the-top way, as some male depictions tended to make them. (Even here, men tended to reach for an ideal villain.) When discussing the rationale for their decisions, students engaged in a lively debate about how they perceived men and women differently. They were able to extrapolate from this discussion that modern attitudes toward the Gothic and its conventions result perhaps from changed views about what is and isn't plausible or probable. (There were complaints on both sides of the aisle that each gender tended to distort the depiction of the other, making the characters of opposite gender implausible.)

Although the novel the class created did not directly subvert patriarchal attitudes—not surprising, given the large number of students participating—students clearly noted the possibilities of the form in this regard. Five women in the class chose to extend the project by creating their own Gothic epistolary project, either by expanding a text we had previously read or by creating one on their own. Each of these texts used subversion in interesting ways. The

Gothic form evidently spoke to the women in the class in ways it did not to men. (One student even tried her hand at responding to the women's poetry we were reading by translating a few of the heterosexual love poems we had read into Gothic-inspired gay love poems and then composing a written rationale for the choices she, and the poets who inspired her, made.)

In the end, such an exercise does not replace more traditional types of assignments. Rather, it complements and enhances them. Engaged writing develops from engaged readers. This exercise promotes both kinds of engagement.

NOTE

I would like to thank Diane Cochrane and Carrie Landi, who pored diligently over numerous drafts of this paper and gave me helpful suggestions along the way. I would also like to thank my colleagues Don Anderson and Ken Moss, whose conversations regarding resistant readers helped spur me on.

APPENDIX 1
Sample Character Clusters from Original Character List

The Beverly Family

Lord Richard Beverly
Lady Matilda, née Thorndyke, his long-suffering wife
Horace, the eldest remaining son, the family's black sheep, a Cambridge grad
Margaret, the Baron's beautiful sixteen-year-old ward
Lawrence, twenty five, a bastard, the product of one of Lord Beverly's youthful indiscretions

The Wilkinsons

Sir Frederick Wilkinson, an eccentric judge, an indulgent father, and by all accounts a good husband
Lady Mary Beverly Wilkinson, his wife, the younger sister of Lord Richard Beverly
Jerry, Sir Frederick's only son, twenty, somewhat affected but not truly foppish
Sarah, the Wilkinsons' youngest child, fifteen, who fancies herself a poetess

A Decadent Circle of Posh Aristocrats

Spencer Truelove, aka Simon Lowell, a handsome rake and college chum of Horace Beverly
William Pitts, a decadent member of Spencer's clique and frequently the foppish companion of Jerry Wilkinson

Hector Jones, Spencer's loyal humpbacked manservant of unusual strength

Clara Galsworthy, a woman of questionable virtue

APPENDIX 2
Examples of Fickle Dame Fortune's Intervention

Lawrence Beverly: Frustrated by Cleland's stonewalling, you break into his London office. While rifling through his papers, you discover a document that indicates you have a twin brother living in France. Then, in a daze, you stumble over something on the floor: Cleland's body. He has been bludgeoned to death. In his hand is clutched an important-looking paper. Escaping from the office, you immediately write to Horace to tell him about this paper's contents.

Margaret Beverly: Truelove has duped you into an elopement. However, you have been left alone for ten minutes. In that time, you write and send off a letter explaining your situation and asking for help. To whom will you write?

Spencer Truelove: You have bribed Margaret Beverly's maid to pass a letter to her expressing how you adore her. Beg for a meeting by the garden wall at midnight. Assure her your intentions are perfectly honorable. Follow this up with a letter to William Pitts, detailing your true intentions and instructing him about what role he should play in Margaret's abduction.

Lady Mary Beverly Wilkinson: You begin traveling with Elizabeth Filcher from London to Pemberton. However, when your coach breaks down, highwaymen rob you and your servant of all your possessions. Strangely, one of them looks familiar behind his mask. After you reach the safety of the next inn, write to your husband of the incident. Then continue your travels.

Sir Frederick Wilkinson: One of your servants has discovered a stash of private letters addressed to your daughter Sarah by an unknown admirer. Alarmed, you are moved to take swift action before it is too late or is it already too late? Your first action is to inform your son Jerry of the danger.

Teaching Gothic Literature
through Filmic Adaptations

Wheeler Winston Dixon

This brief consideration of some of the many filmic adaptations of the Gothic novel for possible use in the classroom should be prefaced by two essential caveats. First, most of the films discussed here vary widely from the source texts. Second, the more recent adaptations often contain sustained sections of graphic violence, which may make them unsuitable for use in the classroom. Instructors are therefore advised to view beforehand each of the films discussed below, to determine whether or not they wish to use them. While many students will willingly attend R-rated features outside the classroom, many others might be offended if such films are introduced in class without explanation or warning.

With older films, of course, the use of graphic violence is not a central concern, but films from the 1930s through the mid-1960s are often in black and white (which, sadly, is often sufficient to keep viewers from appreciating them) and so are sometimes perceived as dull, lacking the gore that avid followers of the *Nightmare on Elm Street*, *Friday the Thirteenth*, and other series have come to expect. Finally, it should be noted that throughout this essay I am very careful to specify both the director and year for each film discussed; other versions are often inferior and should be avoided. For example, Daphne du Maurier's *Rebecca* has been filmed numerous times for television, but only the 1940 Alfred Hitchcock film comes close to achieving any measure of fidelity to the novel.

That said, the two classic American horror films that most inform twentieth-century consciousness of the Gothic cinema are without a doubt James Whale's *Frankenstein* (1931) and Tod Browning's *Dracula* (1931). When screening *Frankenstein* in the classroom, please make sure to obtain the restored version, which includes material cut from the original release; as a result of this material's inclusion, the restored version is both smoother and more gripping. Mention should also be made of George Melford's Spanish-language version of *Dracula* (1931), shot at night on the same sets as Browning's film, starring Carlos Villarías as Dracula. Both the restored *Frankenstein* and the Spanish-language *Dracula* are now readily available on video, in either VHS or DVD format.

Although Whale's *Frankenstein* and Browning's *Dracula* are very freely adapted from their respective novels, audiences will find Bela Lugosi as Dracula and Boris Karloff as the Frankenstein monster entertaining and engaging, even today. Lugosi, for many viewers, "is" Dracula, and tribute was recently paid to the actor in Tim Burton's excellent film *Ed Wood* (1994). Karloff's Frankenstein monster is a true immortal of the screen, even if the monster he portrays bears little relation to Mary Shelley's sentient, philosophical construct. Such classic horror films as Karl Freund's *The Mummy* (1932), Whale's

The Bride of Frankenstein (1935), Lambert Hillyer's *Dracula's Daughter* (1936; an interesting lesbian version of the classic vampire myth), Rowland V. Lee's *Son of Frankenstein* (1939), Erle C. Kenton's *The Ghost of Frankenstein* (1942), Roy William Neill's *Frankenstein Meets the Wolf Man* (1943), Kenton's *House of Frankenstein* (1944) and *House of Dracula* (1945), and other Universal horror films of the 1930s and 1940s are equally engaging and fast-paced and, if presented with sufficient introduction, can easily hold a modern student audience.

It should be noted that perhaps the most successful vampire film from this early period of cinema is F. W. Murnau's silent film *Nosferatu* (1922), an unauthorized adaptation of Bram Stoker's *Dracula* that of all the early versions remains closest to the text. As the undead incarnation of Dracula, king of the vampires, Max Schreck's truly horrific makeup is so effectively cadaverous that it has never been equaled on the screen; *Nosferatu* has served as the prototype for both Francis Ford Coppola's 1992 *Bram Stoker's Dracula* and Werner Herzog's 1979 *Nosferatu*, starring Klaus Kinski in the title role. The original film was nearly destroyed entirely when Stoker's widow sued for damages. Murnau had not bothered to secure the rights to film the novel, which was then still under copyright. As executor of Stoker's estate, his wife sought to have all copies of the film, as well as the negative, destroyed. Happily, several complete versions survived nonetheless, and the film is readily available in VHS or DVD format for use in the classroom. E. Elias Merhige's recent film *Shadow of the Vampire* (2000), with John Malkovich as Murnau and Willem Dafoe as Schreck, is an interesting variation on the 1922 *Nosferatu*, in which Murnau enlists the services of a real vampire to play his leading role.

In 1957, the British firm of Hammer Films began a new cycle of Gothic films, beginning with Terence Fisher's *Curse of Frankenstein* (1957) and *Horror of Dracula* (1958). Both starred Christopher Lee as, respectively, the Frankenstein monster and Dracula, while Peter Cushing tackled the roles of Baron Frankenstein and Dr. Van Helsing. As with the Universal series, Fisher's films take enormous liberties with the original text of both Stoker's and Shelley's novels, but *Horror of Dracula* is perhaps the finest adaptation of *Dracula* to the screen that has ever been made. Working from a carefully crafted screenplay by Jimmy Sangster, Fisher offers us Dracula as a jaded, decadent, yet charismatic aristocrat who seduces his victims solely through the power of his gaze before dispatching them in a suitably violent manner. Fisher's visual style in directing the film, coupled with Bernard Robinson's suitably grandiose sets and James Bernard's ominous musical score, made the film an immediate international success, and film critics even today rank the film as one of the best British productions of the period. *Curse of Frankenstein* is perhaps less successful and slower moving than *Horror of Dracula*, but it is still a superb Gothic entertainment, and Lee is compellingly pathetic as the monster, in sharp contrast to Cushing's Baron Frankenstein, who will stop at nothing to continue his research. When first released, both films received an X for violence, but compared with horror films today *Horror of Dracula* and *Curse of Frankenstein* seem absolutely restrained in their use of on-screen, graphic violence.

Lee's performance as Dracula set the standard for a generation of filmgoers and brought new dimension to the role Lugosi had become irrevocably identified with. Hammer followed up these films with Fisher's *The Revenge of Frankenstein* (1958), *The Mummy* (1959), *The Hound of the Baskervilles* (1959), *The Brides of Dracula* (1960), *Dracula: Prince of Darkness* (1965), *Frankenstein Created Woman* (1967), *Frankenstein Must Be Destroyed* (1969), and *Frankenstein and the Monster from Hell* (1974), as well as Freddie Francis's *The Evil of Frankenstein* (1964)—all of which, thankfully, equaled the stylistic and visual intensity of the first two films in the series. Readily available on video, these are earnestly recommended for pedagogical use, particularly *Horror of Dracula*, because the passage of time has not diluted their collective impact. Sadly, Hammer ceased production in the early 1980s, and another Gothic cycle of cinematic adaptations came to a close.

Frank Langella appeared as Dracula in John Badham's 1979 *Dracula* opposite Sir Laurence Olivier's Van Helsing, but despite its considerable merits, the film failed to spark a Gothic revival, and Langella (notwithstanding his success on Broadway in the same role) never seemed wholly convincing as the undead count. In 1992, Francis Ford Coppola brought Dracula back to the screen in *Bram Stoker's Dracula*, which featured a young cast comprising Winona Ryder, Keanu Reeves, Cary Elwes, Gary Oldman, and Richard E. Grant, with Anthony Hopkins as Van Helsing. Despite the film's title, Coppola's film took even greater liberties with Stoker's text, presenting the audience with a series of pyrotechnic displays in place of a genuine sense of mood and terror. It was little more than a string of spectacularly gruesome prosthetic special effects strung together with rapid MTV-styled editing, remarkable only for Oldman's performance as Dracula.

Even less successful was Kenneth Branagh's 1994 *Mary Shelley's Frankenstein*, in which Branagh's Dr. Frankenstein played opposite Robert De Niro's monster. The film, which also starred Helena Bonham Carter and Monty Python's John Cleese, is full of flashy tracking shots, elaborate sets, and all the usual Gothic locations (deserted castle, mad laboratory, and the like). But even with Branagh's energy in the leading role, the film is sluggish and overly violent and was poorly received on its release.

During this period perhaps the most successful and faithful adaptation of *Frankenstein* was brought to the screen as an independent production: Calvin Floyd's *Victor Frankenstein* (1977), featuring Per Oscarsson as the monster. Shot in Ireland and postproduced in Sweden, this film not only follows Shelley's text almost to the letter but also plays down the violence and focuses audience attention on the humanist plight of a monster thrust into a world not of his making, a monster who can nevertheless speak and reason (in contrast to the mute, shuffling, inarticulate brute of the Universal films) and who not unsurprisingly seeks to exact revenge on his maker. Of all the filmic adaptations of Shelley's novel, this version is the most effective from a pedagogical point of view. *Victor Frankenstein* has recently been released on DVD.

Also during this period, a West German film, *Jonathan* (1970), directed by Hans W. Geissendörfer, offered a fresh take on the Dracula legend, presenting the count as a rapacious nobleman who is nevertheless plagued by a bad conscience and fleeting moments of self-doubt. Intent on increasing the number of living slaves at his command, Geissendörfer's protagonist is nevertheless a three-dimensional creation, capable of pity, remorse, and self-recrimination. Sumptuously photographed in color and staged on a series of suitably crumbling, stylized Gothic sets, *Jonathan* was an art-house hit when first released but failed to find a larger audience. The film is difficult to find on video, but worth the effort. An interesting sidebar to these Gothic films is Ivan Passer's semibiographical 1988 *Haunted Summer*, an evocative and understated version of Anne Edwards's novel about the meeting among Percy Shelley, Byron, Mary Godwin, and John Polidori in Italy in 1816. The film boasts an excellent script by Lewis John Carlino and strong performances from (among others) Philip Anglim as Byron, Alice Krige as Mary Godwin, Eric Stoltz as Shelley, and Alex Winter as John Polidori. Much the same territory is covered in Ken Russell's *Gothic* (1986), featuring Gabriel Byrne as Byron, Julian Sands as Percy Shelley, and Natasha Richardson as Mary Shelley, which re-creates the night during which Mary Shelley first told her tale of *Frankenstein* to amuse her bored companions. Russell also directed the rather stylishly decadent *Lair of the White Worm* (1988), starring Hugh Grant, Amanda Donohoe, and Catherine Oxenberg, based on the novel by Stoker.

H. P. Lovecraft, another Gothic writer whose reputation has increased steadily since his death, has received rather poor treatment from those who seek to adapt his work to the screen, but there are some exceptions. Roger Corman's *The Haunted Palace* (1963) is an effectively understated version of Lovecraft's only novel, *The Case of Charles Dexter Ward*; Daniel Haller's *Die Monster, Die* (1965, from Lovecraft's short story "The Colour out of Space") and *The Dunwich Horror* (1970, based on Lovecraft's short story of the same name) are both ambitious attempts to film Lovecraft's Cthulu mythos; while Stuart Gordon's *Re-animator* (1985, based on Lovecraft's serial novella *Herbert West: Re-animator*) is an all-out splatter film, which despite widespread favorable critical commentary (Pauline Kael singled it out for particular praise in one of her final columns for *The New Yorker*) is really unsuitable for classroom use, featuring as it does endlessly over-the-top Grand Guignol sequences of dismemberment, graphic sexual situations, and spectacularly brutal violence. These comments apply to Gordon's subsequent films, including *From Beyond* (1986) and *The Pit and the Pendulum* (1990); the viewer is hereby warned.

Roger Corman created a stylish series of adaptations based on the stories of Edgar Allan Poe in the early 1960s, including *The Tomb of Ligeia* (1965), *The Masque of the Red Death* (1964), *The Raven* (1963), *The Premature Burial* (1962), *Tales of Terror* (1962), *The Pit and the Pendulum* (1961), and *House of*

Usher (1960); all are in color and Panavision and suitable for use in the classroom to illustrate the visual world inhabited by the protagonists in Poe's phantasmagoric world. *The Pit and the Pendulum* in particular still packs a punch, and many critics consider *The Masque of the Red Death* to be not only Corman's finest film but also the finest adaptation of Poe to the screen. Corman used the actors Vincent Price, Boris Karloff, Basil Rathbone, Peter Lorre, and other veterans of the golden age of horror films in these stylish if often free adaptations of Poe's works, which remain some of the most effective horror films of the era.

More successful adaptations of classic Gothic tales are the numerous versions of Robert Louis Stevenson's *Dr. Jekyll and Mr. Hyde*; perhaps the Rouben Mamoulian version from 1931 with Fredric March is the best. Other versions are Victor Fleming's 1941 film with Spencer Tracy; Terence Fisher's 1960 *The Two Faces of Dr. Jekyll*; and David Wickes's *Jekyll and Hyde*, a 1990 TV movie starring Michael Caine. Albert Lewin directed a stylish 1945 version of Oscar Wilde's *The Picture of Dorian Gray*, a variation on the theme of the duality of human nature, starring Hurd Hatfield and Angela Lansbury; the film is shot in both color and black and white and holds up well today. Less accomplished is Massimo Dallamano's rather lurid Italian-American version *Dorian Gray* (1970), starring Helmut Berger as Dorian. The film is marred by terrible sound recording, has little to do with Wilde's novel, and contains considerable graphic violence; it is not recommended.

A number of other British and American films made during this period warrant our attention; some are adaptations, others are original projects. Jack Clayton's 1961 CinemaScope black-and-white production of *The Innocents*, brilliantly photographed by Freddie Francis and superbly acted by Deborah Kerr, Michael Redgrave, and Martin Stephens, is a faithful and deeply frightening version of Henry James's novella *The Turn of the Screw*; the script is by Truman Capote, William Archibald, and John Mortimer. When using this film, make sure to get a letterbox print: Francis's depthy, swirling black-and-white cinematography deserves to be seen in its entirety rather than cut off by traditional pan-and-scan methods, which eliminate part of the filmic image to fit the size of the standard television screen.

Another superb ghost story from this period is Robert Wise's *The Haunting* (1963), based on Shirley Jackson's novel *The Haunting of Hill House*. Also shot in black-and-white CinemaScope, this film boasts a cast that includes Claire Bloom, Julie Harris, and Valentine Dyall and creates a genuinely sinister mood of evil throughout its compact, epigrammatic running time. (Jan de Bont's 1999 remake of Wise's film, also titled *The Haunting*, is a pale shadow of the original, with additional doses of graphic violence and digital special effects to momentarily dazzle the viewer.) Another excellent Gothic film, slightly earlier, is Lewis Allen's *The Uninvited* (1944), starring Ray Milland, Ruth Hussey, and Donald Crisp in a tale of a brother and sister who unwittingly purchase a haunted house and then must deal with the malign spirits who still inhabit it.

Based on Dorothy Macardle's novel *Uneasy Freehold*, the film stands as one the finest of the 1940s in suggesting rather than explicitly presenting the supernatural on the screen. It holds up well today.

The producer, Val Lewton, who worked at RKO studios during the 1940s, also created a series of deeply felt and now widely revered Gothic films that are among the best made in America during that period, irrespective of genre. These include Robert Wise's *The Body Snatcher* (1945), based on Stevenson's short story, with a superb cast (Boris Karloff, Henry Daniell); Mark Robson's *The Seventh Victim* (1943), in which a young Kim Hunter seeks to rescue her sister from devil worshipers in Greenwich Village; and Jacques Tourneur's *The Cat People* (1942), one of the most famous Gothic films of all time, in which Simone Simon is convinced that she will turn into a leopard if any man so much as kisses her. Paul Schrader directed an updated version of *Cat People* in 1982, starring Nastassja Kinski and Malcolm McDowell, with much less left to the viewer's imagination. Either version can be profitably linked in the classroom to Samuel Taylor Coleridge's 1798 poem "Christabel," a variation on a similar theme, but the 1942 film is clearly superior.

Charlotte Brontë's *Jane Eyre* has been filmed numerous times, as both a feature film and a television adaptation. The most famous version is Robert Stevenson's 1944 film, starring Orson Welles and Joan Fontaine, with a screenplay by John Houseman. More recently, Franco Zeffirelli directed a fine adaptation of *Jane Eyre* in 1996, with William Hurt as Rochester, Charlotte Gainsbourg as Jane Eyre, Joan Plowright as Mrs. Fairfax; the Zeffirelli version is more accessible to modern students. When teaching *Jane Eyre*, one might also consider screening John Duigan's *Wide Sargasso Sea* (1993), based on the novel by Jean Rhys. Set in Jamaica in the early 1800s, the film explores the tempestuous relationship between the native heiress Antoinette Cosway (Karina Lombard) and the very British Edward Rochester (Nathaniel Parker). It is an interesting variation on Brontë's novel, as is Jacques Tourneur's *I Walked with a Zombie* (1943), which transplants Jane Eyre to the West Indies with added Gothic overtones, another of Val Lewton's productions for RKO. In a similar vein, Sheridan Le Fanu's *Uncle Silas* has been adapted twice for the screen. First is the 1947 British feature film *The Inheritance*, directed by Charles Frank, starring Derrick De Marney as Uncle Silas; second is Peter Hammond's excellent 1987 TV movie starring Peter O'Toole and entitled *The Dark Angel*. O'Toole is both convincing and suitably despicable as the corrupt and grasping Uncle Silas; for modern audiences, the PBS version is easily the better choice.

Nathaniel Hawthorne has not fared particularly well on the screen, but there are at least two worthy adaptations of his work available: Joe May's 1940 *The House of the Seven Gables*, starring Vincent Price, George Sanders, Margaret Lindsay, and Cecil Kellaway in an abridged but evocative translation of Hawthorne's source material to the screen; Sidney Salkow's *Twice Told Tales* (1963), a color omnibus film that takes several of Hawthorne's classic tales and brings them to the screen with a cast including Sebastian Cabot, Vincent Price, and Joyce Taylor. One should not forget Alfred Hitchcock's *Rebecca* (1940), the famed director's first American film and the only Hitchcock film ever to win an Academy Award (which went to the producer, David O. Selznick, rather than Hitchcock). Based on Daphne du Maurier's novel, *Rebecca* tells the story of a young, impressionable woman (Joan Fontaine) who is swept off her feet by a dashing aristocrat (Sir Laurence Olivier). Olivier, however, is still haunted by the specter of his first wife, Rebecca, and the gigantic house where the couple attempt to make their home is almost a shrine to her, a shrine dutifully attended by an appropriately sinister Agnes Moorhead.

Of additional interest is the recent wave of feminist horror films that began (with the possible exception of *Dracula's Daughter*, previously mentioned) in the late 1960s and early 1970s, with such films as Kathryn Bigelow's superb modern vampire tale *Near Dark* (1987), in which a group of itinerant vampires seek new victims in the modern American West, set to a hypnotizing score by the pop group Tangerine Dream, and Stephanie Rothman's *The Velvet Vampire* (1971), loosely but effectively based on Sheridan Le Fanu's "Carmilla." "Carmilla" was also brought to the screen in a beautiful film by the underrated director Roger Vadim, entitled *Blood and Roses* (1960), with Mel Ferrer, Annette Vadim, and Elsa Martinelli. Sumptuously photographed in Techniscope and Technicolor, this inventive retelling of Le Fanu's classic tale of a female vampire is enthralling to the eye and also weaves a spell of genuine mystery and suspense throughout its running time.

Charlotte Perkins Gilman's classic feminist short story of incipient insanity, *The Yellow Wallpaper*, has received relatively little attention as film material, perhaps because of its brevity and perhaps because its depiction of the interior states of hallucinatory madness are quite difficult to convey on the screen. However, the producer Sarah Curtis and the director John Clive created a superb adaptation of the work for *Masterpiece Theatre* and the BBC in 1984, featuring Julia Watson in the title role, from a screenplay by Maggie Wadey. Although the eighty-minute film considerably enlarges Gilman's story, it remains true to the core of her vision, the image of a marriage gone hopelessly awry, based in part on Gilman's own marriage, combined with that of her mother. Both as a story and a film, *The Yellow Wallpaper* is a chilling and compelling Victorian Gothic narrative.

This brief survey does not list the many other Gothic films that might profitably be used in the classroom, in conjunction with the source texts that informed their creation. Such little-seen classics as Lew Landers's *Return of the Vampire* (1944); John Brahm's *The Undying Monster* (1942; a tale of lycanthropy set in England in the early 1900s, based on a novel by Jessie Douglas Kerruish and photographed by the great Lucien Ballard); and Henry Levin's *Cry of the Werewolf* (1944), in which a matriarchal group of werewolves terrorize New Orleans during World War II, are equally worthy of consideration when one plans a syllabus for a course in Gothic literature. But again, one should keep in mind that in most of the films described above, the original text serves merely as a springboard for the screenwriter's imagination; the end result, while entertaining, often bears little resemblance to the original. But if one reminds students that a viewing of a film is no substitute for reading the novel itself, the films discussed here may prove to be a useful adjunct to the detailed examination of the many Gothic writers examined in this volume.

NOTES ON CONTRIBUTORS

Stephen C. Behrendt is George Holmes Distinguished University Professor of English at the University of Nebraska, Lincoln. Among his books are *Shelley and His Audiences*, *Reading William Blake*, and *Royal Mourning and Regency Culture: Elegies and Memorials of Princess Charlotte*. He has also edited Percy Bysshe Shelley's *Zastrozzi* and *St. Irvyne*.

Marshall Brown is professor of English and comparative literature at the University of Washington and editor of *Modern Language Quarterly: A Journal of Literary History*. His books include *The Shape of German Romanticism*, *Preromanticism*, *Turning Points: Essays in the History of Cultural Expressions*, and a forthcoming study, *The Gothic Text*.

Ranita Chatterjee is assistant professor of English at California State University, Northridge, where she teaches British Romanticism and critical theory. She has published on Mary Shelley, William Godwin, feminist psychoanalysis, and postcolonial film. Currently, she is working on a book on the politics of erotics in the Godwin-Shelley circle.

Laura Dabundo is professor and chair of the Department of English, Kennesaw State University. She is editor of Garland's *Encyclopedia of Romanticism, 1780s–1830s* and *Jane Austen and Mary Shelley and Their Sisters*, a collection of essays on Romantic women novelists. She is at work on a project on Austen and Wordsworth.

Wheeler Winston Dixon is Ryan Professor of Film Studies, chair of the Film Studies Program, professor of English at the University of Nebraska, Lincoln, and editor-in-chief of *Quarterly Review* and *Film and Video*. His most recent books are *The Second Century of Cinema: The Past and Future of the Moving Image*; *Film Genre 2000: New Critical Essays*; and *Collected Interviews: Voices from Twentieth-Century Cinema*.

Sandy Feinstein is honors coordinator and associate professor of English at Penn State Berks-Lehigh Valley College. Her scholarship on the Middle Ages and early modern literature has appeared in *Chaucer Review*, *Arthuriana*, *Exemplaria*, and *Studies in English Literature*, among others.

Susan Allen Ford is professor of English and writing center coordinator at Delta State University. She has published essays on Jane Austen and her contemporaries, the Gothic, and detective fiction. She teaches courses in these subjects and a variety of writing and introductory literature courses.

Richard Fusco, assistant professor of English at Saint Joseph's University (Philadelphia), is author of *Maupassant and the American Short Story: The Influence of Form at the Turn of the Century* and *Fin de millénaire: Poe's Legacy for the Detective Story*.

Kathy Justice Gentile is associate professor of English and women's and gender studies at the University of Missouri, Saint Louis. She has published a book on Ivy Compton-Burnett and completed a book about the writing of Jane Bowles. She has also published on the Gothic uncanny and teaches courses in female Gothic.

Teresa A. Goddu is associate professor of English at Vanderbilt University. She is author of *Gothic America: Narrative, History, and Nation.*

Tamar Heller is assistant professor at the University of Cincinnati, assistant editor of *Victorian Literature and Culture*, and author of *Dead Secrets: Wilkie Collins and the Female Gothic* and articles on Charlotte Brontë, Oliphant, Le Fanu, and Wharton. She has edited with Patricia Moran the essay collection *Scenes of the Apple: Food and the Female Body in Ninteenth- and Twentieth-Century Women's Writing.*

Mark M. Hennelly, Jr., is department chair and professor of English at California State University, Sacramento. He has published widely in Victorian and Gothic studies. His most recent publications in Gothic appear in *Studies in Romanticism* and in *College Literature.*

Diane Long Hoeveler is professor of English and coordinator of the Women's Studies Program at Marquette University. She is author of *Romantic Androgyny, Gothic Feminism*, coauthor with Lisa Jadwin of *Charlotte Brontë*, and coeditor with Beth Lau of the MLA volume *Approaches to Teaching* Jane Eyre. She is past president of the International Conference of Romanticism.

Jerrold E. Hogle is professor of English and University Distinguished Professor at the University of Arizona. He has published widely on Romantic and Gothic literature and is past president of the International Gothic Association. His newest book is on *The Phantom of the Opera*, and he is the editor of the *Cambridge Companion to Gothic Fiction.*

Patrick M. Horan teaches English literature at Morristown-Beard School and Greenwich University. He received his PhD from Drew University. He has published several articles on Oscar Wilde and is author of *The Importance of Being Paradoxical: Maternal Presence in the Works of Oscar Wilde.*

Tricia Lootens is author of *Lost Saints: Silence, Gender, and Victorian Literary Canonization.* Associate professor of English at the University of Georgia, she writes primarily on nineteenth-century poetry. Her most recent project is a study of the privatization of the "Poetess."

A. A. Markley is associate professor of English at Penn State University, Delaware County. He has published on Mary Shelley's fiction; the poetry of Tennyson, Rossetti, and Morris; and the novels of D. H. Lawrence and E. M. Forster. He has also coedited two of William Godwin's novels and a volume of Mary Shelley's miscellaneous works.

Robert Miles is professor of English at the University of Stirling, Scotland. A past president of the International Gothic Association, he has written extensively on the Gothic. His books include *Gothic Writing, 1750–1820: A Genealogy; Ann Radcliffe: The Great Enchantress; Gothic Documents, 1700–1820: A Source Book*, ed. with E. J. Clery; and *Jane Austen: Writers and Their Works.*

Mark James Morreale is lecturer of English and digital library multimedia specialist for the School of Liberal Arts at Marist College. He is currently developing a course that explores hypertext and its scholarly application to the eighteenth century.

James Norton is assistant professor of British literature and director of the Humanities Program at Marian College, Indianapolis. He has published on William Congreve, John Bunyan, John Milton; on pedagogical theories; and on college administrative practices. He is currently preparing articles on early modern Anglican theology and literature.

Marjean D. Purinton is associate professor of English at Texas Tech University, teaches in the Women's Studies Program and the Comparative Literature Program, and is a member of the Texas Tech University Teaching Academy. She is author of *Romantic Ideology Unmasked: The Mentally Constructed Tyrannies in Dramas of William Wordsworth, Lord Byron, Percy Shelley, and Joanna Baillie.*

Bette B. Roberts, professor emerita at Westfield State College, has taught courses in Victorian literature, Gothic fiction, English composition, and British literature since 1780. She has written a critical study of Anne Rice and articles on eighteenth- and nineteenth-century British Gothic fiction.

Cannon Schmitt, associate professor of English at Wayne State University and editor of *Criticism,* is author of *Alien Nation: Nineteenth-Century Gothic Fictions and English Nationality* and articles in *ELH, Genre, Victorian Literature and Culture.* He is working on a study titled "Savage Mnemonics: South America, Victorian Science, and the Reinvention of the Human."

Daniel Scoggin is headmaster of Tempe Preparatory Academy in Tempe, Arizona. He has published in *Dickens Studies Annual, Victorian Literature and Culture,* and *Negations.*

Carol A. Senf is associate professor of English at the Georgia Institute of Technology. She is author of *Dracula: Between Tradition and Modernism, The Critical Response to Bram Stoker, The Vampire in Nineteenth-Century British Fiction,* and *Science and Social Science in Bram Stoker's Fiction.*

Scott Simpkins, professor of English at the University of North Texas, is author of *Literary Semiotics: A Critical Approach* and has published essays and reviews on Romanticism, modern literature, and semiotics. He is editor of *Studies in the Novel.*

Anne Williams is professor of English at the University of Georgia. She is author of *Prophetic Strain: The Greater Lyric in the Eighteenth Century* and *Art of Darkness: A Poetics of Gothic.* She is currently writing a study of the Gothic, the operatic, and the horror movie.

Judith Wilt is professor of English and Newton College Alumnae Chair in Western Culture at Boston College and a founding member of its Women's Studies Committee. She is author of essays and books on nineteenth-century British literature and in popular culture genres, including *Ghosts of the Gothic: Austen, Eliot, and Lawrence.* She has recently published a new edition of *Frankenstein* and *The Island of Dr. Moreau.*

Angela Wright lectures on eighteenth-century and Romantic literature at the University of Sheffield. She has published on European Gothic, French melodrama, and Sophia Lee. Her current research reexamines radical female Minerva Press authors writing on the cusp of the eighteenth and nineteenth centuries.

SURVEY PARTICIPANTS

Bryan Alexander, *Centenary College*
Kathleen Anderson, *Palm Beach Atlantic College*
Ruth Bienstock Anolik, *Bryn Mawr College*
Chris Baldick, *University of London*
Kate Behr, *Iona College*
Stephen C. Behrendt, *University of Nebraska, Lincoln*
Toby Bielawski, *Chabot College*
Troy Boone, *University of California, Santa Cruz*
Susan Brantly, *University of Wisconsin, Madison*
Marshall Brown, *University of Washington*
Gerald J. Butler, *San Diego State University*
James P. Carson, *Kenyon College*
Alan D. Chalmers, *University of South Carolina, Spartanburg*
Ranita Chatterjee, *University of California, Northridge*
Laura Dabundo, *Kennesaw State University*
Ian Duncan, *University of Oregon*
Thomas Dutoit, *Université de Tours*
Monika Elbert, *Montclair State University*
Kate Ellis, *Rutgers University, New Brunswick*
Sandy Feinstein, *Penn State University, Lehigh*
Maria Aline Salgueiro Seabra Ferreira, *Universidade de Aveiro*
June Foley, *The New School*
Susan Allen Ford, *Delta State University*
Richard Fusco, *Saint Joseph's University*
Michael Gamer, *University of Pennsylvania*
Kathy Justice Gentile, *University of Missouri, Saint Louis*
Maureen Harkin, *Stanford University*
Donna Heiland, *Vassar College*
Tamar Heller, *University of Cincinnati*
Cyndy Hendershot, *Arkansas State University*
Mark M. Hennelly, Jr., *California State University, Sacramento*
Diane Long Hoeveler, *Marquette University*
Patrick M. Horan, *Southern Vermont College*
William Hughes, *Bath Spa University College*
Ann Merrill Ingram, *Davidson College*
Randall Ingram, *Davidson College*
Darryl Jones, *Trinity College, Dublin*
Frank Kelleter, *Johannes Gutenberg Universität*
Elizabeth Godke Koonce, *Ohio University, Athens*
Doug Long, *University of Toledo*
A. A. Markley, *Penn State University, Delaware County*
Sara Martin-Alegre, *Universitat Autònoma de Barcelona*
Karen McGuire, *Pasadena City College*

Robert Miles, *University of Stirling*
Nickianne Moody, *Liverpool John Moores University*
Mark James Morreale, *Marist College*
Nancy Morrow, *University of California, Davis*
James Norton, *Wabash College*
Louis H. Palmer III, *Michigan State University*
Eulalia Pinero-Gil, *Universidad Autónoma de Madrid*
Paul M. Puccio, *University of Central Florida*
David Punter, *University of Bristol*
Marjean D. Purinton, *Texas Tech University*
Doug Rice, *Kent State University, Salem*
Glynis Ridley, *University of Huddersfield*
Bette B. Roberts, *South Portland, ME*
Deborah Rogers, *University of Maine, Orono*
Cannon Schmitt, *Grinnell College*
Beverly Schneller, *Millersville University*
Daniel Scoggin, *Tempe Preparatory Academy*
David Seed, *Liverpool University*
Carol A. Senf, *Georgia Institute of Technology*
Edward A. Shannon, *Ramapo College*
Greg Smith, *Western Michigan University*
John A. Stoler, *University of Texas, San Antonio*
Elizabeth Tilley, *National University of Ireland, Galway*
Brenda Tooley, *Colorado College*
Robert O. Viau, *Georgia College and State University*
Maryanne C. Ward, *Centre College*
Toni Wein, *Gettysburg College*
Kim Wheatley, *College of William and Mary*
Julianne White, *University of New Mexico, Albuquerque*
Anne Williams, *University of Georgia*
Julia M. Wright, *University of Waterloo*

WORKS CITED

Print Sources

Abrams, M. H., ed. *A Glossary of Literary Terms*. 7th ed. Fort Worth: Harcourt, 1998.

Abrams, M. H., et al., eds. *The Renaissance*. New York: Norton, 2000. Vol. 2 of *Norton Anthology of English Literature*.

Aguirre, Manuel. *The Closed Space: Horror Literature and Western Symbolism*. Manchester: Manchester UP; New York: St. Martin's, 1990.

Aiken, John, and Anna Laetitia Aiken. *Sir Bertrand*. Clery and Miles 127–32.

Aiken, Susan Hardy. *Isak Dinesen and the Engendering of Narrative*. Chicago: U of Chicago P, 1990.

Ames, Dianne. "Strawberry Hill: Architecture of the 'As If.'" *Sources in Eighteenth-Century Culture* 8 (1979): 351–63.

Ammons, Elizabeth. *Conflicting Stories: American Writers at the Turn into the Twentieth Century*. New York: Oxford UP, 1991.

Anderson, Sherwood. "The Philosopher." *Winesburg, Ohio*. New York: Dover, 1995. 20–25.

Andriano, Joseph. *Our Ladies of Darkness: Feminine Daemonology in Male Gothic Fiction*. University Park: Penn State UP, 1993.

Andriopoulos, Stefan. "The Invisible Hand: Supernatural Agency in Political Economy and the Gothic Novel." *ELH* 66 (1999): 739–58.

Arata, Stephen D. *Fictions of Loss in the Victorian Fin-de-Siècle*. Cambridge: Cambridge UP, 1996.

———. "The Occidental Tourist: *Dracula* and the Anxiety of Reverse Colonization." *Victorian Studies* 33 (1990): 621–45.

Aristotle. *Aristotle's Metaphysics*. Ed. and trans. John Warrington. New York: Dutton, 1966.

———. *Poetics*. Ed. and trans. Stephen Halliwell. Chapel Hill: U of North Carolina P, 1986.

Armitt, Lucie. "The Magical Realism of Contemporary Gothic." Punter, *Companion* 305–16.

———. *Theorizing the Fantastic*. London: Arnold, 1996.

Armstrong, Nancy. "Emily Brontë in and out of Her Time." *Genre* 15.3 (1982): 243–64.

Arnaud, Pierre. *Ann Radcliffe et le fantastique: Esai de psychobiographie*. Paris: Aubier Montaigne, 1976.

Atwood, Margaret. *Alias Grace*. New York: Doubleday, 1996.

———. *Lady Oracle*. New York: Doubleday, 1976.

———. "A Letter from Margaret Atwood." Reading Group Guides. Amazon.com. 23 Aug. 1999 <www.amazon.com/exec/obidos/s...aliasgrace.html/002–0315306–7477232>.

Auerbach, Nina. *Our Vampires, Ourselves*. Chicago: U of Chicago P, 1995.

Austen, Jane. *Northanger Abbey and Persuasion*. Ed. R. W. Chapman. 3rd ed. Oxford: Oxford UP, 1982. Vol. 5 of *The Novels of Jane Austen*.

Bachelard, Guy. *The Poetics of Space*. 1958. Trans. Maria Jolas. Boston: Beacon, 1994.

Backscheider, Paula R. "Reflections on the Importance of Romantic Drama." *Texas Studies in Literature and Language* 41.4 (1999): 311–29.

———. *Spectacular Politics: Theatrical Power and Mass Culture in Early Modern England*. Baltimore: Johns Hopkins UP, 1993.

Backus, Margot. *The Gothic Family Romance: Heterosexuality, Child Sacrifice, and the Anglo-Irish Colonial Order*. Durham: Duke UP, 1999.

Bailey, Dale. *American Nightmares: The Haunted House Formula in American Popular Culture*. Bowling Green: Bowling Green State U Popular P, 1999.

Baillie, Joanna. *Orra. A Series of Plays*. 1812. Vol. 3. Ed. Donald H. Reiman. New York: Garland, 1977. 1–100.

Bakhtin, Mikhail. *Rabelais and His World*. Trans. Helena Iswolsky. Cambridge: MIT P, 1968.

Baldick, Chris. *In Frankenstein's Shadow: Myth, Monstrosity, and Nineteenth-Century Writing*. Oxford: Clarendon, 1987.

———, ed. *The Oxford Book of Gothic Tales*. 2 vols. Oxford: Oxford UP, 2001.

Baldick, Chris, and Robert Morrison, eds. *Tales of Terror from Blackwood's Magazine*. Oxford: Oxford UP, 1995.

———, eds. *The Vampyre and Other Tales of the Macabre*. Oxford: Oxford UP, 2001.

Balzac, Honoré de. *The Wild Ass's Skin*. Trans. Herbert J. Hunt. Harmondsworth: Penguin, 1977.

Barbauld, Anna Laetitia. "On the Origin and Progress of Novel-Writing." *The British Novelists*. Ed. Barbauld. Vol. 1. London: Rivington, 1810. 1–62.

Barber, Paul. *Vampires, Burial, and Death: Folklore and Reality*. New Haven: Yale UP, 1988.

Barron, Neil, ed. *Fantasy and Horror: A Critical and Historical Guide to Literature, Illustration, Film, TV, Radio, and the Internet*. Lanham: Scarecrow, 1999.

———, ed. *Horror Literature: A Reader's Guide*. New York: Garland, 1990.

Bayer-Berenbaum, Linda. *The Gothic Imagination: Expansion in Gothic Literature and Art*. London: Assoc. UP, 1982.

Becker, Susanne. *Gothic Forms of Feminine Fictions*. Manchester: Manchester UP, 1999.

Beckford, William. *Vathek*. Fairclough 149–255.

Beddoes, Thomas, and James Watt. *Considerations on the Medicinal Use of Factitious Airs and on the Manner of Obtaining Them in Large Quantities*. Bristol: Bulgin, 1794.

Beddoes, Thomas Lovell. *Plays and Poems of Thomas Lovell Beddoes* Ed. Henry Wolfgang Donner. London: Routledge, 1950.

Begnal, Michael H. *Joseph Sheridan LeFanu*. Lewisburg: Bucknell UP, 1971.

Behrendt, Stephen C., ed. *Approaches to Teaching Shelley's Frankenstein*. New York: MLA, 1990.

Belsey, Catherine. "The Romantic Construction of the Unconscious." *1789: Reading, Writing, Revolution: Proceedings of the Essex Conference on the Sociology of Literature*. Ed. Francis Barker, Jay Bernstein, Peter Hulme, Margaret Iverson, and Jennifer Stone. Colchester: U of Essex, 1982. 67–80.

Bendixen, Alfred, ed. *Haunted Women: The Best Supernatural Tales by American Women Writers*. New York: Ungar, 1985.

———. Introduction. Bendixen, *Haunted Women* 1–9.

Benedict, Barbara M. "Pictures of Conformity: Sentiment and Structure in Ann Radcliffe's Style." *Philological Quarterly* 68.3 (1989): 363–77.

Benjamin, Walter. "Hochherrschaftlich Moeblierte Zehnzimmerwohnung." *Einbahnstrasse*. Trans. Tricia Lootens. Ed. Tillman Rexroth. Tuebingen: Suhrkamp, 1972. 83–148. Vol. 4 of *Walter Benjamin: Gesammelte Schriften, unter Mitwirkung von Theodor W. Adorno und Gershom Scholem*.

Bentman, Raymond. "Horace Walpole's Forbidden Passion." *Queer Representations: Reading Lives, Reading Cultures*. Ed. Martin Duberman. New York: New York UP, 1997. 276–89.

Berenstein, Rhona J. *Attack of the Leading Ladies: Gender, Sexuality, and Spectatorship in Classic Horror Cinema*. New York: Columbia UP, 1996.

Bernstein, Stephen. "Form and Ideology in the Gothic Novel." *Essays in Literature* 18 (1991): 151–65.

Bettelheim, Bruno. *Symbolic Wounds: Puberty Rites and the Envious Male*. New York: Collier, 1962.

Bewell, Alan. "An Issue of Monstrous Desire: *Frankenstein* and Obstetrics." *Yale Journal of Criticism* 2 (1988): 105–28.

Bhabha, Homi K. *The Location of Culture*. London: Routledge, 1994.

———. "Signs Taken for Wonders: Questions of Ambivalence and Authority under a Tree Outside Delhi, May 1817." *Critical Inquiry* 12.1 (1985): 144–65. Abbr. rpt. in *The Post-colonial Studies Reader*. Ed. Bill Ashcroft, Gareth Griffiths, and Helen Tiffin. London: Routledge, 1995. 29–35.

Bhalla, Alok. *The Cartographers of Hell: Essays on the Gothic Novel and the Social History of England*. New Delhi: Sterling, 1991.

Birkhead, Edith. *The Tale of Terror: A Study of the Gothic Romance*. London: Constable, 1921.

Blackall, Eric A. *The Novels of the German Romantics*. Ithaca: Cornell UP, 1983.

Blake, William. *Milton. The Complete Poetry and Prose of William Blake*. Ed. David V. Erdman. Rev. ed. New York: Doubleday, 1982. 95–144.

Blatty, William Peter. *The Exorcist*. New York: Bantam, 1972.

Bleiler, E. F., ed. *Three Gothic Novels*. New York: Dover, 1966.

———, ed. *A Treasury of Victorian Ghost Stories*. New York: Scribner's, 1981.

Bloom, Harold. Introduction. Bloom, *Stephen King* 1–3.

———. *A Map of Misreading*. New York: Oxford UP, 1975.

———, ed. *Stephen King*. Modern Critical Views. Philadelphia: Chelsea, 1998.

Boaden, James. *Aurelio and Miranda*. Boaden, *Plays* 1–67.

————. *Memoirs of the Life of John Philip Kemble, Esq. Including a History of the Stage, from the Time of Garrick to the Present Period.* 1825. Vol. 2. New York: Blom, 1969.

————. *The Plays of James Boaden.* Ed. Steven Cohan. New York: Garland, 1980.

Booth, Wayne. "'He Began to Read to Our Hushed Little Circle': Are We Blessed or Cursed by Our Life with *The Turn of the Screw?*" *The Turn of the Screw.* By Henry James. Ed. Peter G. Beidler. Boston: Bedford–St. Martin's, 1995. 163–78.

Botting, Fred. *Gothic.* London: Routledge, 1996.

————, ed. *The Gothic.* Rochester: Boydell, 2001.

Bowen, Elizabeth. "The Big House." *Collected Impressions.* New York: Knopf, 1950. 195–200.

————. Introduction. *Uncle Silas.* By Sheridan Le Fanu. London: Cresset, 1947. 7–23.

Bowlby, Rachel. *Just Looking: Consumer Culture in Dreiser, Gissing, and Zola.* New York: Methuen, 1985.

Boyle, Thomas. *Black Swine in the Sewers of Hampstead: Beneath the Surface of Victorian Sensationalism.* New York: Viking-Penguin, 1989.

Bradbury, Ray. "Marionettes, Inc." *The Illustrated Man.* New York: Bantam, 1967. 156–62.

Braddon, Mary Elizabeth. *Lady Audley's Secret.* Ed. David Skilton. New York: Oxford UP, 1998.

Brantlinger, Patrick. *The Reading Lesson: The Threat of Mass Literacy in Nineteenth-Century British Fiction.* Bloomington: Indiana UP, 1998.

————. *Rule of Darkness: British Literature and Imperialism, 1830–1914.* Ithaca: Cornell UP, 1988.

Brel, Jacques. "La valse à mille temps." 1959. 5 Nov. 2002 <http://www.paroles.net/texte/23545>. "Carousel." *The Songs / Les Chansons.* Trans. Eric Blau and Mort Schuman. 14 Dec. 1998. 5 Nov. 2002 <http://college.holycross.edu/users/staff/bbatty/carousel.htm>.

Brewer, John. *Sinews of Power: War, Money, and the English State, 1688–1783.* London: Routledge, 1994.

Briggs, Julia. *Night Visitors: The Rise and Fall of the English Ghost Story.* London: Faber, 1977.

Brite, Poppy Z. *Exquisite Corpse.* New York: Simon, 1996.

Brogan, Kathleen. "American Stories of Cultural Haunting: Tales of Heirs and Ethnographers." *College English* 57.2 (1995): 149–65.

————. *Cultural Haunting: Ghosts and Ethnicity in Recent American Literature.* Charlottesville: UP of Virginia, 1998.

Bronfen, Elizabeth. *Over Her Dead Body: Death, Femininity, and the Aesthetic.* New York: Routledge, 1992.

Brontë, Charlotte. *Jane Eyre.* Ed. and introd. Q. D. Leavis. London: Penguin, 1986.

————. *Jane Eyre.* Ed. Jane Jack and Margaret Smith. Oxford: Clarendon, 1969.

Brontë, Emily. *Wuthering Heights.* Boston: Houghton, 1956.

————. *Wuthering Heights: Complete Text with Introduction, Contexts, Critical Essays.* New Riverside Eds. Ed. Diane Long Hoeveler. Boston: Houghton, 2002.

Brooks, Peter. *The Melodramatic Imagination: Balzac, Henry James, Melodrama, and the Mode of Excess.* New York: Columbia UP, 1985.

————. "Virtue and Terror: *The Monk*." *ELH* 40 (1973): 249–63.

Brown, Charles Brockden. *Wieland*. Garden City: Anchor, 1973.

Brown, Marshall. "From the Transcendental to the Supernatural: Kant and the Doctors." *Self-Conscious Art: A Tribute to John W. Kronik*. Ed. Susan L. Fischer. *Bucknell Review* 39 (1996): 151–69.

————. "A Philosophical View of the Gothic Novel." *Studies in Romanticism* 26.2 (1987): 275–301.

Browning, Elizabeth Barrett. *Complete Works of Elizabeth Barrett Browning*. Ed. Charlotte Porter and Helen A. Clarke. Vol. 3. New York: Crowell, 1900.

Bruhm, Steven. *Gothic Bodies: The Politics of Pain in Romantic Fiction*. Philadelphia: U of Pennsylvania P, 1994.

————. "Picture This: Stephen King's Queer Gothic." Punter, *Companion* 269–80.

————. "Stephen King's Phallus; or, The Postmodern Gothic." *Narrative* 4.1 (1996): 55–73. Rpt. in Martin and Savoy 75–96.

Burke, Edmund. *A Philosophical Enquiry into the Origin of Our Ideas of the Sublime and the Beautiful*. 1757. Ed. Adam Phillips. Oxford: Oxford UP, 1990.

————. *Reflections on the Revolution in France*. Harvard Classics, vol. 24, pt. 3. Bartleby.com. 17 Oct. 2002 <http://www.bartleby.com/24/3/>.

Butler, Marilyn. *Romantics, Rebels, and Reactionaries: English Literature and Its Background, 1760–1830*. Oxford: Oxford UP, 1981.

————. "The Woman at the Window: Ann Radcliffe in the Novels of Mary Wollstonecraft and Jane Austen." *Women and Literature* 1 (1980): 128–48. Rpt. in *Gender and Literary Voice*. Ed. Janet Todd. New York: Holmes, 1980. 128–48.

Butler, Samuel. *Erewhon*. Ed. Peter Mudford. Baltimore: Penguin, 1976.

Byrd, Max. "The Madhouse, the Whorehouse, and the Convent." *Partisan Review* 44 (1977): 268–78.

Byron, George. "Fragment." M. Shelley, *Frankenstein* [Penguin] 227–32.

Byron, Glennis, and David Punter, eds. *Spectral Readings: Towards a Gothic Geography*. New York: St. Martin's, 1999.

Cahalan, James A. *The Irish Novel: A Critical History*. Boston: Twayne, 1988.

Campbell, Jill. "'I Am No Giant': Horace Walpole, Heterosexual Incest, and Love among Men." *Eighteenth Century* 39.3 (1998): 238–60.

Cardinal, Roger. *German Romantics in Context*. London: Studio Vista, 1975.

Carens, Timothy. "Outlandish English Subjects in *The Moonstone*." Cox and Bachman.

Carlson, Julie A. *In the Theatre of Romanticism: Coleridge, Nationalism, Women*. Cambridge: Cambridge UP, 1994.

Carlyle, Thomas. *Sartor Resartus*. Project Gutenberg. Sept. 1997. 16 Oct. 2002 <http://www.digital.library.upenn.edu/webbin/gutbook/lookup?num=1051>.

Carpenter, Lynette, and Wendy Kolmar, eds. *Haunting the House of Fiction: Feminist Perspectives on Ghost Stories by American Women*. Knoxville: U of Tennessee P, 1994.

Carroll, Noel. *The Philosophy of Horror; or, Paradoxes of the Heart*. New York: Routledge, 1990.

Carter, Angela. Afterword. *Fireworks*. London: Quartet, 1974. Rpt. in Carter, *Burning* 459–60.

———. "The Bloody Chamber." *"The Bloody Chamber" and Other Stories*. 1979. Rpt. in Carter, *Burning* 111–43.

———. *Burning Your Boats: The Collected Short Stories*. New York: Penguin, 1997.

Carter, Margaret, ed. *Dracula: The Vampire and Its Critics*. Ann Arbor: UMI Research, 1988.

———. *Specter or Delusion? The Supernatural in Gothic Fiction*. Ann Arbor: UMI Research, 1987.

Case, Sue-Ellen. "Tracking the Vampire." *Differences* 3 (1991): 1–20.

Casebeer, Edwin F. "The Art of Balance: Stephen King's Canon." Bloom, *Stephen King* 207–18.

Castex, Pierre-Georges. *Le conte fantastique en France de Nodier à Maupassant*. Paris: Corti, 1968.

Castle, Terry. *The Female Thermometer: Eighteenth-Century Culture and the Invention of the Uncanny*. New York. Oxford UP, 1995.

———. "Phantasmagoria and the Metaphorics of Modern Reverie." Castle, *Female Thermometer* 140–67.

———. "The Spectralization of the Other in *The Mysteries of Udolpho*." *The New Eighteenth Century: Theory, Politics, English Literature*. Ed. Felicity Nussbaum and Laura Brown. New York: Methuen, 1987. 231–53.

Ceccio, Joseph F. "Anne Rice's *The Tale of the Body Thief* and the Astral Projection Literary Tradition." *The Gothic World of Anne Rice*. Ed. Gary Hoppenstand and Ray B. Browne. Bowling Green: Bowling Green State U Popular P, 1996. 163–71.

Chard, Chloe. Introduction. Radcliffe, *Romance of the Forest* vii–xxiv.

Cheyne, George. *The English Malady*. Delmar: Scholars' Facsim., 1976.

Child, Lincoln, ed. *Dark Company: The World's Greatest Ghost Stories*. New York: St. Martin's, 1984.

Children's Employment Commission. *First Report of the Commissioners on Mines*. 1842. Shannon: Irish UP, 1968. Vol. 6 of *British Parliamentary Papers: Industrial Revolution: Children's Employment*.

Chopin, Kate. *The Awakening*. New York: Dover, 1993.

———. "A Vocation and a Voice." *Complete Novels and Stories*. Ed. Sandra M. Gilbert. New York: Lib. of Amer., 2002. 839–68.

Cixous, Hélène, and Catherine Clément. *The Newly Born Woman*. Trans. Betsy Wing. Minneapolis: U of Minnesota P, 1986.

Clark, David Lee. *Charles Brockden Brown, Pioneer Voice of America*. Durham: Duke UP, 1952.

Clemens, Valdine. *The Return of the Repressed: Gothic Horror from* The Castle of Otranto *to* Alien. Albany: State U of New York P, 1999.

Clery, Emma J. *The Rise of Supernatural Fiction, 1762–1800*. Cambridge: Cambridge UP, 1995.

———. *Women's Gothic from Clara Reeve to Mary Shelley*. Plymouth, Eng.: Northcote, 2000.

Clery, E. J., and Robert Miles, eds. *Gothic Documents: A Sourcebook, 1700–1820*. Manchester: Manchester UP, 2000.

Clover, Carol J. *Men, Women, and Chain Saws: Gender in the Modern Horror Film.* London: BFI, 1993.

Cohan, Steven. Introduction. Boaden, *Plays* v–lxv.

Cohn, Jan. *Romance and the Erotics of Property: Mass-Market Fiction for Women.* Durham: Duke UP, 1988.

Coleridge, Samuel Taylor. *Biographia Literaria.* 2 vols. Ed. James Engell and W. Jackson Bate. Princeton: Princeton UP, 1983.

———. Rev. of *The Monk*, by Matthew Lewis. *Critical Review* Feb. 1797: 194–200. 7 Mar. 2003 <http://www.english.upenn.edu/~mgamer/Etexts/coleridge.reviews>.

Collins, Thomas J., and Vivienne J. Rundle, eds. *The Broadview Anthology of Victorian Poetry and Poetic Theory.* Peterborough, ON: Broadview, 1999.

Collins, Wilkie. *The Moonstone.* Ed. John Sutherland. Oxford: Oxford UP, 1999.

Colton, J. "Merlin's Cave and Queen Caroline: Garden Art as Political Propaganda." *Eighteenth-Century Studies* 10 (1976): 1–20.

Conger, Syndy McMillen. "Faith and Doubt in *The Castle of Otranto*." *Gothic: The Review of Supernatural Fiction* 1 (1979): 51–79.

Connell, R. W. *Masculinities.* Berkeley: U of California P, 1991.

Conolly, L. W. *The Censorship of English Drama, 1737–1824.* San Marino: Huntington Lib., 1976.

Conrad, Joseph. *Heart of Darkness.* Ed. Ross C. Murfin. Case Studies in Contemporary Criticism. New York: Bedford–St. Martin's, 1989.

———. *The Secret Sharer.* Ed. Daniel R. Schwarz. Case Studies in Contemporary Criticism. Boston: Bedford–St. Martin's, 1997.

Cornwell, Neil. "European Gothic." Punter, *Companion* 27–38.

———. "Gothic and Its Origins in East and West: Vladimir Odoevsky and Fitz-James O'Brian." Tinkler-Villani, Davidson, and Stevenson 117–28.

———. *The Gothic-Fantastic in Nineteenth-Century Russian Literature.* Amsterdam: Rodopi, 1999.

———. *The Literary Fantastic: From Gothic to Postmodernism.* New York: Harvester, 1990.

Cornwell, Patricia. *Point of Origin.* New York: Berkley, 1999.

Cottom, Daniel. *The Civilized Imagination: A Study of Ann Radcliffe, Jane Austen, and Sir Walter Scott.* Cambridge: Cambridge UP, 1985.

Cox, Don Richard, and Maria Bachman, eds. *Reality's Dark Light: The Sensational Wilkie Collins.* Knoxville: U of Tennessee P, forthcoming.

Cox, Jeffrey. "The French Revolution in the English Theatre." *History and Myth: Essays on English Romantic Literature.* Ed. Stephen C. Behrendt. Detroit: Wayne State UP, 1990. 33–52.

———. Introduction. J. Cox, *Seven* 1–77.

———, ed. *Seven Gothic Dramas, 1789–1825.* Athens: Ohio UP, 1992.

Cox, Michael, ed. *Twelve Tales of the Supernatural.* Oxford: Oxford UP, 1997.

———, ed. *Twelve Victorian Ghost Stories*. New York: Oxford UP, 1997.

Cox, Michael, and R. A. Gilbert, eds. *Victorian Ghost Stories: An Oxford Anthology*. Oxford: Oxford UP, 1992.

Craft, Christopher. "'Kiss Me with Those Red Lips': Gender and Inversion in Bram Stoker's *Dracula*." *Representations* 8 (1984): 107–33.

Crane, Jonathan Lake. *Terror and Everyday Life: Singular Moments in the History of the Horror Film*. Thousand Oaks: Sage, 1994.

Crane, Stephen. *"The Monster" and* The Third Violet. Ed. William Follett. *The Works of Stephen Crane*. Vol. 3. New York: Knopf, 1926. New York: Russell, 1963. 25–102.

Crawford, Mary. *Talking Difference: On Gender and Language*. London: Sage, 1995.

Creed, Barbara. *The Monstrous Feminine: Film, Feminism, Psychoanalysis*. London: Routledge, 1993.

Crosby, Christina. "Reading the Gothic Revival: 'History' and *Hints on Household Taste*." *Rewriting the Victorians: Theory, History and the Politics of Gender*. Ed. Linda M. Shires. New York: Routledge, 1992. 101–15.

Crow, Charles, ed. *American Gothic: An Anthology, 1787–1916*. Malden: Blackwell, 1999.

Csicsery-Ronay, Istvan. "Cyberpunk and Neuromanticism." *Mississippi Review* 16.2–3 (1987): 266–78.

Culler, Jonathan. "Reading as a Woman." *On Deconstruction: Theory and Criticism after Structuralism*. Ithaca: Cornell UP, 1982. 43–63.

Cvetcovich, Ann. *Mixed Feelings: Feminism, Mass Culture, and Victorian Sensationalism*. New Brunswick: Rutgers UP, 1992.

Dacre, Charlotte. *Zofloya; or, The Moor*. Ed. Adriana Craciun. Peterborough, ON: Broadview, 1997.

———. *Zofloya; or, The Moor*. Ed. Kim I. Michasiw. Oxford: Oxford UP, 1997.

Dalby, Richard, ed. *Victorian Ghost Stories by Eminent Women Writers*. New York: Carroll, 1989.

Dante. *The Inferno*. Trans. John Ciardi. New York: NAL, 1958.

David, Deirdre. *Rule Britannia: Women, Empire, and Victorian Writing*. Ithaca: Cornell UP, 1995.

Davidoff, Leonore, and Catherine Hall. *Family Fortunes: Men and Women of the English Middle Class, 1780–1850*. London: Hutchinson, 1987.

Day, Aidan. *Romanticism*. New York: Routledge, 1996.

Day, William Patrick. *In the Circles of Fear and Desire: A Study of Gothic Fantasy*. Chicago: U of Chicago P, 1985.

Dayan, Joan. "Amorous Bondage: Poe, Ladies, and Slaves." *American Literature* 66 (1994): 239–73.

DeLamotte, Eugenia C. "Male and Female Mysteries in *The Yellow Wallpaper*." *Legacy* 5 (1988): 3–14.

———. *Perils of the Night: A Feminist Study of Nineteenth-Century Gothic*. New York: Oxford UP, 1990.

De Quincey, Thomas. "On the Knocking at the Gate in *Macbeth*." *The Works of Thomas De Quincey*. Vol. 3. Ed. Frederick Burwick. London: Pickering, 2000. 150–54.

Derrida, Jacques. *Of Spirit: Heidegger and the Question*. Trans. Geoffrey Bennington and Rachel Bowlby. Chicago: U of Chicago P, 1989.

——. *Specters of Marx: The State of the Debt, the Work of Mourning, and the New International*. Trans. Peggy Kamuf. New York: Routledge, 1994.

D'Haen, Theo. "Postmodern Gothic." Tinkler-Villani, Davidson, and Stevenson 283–94.

Dick, Philip K. *Do Androids Dream of Electric Sheep?* New York: Doubleday, 1968.

Dickens, Charles. *Bleak House*. Ed. George Ford and Sylvere Monod. New York: Norton, 1977.

——. *A Christmas Carol*. An Online Lib. of Lit. Knowledge Matters. 8 Jan. 2002. 5 June 2003 <http://www.literature.org/authors/dickens-charles/christmas-carol/>.

——. "The Ghost of Art." *Reprinted Pieces*. Introd. Michael Foss. Geneva: Heron, 1969. 85–93.

Dickens, Charles, and Wilkie Collins. *The Perils of Certain English Prisoners*. *"The Lazy Tour of Two Idle Apprentices" and Other Stories*. London: Chapman, 1890. 237–327.

Dickerson, Vanessa R. *Victorian Ghosts in the Noontide: Women Writers and the Supernatural*. Columbia: U of Missouri P, 1996.

Dika, Vera. *Games of Terror: Halloween, Friday the Thirteenth, and the Films of the Stalker Cycle*. Rutherford: Fairleigh Dickinson UP, 1990.

Dixon, Wheeler Winston. "Gender Approaches to Directing the Horror Film: Women Filmmakers and the Mechanisms of the Gothic." *Popular Culture Review* 7.1 (1996): 121–34.

Docherty, Brian, ed. *American Horror Fiction: From Brockden Brown to Stephen King*. New York: St. Martin's, 1990.

Dock, Julie Bates, ed. *Charlotte Perkins Gilman's "The Yellow Wall-paper" and the History of Its Publication and Reception.* University Park: Penn State UP, 1998.

Donohue, Joseph. *Theatre in the Age of Kean*. Oxford: Blackwell, 1975.

Donovan, Josephine. *New England Local Color Literature: A Women's Tradition*. New York: Ungar, 1983.

Doody, Margaret Anne. "Deserts, Ruins, and Troubled Waters: Female Dreams in Fiction and the Development of the Gothic Novel." *Genre* 10 (1977): 529–72.

Douglass, Frederick. *Narrative of the Life of Frederick Douglass, an American Slave*. Ed. Houston Baker. New York: Penguin, 1982.

Doyle, Arthur Conan. *Complete Novels and Stories*. Vol. 1. Introd. Loren D. Estleman. New York: Bantam, 1986.

——. "The Man with the Twisted Lip." Doyle, *Complete Novels* 306–27.

——. *The Sign of Four*. Doyle, *Complete Novels* 105–205.

Duncan, Ian. *Modern Romance and Transformations of the Novel: The Gothic, Scott, Dickens*. Cambridge: Cambridge UP, 1992.

——. "Walter Scott, James Hogg, and Scottish Gothic." Punter, *Companion* 70–80.

Durant, David. "Ann Radcliffe and the Conservative Gothic." *Studies in English Literature* 22 (1982): 519–30.

Eagleton, Terry. *Heathcliff and the Great Hunger: Studies in Irish Culture*. London: Verso, 1996.

Easton, Allison. Introduction. Jewett, Country vii–xxii.

Edgeworth, Maria. *Castle Rackrent*. Ed. George Watson. Introd. Kathryn J. Kirk-patrick. New York: Oxford UP, 1995.

Edmundson, Mark. *Nightmare on Main Street: Angels, Sadomasochism, and the Culture of Gothic*. Cambridge: Harvard UP, 1997.

Edwards, Anne. *Haunted Summer*. New York: Putnam, 1972.

Egan, James. "Technohorror: The Dystopian Vision of Stephen King." Bloom, *Stephen King* 47–58.

Elias, Norbert. *The Civilizing Process*. Trans. Edmund Jephcott. New York: Pantheon, 1978. Vol. 1 of *The History of Manners*.

Eliot, George. *Middlemarch*. Ed. David Carroll. New York: Oxford UP, 1988.

Ellis, Kate Ferguson. *The Contested Castle: Gothic Novels and the Subversion of Domestic Ideology*. Urbana: U of Illinois P, 1989.

Ellis, Markman. *The History of Gothic Fiction*. Edinburgh: Edinburgh UP, 2001.

Ellison, Harlan. "Bleeding Stones." *The Deathbird Stories*. New York: Harper, 1975. 180–85.

Engels, Friedrich. *The Condition of the Working Class in England*. Trans. and ed. W. O. Henderson and W. H. Chaloner. Stanford: Stanford UP, 1958.

Epstein, Lynne. "Mrs. Radcliffe's Landscapes: The Influence of Three Landscape Painters on Her Nature Descriptions." *University of Hartford Studies in Literature* 1 (1969): 107–20.

Evans, Bertrand. *Gothic Drama from Walpole to Shelley*. U of California Pubs. in English 18. Berkeley: U of California P, 1947.

Evans, David Morier. *Speculative Notes and Notes on Speculation*. New York: Franklin, 1968.

Everson, William K. *Classics of the Horror Film*. Secaucus: Citadel, 1990.

Fairclough, Peter, ed. *Three Gothic Novels*. New York: Penguin, 1986.

Faulkner, William. Absalom! Absalom! *The Corrected Text*. Ed. Noel Polk et al. New York: Vintage, 1986.

——. *Light in August*. Introd. Cleanth Brooks. New York: Modern Lib., 1968.

——. "Pantaloon in Black." *Go Down, Moses*. New York: Vintage, 1973. 135–59.

Fawcett, Mary Laughlin. "*Udolpho*'s Primal Mystery." *Studies in English Literature* 23 (1983): 481–94.

Fedorko, Kathy. *Gender and the Gothic in the Fiction of Edith Wharton*. Tuscaloosa: U of Alabama P, 1995.

Female Gothic Writing. Spec. issue of *Women's Writing* 1.2 (1994): 131–253.

Ferguson, Frances. *Solitude and the Sublime: Romanticism and the Aesthetics of Individualism*. New York: Routledge, 1992.

Ferraro, Susan. "Novels You Can Sink Your Teeth Into." *New York Times Book Review* 14 Oct. 1990: 27+.

Fichte, Johann Gottlieb. *The Vocation of Man*. Trans. Peter Preuss. Indianapolis: Hackett, 1987.

Fiedler, Leslie. *Love and Death in the American Novel*. Cleveland: World, 1962.

Field, Michael. "La Gioconda: Leonardo Da Vinci." Collins and Rundle 1077.

Fierobe, Claude. *Charles Robert Maturin: L'homme et l'œuvre.* Lille: PU de Lille, 1974.

Figes, Eva. *Sex and Subterfuge: Women Writers to 1850.* London: Pandora, 1990.

Fisch, Audrey. "Wilkie Collins, Race, and Slavery." Cox and Bachman.

Fischer, Dennis. *Horror Film Directors, 1931–1990.* Jefferson: McFarland, 1991.

Fisher, Benjamin F. *The Gothic's Gothic: Study Aids to the Tradition of the Tale of Terror.* New York: Garland, 1988.

Flaxman, Rhoda L. "Radcliffe's Dual Modes of Vision." *Fetter'd or Free? British Women Novelists, 1670–1815.* Ed. Mary Anne Schofield and Cecilia Macheski. Athens: Ohio UP, 1986. 124–33.

Fleenor, Juliann E., ed. *The Female Gothic.* Montreal: Eden, 1983.

Flint, Kate. "Romance, Post-modernism, and the Gothic: Fictional Challenges to Theories of Women and Reading, 1790–1830." *Literatur und erfahrungswandel, 1789–1830.* Ed. Rainer Schöwerling, Hartmut Steinecke, and Günter Tiggesbäumker. Munich: Fink, 1996. 269–79.

Folsom, James K. "Beckford's *Vathek* and the Tradition of Oriental Satire." *Criticism* 6 (1964): 53–69.

Forry, Steven Earl. *Hideous Progenies: Dramatizations of* Frankenstein *from Mary Shelley to the Present.* Philadelphia: U of Pennsylvania P, 1990.

Forster, E. M. *Aspects of the Novel.* 1927. London: Arnold, 1974.

Fothergill, Brian. *Beckford of Fonthill.* London: Faber, 1979.

———. *The Strawberry Hill Set: Horace Walpole and His Circle.* London: Faber, 1983.

Foucault, Michel. *Discipline and Punish: The Birth of the Prison.* Trans. Alan Sheridan. New York: Vintage, 1979.

———. *Histoire de la folie à l'âge classique.* Paris: Gallimard, 1972.

———. *The History of Sexuality.* Trans. Robert Hurley. 3 vols. New York: Pantheon, 1978–87.

———. *An Introduction.* Trans. Robert Hurley. New York: Vintage, 1980. Vol. 1 of *The History of Sexuality.*

———. *Madness and Civilization: A History of Insanity in the Age of Reason.* Trans. Richard Howard. New York: Vintage, 1988.

———. *Power/Knowledge: Selected Interviews and Other Writings, 1972–1977.* New York: Pantheon, 1980.

———. "What Is an Author?" *Language, Counter-memory, Practice: Selected Essays and Interviews.* Ed. Donald F. Bouchard. Trans. Bouchard and Sherry Simon. Ithaca: Cornell UP, 1977. 113–38.

Four Gothic Novels. Oxford: Oxford UP, 1994.

Fowler, Kathleen. "Hieroglyphics in Fire: *Melmoth the Wanderer.*" *Studies in Romanticism* 25 (1986): 521–39.

Franceschina, John, ed. *Sisters of Gore: Seven Gothic Melodramas by British Women, 1790–1843.* New York: Routledge, 2000.

Frank, Frederick. *The First Gothics: A Critical Guide to the English Gothic Novel.* New York: Garland, 1987.

————, ed. *Gothic Fiction: A Master List of Twentieth-Century Criticism and Research.* Westport: Meckler, 1988.

————, ed. *The Guide to the Gothic II: An Annotated Bibliography of Criticism, 1983–1993.* Lanham: Scarecrow, 1995.

————. "Illustrations from Early Gothic Novels." Graham, *Gothic Fictions* 270–87.

————, ed. *Matthew Lewis's* The Monk. Spec. issue of *Romanticism on the Net* 8 (Nov. 1997). 25 Mar. 2003 <http://www-sul.stanford.edu/mirrors/romnet/guest2.html>.

————. "*The Monk*: A Bicentenary Bibliography." Frank, *Matthew Lewis's* The Monk. 25 Mar. 2003 <http://www-sul.stanford.edu/mirrors/romnet/monkbiblio.html>.

————. *Through the Pale Door: A Guide to and through the American Gothic.* New York: Greenwood, 1990.

Frankl, Paul. *The Gothic: Literary Sources and Interpretations through Eight Centuries.* Princeton: Princeton UP, 1960.

Franklin, Benjamin. *The Autobiography.* Ed. J. A. Leo Lemay and P. M. Zall. New York: Norton, 1986.

Frayling, Christopher, ed. *Vampyres: Lord Byron to Count Dracula.* London: Faber, 1991.

Freeman, Barbara Claire. *The Feminine Sublime: Gender and Excess in Women's Fiction.* Berkeley: U of California P, 1995.

Freeman, Mary Wilkins. *"The Wind in the Rose-Bush" and Other Stories of the Supernatural.* Chicago: Acad. Chicago, 1986.

Freud, Sigmund. *Beyond the Pleasure Principle.* Freud, *Standard Edition* 18: 1–64.

————. "A Child Is Being Beaten." Freud, *Standard Edition* 17: 175–204.

————. *The Interpretation of Dreams.* 1900. Freud, *Standard Edition* 5: 1–338.

————. *The Standard Edition of the Complete Psychological Works of Sigmund Freud.* 24 vols. Trans. James Strachey et al. Ed. Strachey. London: Hogarth; Inst. of Psychoanalysis, 1986.

————. "The Uncanny." Freud, *Standard Edition* 17: 217–52.

Frye, Northrop, Sheridan Baker, George Perkins, and Barbara M. Perkins. *The Harper Handbook to Literature.* 2nd ed. New York: Longman, 1997.

Fulford, Tim. *Romanticism and Masculinity.* New York: St. Martin's, 1999.

Fusco, Richard. *Maupassant and the American Short Story: The Influence of Form at the Turn of the Century.* University Park: Penn State UP, 1994.

Fuseli, Henry. *The Nightmare.* Detroit Inst. of Arts. Photograph 1 of *Henry Fuseli.* By Martin Myrone. Princeton: Princeton UP, 2001.

Gamer, Michael. "Authors in Effect: Lewis, Scott, and the Gothic Drama." *ELH* 66 (1999): 831–61.

————. "Genres for the Prosecution: Pornography and the Gothic." *PMLA* 114 (1999): 1043–54.

————. "National Supernaturalism: Joanna Baillie, Germany, and the Gothic Drama." *Theatre Survey* 38 (1997): 49–88.

————. *Romanticism and the Gothic: Genre, Reception, and Canon Formation.* Cambridge: Cambridge UP, 2000.

Garnett, Rhys. "*Dracula* and *The Beetle*: Imperial and Sexual Guilt and Fear in Late Victorian Fantasy." *Science Fiction Roots and Branches: Contemporary Critical Approaches*. Ed. Garnett and R. J. Ellis. Basingstoke, Eng.: Macmillan, 1990. 30–54.

Gates, Henry Louis, Jr., and Nellie Y. McKay, eds. *The Norton Anthology of African-American Literature*. New York: Norton, 1997.

Gaull, Marilyn. *English Romanticism: The Human Context*. New York: Norton, 1988.

Gelder, Ken. *Reading the Vampire*. London: Routledge, 1994.

Genet, Jacqueline, ed. *The Big House in Ireland*. Savage: Barnes, 1991.

Gibson, William. *Neuromancer*. New York: Ace, 1984.

Gilbert, Pamela K. *Disease, Desire, and the Body in Victorian Women's Popular Novels*. Cambridge: Cambridge UP, 1997.

Gilbert, Sandra M., and Susan Gubar. *The Madwoman in the Attic: The Woman Writer and the Nineteenth-Century Literary Imagination*. New Haven: Yale UP, 1979.

——, eds. *The Norton Anthology of Literature by Women: The Traditions in English*. 2nd ed. New York: Norton, 1996.

——. *Sexchanges*. New Haven: Yale UP, 1989. Vol. 2 of *No Man's Land: The Place of the Woman Writer in the Twentieth Century*.

Gilman, Charlotte Perkins. *The Yellow Wall-Paper*. Rev. ed. New York: Feminist, 1996.

Gilman, Sander L. "The Hottentot and the Prostitute: Toward an Iconography of Female Sexuality." *Difference and Pathology: Stereotypes of Sexuality, Race, and Madness*. Ithaca: Cornell UP, 1985. 76–108.

——. *The Jew's Body*. New York: Routledge, 1991.

Ginsberg, Lesley. "Slavery and the Gothic Horror of Poe's 'The Black Cat.'" Martin and Savoy 99–128.

Glover, David. "Bram Stoker and the Crisis of the Liberal Subject." *New Literary History* 23 (1992): 983–1002.

Goddu, Teresa. *Gothic America: Narrative, History, and Nation*. New York: Columbia UP, 1999.

Godwin, William. *Caleb Williams*. 1794. Ed. David McCracken. Oxford: Oxford UP, 1988.

Goethe, Johann Wolfgang von. *Faust: Gesamtausgabe*. Leipzig: Insel, 1975.

Gold, Alex, Jr. "It's Only Love: The Politics of Passion in Godwin's *Caleb Williams*." *Texas Studies in Literature and Language* 19.2 (1977): 135–60.

Gonda, Caroline. *Reading Daughters' Fictions, 1709–1834*. Cambridge: Cambridge UP, 1996.

Gordon, Jan B. "Narrative Enclosure as Textual Ruin: An Archaeology of Gothic Consciousness." *Dickens Studies Annual* 11 (1983): 209–38.

Gordon, Joan, and Veronica Hollinger, eds. *Blood Read: The Vampire as Metaphor in Contemporary Culture*. Philadelphia: U of Pennsylvania P, 1997.

Gorp, Hendrik van. "The Sublime and the Gothic." *Sense and Transcendence: Essays in Honor of Herman Servotte*. Ed. Ortwin de Graef et al. Leuven, Belg.: Leuven UP, 1995. 175–85.

"Gothic." "Gothicism." "Gothicize." *The Oxford English Dictionary*. 2nd ed. 1989.

Gould, Stephen Jay. "Bound by the Great Chain." *The Flamingo's Smile: Reflections in Natural History*. New York: Norton, 1987. 281–90.

——. *The Mismeasure of Man*. New York: Norton, 1981.

Graddol, David, and Joan Swann. *Gender Voices*. Cambridge: Blackwell, 1989.

Graham, Kenneth W. "Beckford's *Vathek*: A Study in Ironic Dissonance." *Criticism* 14 (1972): 243–52.

——, ed. *Gothic Fictions: Prohibition/Transgression*. New York: AMS, 1989.

——, ed. Vathek *and the Escape from Time: Bicentenary Revaluations*. New York: AMS, 1990.

Grant, Barry Keith, ed. *The Dread of Difference: Gender and the Horror Film*. Austin: U of Texas P, 1996.

Grixti, Joseph. *Terrors of Uncertainty: The Cultural Contexts of Horror Fiction*. New York: Routledge, 1989.

Gross, Lewis S. *Redefining the American Gothic: From* Wieland *to* Day of the Dead. Ann Arbor: UMI Research, 1989.

Grosz, Elizabeth. *Jacques Lacan: A Feminist Introduction*. London: Routledge, 1990.

Grudin, Peter. "*The Monk*: Mathilda and the Rhetoric of Deceit." *Journal of Narrative Technique* 5.2 (1975): 136–46.

Guest, Harriet. "The Wanton Muse: Politics and Gender in Gothic Theory after 1790." *Beyond Romanticism: New Approaches to Texts and Contexts, 1780–1832*. Ed. Stephen Copley and John Whale. Syracuse: Syracuse UP, 1991. 118–39.

Haggard, H. Rider. *She*. Ed. Daniel Karlin. Oxford: Oxford UP, 1991.

Haggerty, George. *Gothic Fiction / Gothic Form*. University Park: Penn State UP, 1989.

——. "Literature and Homosexuality in the Late Eighteenth Century: Walpole, Beckford, Lewis." *Studies in the* Novel 18 (1986): 341–52. Rpt. in *Homosexual Themes in Literary Studies*. Ed. Wayne R. Dynes and Stephen Donaldson. New York: Garland, 1992. 167–78.

——. *Unnatural Affections: Women and Fiction in the Later Eighteenth Century*. Bloomington: Indiana UP, 1998.

Haining, Peter, ed. *The Gentlewomen of Evil: An Anthology of Rare Supernatural Stories from the Pens of Victorian Ladies*. London: Hale, 1967.

Halberstam, Judith. *Skin Shows: Gothic Horror and the Technology of Monsters*. Durham: Duke UP, 1995.

Hallam, Clifford. "The Double as Incomplete Self: Toward a Definition of Doppelgänger." *Fearful Symmetry: Doubles and Doubling in Literature and Film: Papers from the Fifth Annual Florida State University Conference on Literature and Film*. Ed. Eugene Joseph Crook. Tallahassee: UP of Florida, 1982. 1–31.

Halttunen, Karen. *Murder Most Foul: The Killer and the American Gothic*. Cambridge: Harvard UP, 1998.

Hanke, Ken. *A Critical Guide to Horror Film Series*. New York: Garland, 1991.

Harfst, Betsy. *Horace Walpole and the Unconscious: An Experiment in Freudian Analysis*. New York: Arno, 1980.

Harris, Thomas. *Hannibal*. New York: St. Martin's, 1999.

——. *The Silence of the Lambs*. New York: St. Martin's, 1989.

Hawthorne, Nathaniel. "The Custom-House." *The Scarlet Letter*. Bartleby.com. Great Books Online. 6 Nov. 2002 <http://www.bartleby.com/83/101.html>.

——. *The House of the Seven Gables*. Introd. Richard Horter Fogle. London: Macmillan, 1962.

——. *The Marble Faun; or, The Romance of the Monte Beni*. New York: Penguin, 1990.

——. *Rappaccini's Daughter*. *Bartleby.com* 4 June 2003 <http://www.bartleby.com/310/1/3000.html>.

Hazlitt, William. *Lectures on the Comic Writers*. London: Oxford UP, 1907.

Heiland, Donna. *Gothic Novels: A Feminist Introduction*. Oxford: Blackwell, forthcoming.

Heilman, Robert B. "Charlotte Brontë's 'New' Gothic." *From Jane Austen to Joseph Conrad*. Ed. Robert C. Rathburn and Martin Steinmann, Jr. Minneapolis: U of Minnesota P, 1958. 118–32.

Heller, Janet Ruth. *Coleridge, Lamb, Hazlitt, and the Reader of Drama*. Columbia: U of Missouri P, 1990.

Heller, Lee. "*Frankenstein* and the Cultural Uses of Gothic." M. Shelley, *Frankenstein* [Smith] 325–41.

Heller, Tamar. *Dead Secrets: Wilkie Collins and the Female Gothic*. New Haven: Yale UP, 1992.

——. "The Vampire in the House: Hysteria, Female Sexuality, and Female Knowledge in J. S. Le Fanu's 'Carmilla.'" *The New Nineteenth Century: Feminist Readings of Underread Victorian Fiction*. Ed. Barbara Harman and Susan Meyer. New York: Garland, 1996. 77–95.

Heller, Terry. *The Delights of Terror: An Aesthetics of the Tale of Terror*. Urbana: U of Illinois P, 1987.

Helsinger, Elizabeth K., Robin Lauterbach Sheets, and William Veeder, eds. *The Woman Question: Society and Literature in Britain and America, 1837–1883*. 3 vols. New York: Garland, 1983. Chicago: U of Chicago P, 1989.

Hendershot, Cyndy. *The Animal Within: Masculinity and the Gothic*. Ann Arbor: U of Michigan P, 1998.

Henderson, Andrea. "'An Embarrassing Subject': Use Value and Exchange Value in Early Gothic Characterization." *At the Limits of Romanticism: Essays in Cultural, Feminist, and Materialist Criticism*. Ed. Mary A. Favret and Nicola J. Watson. Bloomington: Indiana UP, 1994. 225–45.

Hennelly, Mark M., Jr. "Framing the Gothic: From Pillar to Post-structuralism." *College Literature* 28 (2001): 68–87.

——. "*Melmoth the Wanderer* and Gothic Existentialism." *Studies in English Literature* 21 (1981): 665–79.

Hennessy, Brendan. *The Gothic Novel*. Harlow, Eng.: Longman for the British Council, 1978.

Herder, Johann Gottfried. *Briefe*. Ed. Wilhelm Dobbek. Weimar: Volksverlag Weimar, 1959.

Hilton, Boyd. *The Age of Atonement: The Influence of Evangelicalism on Social and Economic Thought, 1785–1865*. Oxford: Clarendon, 1991.

Hipple, Walter J. *The Beautiful, the Sublime, and the Picturesque in Eighteenth-Century British Aesthetic Theory*. Carbondale: Southern Illinois UP, 1957.

Hirsch, Gordon. "*Frankenstein*, Detective Fiction, and *Jekyll and Hyde*." Veeder and Hirsch 223–46.

Hoeveler, Diane Long. "Charlotte Dacre's *Zofloya*: A Case Study in Miscegenation as Sexual and Racial Nausea." *European Romantic Review* 6 (1997): 184–98.

———. "Gendering the Scottish Ballad: The Case of Anne Bannerman's *Tales of Superstition and Chivalry*." *Wordsworth Circle* 31 (2000): 97–102.

———. "Gothic Drama as Nationalistic Catharsis." *Wordsworth Circle* 31 (2000): 169–72.

———. *Gothic Feminism: The Professionalization of Gender from Charlotte Smith to the Brontës*. University Park: Penn State UP, 1998.

———. "Postgothic Fiction: Joyce Carol Oates Turns the Screw on Henry James." *Studies in Short Fiction* 35 (1998): 355–71.

———. "Reading the Wound: Wollstonecraft's *The Wrongs of Woman; or, Maria* and Trauma Theory." *Studies in the Novel* 31 (1999). 387–408.

———. "The Tyranny of Sentimental Form: Wollstonecraft's *Mary* and the Gendering of Anxiety." *Eighteenth-Century Novel* 3 (2003): 218–41.

———, ed. *Emily Brontë's* Wuthering Heights. Boston: Houghton, 2001.

Hoeveler, Diane Long, and Beth Lau, eds. *Approaches to Teaching Brontë's* Jane Eyre. New York: MLA, 1993.

Hoffmann, E. T. A. *The Devil's Elixirs*. Trans. Ronald Taylor. London: Calder, 1963.

———. *Die Elixiere des Teufels [and] Lebens-Ansichten des Katers Murr*. Ed. Walter Müller-Seidel. Darmstadt: Wissenschaftliche Buchgesellschaft, 1970.

Hogg, James. *The Private Memoirs and Confessions of a Justified Sinner*. London: Oxford UP, 1969.

Hogle, Jerrold E. "The Gothic and the 'Otherings' of Ascendant Culture: The Original *Phantom of the Opera*." Byron and Punter 177–201.

———. "The Gothic Ghost of the Counterfeit and the Progress of Abjection." Punter, *Companion* 293–304.

———. "Introduction: Gothic Studies Past, Present and Future." *Gothic Studies* 1 (1999): 1–9.

———. "The Restless Labyrinth: Cryptonymy in the Gothic Novel." *Arizona Quarterly* 36 (1980): 330–58.

Holland, Norman, and Leona F. Sherman. "Gothic Possibilities." *New Literary History* 8 (1977): 278–94. Rpt. in *Gender and Reading*. Ed. Elizabeth A. Flynn and Patrocinio P. Schweickart. Baltimore: Johns Hopkins UP, 1986. 215–33.

Homans, Margaret. *Bearing the Word: Language and Female Experience in Nineteenth-Century Women's Writing*. Chicago: U of Chicago P, 1986.

———. "The Women in the Cave: Recent Feminist Fictions and the Classical Underworld." *Contemporary Literature* 29 (1988): 369–402.

Homer. *Iliad*. Trans. Richard Lattimore. Chicago: U of Chicago P, 1966.

Hood, Thomas. "The Song of the Shirt." *Selected Poems of Thomas Hood*. Ed. John Clubbe. Cambridge: Harvard UP, 1970. 304–07.

hooks, bell. "Thinking past Censorship: Having the Courage to Criticize Our Allies." *On the Issues* 25 (1992): 4, 58.

Hopkins, Pauline. *Contending Forces: A Romance Illustrative of Life North and South.* Introd. Richard Yarborough. New York: Oxford UP, 1988.

Horne, R. H. "Children's Employment Commission Report." 1843. *British Parliamentary Papers: Industrial Revolution: Children's Employment.* Vol. 11. Shannon: Irish UP, 1968. Q1–Q95.

———. "Evidence." 1843. *British Parliamentary Papers: Industrial Revolution: Children's Employment.* Vol. 11. Shannon: Irish UP, 1968. q1–q84.

Horner, Avril, and Sue Zlosnik. *Daphne du Maurier: Writing, Identity, and the Gothic Imagination.* New York: St. Martin's, 1998.

Howard, Jacqueline. *Reading Gothic Fiction: A Bakhtinian Approach.* Oxford: Clarendon, 1994.

Howells, Coral Ann. *Love, Mystery, and Misery: Feeling in Gothic Fiction.* London: Athlone, 1978.

Howes, Marjorie. "Misalliance and Anglo-Irish Tradition in Le Fanu's *Uncle Silas.*" *Nineteenth-Century Literature* 47 (1992): 164–86.

Hughes, Glyn Tegai. *Romantic German Literature.* New York: Holmes, 1979.

Hughes, Winifred. *The Maniac in the Cellar: Sensation Novels of the 1860s.* Princeton: Princeton UP, 1980.

Hume, Robert D. "Gothic versus Romantic: A Revaluation of the Gothic Novel." *PMLA* 84 (1969): 282–90.

Hume, Robert D., and Robert L. Platzner. "'Gothic versus Romantic': A Rejoinder." *PMLA* 86 (1971): 266–74.

Hunt, John Dixon. *Gardens and the Picturesque: Studies in the History of Landscape Architecture.* Cambridge: MIT P, 1994.

Hurd, Richard. *Letters on Chivalry and Romance.* Ed. Edith Morely. London: Frowde, 1911.

Hurley, Kelly. *The Gothic Body: Sexuality, Materialism, and Degeneration at the Fin de Siècle.* Cambridge: Cambridge UP, 1996.

Hussey, Christopher. *The Picturesque: Studies in a Point of View.* London: Putnam's, 1927.

Idman, Niilo. *Charles Robert Maturin: His Life and Works.* London: Constable, 1923.

Ingebretsen, Edward J. *Maps of Heaven, Maps of Hell: Religious Terror as Memory from the Puritans to Stephen King.* Armonk: Sharpe, 1996.

Ireland, S. *An Investigation of Malone's Claim to the Character of Scholar, or Critic, Being an Examination of His Inquiry into the Authenticity of the Shakespeare Manuscripts, et Cetera.* London, 1798.

Jackson, Rosemary. *Fantasy: The Literature of Subversion.* London: Methuen, 1981.

———. "Narcissism and Beyond: A Psychoanalytic Reading of *Frankenstein* and Fantasies of the Double." *Aspects of Fantasy: Selected Essays from the International Conference on the Fantastic in Literature and Film.* Ed. William Coyle. Westport: Greenwood, 1986. 43–53.

Jackson, Shirley. *The Haunting of Hill House.* New York: Penguin, 1984.

——. *We Have Always Lived in the Castle*. New York: Popular Lib., 1962.

Jacobs, Edward. *Accidental Migrations: An Archaeology of Gothic Discourse*. Lewisburg: Bucknell UP, 2000.

——. "Anonymous Signatures: Circulating Libraries, Conventionality, and the Production of Gothic Romances." *ELH* 62 (1995): 603–29.

Jacobs, Harriet. *Incidents in the Life of a Slave Girl*. Ed. Nellie Y. McKay and Frances Smith Foster. Norton Critical Ed. New York: Norton, 2001.

James, Henry. *Complete Stories*. 5 vols. New York: Lib. of Amer., 1996.

——. *The Turn of the Screw*. Ed. Peter G. Beidler. Case Studies in Contemporary Criticism 1. New York: St. Martin's, 1994.

James, Sibyl. "Gothic Transformations: Isak Dinesen and the Gothic." Fleenor 139–52.

Jann, Rosemary. "Saved by Science? The Mixed Messages of Stoker's *Dracula*." *Texas Studies in Literature and Language* 31.2 (1989): 273–86.

Janowitz, Anne. *England's Ruins: Poetic Purpose and the National Landscape*. Oxford: Blackwell, 1990.

Jarrett, David. *The Gothic Form in Fiction and Its Relation to History*. Winchester, Eng.: King Alfred's Coll., 1980.

Jewett, Sarah Orne. The Country of the Pointed Firs *and Other Stories*. London: Penguin, 1995.

——. "The Foreigner." Jewett, Country 225–46.

Johnson, Anthony. "Gaps and Gothic Sensibility: Walpole, Lewis, Mary Shelley, and Maturin." Tinkler-Villani, Davidson, and Stevenson 7–24.

Johnson, Claudia. *Equivocal Beings: Politics, Gender, and Sentimentality in the 1790s: Wollstonecraft, Radcliffe, Burney, Austen*. Chicago: U of Chicago P, 1995.

Jones, Chris. *Radical Sensibility: Literature and Ideas in the 1790s*. London: Routledge, 1993.

Jones, Ernest. *The Life and Work of Sigmund Freud*. Vol. 2. New York: Basic, 1955.

——. *On the Nightmare*. 1931. New York: Liveright, 1951.

Jones, Wendy. "Stories of Desire in *The Monk*." *ELH* 57 (1990): 129–50.

Joyce, James. "The Dead." *Dubliners*. New York: Penguin, 1976. 175–223.

——. *Ulysses*. Ed. Morris L. Ernst. New York: Modern Lib., 1961.

Jung, Carl Gustav. "Aion: Contributions to the Symbolism of Self." *Psyche and Symbol: A Selection from the Writings of C. G. Jung*. Ed. Violet de Lazlo. New York: Anchor, 1958. 1–22.

——. *The Archetypes and the Collective Unconscious*. Trans. R. F. C. Hull. Princeton: Princeton UP, 1971.

Kahane, Claire. "The Gothic Mirror." *The (M)Other Tongue: Essays in Feminist Psychoanalytical Interpretation*. Ed. Shirley Nelson Garner, Kahane, and Madelon Sprengnether. Ithaca: Cornell UP, 1985. 334–52.

Kalikoff, Beth. *Murder and Moral Decay in Victorian Popular Literature*. Ann Arbor: UMI Research, 1986.

Kant, Immanuel. *Critique of Pure Reason*. Trans. F. Max Müller. Garden City: Doubleday, 1966.

——. *Prolegomena zu einer jeden künftigen Metaphysik*. Dept. of Philosophy. Peking U. 16 Oct. 2002 <http://www.phil.pku.edu.cn/resguide/kant/proleg/_index.htm>.

——. "What Is Orientation in Thinking?" *Critique of Practical Reason and Other Writings in Moral Philosophy*. Trans. Lewis White Beck. Chicago: U of Chicago P, 1949. 293–305.

Kaufman, Pamela. "Burke, Freud, and the Gothic." *Studies in Burke and His Time* 13 (1972): 2178–92.

Kayman, Martin A. *From Bow Street to Baker Street: Mystery, Detection, and Narrative*. New York: St. Martin's, 1992.

Keats, John. "La Belle Dame sans Merci." *Selected Poetry of John Keats (1795–1821)*. U of Toronto English Lib. Ed. J. R. MacGillivray and Ian Lancashire. 1994–98. 18 Oct. 2002 <http://www.library.utoronto.ca/utel/rp/poems/keats15.html>.

Kelly, Gary. *English Fiction of the Romantic Period, 1789–1830*. London: Longman, 1989.

——, gen. ed. *Varieties of Female Gothic*. 6 vols. London: Chatto, 2001.

——. *Women, Writing, and Revolution, 1790–1827*. Oxford: Clarendon, 1993.

Kelly, James Patrick. "Solstice." Sterling 66–104.

Kelly, Patricia. "The Big House in Contemporary Anglo-Irish Literature." Zach and Kosok 229–34.

Keppler, Carl. *The Literature of the Second Self*. Tucson: U of Arizona P, 1987.

Kerr, Howard. *Mediums, and Spirit-Rappers, and Roaring Radicals: Spiritualism in American Literature, 1850–1900*. Urbana: U of Illinois P, 1972.

Kerr, Howard, and John William Crowley, eds. *The Haunted Dusk: American Supernatural Fiction, 1820–1920*. Athens: U of Georgia P, 1983.

Ketterer, David. *Frankenstein's Creation: The Book, the Monster, and the Human Reality*. Victoria, BC: U of Victoria P, 1979.

Ketton-Cremer, R. W. *Horace Walpole: A Biography*. 3rd ed. Ithaca: Cornell UP, 1964.

Kiberd, Declan. *Inventing Ireland: The Literature of the Modern Nation*. Cambridge: Harvard UP, 1996.

Kiely, Robert. *The Romantic Novel in England*. Cambridge: Harvard UP, 1972.

Kilgour, Maggie. *The Rise of the Gothic Novel*. London: Routledge, 1995.

King, Stephen. *Carrie*. New York: Signet, 1975.

——. *Christine*. New York: Viking, 1983.

——. *Danse Macabre*. New York: Everest, 1981.

——. Introduction. *Frankenstein; Dracula; Dr. Jekyll and Mr. Hyde*. New York: Signet, 1978.

——. *It*. New York: New Amer. Lib.–Penguin, 1987.

——. *'Salem's Lot*. New York: Signet, 1975.

——. "Why We Crave Horror Movies." *The St. Martin's Guide to Writing*. 5th ed. Ed. Rise Axelrod and Charles R. Cooper. New York: St. Martin's, 1997. 339–41.

Kliger, Samuel. *The Goths in England*. Cambridge: Harvard UP, 1952.

Knapp, Bettina L. *Archetype, Architecture, and the Writer*. Bloomington: Indiana UP, 1986.

Kostelnick, Charles. "From Picturesque View to Picturesque Vision: William Gilpin and Ann Radcliffe." *Mosaic* 18.3 (1985): 31–48.

Kramer, Dale. *Charles Robert Maturin.* New York: Twayne, 1973.

Kramnick, Isaac. *Republicanism and Bourgeois Radicalism: Political Ideology in Late-Eighteenth-Century England and America.* Ithaca: Cornell UP, 1990.

Kristeva, Julia. *Black Sun: Depression and Melancholia.* Trans. Louis A. Roudiez. New York: Columbia UP, 1989.

———. *Powers of Horror: An Essay on Abjection.* Trans. Louis A. Roudiez. New York: Columbia UP, 1980.

———. *Revolution in Poetic Language.* Trans. and introd. Louis A. Roudiez. New York: Columbia UP, 1984.

———. *Tales of Love.* Trans. Louis A. Roudiez. New York: Columbia UP, 1987.

Kropf, David Glenn. *Authorship as Alchemy: Subversive Writing in Pushkin, Scott, Hoffmann.* Stanford: Stanford UP, 1994.

Lacan, Jacques. *Ecrits: A Selection.* Trans. Alan Sheridan. London: Tavistock, 1977.

———. "Of the Gaze as Objet Petit a." *The Four Fundamental Concepts of Psychoanalysis.* Ed. Jacques-Alain Miller. Trans. Alan Sheridan. New York: Norton, 1981. 65–119.

Lamb, Charles. "Witches, and Other Night-Fears." *Essays of Elia.* New York: Dutton, 1978. 76–82.

Langbaum, Robert. *The Gayety of Vision: A Study of Isak Dinesen's Art.* New York: Random, 1964.

Laplanche, Jean, and J.-B. Pontalis. *The Language of Psycho-analysis.* Trans. Donald Nicholson-Smith. New York: Norton, 1973.

Laqueur, Thomas. *Making Sex: Body and Gender from the Greeks to Freud.* Cambridge: Harvard UP, 1990.

Lautréamont, Comte de. Maldoror *and the Complete Works of the Comte de Lautréamont.* Trans. Alexis Lykiard. Berkeley: Exact Change, 1994.

Leacroft, Richard. *The Development of the English Playhouse: An Illustrated Survey of Theatre Building in England from Medieval to Modern Times.* London: Methuen, 1988.

Lechte, John. *Julia Kristeva.* London: Routledge, 1990.

Lee, Sophia. *The Recess; or, A Tale of Other Times.* 3 vols. London, 1785. Ed. April Alliston. Lexington: UP of Kentucky, 2000.

Lees-Milne, James. *William Beckford.* 1976. London: Century, 1990.

Le Fanu, Sheridan. "Carmilla." *Novels of Mystery from the Victorian Age.* Ed. Maurice Richardson. London: Pilot, 1945. 573–628.

———. *Uncle Silas: A Tale of Bartram-Haugh.* Introd. Frederick Shroyer. New York: Dover, 1966.

Levin, Ira. *Rosemary's Baby.* 1967. New York: Signet, 1997.

Levine, George, and U. C. Knoepflmacher, eds. *The Endurance of* Frankenstein: *Essays on Mary Shelley's Novel.* Berkeley: U of California P, 1979.

Lévi-Strauss, Claude. *The Elementary Structure of Kinship.* Trans. James Harle Belle and John Richard Von Sturmer. Rev. ed. Boston: Beacon, 1969.

Lévy, Maurice. "'Gothic' and the Critical Idiom." Smith and Sage 1–15.

———. *Le roman "gothique" anglais, 1764–1824*. 1968. Paris: Albin, 1995.

Lew, Joseph W. "Unprepared for Sudden Transformations: Identity and Politics in *Melmoth the Wanderer*." *Studies in the Novel* 26 (1994): 173–95.

Lewis, Matthew Gregory. *Journal of a West-India Proprietor, Kept during a Residence in the Island of Jamaica*. London: Murray, 1834.

———. *The Monk*. Ed. Howard Anderson. Oxford: Oxford UP, 1990.

Light, Alison. "'Returning to Manderley': Romance Fiction, Female Sexuality, and Class." *Feminist Review* 16 (1984): 7–25.

Litvak, Joseph. *Caught in the Act: Theatricality in the Nineteenth-Century English Novel*. Berkeley: U of California P, 1992.

Lloyd, David. *Anomalous States: Irish Writing and the Post-colonial Moment*. Durham: Duke UP, 1993.

London, April. "Ann Radcliffe in Context: Marking the Boundaries of *The Mysteries of Udolpho*." *Eighteenth-Century Life* 10.1 (1986): 35–47.

Lorber, Judith, and Susan A. Farrell, eds. *The Social Construction of Gender*. London: Sage, 1991.

Lougy, Robert E. *Charles Robert Maturin*. Lewisburg: Bucknell UP, 1975.

Lovecraft, H. P. *The Supernatural in Horror Literature*. New York: Dover, 1973.

Lovejoy, Arthur O. "The First Gothic Revival and the Return to Nature." *Modern Language Notes* 47 (1932): 419–46.

———. *The Great Chain of Being: A Study of the History of an Idea*. 1936. Cambridge: Harvard UP, 1957.

Lovell, Terry. *Consuming Fiction*. London: Verso, 1987.

Lowe-Evans, Mary. "Reading with a 'Nicer Eye': Responding to *Frankenstein*." M. Shelley, *Frankenstein* [Smith] 215–29.

Lundie, Catherine A., ed. *Restless Spirits: Ghost Stories by American Women, 1872–1926*. Amherst: U of Massachusetts P, 1996.

Lyotard, Jean-François. *The Inhuman: Reflections on Time*. Trans. Geoffrey Bennington and Rachel Bowlby. Stanford: Stanford UP, 1991.

MacAndrew, Elizabeth. *The Gothic Tradition in Fiction*. New York: Columbia UP, 1979.

Mac Aodha, Breandán. "The Big House in Western Ireland." Genet 19–29.

Macaulay, James. *The Gothic Revival, 1745–1845*. London: Blackie, 1975.

Macauley, Rose. *The Pleasure of Ruins*. London: Thames, 1966.

MacDonald, D. L. *Poor Polidori: A Critical Biography of the Author of* The Vampyre. Toronto: U of Toronto P, 1991.

Madden-Simpson, Janet. "Haunted Houses: The Image of the Anglo-Irish in Anglo-Irish Literature." Zach and Kosok 41–46.

Maddox, Tom. "Snake Eyes." Sterling 12–33.

Magistrale, Tony, and Michael Morrison. *A Dark Night's Dreaming: Contemporary American Horror Fiction*. Columbia: U of South Carolina P, 1996.

Magnuson, Paul. *Coleridge and Wordsworth: A Lyrical Dialogue*. Princeton: Princeton UP, 1988.

Mahmoud, Fatma Moussa, ed. *William Beckford of Fonthill, 1760–1844: Bicentenary Essays*. Cairo: n.p., 1960.

Malchow, H. L. *Gothic Images of Race in Nineteenth-Century Britain*. Stanford: Stanford UP, 1996.

Mansfield, Katherine. "The Garden-Party." *Stories*. Ed. Elizabeth Bowen. New York: Vintage, 1956. 285–301.

Manwaring, Elisabeth. *Italian Landscape in Eighteenth-Century England: A Study Chiefly of Claude Lorraine and Salvator Rosa on English Taste, 1700–1800*. London: Oxford UP, 1925.

Marcet, Jane [Mrs. Haldimand]. *Conversations on Chemistry, in Which the Elements of That Science Are Familiarly Explained and Illustrated by Experiments*. 2 vols. London: Longman, 1806.

Martin, Robert K. "Haunted by Jim Crow: Gothic Fictions by Hawthorne and Faulkner." Martin and Savoy 129–42.

Martin, Robert K., and Eric Savoy, eds. *The American Gothic: New Interventions in a National Narrative*. Iowa City: U of Iowa P, 1998.

Marx, Karl. *Capital: A Critique of Political Economy*. Vol. 1. Introd. Ernest Mandel. Trans. Ben Fowkes. London: Penguin, 1990.

———. *Marx's* Capital: *A Student Edition*. Ed. C. J. Arthur. London: Lawrence, 1992.

Massé, Michelle A. "Gothic Repetition: Husbands, Horrors, and Things That Go Bump in the Night." *Signs* 15 (1990): 679–709.

———. *In the Name of Love: Women, Masochism, and the Gothic*. Ithaca: Cornell UP, 1992.

———. "Psychoanalysis and the Gothic." Punter, *Companion* 229–41.

Maturin, Charles Robert. *Melmoth the Wanderer*. Introd. William F. Axton. Lincoln: U of Nebraska P, 1961.

Maupassant, Guy de. "The Horla." *Selected Short Stories*. Ed. and trans. Roger Colet. New York: Penguin, 1971. 313–44.

Mbiti, John. *African Religions and Philosophy*. New York: Praeger, 1969.

McCarthy, Michael. *The Origins of the Gothic Revival*. New Haven: Yale UP, 1987.

McCarty, John, ed. *The Fearmakers: The Screen's Directorial Masters of Suspense and Terror*. London: St. Martin's, 1994.

McClintock, Anne. *Imperial Leather: Race, Gender, and Sexuality in the Colonial Contest*. New York: Routledge, 1995.

McCormack, William J. "Irish Gothic." Mulvey-Roberts, *Handbook* 135–37.

———. "Irish Gothic and After (1820–1945)." *The Field Day of Irish Writing*. Ed. Seamus Deane. Vol. 2. Derry: Field Day, 1991. 831–54.

———. *Sheridan Le Fanu and Victorian Ireland*. Oxford: Clarendon, 1980.

McGrath, Patrick, and Bradford Morrow, eds. *The New Gothic: A Collection of Contemporary Gothic Fiction*. New York: Vintage, 1992.

McKendrick, Neil, John Brewer, and J. H. Plumb. *The Birth of a Consumer Society: The Commercialization of Eighteenth-Century England*. Bloomington: Indiana UP, 1985.

McKillop, Alan D. "Mrs. Radcliffe on the Supernatural in Poetry." *Journal of English and Germanic Philology* 31 (1932): 352–59.

McKinney, D. D. "The Castle of My Ancestors: Horace Walpole and Strawberry Hill." *British Journal for Eighteenth-Century Studies* 13.2 (1990): 199–214.

McNutt, Dan. *The Eighteenth-Century Gothic Novel: An Annotated Bibliography of Criticism and Selected Texts*. New York: Garland, 1974.

McWhir, Anne. "The Gothic Transgression of Disbelief: Walpole, Radcliffe, and Lewis." Graham, *Gothic Fictions* 29–47.

Mehrotra, Kevala-Krishna. *Horace Walpole and the English Novel: A Study of the Influence of* The Castle of Otranto, *1764–1820*. Oxford: Blackwell, 1934.

Mehta, Jaya. "English Romance, Indian Violence." *Centennial Review* 39 (1995): 611–57.

Melada, Ivan. *Sheridan Le Fanu*. Boston: Twayne, 1987.

Mellor, Anne K. *Mary Shelley: Her Life, Her Fiction, Her Monsters*. New York: Methuen, 1988.

———. *Romanticism and Gender*. New York: Routledge, 1993.

Melville, Herman. *Melville's Letters to Hawthorne*. 25 July 2000 <http://www.melville.org/corresp.htm>.

———. *Pierre; or, The Ambiguities*. New York: Penguin, 1996.

Melzer, Françoise. "Unconscious." *Critical Terms for Literary Study*. Ed. Frank Lentricchia and Thomas MacLaughlin. 2nd ed. Chicago: U of Chicago P, 1995. 147–62.

Mesmer, Franz Anton. "Dissertation on the Discovery of Animal Magnetism." *Mesmerism: A Translation of the Original Scientific and Medical Writings of F. A. Mesmer*. Trans. and comp. George Bloch. Los Altos: Kaufmann, 1980. 43–78.

Meyer, Susan. *Imperialism at Home: Race and Victorian Women's Fiction*. Ithaca: Cornell UP, 1996.

Michasiw, Kim Ian. "Ann Radcliffe and the Terrors of Power." *Eighteenth-Century Fiction* 6.4 (1994): 327–46.

Michie, Elsie B. "Production Replaces Creation: Market Forces and *Frankenstein* as a Critique of Romanticism." *Nineteenth-Century Contexts* 12.1 (1988): 27–33.

Mighall, Robert. *A Geography of Victorian Gothic Fiction: Mapping History's Nightmares*. Oxford: Oxford UP, 1999.

Milbank, Alison. *Daughters of the House: Modes of the Gothic in Victorian Fiction*. New York: St. Martin's, 1992.

———. "Doubting Castle: Gothic Modes of Questioning." *The Critical Spirit and the Will to Believe: Essays in Nineteenth-Century Literature and Religion*. Ed. David Jasper and T. R. Wright. New York: St. Martin's, 1989. 105–19.

———. "The Haunted House: Sheridan Le Fanu." Milbank, *Daughters* 158–73.

———. "Through a Glass Darkly: *Uncle Silas*." Milbank, *Daughters* 174–97.

Miles, Robert. *Ann Radcliffe: The Great Enchantress*. Manchester: Manchester UP, 1995.

———. "The Eye of Power: Ideal Presence and Gothic Romance." *Gothic Studies* 1 (1999): 10–30.

———. *Gothic Writing, 1750–1820: A Genealogy*. London: Routledge, 1993.

Miller, Andrew H. *Novels behind Glass: Commodity, Culture, and Victorian Narrative*. New York: Cambridge UP, 1995.

Miller, Anita, ed. *Four Classic Ghostly Tales*. Chicago: Acad. Chicago, 1993.

Miller, D. A. "*Cage aux Folles*: Sensation and Gender in Wilkie Collins's *The Woman in White*." *The Making of the Modern Body: Sexuality and Society in the Nineteenth Century*. Ed. Catherine Gallagher and Thomas Laqueur. Berkeley: U of California P, 1987. 107–36.

———. *The Novel and the Police*. Berkeley: U of California P, 1988.

Miller, Karl. *Doubles: Studies in Literary History*. Oxford: Oxford UP, 1987.

Milton, John. *Paradise Lost*. Ed. Merritt Y. Hughes. Indianapolis: Bobbs, 1975.

Mishra, Vijay. *The Gothic Sublime*. New York: State U of New York P, 1994.

Miyoshi, Masao. *The Divided Self: A Perspective on the Literature of the Victorians*. New York: New York UP, 1969.

Modleski, Tania. "The Female Uncanny: Gothic Novels for Women." Modleski, *Loving* 59–85.

———. *Loving with a Vengeance: Mass-Produced Fantasies for Women*. 1982. New York: Methuen, 1984.

———. *The Women Who Knew Too Much: Hitchcock and Feminist Theory*. New York: Methuen, 1988.

Moers, Ellen. "Female Gothic." Levine and Knoepflmacher 77–87.

———. *Literary Women: The Great Writers*. New York: Doubleday, 1977.

Mogen, David, Scott Patrick Sanders, and Joanne B. Karpinski, eds. *Frontier Gothic: Terror and Wonder at the Frontier in American Literature*. Ed. Mogen, Sanders, and Karpinski. Rutherford: Fairleigh Dickinson UP, 1993.

Moi, Toril, ed. *The Kristeva Reader*. New York: Columbia UP, 1986.

———. *Sexual/Textual Politics: Feminist Literary Theory*. London: Routledge, 1985.

Monk, Samuel. *The Sublime: A Study of Critical Theories in Eighteenth-Century England*. Ann Arbor: U of Michigan P, 1960.

Montag, Warren. "The 'Workshop of Filthy Creation': A Marxist Reading of *Frankenstein*." M. Shelley, *Frankenstein* [Smith] 384–95.

Moody, Jane. *Illegitimate Theatre in London, 1777–1840*. Cambridge: Cambridge UP, 2000.

Moody, Nickianne. "Visible Margins: Women Writers and the English Ghost Story." *Image and Power: Women in Fiction in the Twentieth Century*. Ed. Sarah Sceats and Gail Cunningham. London: Longman, 1996. 77–90.

Moretti, Franco. *Signs Taken for Wonders: Essays in the Sociology of Literary Forms*. Trans. Susan Fischer et al. London: Verso, 1983.

Moritz, Karl Philipp. *Anton Reiser: Ein psychologischer Roman*. Leipzig: Insel, 1987.

———. "Fragmente aus dem Tagebuch eines Beobachters Seinselbst." *Magazin zur Erfahrungsseelenkunde* 6 (1788): 55–61.

Morris, David. "Gothic Sublimity." *New Literary History* 16 (1985): 299–319.

Morrish, Robert, and Mike Ashley. "Fantasy and Horror Magazines." Barron, *Fantasy* 633–46.

Morrissey, Lee. "'To Invent in Art and Folly': Postmodernism and Walpole's *The Castle of Otranto*." *Bucknell Review* 41.2 (1998): 86–99. Rpt. in *From the Temple to the Castle: An Architectural History of British Literature, 1660–1760.* Charlottesville: U of Virginia P, 1999. 108–30.

Morrison, Paul. "Enclosed in Openness: *Northanger Abbey* and the Domestic Carceral." *Texas Studies in Literature and Language* 33.1 (1991): 1–23.

Morrison, Toni. *Beloved.* New York: Penguin, 1988.

——. *Playing in the Dark: Whiteness and the Literary Imagination.* Cambridge: Harvard UP, 1992.

Moses, Michael Valdez. "The Irish Vampire: *Dracula*, Parnell, and the Troubled Dream of Nationhood." *Journal X* 2 (1997): 66–111.

Most, Glenn W., and William W. Stowe, eds. *The Poetics of Murder: Detective Fiction and Literary Theory.* New York: Harcourt, 1983.

Mowl, Timothy. *Horace Walpole: The Great Outsider.* London: Murray, 1996.

Moynahan, Julian. *Anglo-Irish: The Literary Imagination in a Hyphenated Culture.* Princeton: Princeton UP, 1995.

——. "The Politics of Anglo-Irish Gothic: Maturin, Le Fanu, and *The Return of the Repressed*." *Studies in Anglo-Irish Literature.* Ed. Heinz Kosok. Bonn: Bouvier, 1982. 43–53.

Mudge, Bradford K. "The Man with Two Brains: Gothic Novels, Popular Culture, Literary History." *PMLA* 107 (1992): 92–104.

Mulvey-Roberts, Marie. *Gothic Immortals: The Fiction of the Brotherhood of the Rosy Cross.* London: Routledge, 1989.

——, ed. *The Handbook to Gothic Literature.* New York: New York UP, 1998.

Murdoch, Iris. *The Unicorn.* New York: Viking, 1987.

Murphy, John V. *The Dark Angel: Gothic Elements in Shelley's Works.* Lewisburg: Bucknell UP, 1975.

Mussell, Kay. *Fantasy and Reconciliation: Contemporary Formulas of Women's Romance Fiction.* Westport: Greenwood, 1984.

——. *Women's Gothic and Romantic Fiction: A Reference Guide.* Westport: Greenwood, 1981.

Nancy, Jean-Luc. *Discours de la syncope.* Paris: Flammarion, 1976. Vol. 1 of *Logodaedalus.*

——. "Logodaedalus." *Poétique* 21 (1975): 24–52.

Napier, Elizabeth R. *The Failure of Gothic: Problems of Disjunction in an Eighteenth-Century Form.* Oxford: Clarendon, 1987.

Nayder, Lillian. *Unequal Partners: Charles Dickens, Wilkie Collins, and Victorian Authorship.* Ithaca: Cornell UP, 2002.

——. *Wilkie Collins.* New York: Twayne, 1997.

Naylor, Gloria. *Linden Hills.* New York: Penguin, 1986.

Nelson, Lowry, Jr. "Night Thoughts on the Gothic Novel." *Yale Review* 52 (1962): 236–57.

Nemoianu, Virgil. *The Taming of Romanticism: European Literature and the Age of Biedermeier.* Cambridge: Harvard UP, 1984.

Newman, Judie. "Postcolonial Gothic: Ruth Prawer Jhabvala and the Sobhraj Case." *Modern Fiction Studies* 40 (1994): 85–100.

Norton, Rictor. *Mistress of Udolpho: The Life of Ann Radcliffe*. London: Leicester UP, 1999.

Null, Jack. "Structure and Theme in *Melmoth the Wanderer*." *Papers on Language and Literature* 13 (1977): 136–47.

Oates, Joyce Carol, ed. *American Gothic Tales*. New York: Plume, 1996.

———. Introduction. Oates, *Tales* 1–9.

Oost, Regina. "Servility and Command: Authorship in *Melmoth the Wanderer*." *Papers on Language and Literature* 31 (1995): 291–312.

Ousby, Ian. *Bloodhounds of Heaven: The Detective in English Fiction from Godwin to Doyle*. Cambridge: Harvard UP, 1976.

Owens, E. Suzanne. "The Ghostly Double behind the Wallpaper in Charlotte Perkins Gilman's *The Yellow Wallpaper*." Carpenter and Kolmar 64–79.

Pal-Lapinski, Piya. "Chemical Seductions: Exoticism, Toxicology, and the Female Poisoner in *Armadale* and *The Legacy of Cain*." Cox and Bachman.

Palmer, Paulina. *Lesbian Gothic: Transgressive Fictions*. London: Cassell, 1999.

Parreaux, Andre. "Beckford: Bibliographie selective et critique." *Bulletin de la société d'études anglo-americaines des XVIIième et XVIIIième siècles* 3 (1976): 45–55.

———. *The Publication of* The Monk: *A Literary Event, 1796–1798*. Paris: Librairie Marcel Didier, 1960.

———. *William Beckford, auteur de* Vathek *(1760–1844): Etude de la création littéraire*. Paris: Nizet, 1960.

Pater, Walter. "La Gioconda." Abrams et al. 1641–42.

Paulson, Ronald. "Gothic Fiction and the French Revolution." *ELH* 48 (1981): 532–54.

———. *Representations of Revolution, 1789–1820*. New Haven: Yale UP, 1983.

Paxton, Nancy. "Mobilizing Chivalry: Rape in British Novels about the Indian Uprising of 1857." *Victorian Studies* 36.1 (1992): 5–30.

———. *Writing under the Raj: Gender, Culture, and Rape in the British Colonial Imagination*. New Brunswick: Rutgers UP, 1999.

Peacock, Thomas Love. *Nightmare Abbey*. Harmondsworth: Penguin, 1986.

Peake, Richard Brinsley. *Presumption; or, The Fate of Frankenstein*. J. Cox, *Seven* 385–425.

Peck, Louis F. *A Life of Matthew G. Lewis*. Cambridge: Harvard UP, 1961.

Perkin, Harold. *Origins of Modern English Society*. 1969. London: Routledge, 1991.

Perrault, Charles. "Bluebeard." *The Fairy Tales of Charles Perrault*. Trans. Angela Carter. New York: Avon, 1979. 29–41.

Perry, Ruth. "Incest as the Meaning of the Gothic Novel." *Eighteenth Century* 39.3 (1998): 261–78.

Petry, Alice Hall. "Jamesian Parody, *Jane Eyre*, and 'The Turn of the Screw.'" *Modern Language Studies* 13 (1983): 61–78.

Piercy, Marge. *He, She, and It*. New York: Knopf, 1991.

Pinch, Adela. *Strange Fits of Passion: Epistemologies of Emotion, Hume to Austen*. Stanford: Stanford UP, 1996.

Pinedo, Isabel Cristina. *Recreational Terror: Women and the Pleasures of Horror Film Viewing*. Albany: State U of New York P, 1997.

Pirie, David. *A Heritage of Horror: The English Gothic Cinema, 1946–1972*. New York: Equinox, 1974.

Plato. *The Republic*. Trans. Richard W. Sterling and William C. Scott. New York: Norton, 1985.

Plumb, J. H. *England in the Eighteenth Century*. 1950. Harmondsworth: Penguin, 1990.

Pochmann, Henry A. *German Culture in America: Philosophical and Literary Influences*. Madison: U of Wisconsin P, 1961.

Poe, Edgar Allan. *Great Short Works of Edgar Allan Poe*. Ed. G. R. Thompson. New York: Harper, 1970.

———. *Tales and Sketches*. Ed. Thomas Ollive Mabbott. Vol. 1. Urbana: U of Illinois P, 2000.

———. *Works*. 5 vols. New York: Collier, 1904.

Polidori, John. "The Vampyre: A Tale." M. Shelley, *Frankenstein* [Penguin] 233–55.

Poovey, Mary. "Ideology and *The Mysteries of Udolpho*." *Criticism* 21 (1979): 307–30.

———. *The Proper Lady and the Woman Writer: Ideology as Style in the Works of Mary Wollstonecraft, Mary Shelley, and Jane Austen*. Chicago: U of Chicago P, 1984.

Pope, Alexander. "Eloisa to Abelard." *Selected Poetry and Prose of Alexander Pope (1688–1744)*. Ed. Ian Lancashire and D. F. Theall. U of Toronto English Lib. 1994–2000. 18 Oct. 2002 <http://www.library.utoronto.ca/utel/rp/poems/pope9.html>.

Porte, Joel. "In the Hands of an Angry God: Religious Terror in Gothic Fiction." G. Thompson, *Gothic Imagination* 42–64.

Porter, Dennis. *The Pursuit of Crime: Art and Ideology in Detective Fiction*. New Haven: Yale UP, 1981.

Porter, Roy. *English Society in the Eighteenth Century*. Harmondsworth: Penguin, 1985.

Prévost, Antoine François. *Le philosophe anglais ou Histoire de M. Cleveland*. Ed. J. Sgard. Grenoble: PUG, 1978.

Probyn, May. "The Model." *Victorian Women Poets: An Anthology*. Ed. Angela Leighton and Margaret Reynolds. Cambridge: Blackwell, 1995. 526–29.

Punter, David. "Ceremonial Gothic." Byron and Punter 37–53.

———, ed. *A Companion to the Gothic*. Oxford: Blackwell, 2000.

———. *Gothic Pathologies: The Text, the Body, the Law*. Basingstoke, Eng.: Macmillan, 1998.

———. *The Gothic Tradition*. London: Longman, 1996. Vol. 1 of *The Literature of Terror*, 2nd ed.

———. "Heartlands: Contemporary Scottish Gothic." *Gothic Studies* 1.1 (1999): 101–18.

———. *The Literature of Terror: A History of Gothic Fictions from 1765 to the Present Day*. 1st ed. London: Longman, 1980.

———. *The Modern Gothic*. London: Longman, 1996. Vol. 2 of *The Literature of Terror*, 2nd ed.

———. *The Romantic Unconscious: A Study in Narcissism and Patriarchy.* New York: Harvester Wheatsheaf, 1989.

———. "Scottish and Irish Gothic." *The Cambridge Companion to Gothic Fiction.* Ed. Jerrold E. Hogle. Cambridge: Cambridge UP, 2002. 105–23.

———. "Social Relations of Gothic Fiction." *Romanticism and Ideology: Studies in English Writing, 1765–1830.* Ed. David Aers, Jonathan Cook, and Punter. London: Routledge, 1981. 103–17.

Purinton, Marjean D. "Theatricalized Bodies and Spirits: Gothic as Performance in Romantic Drama." *Gothic Studies* 3.2 (2001): 134–55.

Pykett, Lyn. *The "Improper" Feminine: The Women's Sensation Novel and the New Woman Writing.* London: Routledge, 1992.

Radcliffe, Ann. *The Castles of Athlin and Dunbayne.* Ed. Alison Milbank. Oxford World's Classics. Oxford: Oxford UP, 1995.

———. *The Italian; or, The Confessional of the Black Penitents, a Romance.* 1797. Ed. Frederick Garber. Oxford: Oxford UP, 1968.

———. *The Mysteries of Udolpho, a Romance.* 1794. Ed. Bonamy Dobrée. London: Oxford UP, 1966.

———. *The Romance of the Forest.* 1791. Ed. Chloe Chard. Oxford: Oxford UP, 1986.

———. *A Sicilian Romance.* 1790. Ed. Alison Milbank. Oxford: Oxford UP, 1993.

Radway, Janice. *Reading the Romance: Women, Patriarchy, and Popular Literature.* Chapel Hill: U of North Carolina P, 1984.

———. "The Utopian Impulse in Popular Literature: Gothic Romances and Feminist Protest." *Locating American Studies: The Evolution of a Discipline.* Ed. Lucy Maddox. Baltimore: Johns Hopkins UP, 1999. 235–60.

Railo, Eino. *The Haunted Castle: A Study of the Elements of English Romanticism.* 1927. New York: Humanities, 1964.

Ramsland, Katherine. *The Vampire Companion: The Official Guide to Anne Rice's The Vampire Chronicles.* New York: Ballantine, 1993.

Rance, Nicholas. *Wilkie Collins and Other Sensation Novelists: Walking the Moral Hospital.* Rutherford: Fairleigh Dickinson UP, 1991.

Ranger, Paul. *"Terror and Pity Reign in Every Breast": Gothic Drama in the London Patent Theatre, 1750–1820.* London: Soc. for Theatre Research, 1991.

Rank, Otto. *Beyond Psychology.* New York: Dover, 1958.

———. *The Double: A Psychoanalytic Study.* Trans. Harry Tucker. Chapel Hill: U of North Carolina P, 1971.

Reeve, Clara. *The Old English Baron: A Gothic Story.* 1778. Ed. and introd. J. Trainer. Oxford: Oxford UP, 1967.

Reil, Johann Christian. "Das Zerfallen der Einheit unsers Körpers im Selbstbewusstseyn." *Beyträge zur Beförderung einer Kurmethode auf psychischem Wege* 1 (1808): 550–85.

Restuccia, Frances. "Female Gothic Writing: 'Under Cover to Alice.'" *Genre* 19 (1986): 245–66.

Rice, Anne. *Interview with the Vampire.* New York: Knopf, 1976.

———. *The Tale of the Body Thief.* New York: Knopf, 1992.

Richards, Thomas. *The Commodity Culture of Victorian England: Advertising and Spectacle, 1851–1914*. Stanford: Stanford UP, 1990.

Richter, David. *The Progress of Romance: Literary Historiography and the Gothic Novel*. Columbus: Ohio State UP, 1996.

———. "The Reception of the Gothic Novel in the 1790s." *The Idea of the Novel in the Eighteenth Century*. Ed. Robert W. Uphaus. East Lansing: Colleagues, 1988. 117–37.

———. "The Unguarded Prison: Reception Theory, Structural Marxism, and the History of the Gothic Novel." *Eighteenth Century* 30.3 (1989): 3–17.

Ringe, Donald A. *American Gothic: Imagination and Reason in Nineteenth-Century Fiction*. Lexington: UP of Kentucky, 1982.

Riquelme, John Paul, ed. *Gothic and Modernism*. Spec. issue of *Modern Fiction Studies* 46 (2000): 585–799.

———. "Toward a History of Gothic and Modernism: Dark Modernity from Bram Stoker to Samuel Beckett." Riquelme, *Gothic* 585–605.

Robbins, Ruth, and Julian Wolfreys, eds. *Victorian Gothic: Literary and Cultural Manifestations in the Nineteenth Century*. New York: Palgrave–St. Martin's, 2000.

Roberts, Adam, and Eric Robertson. "The Giaour's Sabre: A Reading of Beckford's *Vathek*." *Studies in Romanticism* 35.2 (1996): 199–211.

Roberts, Bette B. *Anne Rice*. United States Authors Ser. Ed. Frank Day. New York: Twayne, 1994.

———. *The Gothic Romance: Its Appeal to Women Writers and Readers in Late-Eighteenth-Century England*. New York: Arno, 1980.

———. "Sophia Lee's *The Recess* (1785): The Ambivalence of Female Gothicism." *Massachussetts Studies in English* 6 (1979): 68–82.

———. *Victorian Britain: An Encyclopedia*. Ed. Sally Mitchell. New York: Garland, 1988.

Robertson, Fiona. *Legitimate Histories: Scott, Gothic, and the Authorities of Fiction*. Oxford: Clarendon, 1994.

Robinson, J. M. *Temples of Delight: Stowe Landscape Gardens*. Andover, Eng.: Pitkin, 1990.

Robinson, Marilynn. *Housekeeping*. New York: Farrar, 1980.

Rockett, Will H. *Devouring Whirlwind: Terror and Transcendence in the Cinema of Cruelty*. New York: Greenwood, 1988.

Rogers, Deborah, ed. *Ann Radcliffe: A Bio-bibilography*. Westport: Greenwood, 1996.

———, ed. *The Critical Response to Ann Radcliffe*. Westport: Greenwood, 1994.

———, ed. *Two Gothic Classics by Women:* The Italian *by Ann Radcliffe and* Northanger Abbey *by Jane Austen*. New York: Signet, 1995.

Rogers, Robert. *A Psychoanalytic Study of the Double in Literature*. Detroit: Wayne State UP, 1970.

Rosen, David. *The Changing Fictions of Masculinity*. Urbana: U of Illinois P, 1993.

Rosenthal, Bernice Glatzer. *The Occult in Russian and Soviet Culture*. Ithaca: Cornell UP, 1997.

Ross, Marlon. *The Contours of Masculine Desire: Romanticism and the Rise of Women's Poetry*. New York: Oxford UP, 1989.

Rossetti, Christina. "Goblin Market." Abrams et al. 1589–601.

Roth, Phyllis A. "Suddenly Sexual Women in Bram Stoker's *Dracula*." *Literature and Psychology* 27.3 (1977): 113–20.

Roy, Donald, ed. *Plays by James Robinson Planché*. Cambridge: Cambridge UP, 1986.

Rudd, Joy. "'Cast a Cold Eye': A Sociological Approach." Genet 31–42.

Ruskin, John. "Second, or Gothic, Period: Chapter VI: The Nature of Gothic." *The Stones of Venice*. Ed. E. T. Cook and Alexander Wedderburn. London: Allen, 1904. 180–215. Vol. 10 of *Complete Works*.

Russ, Joanna. "Somebody's Trying to Kill Me and I Think It's My Husband: The Modern Gothic." Fleenor 31–56.

Russett, Cynthia Eagle. *Sexual Science: The Victorian Construction of Womanhood*. Cambridge: Harvard UP, 1989.

Ryan, Alan, ed. *The Penguin Book of Vampire Stories*. London: Penguin, 1988.

Rymer, James Malcolm. *Varney the Vampire; or, The Feast of Blood*. 1847. Introd. E. F. Bleiler. 2 vols. New York: Dover, 1972.

Sabor, Peter, ed. *Horace Walpole: The Critical Heritage*. London: Routledge, 1987.

Sadleir, Michael. *The Northanger Novels: A Footnote to Jane Austen*. English Pamphlet 68. London: Oxford UP, 1927.

Sage, Victor, ed. *The Gothick Novel: A Casebook*. Basingstoke, Eng.: Macmillan, 1990.

———. *Horror Fiction in the Protestant Tradition*. London: Macmillan, 1998.

———. "Irish Gothic: C. R. Maturin, J. S. LeFanu." Punter, *Companion* 81–93.

Sage, Victor, and Allan Lloyd Smith, eds. *Modern Gothic: A Reader*. Manchester: Manchester UP, 1996.

Said, Edward W. *Culture and Imperialism*. New York: Knopf, 1993.

———. *Orientalism*. New York: Vintage, 1978.

Salmonson, Jessica Amanda, ed. *What Did Miss Darrington See? An Anthology of Feminist Supernatural Fiction*. New York: Feminist, 1989.

Savoy, Eric. "The Face of the Tenant: A Theory of American Gothic." Martin and Savoy 3–19.

Schaffer, Talia. "A Wilde Desire Took Me: The Homoerotic History of *Dracula*." *ELH* 61 (1994): 381–425.

Schmitt, Cannon. *Alien Nation: Nineteenth-Century Gothic Fictions and English Nationality*. Philadelphia: U of Pennsylvania P, 1997.

———. "Mother Dracula: Orientalism, Degeneration, and Anglo-Irish Subjectivity at the Fin-de-Siècle." *Bucknell Review* 38 (1994): 25–43.

Scholes, Robert. *Fabulation and Metafiction*. Urbana: U of Illinois P, 1979.

Schwartzmantel, John. *The Age of Ideology: Political Ideologies from the American Revolution to Post-modern Times*. Basingstoke, Eng.: Macmillan, 1998.

Scott, Walter. *Lives of the Novelists*. London: Dent, 1910.

———. *The Miscellaneous Prose Works of Sir Walter Scott*. 3 vols. Edinburgh, 1841.

Scruggs, Charles. "The Invisible City in Toni Morrison's *Beloved.*" *Arizona Quarterly* 48 (1992): 95–132.

Sedgwick, Eve Kosofsky. *Between Men: English Literature and Male Homosocial Desire.* New York: Columbia UP, 1985.

———. "The Character in the Veil: Imagery of the Surface in the Gothic Novel." *PMLA* 96 (1981): 255–70.

———. *The Coherence of Gothic Conventions.* New York: Methuen, 1986.

———. "A Poem Is Being Written." *Representations* 17 (1987): 115–43.

Senf, Carol A. "'Dracula': Stoker's Response to the New Woman." *Victorian Studies* 26.1 (1982): 33–49.

———. "*Dracula*: The Unseen Face in the Mirror." *Journal of Narrative Technique* 9.3 (1979): 160–70.

———. "Polidori's *The Vampyre*: Combining the Gothic with Realism." *North Dakota Quarterly* 56.1 (1988): 197–208.

———. "The Vampire in *Middlemarch* and George Eliot's Quest for Historical Reality." *New Orleans Review* 14.1 (1987): 87–97.

———. *The Vampire in Nineteenth-Century English Literature.* Bowling Green: Bowling Green State U Popular P, 1988.

Shakespeare, William. *Hamlet.* Ed. Tucker Brooke and Jack Randall Crawford. New Haven: Yale UP, 1966.

———. *Macbeth.* Ed. Tucker Brooke and Jack Randall Crawford. New Haven: Yale UP, 1966.

Shattuck, Roger. *Forbidden Knowledge from Prometheus to Pornography.* New York: Harcourt, 1997.

Shelley, Mary Wollstonecraft. *Frankenstein.* 1818. New York: Penguin, 1992.

———. *Frankenstein.* Ed. Nora Crook. London: Pickering, 1995.

———. *Frankenstein.* Ed. Johanna M. Smith. 2nd ed. Bedford Case Studies in Contemporary Criticism. Boston: Bedford–St. Martin's, 2000.

———. Frankenstein; or, The Modern Prometheus: *The 1818 Text.* Ed. James Reiger. Chicago: U of Chicago P, 1982.

———. *The Letters of Mary Wollstonecraft Shelley.* Vol. 1. Ed. Betty T. Bennett. Baltimore: Johns Hopkins UP, 1980. 3 vols.

———. *Matilda. Mary Wollstonecraft's* Mary *and* Maria *and Mary Shelley's* Matilda. Ed. Janet Todd. London: Penguin, 1991. 149–210.

———. "Transformation." *Collected Tales and Stories.* Ed. Charles E. Robinson. Baltimore: Johns Hopkins UP, 1976. 121–35.

———. *Valperga; or, The Life and Adventures of Castruccio, Prince of Lucca.* Ed. Stuart Curran. New York: Oxford UP, 1997.

Shelley, Percy Bysshe. Zastrozzi *and* St. Irvyne. Ed. Stephen C. Behrendt. Peterborough, ON: Broadview, 2002.

Showalter, Elaine. *The Female Malady: Women, Madness, and English Culture, 1830–1980.* New York: Penguin, 1985.

———. *A Literature of Their Own: British Women Novelists from Brontë to Lessing.* 1977. Rev. and expanded ed. Princeton: Princeton UP, 1998.

———. *Sexual Anarchy: Gender and Culture at the Fin de Siècle.* New York: Viking, 1990.

———. *Sister's Choice: Tradition and Change in American Women's Writing.* Oxford: Oxford UP, 1991.

Siddons, Henry. *A Sicilian Romance; or, The Apparition of the Cliff. Three Centuries of Drama.* Larpent Collection of Manuscript Plays, 1737–1800. Henry E. Huntington Lib. New York: Readex Microprint Corp., 1955–56. Microprint-microfiche. 6–44.

Sitwell, Sacheverall. *The Gothick North: A Study of Medieval Life, Art, and Thought.* London: Duckworth, 1929.

Skal, David J. *Hollywood Gothic: The Tangled Web of Dracula from Novel to Stage to Screen.* New York: Norton, 1991.

———. *The Monster Show: A Cultural History of Horror.* New York: Penguin, 1994.

Smith, Allan Lloyd, and Victor Sage, eds. *Gothick Origins and Innovations.* Amsterdam: Rodopi, 1994.

Smith, Amy Elizabeth. "Experimentation and 'Horrid Curiosity' in Maturin's *Melmoth the Wanderer*." *English Studies* 74 (1993): 524–35.

Smith, Johanna M. "'Too Beautiful Altogether': Patriarchal Ideology in *Heart of Darkness*." Conrad, *Heart* 179–95.

Smith, Nelson C. "Sense, Sensibility, and Ann Radcliffe." *Studies in English Literature* 13 (1973): 577–90.

Smith, Paul. "Vas." *Feminisms: An Anthology of Literary Theory and Criticism.* Ed. Robyn Warhol and Diane Price Herndl. New Brunswick: Rutgers UP, 1991. 1011–29.

Smith, R. J. *The Gothic Bequest: Medieval Institutions in British Thought, 1688–1863.* Cambridge: Cambridge UP, 1987.

Sontag, Susan. *A Susan Sontag Reader.* New York: Farrar, 1982.

Spector, Robert Donald. *The English Gothic: A Bibliographical Guide to Writers from Horace Walpole to Mary Shelley.* Westport: Greenwood, 1984.

Spencer, Jane. *The Rise of the Woman Novelist: From Aphra Behn to Jane Austen.* Oxford: Blackwell, 1986.

Spencer, Kathleen L. "Purity and Danger: *Dracula*, the Urban Gothic, and the Late Victorian Degeneracy Crisis." *ELH* 59 (1992): 197–225.

Sprengnether, Madelon. *The Spectral Mother: Freud, Feminism, Psychoanalysis.* Ithaca: Cornell UP, 1990.

Sterling, Bruce, ed. *Mirrorshades: The Cyberpunk Anthology.* New York: Ace, 1988.

Sterrenburg, Lee. "Mary Shelley's Monster: Politics and Psyche in *Frankenstein*." Levine and Knoepflmacher 143–71.

Stevenson, Robert Louis. *The Strange Case of Dr. Jekyll and Mr. Hyde.* London: Longmans, 1886.

———. *The Strange Case of Dr. Jekyll and Mr. Hyde.* New York: Bantam, 1977.

———. *The Strange Case of Dr. Jekyll and Mr. Hyde.* London: Penguin, 1979.

Stewart, Susan. "The Epistemology of the Horror Story." *Journal of American Folklore* 95 (1982): 33–50.

Stoker, Bram. *Dracula*. New York: Modern Lib., 1897.

———. *Dracula*. Bantam Classics. New York: Bantam, 1981.

———. *Dracula*. Ed. Nina Auerbach and David J. Skal. Norton Critical Ed. New York: Norton, 1997.

———. *Dracula*. Oxford World's Classics. Ed.Maud Ellmann. Oxford: Oxford UP, 1996.

———. *Dracula*. Ed. John P. Riquelme. Case Studies in Contemporary Criticism. New York: Bedford–St. Martin's, 2001.

———. *The Jewel of Seven Stars*. London: Heineman, 1903.

———. *The Lair of the White Worm*. London: Rider, 1911.

Stowe, Harriet Beecher. *Uncle Tom's Cabin*. Introd. Langston Hughes. New York: Dodd, 1952.

Stuart, Roxana. *Stage Blood: Vampires of the Nineteenth-Century Stage*. Bowling Green: Bowling Green State U Popular P, 1994.

Stoppard, Tom. *Arcadia*. Boston: Faber, 1993.

Sullivan, Jack. *Elegant Nightmares: The English Ghost Story from Le Fanu to Blackwood*. Athens: Ohio UP, 1978.

Summers, Claude. *Gay Fictions: Wilde to Stonewall*. New York: Continuum, 1990.

Summers, Montague, ed. *A Gothic Bibliography*. 1941. New York: Russell, 1964.

———. *The Gothic Quest: A History of the Gothic Novel*. 1938. New York: Russell, 1964.

Tatar, Maria. "The Houses of Fiction: Toward a Definition of the Uncanny." *Comparative Literature* 33.2 (1981): 167–82.

Tennyson, Alfred. "The Palace of Art." Collins and Rundle 165–70.

Thelwall, John. *The Rights of Nature against the Usurpation of Establishments: A Series of Letters to the People of Britain, Occasioned by the Recent Effusions of the Right Honourable Edmund Burke*. London: Symonds, 1796.

Thomas, Ronald R. *Dreams of Authority: Freud and the Fictions of the Unconscious*. Ithaca: Cornell UP, 1990.

———. "Minding the Body Politic: The Romance of Science and the Revision of History in Victorian Detective Fiction." *Victorian Literature and Culture* 19 (1991): 233–54.

Thompson, G. R., ed. *The Gothic Imagination: Essays in Dark Romanticism*. Pullman: Washington State UP, 1974.

———, ed. *Romantic Gothic Tales, 1790–1840*. New York: Harper, 1979.

Thompson, Jon. *Fiction, Crime, and Empire: Clues to Modernity and Postmodernism*. Urbana: U of Illinois P, 1993.

Thomson, Douglass H., Jack G. Voller, and Frederick S. Frank, eds. *Gothic Writers: A Critical and Bibliographic Guide*. Westport: Greenwood, 2002.

Thoreau, Henry David. *Walden and Other Writings*. Ed. Brooks Atkinson. New York: Random, 1950.

Thornburg, Mary K. Patterson. *The Monster in the Mirror: Gender and the Sentimental/Gothic Myth in* Frankenstein. Ann Arbor: UMI Research, 1987.

Thorslev, Peter, Jr. *Romantic Contraries: Freedom versus Destiny*. New Haven: Yale UP, 1984.

Thurston, Carol. *The Romance Revolution: Erotic Novels for Women and the Quest for a New Sexual Identity*. Urbana: U of Illinois P, 1987.

Tinkler-Villani, Valeria, Peter Davidson, and Jane Stevenson, eds. *Exhibited by Candlelight: Sources and Development in the Gothic Tradition*. Amsterdam: Rodopi, 1995.

Todd, Janet. *The Sign of Angellica: Women, Writing, and Fiction, 1660–1800*. New York: Columbia UP, 1989.

Todorov, Tzvetan. *The Fantastic: A Structural Approach to a Literary Genre*. Ithaca: Cornell UP, 1975.

Tompkins, J. M. S. *The Popular Novel in England, 1770–1800*. London: Methuen, 1932.

Tompkins, Jane. *Sensational Designs: The Cultural Work of American Fiction, 1790–1860*. New York: Oxford UP, 1985.

Toufic, Jalal. *Vampires: An Uneasy Essay on the Undead in Film*. Barrytown: Station Hill, 1993.

Tracy, Ann Blaisdell. *The Gothic Novel, 1790–1830: Plot Summaries and an Index to Motifs*. Lexington: UP of Kentucky, 1981.

——. *Patterns of Fear in the Gothic Novel, 1790–1830*. New York: Arno, 1980.

Tromp, Marlene. *The Private Rod: Marital Violence, Sensation, and the Law in Victorian Britain*. Charlottesville: UP of Virginia, 2000.

Tromp, Marlene, Pamela K. Gilbert, and Aeron Haynie. *Beyond Sensation: Mary Elizabeth Braddon in Context*. Albany: State U of New York P, 2000.

Tropp, Martin. *Images of Fear: How Horror Stories Helped Shape Modern Culture (1818–1919)*. Jefferson: McFarland, 1990.

Trott, Nicola, ed. *Gothic Novels: An Anthology*. Oxford: Blackwell, 1997.

Trotter, Thomas. *A View of the Nervous Temperament: Being a Practical Enquiry into the Increasing Prevalence, Prevention, and Treatment of Those Diseases Commonly Called Nervous, Bilious, Stomach and Liver Complaints; Indigestion; Low Spirits; Gout, et Cetera*. London: Longman, 1807.

Tudor, Andrew. *Monsters and Mad Scientists: A Cultural History of the Horror Movie*. Oxford: Blackwell, 1989.

Turgenev, Ivan. "Clatter of Wheels." *Sketches from a Hunter's Album*. Ed. and trans. Richard Freeborn. New York: Penguin, 1967. 227–44.

Twitchell, James B. *Dreadful Pleasures: An Anatomy of Modern Horror*. Oxford: Oxford UP, 1985.

——. "*Frankenstein* and the Anatomy of Horror." *Georgia Review* 37.1 (1983): 41–84.

——. *The Living Dead: A Study of the Vampire in Romantic Literature*. Durham: Duke UP, 1981.

Tymn, Marshall B., ed. *Horror Literature: A Core Collection and Reference Guide*. New York: Bowker, 1981.

Ursini, James, and Alain Silver. *More Things Than Are Dreamt Of: Masterpieces of Supernatural Horror, from Mary Shelley to Stephen King, in Literature and Film*. New York: Limelight, 1994.

Valente, Joseph. "'Double Born': Bram Stoker and the Metrocolonial Gothic." Riquelme, *Gothic* 632–45.

——. *Dracula's Crypt: Bram Stoker, Irishness, and the Question of Blood*. Champaign: U of Illinois P, 2002.

Varma, Devendra P. *The Gothic Flame: Being a History of the Gothic Novel in England:*

Its Origins, Efflorescence, Disintegration, and Residuary Influences. London: Barker, 1957.

———. Introduction. *The Collected Works of J. Sheridan Le Fanu.* New York: Arno, 1977. i–xxiii.

Varnado, S. L. *Haunted Presence: The Numinous in Gothic Fiction.* Tuscaloosa: U of Alabama P, 1987.

Veeder, William, and Gordon Hirsch, eds. Dr. Jekyll and Mr. Hyde *after One Hundred Years.* Chicago: U of Chicago P, 1988.

Vidler, Anthony. *The Architectural Uncanny: Essays in the Modern Unhomely.* Cambridge: MIT P, 1992.

Voller, Jack. *The Supernatural Sublime: The Metaphysics of Terror in Anglo-American Romanticism.* DeKalb: Northern Illinois UP, 1994.

Walkley, Christina. *The Ghost in the Looking Glass: The Victorian Seamstress.* London: Owen, 1981.

Waller, Gregory A. *The Living and the Undead: From Stoker's* Dracula *to Romero's* Dawn of the Dead. Urbana: U of Illinois P, 1986.

Walpole, Horace. *The Castle of Otranto.* 1764. Rev. ed. Ed. W. S. Lewis and E. J. Clery. Oxford: Oxford UP, 1996.

———. *The Castle of Otranto, a Gothic Story.* Ed. W. S. Lewis. Oxford: Oxford UP, 1982.

———. The Castle of Otranto *and* Hieroglyphic Tales. Ed. Robert Mack. London: Dent, 1993.

———. *The Castle of Otranto: A Gothic Story.* Ed. Sir Walter Scott. Edinburgh: Ballantyne, 1811.

———. *Letters from the Hon. Horace Walpole, to the Rev. William Cole, and Others (1745–1782).* London: Rodwell, 1818.

———. *The Works of Horatio Walpole.* 5 vols. London: Robinson, 1798.

———. *The Yale Edition of Horace Walpole's Correspondence.* Ed. W. S. Lewis. 48 vols. Yale UP, 1937–83.

Ward, Catherine C. "Gloria Naylor's *Linden Hills:* A Modern *Inferno.*" *Contemporary Literature* 28 (1987): 67–81.

Warner, Marina. *From the Beast to the Blonde: On Fairy Tales and Their Tellers.* New York: Farrar, 1995.

Watt, Ian P. "Time and Family in the Gothic Novel: *The Castle of Otranto.*" *Eighteenth-Century Life* 10.3 (1986): 159–71.

Watt, James. *Contesting the Gothic: Fiction, Genre, and Cultural Conflict.* Cambridge: Cambridge UP, 1999.

Webster, Noah. Preface. *An American Dictionary of the English Language.* 1828. 31 Oct. 2002 <http://www.webincunabula.com/html/we/webster1.htm>.

Wein, Toni. "Tangled Webs: Horace Walpole and the Practice of History in *The Castle of Otranto.*" *English Language Notes* 35.4 (1998): 12–21.

Weiner, Stephen. "Beyond Superheroes: Comics Get Serious." *Library Journal* 1 Feb. 2002: 55–58.

Wells, H. G. *The Invisible Man.* 1897. New York: Signet, 2002.

——. *The Island of Dr. Moreau*. 1896. New York: Bantam, 1994

——. *The Time Machine*. 1895. Ed. Nicholas Ruddick. Orchard Park: Broadview, 2001.

——. *War of the Worlds*. 1898. New York: Signet, 1986.

Wharton, Edith. *The Ghost Stories of Edith Wharton*. New York: Scribner's, 1973.

White, Hayden. *Metahistory: The Historical Imagination in Nineteenth-Century Europe*. Baltimore: Johns Hopkins UP, 1973.

Wicke, Jennifer. "Vampiric Typewriting: *Dracula* and Its Media." *ELH* 59 (1992): 467–93.

Wiesenfarth, Joseph. *Gothic Manners and the Classic English Novel*. Madison: U of Wisconsin P, 1988.

Wigley, Mark. *The Architecture of Deconstruction: Derrida's Haunt*. Cambridge: MIT P, 1993.

Wilde, Oscar. *The Complete Works of Oscar Wilde*. Ed. J. B. Foreman. New York: Harper, 1989.

——. *The Picture of Dorian Gray*. New York: Dell, 1973.

——. *The Picture of Dorian Gray*. Ed. Richard Ellmann. New York: Bantam, 1982.

Wiley, Basil. *The Eighteenth-Century Background: Studies in the Idea of Nature in the Thought of the Period*. 1940. London: Ark, 1986.

Williams, Anne. *Art of Darkness: A Poetics of Gothic*. Chicago: U of Chicago P, 1995.

Wilson, Harriet E. *Our Nig; or, Sketches from the Life of a Free Black*. Ed. Henry Louis Gates, Jr. New York: Random, 1983.

Wilt, Judith. *Ghosts of the Gothic: Austen, Eliot, and Lawrence*. Princeton: Princeton UP, 1980

——. "The Imperial Mouth: Imperialism, the Gothic, and Science Fiction." *Journal of Popular Culture* 4 (1981): 618–28.

Winsbro, Bonnie. *Supernatural Forces: Belief, Difference, and Power in Contemporary Works by Ethnic Women*. Amherst: U of Massachusetts P, 1993.

Winter, Kari J. "Sexual/Textual Politics of Terror: Rewriting the Gothic Genre in the 1790s." *Misogyny in Literature: An Essay Collection*. Ed. Katherine Ackley. New York: Garland, 1992. 89–103.

——. *Subjects of Slavery, Agents of Change: Women and Power in Gothic Novels and Slave Narratives, 1790–1865*. Athens: U of Georgia P, 1992.

Wisker, Gina. "Love Bites: Contemporary Women's Vampire Fictions." Punter, *Companion* 167–79.

Wolf, Leonard. *Blood Thirst: One Hundred Years of Vampire Fiction*. Oxford: Oxford UP, 1999.

——, ed. *The Essential* Dracula: *Including the Complete Novel by Bram Stoker*. New York: Plume, 1993.

——, ed. *The Essential* Frankenstein: *Including the Complete Novel by Mary Shelley*. New York: Plume, 1993.

Wolff, Cynthia Griffin. "The Radcliffean Gothic Model: A Form for Feminine Sexuality." Fleenor 207–23.

Wollstonecraft, Mary. *Maria; or, The Wrongs of Woman*. 1798. New York: Norton, 1994.

———. *A Vindication of the Rights of Woman.* Oregon State U. 23 Oct. 2002 <http://www.orst.edu/instruct/ph1302/texts/wollstonecraft/woman-contents.html>.

Wolman, Benjamin B., ed. *International Encyclopedia of Psychiatry, Psychology, Psychoanalysis, and Neurology.* 12 vols. New York: Aesculapius, 1977.

Wolstenholme, Susan. *Gothic (Re)Visions: Writing Women as Readers.* Albany: State U of New York P, 1993.

Wordsworth, William. *Ode: Intimations of Immortality from Recollections of Early Childhood.* Bartleby.com. July 1999. 16 Oct. 2002 <http://www.bartleby.com/145/ww331.html>.

Wordsworth, William, and Samuel Taylor Coleridge. *Lyrical Ballads.* Ed. R. L. Brett and A. R. Jones. London: Routledge, 1991.

Worrall, David. "The Political Culture of Gothic Drama." Punter, *Companion* 94–106.

Wright, Bruce Lanier. *Nightwalkers: Gothic Horror Movies: The Modern Era.* Dallas: Taylor, 1995.

Yeats, William Butler. The Celtic Twilight *and a Selection of Early Poems.* Introd. Walter Starkie. New York: Signet, 1962.

———. *The Collected Plays of W. B. Yeats.* New York: Macmillan, 1953.

Zach, Wolfgang, and Heinz Kosok, eds. *Literary Interrelations: Ireland, England, and the World.* Tübingen: Narr, 1987. Vol. 3 of *National Images and Stereotypes.*

Zimmermann, Johann Georg. *Ueber die Einsamkeit.* 4 vols. Leipzig: Heidmann, 1784–85.

Films Cited or Recommended

Alien. Dir. Ridley Scott. 1979.

Alien: Resurrection. Dir. Jean-Pierre Jeunet. 1997.

Alien 3. Dir. David Fincher. 1992.

Beloved. Dir. Jonathan Demme. 1998.

Blacula. Dir. William Crain. 1972.

Blade Runner. Dir. Ridley Scott. 1982.

Blood and Roses. Dir. Roger Vadim. 1960.

Blue Velvet. Dir. David Lynch. 1986.

The Body Snatcher. Dir. Robert Wise. 1945.

Bram Stoker's Dracula. Dir. Francis Ford Coppola. 1992.

The Bride of Frankenstein. Dir. James Whale. 1935.

The Brides of Dracula. Dir. Terence Fisher. 1960.

The Car. Dir. Elliot Silverstein. 1977.

Carmilla. Dir. Gabrielle Beaumont. 1989.

Carnival of Souls. Dir. Herk Harvey. 1962.

The Cat People. Dir. Jacques Tourneur. 1942.

The Cat People. Dir. Paul Schrader. 1982.

Christine. Dir. John Carpenter. 1983.

Cry of the Werewolf. Dir. Henry Levin. 1944.

Curse of Frankenstein. Dir. Terence Fisher. 1957.

The Dark Angel. Dir. Peter Hammond. 1987.

Dead Ringers. Dir. David Cronenberg. 1988.

Die, Monster, Die. Dir. Daniel Haller. 1965.

Dorian Gray. Dir. Massimo Dallamano. 1970.

Dracula. Dir. Tod Browning. 1931.

Dracula (Spanish). Dir. George Melford. 1931.

Dracula. Dir. John Badham. 1979.

Dracula: Prince of Darkness. Dir. Terence Fisher. 1965.

Dracula's Daughter. Dir. Lambert Hillyer. 1936.

Dr. Jekyll and Mr. Hyde. Dir. Rouben Mamoulian. 1931.

Dr. Jekyll and Mr. Hyde. Dir. Victor Fleming. 1941.

The Dunwich Horror. Dir. Daniel Haller. 1970.

Edward Scissorhands. Dir. Tim Burton. 1990.

Ed Wood. Dir. Tim Burton. 1994.

The Empire Strikes Back. Dir. George Lucas. 1980.

The Exorcist. Dir. William Friedkin. 1973.

The Fly. Dir. David Cronenberg. 1986.

Frankenstein. Dir. James Whale. 1931.

Frankenstein. Dir. David Wickes. 1993.

Frankenstein and the Monster from Hell. Dir. Terence Fisher. 1974.

Frankenstein Created Woman. Dir. Terence Fisher. 1967.

Frankenstein Meets the Wolf Man. Dir. Roy William Neill. 1943.

Frankenstein Must Be Destroyed. Dir. Terence Fisher. 1969.

Friday the Thirteenth. Dir. Sean S. Cunningham. 1980.

From Beyond. Dir. Stuart Gordon. 1986.

The Ghost of Frankenstein. Dir. Erle C. Kenton. 1942.

Gothic. Dir. Ken Russell. 1986.

Hannibal. Dir. Ridley Scott. 2000.

The Haunted Palace. Dir. Roger Corman. 1963.

Haunted Summer. Dir. Ivan Passer. 1988.

The Haunting. Dir. Robert Wise. 1963.

The Haunting. Dir. Jan de Bont. 1999.

Hellraiser. Dir. Clive Barker. 1988.

Horror of Dracula. Dir. Terence Fisher. 1958.

The Hound of the Baskervilles. Dir. Terence Fisher. 1959.

House of Dracula. Dir. Erle C. Kenton. 1945.

House of Frankenstein. Dir. Erle C. Kenton. 1944.

The House of the Seven Gables. Dir. Joe May. 1940.

House of Usher. Dir. Roger Corman. 1960.

The Hunger. Dir. Tony Scott. 1983.

The Inheritance. Dir. Charles Frank. 1947.

The Innocents. Dir. Jack Clayton. 1961.

Interview with the Vampire. Dir. Neil Jordan. 1994.

I Walked with a Zombie. Dir. Jacques Tourneur. 1943.

Jane Eyre. Dir. Robert Stevenson. 1944.

Jane Eyre. Dir. Franco Zeffirelli. 1996.

Jekyll and Hyde. Dir. David Wickes. 1990.

Jonathan. Dir. Hans W. Geissendörfer. 1970.

Lair of the White Worm. Dir. Ken Russell. 1988.

Marnie. Dir. Alfred Hitchcock. 1964.

Mary Shelley's Frankenstein. Dir. Kenneth Branagh. 1994.

The Masque of the Red Death. Dir. Roger Corman. 1964.

The Matrix. Dir. Andy Wachowski and Larry Wachowski. 1999.

Maximum Overdrive. Dir. Stephen King. 1986.

The Mummy. Dir. Karl Freund. 1932.

The Mummy. Dir. Terence Fisher. 1959.

Near Dark. Dir. Kathryn Bigelow. 1987.

Nightmare on Elm Street. Dir. Wes Craven. 1984.

Night of the Demons. Dir. Jacques Tourneau. 1958. (Also known as *Curse of the Demon.*)

Nosferatu. Dir. F. W. Murnau. 1922.

Nosferatu. Dir. Werner Herzog. 1979.

The Picture of Dorian Gray. Dir. Albert Lewin. 1945.

The Pit and the Pendulum. Dir. Roger Corman. 1961.

The Pit and the Pendulum. Dir. Stuart Gordon. 1990.

The Premature Burial. Dir. Roger Corman. 1962.

Psycho. Dir. Alfred Hitchcock. 1960.

The Raven. Dir. Roger Corman. 1963.

Re-animator. Dir. Stuart Gordon. 1985.

Rebecca. Dir. Alfred Hitchcock. 1940.

Return of the Vampire. Dir. Lew Landers. 1944.

Revenge of Frankenstein. Dir. Terence Fisher. 1958.

RoboCop. Dir. Paul Verhoeven. 1987.

Rosemary's Baby. Dir. Roman Polanski. 1968.

Scream. Dir. Wes Craven. 1996.

Seven. Dir. David Fincher. 1995.

The Seventh Victim. Dir. Mark Robson. 1943.

Shadow of the Vampire. Dir. Elias Merhige. 2000.

The Shining. Dir. Stanley Kubrick. 1980.

The Silence of the Lambs. Dir. Jonathan Demme. 1991.

The Sixth Sense. Dir. M. Night Shyamalan. 1999.

Son of Frankenstein. Dir. Roland V. Lee. 1939.

Tales of Terror. Dir. Roger Corman. 1962.

The Terminator. Dir. James Cameron. 1984.

Terminator 2: Judgment Day. Dir. James Cameron. 1991.

The Time Machine. Dir. George Pal. 1960.

The Tomb of Ligeia. Dir. Roger Corman. 1965.

Twice Told Tales. Dir. Sidney Salkow. 1963.

The Two Faces of Dr. Jekyll. Dir. Terence Fisher. 1960.

2001. Dir. Stanley Kubrick. 1968.

The Undying Monster. Dir. John Brahm. 1942.

The Uninvited. Dir. Lewis Allen. 1944.

The Velvet Vampire. Dir. Stephanie Rothman. 1971.

Vertigo. Dir. Alfred Hitchcock. 1958.

Victor Frankenstein. Dir. Calvin Floyd. 1977.

Wide Sargasso Sea. Dir. John Duigan. 1993.

The Wraith. Dir. Mike Marvin. 1986.

Wuthering Heights. Dir. William Wyler. 1939.

Young Frankenstein. Dir. Mel Brooks. 1974.

Audiovisual Resources Cited or Recommended

Aspects of Jane Eyre. Videotape. BBC Educ. Publishing, 1998.

Birth of a Gothic Novel. 18 microfilm reels. Research Pubs., Woodbridge, CT, 1996.

Dark Angel. BBC film adaptation of Le Fanu's novel *Uncle Silas* available on video.

Dracula. Videotape. Films for the Humanities and Sciences.

Dracula: A Cinematic Scrapbook. Rhino Home Video. UNI Distribution, 1991.

Frankenstein: A Cinematic Scrapbook. Rhino Home Video, UNI Distribution, 1991.

Frankenstein: The Making of a Monster. Videotape. Films for the Humanities and Sciences.

The Jolly Corner. PBS film adaptation of Henry James's short story.

Joseph Conrad: Heart of Darkness. CD-ROM and videotape. Films for the Humanities and Sciences.

Mary Wollstonecraft Shelley: Frankenstein, *the Making of the Monster*. Videotape. Films for the Humanities and Sciences. 1994.

The Moonstone. BBC film adaptation of Wilkie Collins's novel. 1972.

Northanger Abbey. BBC film adaptation of Austen's novel available on video.

Rebecca. BBC film adaptation of Daphne du Maurier's novel.

Terror and the Gothic Novel. CBC Learning Systems audiocassette. Lecture by Devendra Varma.

Turn of the Screw. BBC film adaptation of Henry James's short story.

The Woman in White. BBC film adaptation of Wilkie Collins's short story.

Wuthering Heights. BBC film adaptation of Emily Brontë's novel.

Wuthering Heights: *A Critical Guide*. Videotape. Films for the Humanities and Sciences.

The Yellow Wallpaper. BBC television adaptation of Gilman's short story.

INDEX

Approaches to Teaching World Literature

Marguerite de Navarre's Heptameron. Ed. Colette H. Winn. 2007.
Medieval English Drama. Ed. Richard K. Emmerson. 1990.
Melville's Moby-Dick. Ed. Martin Bickman. 1985.
Metaphysical Poets. Ed. Sidney Gottlieb. 1990.
Miller's Death of a Salesman. Ed. Matthew C. Roudané. 1995.
Milton's Paradise Lost. First edition. Ed. Galbraith M. Crump. 1986.
Milton's Paradise Lost. Second edition. Ed. Peter C. Herman. 2012.
Milton's Shorter Poetry and Prose. Ed. Peter C. Herman. 2007.
Molière's Tartuffe *and Other Plays*. Ed. James F. Gaines and
     Michael S. Koppisch. 1995.
Momaday's The Way to Rainy Mountain. Ed. Kenneth M. Roemer. 1988.
Montaigne's Essays. Ed. Patrick Henry. 1994.
Novels of Toni Morrison. Ed. Nellie Y. McKay and Kathryn Earle. 1997.
Murasaki Shikibu's The Tale of Genji. Ed. Edward Kamens. 1993.
Nabokov's Lolita. Ed. Zoran Kuzmanovich and Galya Diment. 2008.
Works of Ngũgĩ wa Thiong'o. Ed. Oliver Lovesey. 2012.
Works of Tim O'Brien. Ed. Alex Vernon and Catherine Calloway. 2010.
Works of Ovid and the Ovidian Tradition. Ed. Barbara Weiden Boyd and
     Cora Fox. 2010.
Poe's Prose and Poetry. Ed. Jeffrey Andrew Weinstock and Tony Magistrale. 2008.
Pope's Poetry. Ed. Wallace Jackson and R. Paul Yoder. 1993.
Proust's Fiction and Criticism. Ed. Elyane Dezon-Jones and
     Inge Crosman Wimmers. 2003.
Puig's Kiss of the Spider Woman. Ed. Daniel Balderston and Francine Masiello. 2007.
Pynchon's The Crying of Lot 49 *and Other Works*. Ed. Thomas H. Schaub. 2008.
Works of François Rabelais. Ed. Todd W. Reeser and Floyd Gray. 2011.
Novels of Samuel Richardson. Ed. Lisa Zunshine and Jocelyn Harris. 2006.
Rousseau's Confessions *and* Reveries of the Solitary Walker. Ed. John C. O'Neal
     and Ourida Mostefai. 2003.
Scott's Waverley Novels. Ed. Evan Gottlieb and Ian Duncan. 2009.
Shakespeare's Hamlet. Ed. Bernice W. Kliman. 2001.
Shakespeare's King Lear. Ed. Robert H. Ray. 1986.
Shakespeare's Othello. Ed. Peter Erickson and Maurice Hunt. 2005.
Shakespeare's Romeo and Juliet. Ed. Maurice Hunt. 2000.
Shakespeare's The Tempest *and Other Late Romances*. Ed. Maurice Hunt. 1992.
Shelley's Frankenstein. Ed. Stephen C. Behrendt. 1990.
Shelley's Poetry. Ed. Spencer Hall. 1990.
Sir Gawain and the Green Knight. Ed. Miriam Youngerman Miller and
     Jane Chance. 1986.
Song of Roland. Ed. William W. Kibler and Leslie Zarker Morgan. 2006.
Spenser's Faerie Queene. Ed. David Lee Miller and Alexander Dunlop. 1994.
Stendhal's The Red and the Black. Ed. Dean de la Motte and Stirling Haig. 1999.

Sterne's Tristram Shandy. Ed. Melvyn New. 1989.

Works of Robert Louis Stevenson. Ed. Caroline McCracken-Flesher. 2013.

The Story of the Stone (Dream of the Red Chamber). Ed. Andrew Schonebaum and Tina Lu. 2012.

Stowe's Uncle Tom's Cabin. Ed. Elizabeth Ammons and Susan Belasco. 2000.

Swift's Gulliver's Travels. Ed. Edward J. Rielly. 1988.

Teresa of Ávila and the Spanish Mystics. Ed. Alison Weber. 2009.

Thoreau's Walden *and Other Works.* Ed. Richard J. Schneider. 1996.

Tolstoy's Anna Karenina. Ed. Liza Knapp and Amy Mandelker. 2003.

Vergil's Aeneid. Ed. William S. Anderson and Lorina N. Quartarone. 2002.

Voltaire's Candide. Ed. Renée Waldinger. 1987.

Whitman's Leaves of Grass. Ed. Donald D. Kummings. 1990.

Wiesel's Night. Ed. Alan Rosen. 2007.

Works of Oscar Wilde. Ed. Philip E. Smith II. 2008.

Woolf's Mrs. Dalloway. Ed. Eileen Barrett and Ruth O. Saxton. 2009.

Woolf's To the Lighthouse. Ed. Beth Rigel Daugherty and Mary Beth Pringle. 2001.

Wordsworth's Poetry. Ed. Spencer Hall, with Jonathan Ramsey. 1986.

Wright's Native Son. Ed. James A. Miller. 1997.